To War
with Whitaker

The Countess of Ranfurly
is eighty-one years old
and lives in Buckinghamshire.

TO WAR WITH WHITAKER

*The Wartime Diaries
of the Countess of Ranfurly
1939–1945*

Mandarin

A Mandarin Paperback
TO WAR WITH WHITAKER

First published in Great Britain 1994
by William Heinemann Ltd
This edition published 1995
by Mandarin Paperbacks
an imprint of Reed International Books Ltd
Michelin House, 81 Fulham Road, London SW3 6RB
and Auckland, Melbourne, Singapore and Toronto

Reprinted 1995 (six times), 1996 (twice)

A CIP catalogue record for this title
is available from the British Library
ISBN 0 7493 1954 2

Printed and bound in Great Britain
by Cox & Wyman Ltd, Reading, Berkshire

Contents

Preface

Since I was about five years old I have kept a diary. Though I am now eighty, most of these have survived my many adventures and travels and sometimes I glance at them to remember with laughter.

Growing up is like entering a jungle where some of the larger creatures look alarming and possible man-eaters; and most of the smaller ones – like insects – go unnoticed. As one grows up the jungle gets denser and so, most likely, do you.

But now I am old and in the Departure Lounge – though certainly still growing up – I look back with amusement at how 'cock-sure' I became and how often wrong; so many of those creatures who, at first, looked big and fierce became my life-long friends; so many 'insects' turned out to be brilliant, fascinating and kind companions.

My diaries, written mostly at night and always in haste, in nurseries, school rooms, cars, boats, aeroplanes and sometimes in loos, expose how we all arrive, helpless, innocent and ignorant; and then, as we step gingerly into the jungle, show how afraid, selfish, show-off and silly we often are. Mine also prove how lucky I have always been. Most of the creatures in my jungle have been extra special.

Two friends who helped me through thick and thin I never met: Alexander the Great, who said, 'One must live every day as if it were one's last, and as if one would live forever, both at the same time,' and Oscar Wilde, who said, 'All of us are standing in the gutter but a few of us are looking at the stars.' These two remarks should get anyone through their jungle.

Then, of course, there was Dan; forever the best human being I'll ever know.

I have only one regret: that soon the diaries must stop and no longer record – with laughter – what happened next. This is an account of my life during the six years of World War II.

1

The Storm breaks

Dan Ranfurly and I were married in London on 17 January 1939. We were both twenty-five years old. We had met in Australia in 1937 when he was Aide-de-Camp to Lord Gowrie, the Governor-General, and I was personal Assistant to Lord and Lady Wakehurst, Governor of New South Wales.

When our different terms were up and we met again in Europe we heard much talk of war – Hitler was on the prowl. We knew that England had given a guarantee to Poland but, like most other people, we could not believe that Hitler would risk war with Britain and France. In late August 1939, when the German-Soviet agreement was broadcast to the world, people in the know looked grim but we, and our generation, took little heed. In that lovely hot summer Dan and I left our small flat in London and drove up to the highlands of Scotland for a holiday. The countryside looked more beautiful than ever. We were supremely happy and carefree when we arrived to stay with Joe and Ann Laycock beside Loch Torridon in Ross-shire to fish and stalk deer.

31 August 1939   *Upper Loch Torridon, Scotland*

Dan, Andrew the Ghillie and I set off early this morning. We took the mountain track through the wood. Cobwebs glittered on the grass and brambles, rabbits thumped their warnings and hustled away into the bushes.

Soon we began wading up steep heathered hills, catching our toes in roots and tufts, leaving deep marks in the peat hags. Andrew went easily ahead – his rifle slung on his shoulder, his lunch bulging his pocket. Several times I slumped to the ground and looked back at the blue loch water below. I wondered if I was tired after the the long drive from London yesterday – or am just lazy. How does one know the difference? I counted three out loud to make myself get up and each time Andrew looked back and grinned.

Presently we reached bare rock and began to climb. It took ages to reach the top. There we lay in the sun and spied for stags through a telescope while we ate our lunch, each with a halo of midges. Deer were grazing in a corrie far beyond and below us, and through the long hot afternoon we made a great detour and stalked them, finally crawling along a burn over shining brown pebbles till we were in range. Dan fired and missed. I was glad – the stag looked so beautiful.

Long after the sun went down we were still walking home. We discussed whether toenails came off after slithering down steep slopes in sodden shoes. They laughed at me for wearing tennis shoes, which I always use for mountains. We talked about our wedding in January and this, our second honeymoon. Andrew told us all about his job and his family.

When we came out of the wood and crossed the lawn it was dusk. Lights were on in the house. We opened the front door and were surprised to see suitcases in the hall. General Joe Laycock came out of his study and for a moment I thought he was going to be cross because we were nearly late for dinner. He looked tired, or older than he did at breakfast. 'Dear Dan and Hermione, welcome back,' he said. 'We are not changing for dinner.' He hesitated, and then said very slowly – as if it hurt him – 'I want you to give me a lift in your car at day-break tomorrow. I must go south and so must you. Bob has telephoned from the War Office: the Germans are marching on Poland.'

No one spoke or ate much at dinner and immediately afterwards we went upstairs to pack and go to bed. Soon it will be dawn. Dan is fast asleep. I have counted sheep in vain – they all turned into Germans.

3 September 1939   *Melton Mowbray, Leicestershire*

Two days ago we left Torridon. It seems an age. As we stacked our guns, golf-clubs and fishing rods into the back of our Buick, fear pinched my heart: those are the toys of yesterday I thought; they belong to another world. General Laycock, Dan and I sat in front. We hardly spoke. No doubt the General was thinking of his sons, Bob, Peter and Michael, who will all have to go to the war. Questions teemed through my mind: where will Dan's Yeomanry, the Notts Sherwood Rangers, go? Will I be able to see him? Mummy, ill in hospital in Switzerland – should I fetch her back to England? And Whitaker – our cook-butler – perhaps he is too old to be a soldier? It was raining. The windscreen wipers ticked to and fro' and it seemed as if each swipe brought a new and more horrifying thought to me. We had started on a journey – but to where? And for how long?

We sent a telegram from Inverness to our flat in London and drove on to Edinburgh where we were surprised to find the street lamps out. All night we drove slowly, through thick fog. It was hard to see without headlights. None of us slept.

We dropped the General at his house, Wiseton, near Doncaster, where we ate a hurried breakfast and then drove on to London. Whitaker and Mrs Sparrow, our charlady, were waiting for us, and a telegram from Dan's Yeomanry saying he must report immediately at Retford in Nottinghamshire. After reading this Dan asked Whitaker if he would like to go with him. The old fatty looked over the top of his spectacles and said, 'To the War, my Lord? Very good, my Lord.' Then we started to pack.

Short and stout, his huge face much creased from smiling, Whitaker has many abilities – all self-taught – but I just can't imagine him going to war on a horse.[1]

---

[1] The Notts Sherwood Rangers Yeomanry was part of 1st Cavalry Division, the only horsed formation at that time in the British Army. Later, it became 10th Armoured Division.

This morning we piled camp beds, saddle and saddle bags into the back of the Buick and started: Dan in uniform, Whitaker in his best navy pinstripe suit and myself in a fuss. We listened to Mr Chamberlain broadcasting that 'a state of war exists' as we sped up the Great North Road.

Dan left me here with Hilda, his Mother. She offered him her beautiful chestnut mare to be his second charger and he accepted gratefully. In twenty minutes, he and Whitaker were gone . . .

Thousands of children are being evacuated from London to the country. They, and their parents, must feel as desolate as me.

7 September 1939   *9 Clarges Street, London, W1*

I came to London this morning to fix up our small flat so that we can let it furnished at a moment's notice if necessary. Mrs Sparrow helped me pack up our few treasures and our wedding presents – it seemed strange to be sending them to store. She asked me all the questions I have been asking myself: How long will it last? Will they bomb London? What shall I do now? I promised her I will 'let' her with our flat or not let it at all – so she may be sure of work.

I lunched with Dan's Grannie Cooper who told me that this morning she put her name down for war work and described herself as 'Eighty but active'. We talked of Poland. Afterwards I walked to the gun shop in Pall Mall and bought a small .25 Colt revolver. The shopkeeper said I may not take possession of it until I get a licence. Then I went to Whitaker's flat near the Tottenham Court Road and arranged for all his things to be stored. The piano he was buying on the instalment system from Selfridges will have to be returned. On my way home I bought two 'safari' beds made of canvas with slim detachable steel feet. They fold into a neat bundle and are lighter than the old wooden ones. Tomorrow I begin training to be an ambulance driver – in gumboots and gas-mask.

Russian troops have entered Poland. Tragic we can do nothing to help the Poles. Warsaw is being bombed.

The Sherwood Rangers have moved from Retford to Malton in Yorkshire. I managed, by telephone, to book a room in this small hotel. It was their last. Michael Laycock, who is with Dan, had asked me to collect his car from Wiseton together with jerry cans of petrol from their estate pump, and so I went by train to Doncaster and thence by taxi, to pick these up. I found the boot and back seat of Michael's car crammed with jerry cans and so I borrowed rugs to cover them, and set off slowly on the Great North Road. At Ferrybridge a cyclist shot out of a side road straight across the major road. I swerved and just managed to miss him by inches. He pedalled on furiously and went head-first into iron railings on the far side verge. I stopped, and so did the driver behind me who kindly bore witness that this was not my fault. Police, a doctor and an ambulance arrived quickly and the old cyclist was rushed to hospital: his face looked ghastly – deeply gashed. The police told me that if he died I would be called as a witness. They did not notice my illicit cargo and I drove on – cold and shivering from shock.

The whole division of cavalry is assembling in and around Malton. A lot of Yeomanry wives have rented houses nearby and Toby Wallace is one of them. She asked Dan and me to dine tonight. She thinks the Sherwood Rangers will be sent abroad soon – to the Near East, as horse cavalry was in the last war. I asked her what she would do then. 'Go too,' she said. 'You and I will go together.'

Toby has a prominent nose and chin and is rather round shouldered hence, perhaps, her name. But she has beautiful eyes and voice and is intelligent and kind. She is braver than me. Dandy, her husband, is very amusing but, I suspect, unreliable. They have two little children and two large houses. Awful she must choose between staying with her children or her husband.

The days seem long because we live in suspense, asking ourselves when the war will end, though it has not really begun. Each hour I expect to hear that the Sherwood Rangers are going overseas. Dan is a Second Lieutenant in 'C' Squadron and now has two horses, one requisitioned. He is very busy so I see him only occasionally. His Squadron Leader has asked me to go to York and buy cheap second-hand tables and chairs to furnish their Mess.

I ride whenever I can borrow Dan's mare. This is lovely country and it is fun to canter over the golden stubble fields and jump stone walls.

Today I was thankful to hear that the old cyclist from Ferrybridge is going to survive. The matron of the hospital told me that his son had been killed on that cross-roads quite recently and the old man had sworn never to stop for a car ever again in his life.

Warsaw must fall soon: it is being bombed incessantly. Hideous news keeps coming about Poland.

Warsaw has surrendered. Poland is being partitioned by Germany and Russia. I telephoned Jan Smeterlin[1] in London. He was so upset he could hardly speak. 'Hold on,' he said. 'I'll put the receiver down on my piano.' He played me a little sad Chopin and then came back on the line – 'That's how I feel,' he said, and hung up.

Firearm Certificate No. 2802 has arrived from the Leicestershire Police. A note was enclosed: 'We had a good laugh over your application – "For use against parachutists".' Now I can collect my revolver and ten rounds of ammunition.

[1.] A well-known Polish pianist.

Yesterday Dan, Whitaker and I left Malton. We stayed the night in London on our way to Netheravon where Dan is to spend a month doing a machine gun course.

Early this morning we drove to Netheravon in search of a room, a flat, or cottage. It rained incessantly and we spent a depressing day being told by house agents and pubs alike that thousands of soldiers and airmen are being trained on Salisbury Plain, and there was no hope of getting accommodation. Towards 6 p.m., just when we thought we must give up, we saw a notice on a small wooden cottage: 'To let furnished – apply next door'. The kind owner allowed us to move in then and there. It is a humble place, four miles from Netheravon, but to us it is a palace – two bedrooms, a sitting room, a bath and kitchen. We lit the stove. A few rats belted out of the kitchen into the garden. We are warm, happy, grateful and together.

Dan started work and took the car. I walked up the valley to Upavon to buy food and try to buy a bicycle. Since petrol rationing came in, these are hard to find. I was lucky and found one, the last in a small shed shop. I arranged with the Upavon Garage to go there three mornings a week to learn how to do running repairs on cars. This is necessary if I am to become an ambulance driver. I pedalled home to find Whitaker had spring-cleaned the cottage but was in a great fuss about rats. I shall write to London for a copy of *The Wind in the Willows*. Perhaps Ratty will help him to like rats.

There are three aerodromes nearby and yellow training planes pass overhead all the time.

The kind farmer who lives nearby has lent me his cob for afternoons so that I can teach Whitaker to ride. It is a big, lazy animal with a Roman nose, called Dulcie. Today when I was saddling her Whitaker announced he did not know which end of her frightened him most. Then our troubles began: Whitaker's legs are so short he could not reach the stirrup to mount, and I found him too heavy for me to give him a 'leg-up'. We built a pile of logs quite high and from it Whitaker scrambled into the saddle, only to topple off on the other side. After several attempts we set off with Whitaker perched and petrified in the saddle and me holding the bridle. We walked slowly along the cart track which leads to Salisbury Plain and I had a struggle not to laugh; he looked so funny with his fat face stiff with fear, his hair tousled and his mouth screwed into a button. All went well until we turned to go home, when Dulcie made a tremendous fart, plunged forward and departed at a gallop with Whitaker clutching the saddle. I could not run for laughing. When I reached the farmyard I found Whitaker seated on the ground and Dulcie grazing. 'I made the trip and then slid down its neck,' he said cheerfully and added, 'I can assure your Ladyship I did not make that horrible rude noise.'

Dan brought friends from the Gunnery School to dinner and Whitaker excelled himself – when dinner was ready he announced in his best French: 'Sole à la Shrimpy, Chicken Hellsmere, and Chocolate Manure'.

26 October 1939   *East Chisenbury, Wiltshire*

Today it rained so I stayed indoors and Whitaker showed me how to roast a chicken. When he had put it in the oven I sat down on the kitchen table and asked him to tell me what he did before he came to work for Dan's family twelve years ago.

He was born in Sunderland in 1900 on the night of the relief of Mafeking. He was christened George Gibbon. His father, a shipwright, had ten children and all of his five sons, when they reached the age of fourteen, became apprentices at the same shipyard. When it was George Gibbon's turn to go he hated it and ran away to London to see the sights. He worked in a bar, a grocer's shop and delivered laundry.

Eventually he returned home. His family was dreadfully poor and one cold winter his mother cut the legs off all their furniture to make a fire to keep them warm. Soon his father sent him to work on a refrigerator ship, where he stayed until 1917 when he returned home to join the Army. He was too young to go to the Front. When the Armistice came, he deserted and signed on as a greaser in a ship going to America. He worked on various cargo boats travelling between America, Italy and South America but in 1921 he got caught in the big shipping strike and, like many others, found himself without a job. When his money ran out he pawned his watch and some of his clothes and washed dishes in cafés in exchange for meals. He continued to search for a job and ended up in Pensacola playing the piano in a brothel. Eventually he got work on a ship going to England and when it reached port he left it and went to visit his family. He returned to London and became a silver cleaner at the Bath Club but soon, for better wages, he moved to Service Chambers near St James's Street as a valet. There he met Dan's stepfather, Lizzie Lezard, who took him on as his personal valet. When he joined our family Dan was fifteen and still at Eton.

As he ended his story Whitaker remarked, 'The difference between His Lordship and me is that he was brought up and I was dragged up. I've had to educate myself in every respect.' Fascinating, but sad, to think of what Whitaker might have achieved if he had gone to a good prep school, Eton and Cambridge, like Dan. He is talented – intelligent, witty, energetic and a brilliant piano player and cook.

1 November 1939   *East Chisenbury, Wiltshire*

Mrs Sparrow has forwarded our mail from London. One letter was from Monty Moore Montgomery:[1]

[1.] An amusing, sophisticated, travelled American to whom I had an introduction and who took me dining and dancing during my week in New York on my way back from Australia.

Wall Street, New York   10 October 1939

It was perfectly grand hearing from you, Hermione, and I am glad you are doing a job of protecting your virtue, as the Victorians might say. But if you are counting on us Americans to come over and liquidate the stupidities of your post-war British Governments I suspicion you will be disappointed. The feeling here is intense against involvement although sentiment is pro-Ally. Americans, you know, revere sagacity – and there are some of us who think Hitler has the finest brain in Europe, if not in the world today – and that with such a leader Germany is sufficiently powerful to do a lot of unpleasant things if you insist. It would seem foolish to me to go on, killing hundreds of thousands and squandering pounds sterling to the ultimate end of fostering communism in all Europe.

I honestly don't think you have a chance of defeating Germany, and if you do, the communists will take over.

Of course this does not make pleasant reading, but I must say, after the Baldwins and MacDonalds, etc., you English should enjoy a little realism.

Life here is about as usual, all the night clubs are opening up in new decor, Martinique, Hawaii and other exotic islands – morals are a little freer lest somebody bomb us before we've equalled our quota of ecstasy. The theatre has barely opened but swing and symphony are in third speed.

And just so you won't dislike me too much for my political views, I'd better say that I feel damn sorry for all the poor devils in uniform whatever their nationality is.

If England doesn't negotiate a peace within six months, I shall be both surprised and shocked. False pride and foolish alliances are no reason for a war – and when it comes to broken promises, well, Hitler may have the high score but England and France are close seconds . . .

13 November 1939   *Brigg, Lincolnshire*

Our pleasant month at East Chisenbury is ended. We left that sheltered valley last week and Dan and Whitaker rejoined the Sherwood Rangers at Brocklesby Park, near Grimsby, the home of the Colonel, Lord Yarborough. I have a room in a pub ten miles away. By bus and bike I have searched for a room nearer to Dan without success. This is bleak country with large farmhouses but their owners are unfriendly and refuse to rent a room. Today is my twenty-sixth birthday – no presents or cards because no one knows where I am except Dan who cannot get time off to see me – and Toby who telephoned to ask me to find her a room. She has heard a rumour that no Yeomanry wives will be permitted to go overseas though regular Army wives are allowed.

20 November 1939   *Brocklesby Park, Lincolnshire*

The Yarboroughs have invited me to stay for a week while I try to find rooms nearby. Brocklesby is a large house and estate, most of which has been lent to the Yeomanry. My host has his own pack of foxhounds and today I went hunting in borrowed clothes on a troop horse called Number Nine. This is a surprising country to ride over – I came across iron bedsteads, baths and broken chamber pots in the fences. This evening Dan came to tell me it is now official that Yeomanry wives will not be allowed to go overseas. Grannies, sisters, mothers, mistresses and regular Army wives may go – only Yeomanry wives are banned.

28 November 1939   *A Farmhouse in Lincolnshire*

I have managed to rent rooms for Toby, Rona Trotter and myself in a big farmhouse. The farmer charges us seven guineas a week each for bed and breakfast. The lavatory is ghastly. We cook our other meals on a small wood fire in my bedroom. Today Dan stole half an hour to come and see me. He told me that when the whole Regiment paraded recently, Whitaker appeared on a large horse in his best pinstripe suit and a tin hat, which caused considerable mirth. No uniform has yet been found big enough to fit him.

1 December 1939   *A Farmhouse in Lincolnshire*

Today I went hunting on Dan's mare – a brilliant jumper. Dan rode Horse Number Nine, which was generous of him because she only jumps with her front legs. A lot of Sherwood Rangers were out including the Padre Hughes[1] who goes like a bomb and is most amusing.

On Sundays we walk to church to hear his sermons – we have to start early because such a mass of soldiers attend and even the churchyard gets crowded. My bicycle is our life-line; we take turns to go to the village post-office shop to buy necessities and newspapers. The rest of the time we knit khaki socks and discuss endlessly where the Yeomanry may be sent and how we could follow. There is a leak in the ceiling over my bed and when it rains I get soaked.

Russia has invaded Finland. This awful news reached us tonight. This will be a David v Goliath struggle – the Finns are so brave.

19 December 1939   *A Farmhouse in Lincolnshire*

We have won a sea battle off the River Plate.

This morning we watched our host, the farmer, hoovering his cart-horse in the back yard. The horse stood quite still and seemed to enjoy it. Dan had taken my bicycle to Brocklesby in the back of the Buick so that Whitaker could pedal over and see us. Today he came, with Higgs, Toby's butler, on the rear seat. Their comments on life in the cavalry kept us in fits of laughter: Whitaker said he's got used to horses and rats now. They departed with little Higgs pedalling and Whitaker, like a balloon, on the back.

21 December 1939   *A Farmhouse in Lincolnshire*

Each morning we huddle round my small fire and Toby reads the newspaper out loud while Rona knits and I take down the news in shorthand for practice. 'The Captain of the German pocket battleship, *Admiral Graf Spee*, shot himself last night . . . Perhaps he was outraged by Hitler's order that he should

---

[1.] Later to be Senior Chaplain, Eighth Army, 21st Army Group and then Chaplain-General of the Army.

scuttle his ship . . . The Russians are trying to break the Mannerheim Line in Finland. The Finns are fighting brilliantly . . . Admiral Darlan, the Commander-in-Chief of the French Navy, has arrived in England. Mr Chamberlain and Monsieur Daladier are at the Supreme War Council in Paris . . .' Today that is as far as Toby got because Dan, Dandy Wallace and Henry Trotter arrived – jubilant – to say we are all to get three days' leave for Christmas. Toby set off at once to join her children. As she left she said, 'Be brave. This could be embarkation leave.' I telephoned Hilda from a call box to tell her Dan and I will arrive on Christmas Eve. For all our efforts to be near our husbands we hardly ever see them, so this is marvellous news.

1 January 1940   *A Farmhouse in Lincolnshire*

Last night the Yarboroughs gave a New Year's Eve Dance. Their ballroom looked splendid filled with officers in their Sherwood green tunics with yellow facings and chain epaulettes, and their wives in long, beautiful dresses. I wore my wedding dress with the train chopped off. Toby said, 'This could be a farewell party.'

Whitaker worked at the bar. I missed just one dance to sit with him on the back stairs and give him a drink. He said to me, 'If you get separated from His Lordship be sure I'll stay with him come what may. I won't desert in this war.'

Cheek to cheek Dan and I danced into the dawn of 1940.

10 January 1940   *A Farmhouse in Lincolnshire*

Nancye Yarborough has organised a canteen at Brocklesby Station for the Sherwood Rangers, who are leaving in batches all this week. I bicycled over to help her. We doled out tea and buns on a long trestle table and watched horses being loaded on to the train – some of them were terrified and took ages. Straw had been laid down everywhere to prevent the horses from slipping on the icy roads and platform. There are about 1000 horses to be moved.

It is bitterly cold – the newspapers say, 'It's the coldest snap in this country since 1815, the year of Waterloo.'

18 January 1940   *London*

Yesterday was our first wedding anniversary. Dan left with the last of the Sherwood Rangers ... I worked on the cold platform with the other wives – we handed out tea and watched kit bags being loaded. It was torture. Whitaker, looking incredibly fat in his new uniform hung all over with kit, came along the platform to say goodbye. 'Don't worry, I will look after His Lordship,' he said, while I struggled with my laughter and my tears.

The train chugged slowly out of the little station with hands waving from every window. Then I filled our car with all the paraphernalia that Dan and Whitaker were not taking with them and drove away over the frozen roads for London. Halfway down a steep hill I put on the brakes and skidded. The heavy car turned over and buckled both back wheels. It did not seem to matter. I sat on a heap of snow till a car came by and gave me a lift to Grantham Station. When I arrived in London I found Toby and Mrs Sparrow in our flat. They had bought me a bowl of white hyacinths for our wedding anniversary.

This morning, early, the telephone woke me. It was Dan at the port of embarkation. I was surprised and could think of nothing to say until he rang off. He could not tell me where he was – just said it was desperately cold. It seems to be weeks since he left.

Later I telephoned Dan's friend, Lord Lloyd,[1] to ask whether I could get a job with the British Council in the Near East. He was very kind – said he could not do anything unorthodox but the Head of the Middle East Section will be in London soon and if staff are needed there he will tell me. I told Toby about this, but she said that non-regular Army wives are being prevented from going oversees whatever pretext they give.

[1.] Family friend, distinguished proconsul, and at this time head of the British Council.

14

Tomorrow, with an instructor, I am to drive an ambulance round Central London. I hate driving in gumboots and find it difficult to reverse with a gas-mask round my neck.

25 January 1940   *London*

Toby and I have been injected and vaccinated. We have paid our bills, visited the dentist and had permanent waves. I have typed out copies of my secretarial references – from the *Spectator*, the War Office, and Lord Wakehurst in Government House, New South Wales. I am having paid dictation to accelerate my shorthand and have reached a good speed.

I have been to see Cator Holland, Dan's Trustee, to ask if we have enough money for me to go to the Middle East. He is a charming man. He explained our poverty position and did not laugh when I said it would be best if I pawned our family jewellery. Also, he promised, should I leave in a hurry, he would redeem the jewellery and take care of Mrs Sparrow. His clerk told us there is a good pawn shop near Victoria Station.

Toby took me to lunch at the Ritz and there we found old Lady Oxford, resplendent in scarlet. She told us cheerfully she intends to stay in London, come what may. Old people are being marvellous: they are well aware they may not see the end of the war and that all their young are at risk, but they ask no quarter – they remain elegant, resolute and charming.

Afterwards I saw Toby off on a train to Scotland – she wants to spend as much time as possible with her children. I returned to our flat to read the newspapers and think. News from everywhere is awful and specially from Poland, where the Nazis are doing most terrible things to the Poles. Even London has changed: huge barrage balloons hover in the sky to keep enemy planes high up; the black-out has encouraged a rash of robberies; and now it is unwise to go out alone after dark. Petrol rationing has made everyone think twice about using their cars; people are buying food to hoard; many houses are empty – their owners being called up or retreated to the country; families and friends are so scattered that telephone directories and address books are now pretty useless, and even

15

if one knows where people have gone it is dangerous to say so. Though we dress well and talk as cheerfully as ever the disguise of our loneliness and anxiety is thin.

Someone has tried to break into our flat. Mrs Sparrow wants me to go and stay with Dan's Grannie.

28 January 1940   *London*

Toby telephoned: she has received a telegram from Dandy. It conveyed that he and the advance party have arrived in Palestine.

Last night the First Lord of the Admiralty, Mr Winston Churchill, made a speech in Manchester. It was stupendous and made me feel quite brave. '. . . Come, then: let us to the task, to the battle, to the toil . . . each to our part, each to our station. Fill the armies, rule the air, pour out the munitions, strangle the U-boats, sweep the mines, plough the land, build the ships, guard the streets, succour the wounded, uplift the downcast, and honour the brave. Let us go forward together in all parts of the Empire, in all parts of the Island. There is not a week, nor a day, nor an hour to be lost.'

It's been snowing. Berkeley Square looks like Gay Vienna. The pipes in our flat are frozen, so I have to go out to wash, etc.

2 February 1940   *London*

I had an interview with the British Council Middle East representative, a tall, sallow, sour man, in an over-heated room. He would not read my references and said my name and appearance are a great disadvantage. After a few rather acid remarks he said he will take me on trial as a secretary for three weeks. I must work from 9 a.m. till 9 p.m. – no pay. At the end of that time – if he thinks me suitable – he said it would be easy to get me a visa to go and work in Cairo. I agreed to start work tomorrow. I have no alternative.

A letter came from Dan dated January 24th.

> . . . We left the port yesterday. It was incredibly cold, fourteen
> degrees of frost one night and a terrible gale. The horses
> had an awful time – all their rugs were blown off and some of
> them died of exposure. For twenty-four hours this gale has
> blown and the noise of crockery being broken and tins rolling
> about at night is enough to waken the dead. Yesterday I was
> orderly officer and had to stagger round the ship every hour
> till midnight. The men who went with the horses had a
> dreadful journey across France. Since I saw you we have heard
> no news – we are not allowed to use wireless . . .
>
> It is a fine sight to see six ships steaming three abreast with
> Destroyers sweeping round them. You must hurry. If Italy
> comes into the War it will be much more difficult, perhaps
> impossible, for you to reach us . . .

Last night Rona Trotter telephoned me. She wanted to see me
urgently. I set forth in the black-out and found her in a state of
wild excitement: she is leaving tomorrow for Palestine. Under
vows of secrecy she gave me an address to go to but she made
me promise not to use it until she has time to reach her destination by air.

A letter came from Dan, dated January 29th: 'We have arrived
and our official address is Notts Sherwood Rangers Yeomanry,
Palestine. Letters by airmail take about a week.' I also had a
letter from Whitaker. It was completely blacked out by a censor
except for 'My Lady' at the top. I wonder what he wrote.

Now it is light until 5 p.m., and there are tulips and daffodils
on the street barrows. Each evening, after work, I go to see, or I
telephone, one or other of our family. I feel dreadfully sad
I must leave them.

Today, again, my boss asked me out – to dine and dance. I made another feeble excuse and refused. Most embarrassing.

In my lunch hour I went to the address Rona gave me. It is a small travel agency – just one room with a man and a typist in it. I explained that I want to go to Palestine, but as Dan is a soldier I come under the War Office ruling on war wives. 'Don't look so worried,' he said cheerfully. 'That can be arranged.' He took my particulars, passport and telephone number and told me to get ready to leave at short notice. I asked him if he would help Toby. 'On no account must you travel together,' he said. 'I'll help her when we've got you away. Don't tell anyone you've been here.'

When I got home I found several letters from Dan.

> . . . If you go to Cairo I shall never see you. Jerusalem would be
> nearly as bad because, owing to the Troubles, there is a
> curfew on the roads. We get only two half days off a week. The
> rest of the time we work really hard – I was in the saddle for
> seven hours today and have been out of bed for seventeen. I
> have written to you every day since we left . . .

I also got a letter from Lord Lloyd offering me a contract to work in Cairo. 'Our Middle East Representative tells me your shorthand is not fast enough for him, but we can offer you a post as an archivist at three pounds a week.' I telephoned and thanked him warmly for his help and kindness but turned down the offer and told him why. It seems his Representative is too fast for me in every respect.

17 February 1940   *London*

The travel agent telephoned this morning and asked me to go to his office at once. I found he had obtained all necessary papers for me to leave, a transit visa for France and a visa for Egypt. He handed me my tickets from London to Alexandria – and the bill – forty pounds, ten shillings and five pence. He advised me to leave tonight. I asked him what money I should give him for his trouble and how this had been fixed. 'As you are travelling third class I would be happy with five pounds,' he said, and added, 'My brother works in the Passport Office.' He promised to take care of Toby. We shook hands. 'Remember there is a strong possibility you may be stopped on the way and returned to England. Send me a postcard of the Sphinx – if you make it,' he said.

I packed quickly: two suitcases, an overnight bag, my portable wireless, Dan's Leica and his shotguns in their case. I hid my revolver in my elastic girdle in case one is not allowed to carry fire-arms abroad. Then I telephoned Toby, Cator Holland, Dan's family and mine and kissed Mrs Sparrow goodbye. Her fierce old face puckered as she fought back her tears.

At Victoria Station I was already petrified of being discovered. I huddled in a corner seat behind the *Evening Standard*. Now I am on the Channel in thick fog – somewhere between Newhaven and Dieppe. I've managed to get a bunk and a blanket. The stewards in the gangway keep chatting about mines. I am filled with fears: of being caught; of drowning; of never seeing our families again; of not reaching Dan; of the war going on for years and years . . .

19 February 1940   *Marseilles*

It was snowing when I reached Paris. I sent a telegram to Dan saying 'I love you', hoping he will realise from the postmark that I have started. In the evening I continued my journey sitting up in a crowded, wooden-seated carriage.

I arrived here this morning and went straight to the docks. I found my boat but was not allowed to board it – it is held up as it may be turned into a troop ship. Marseilles is full of soldiers and sailors and many are British so I dared not go for a walk or to a cinema in case I be questioned. I have stayed all day in a small dock-side hotel bedroom, reading a paper book lent me by the concierge. It is called *Bessie Cotter*, and is all about a brothel. Waiting is awful and, to make things worse, the extreme cold has made my nose bleed.

20 February 1940   *Marseilles. Khedival Mail Steamer*
                              s.s. Mohammed Ali El Kebir

This ship is still delayed but I am on board which is something. There are few other passengers. Meals are a nightmare because I am seated between the Captain and an English Colonel Jackson. Both ply me with questions which I cannot answer truthfully. There seems to be a good chance we may sail tomorrow.

22 February 1940   *s.s. Mohammed Ali El Kebir*

I am love-sick, home-sick and now . . . seasick.

23 February 1940   *s.s. Mohammed Ali El Kebir*

Today we reached Malta. Two of our destroyers and a submarine passed us as we entered the harbour. Valetta looked lovely in the sunshine: brilliant coloured boats, tugs, and grey warships all around us and yellow stone buildings packed tight up the hill behind the harbour. I went ashore and ran up steep stone steps to the top of the town. The narrow streets were crowded with sailors and soldiers, ponies and donkeys, and merchants calling their wares. I saw a fisherman followed by some twenty cats. I bought a small bunch of fresias which smell wonderful – and a budgerigar in a paper bag – all for two shillings. The Maltese are ugly but they are smiling people so it does not seem to matter.

It is five weeks since I saw Dan. I dread the Customs at Alexandria and wonder if British military check the port and arrivals.

26 February 1940   *Egypt*

We docked at Alexandria this morning. When I walked down the gang plank a grand-looking Egyptian official approached me, bowed and led me away by the arm to a different building from the other passengers. I thought, 'I'm caught.' In his office I was given a chair and a cup of Turkish coffee while he spoke rapidly and long. I could not understand what he was saying and so just sat and grinned. After a second cup of coffee, more bows, and in spite of my guilty face, he led me off again – this time to the Customs shed where he waved his arms about and I was let through and none of my cases were opened.

I came by train to Cairo. The carriage was filled with Egyptians wearing tarbooshes – they read their newspapers from right to left. It was exciting looking out of the window. I drove from Cairo station to the Continental Hotel in a gharry drawn by two grey ponies. There, on the terrace in his cherry red trousers, I found Robin Stuart French waiting for me. He had got my telegram from Malta asking him to book me a room and contact Dan. He is on sick leave. He introduced me to Freddie Hoffman, the Swiss hotel manager, and I found a telegram from Dan: 'Rona wants you to stay with her at Rehovoth near Tel Aviv.' We dumped my luggage, released the budgerigar from my pocket and let it fly round my room, and went to the American Express office who said they could get me a visa for Palestine in a few days.

At dinner Robin talked about his Regiment, the 11th Hussars, which is in the Desert patrolling the Egyptian frontier – 'where a great wire fence runs for two hundred miles, southwards, from the sea at Sollum, along the edge of Libya.' He told me that the 11th Hussars are using the same old vehicles they had in 1935 during the Italian-Abyssinian crisis. He talked of Mersa Matruh, sand storms, ice cold nights, scorching days and a wind called Khamsin . . . He said, 'If trouble comes we'll be dangerously short of men and equipment.'

Robin had a friend going to Palestine tomorrow so I gave him a note to get to Dan by hand – I dared not send a telegram.

28 Febuary 1940 *Cairo*

When I asked Robin what Cairo was like he said, 'A filthy, Frenchy, modern town – an ancient, elegant, primitive city.' Then he showed it to me.

We went to the Musqi, which is a labyrinth of tiny streets in the poor quarter where are crammed shops of every conceivable kind. We looked at piles of rugs, watched craftsmen tapping out patterns on brass and other metals, stared up at high bales of silks and cottons, explored jewellery shops where many treasures from refugees are on sale, tried some of the perfumes they sell in pretty bottles and laughed at the conversation of the shopkeepers – 'Sir, Sir, you buy amber grease – will make you powerful lover – you need aphrodisiac seriously, Sir.'

We drove across the city to the museum to see the wonders from Tutankhamen's tomb: fabulous gold ornaments, alabaster vases, mummy cases, all the magnificence of three thousand years ago. We crossed the Kasr el Nil bridge which is guarded on either side by two great marble lions – Robin said they only smile if a virgin crosses the bridge. Thence to Mena to see the Pyramids and the Sphinx and I bought a postcard to send to the travel agent in London. We drove past the King's Palace which is surrounded by slums, past the Citadel where once Napoleon's troops were garrisoned, to the Ibn Touloun Mosque. We crossed its great courtyard and climbed the little haunted minaret from where we could see for miles – the desert, the brown waters of the Nile, the emerald green Delta and this vast city. Next we went to the Sultan Hassan Mosque which has the loveliest ceiling I ever saw: the sky.

Through overcrowded streets, where horse-drawn vehicles, dilapidated taxis, trams hung about with people, army trucks and the seething populace struggle to move around, we made our way past modern stores, luxury flats and piteous dwellings, to Gezirah island where there is a golf course, polo ground and Club House. In Cairo the ancient and the new world, riches and poverty, peace and war, are cheek by jowl. It is a very noisy city.

This morning I got my visa for Palestine. Robin sent Dan a telegram: 'Your baggage arrives Rehovoth March 2nd eleven a.m.'

I caught the evening train. In the low sun the glossy green of the Delta and the red brown trunks of the palm trees looked lovely. Peasants were still working on the land, ploughing with oxen and donkeys and driving high-wheeled carts along sun-baked tracks to little towns. Barges and feluccas, laden with bricks and bales, slid along the canals.

We passed a station called Zagazig and soon after reached Kantara where I discovered I must change trains. Porters seized my luggage and waved me to a ferry which took me across the Suez Canal. Hundreds of frogs were croaking. On the other side I found passport officials and Customs. Unfortunately they opened Dan's gun case and a hullaballoo began in Arabic and broken English. Eventually I convinced them that the guns were for 'Engleesh Officer' and was allowed through. In the excitement they forgot to look at the rest of my luggage. I found a seat in a third-class carriage. The coach was filled with Australian soldiers returning to Gaza from a course in Egypt. After an age the train started and just as we left Kantara my budgerigar escaped from my pocket and flew out of the open window into the warm summer night. 'At home those fly about wild,' said my neighbour, showing not the slightest surprise. After that we talked about New South Wales – from Bondi Beach to Tibooburra where I once rode in a camel race.

Probably because I had sat up all night on a hard seat being serenaded by the Australian soldiers singing 'Waltzing Matilda' and 'We're the boys from way down under' I found Palestine in the dawn rather disappointing – it was flat and less colourful than I expected. I ate breakfast on the train and reached Rehovoth at eleven. I climbed out on to sand, hardly daring to believe I was going to see Dan.

I saw him a long way down the train looking up at the carriages. Tall, bronzed by the sun, wearing khaki shorts and tunic, marvellously good-looking . . . I stood and watched him, spellbound. I thought my heart would burst . . . Heaven is being together.

2

Rough Justice

4 March 1940   *Rehovoth, Palestine*

I am staying in Rona Trotter's rented, unfurnished bungalow on the edge of Rehovoth alongside an orange grove which smells wonderful by day but seems creepy after dark. With camp beds, orange boxes, and a table, two chairs and some blankets lent by the Royal Scots Greys' wives who live nearby, we are quite comfortable. Dan and Henry Trotter are camped at Latrun some distance away. They can come and see us on their two half-days off a week.

The worst of the Troubles in Palestine are supposed to be over but tensions still exist. Rona and I have been warned not to stray off main roads or go out after dusk. There is still risk of roads being mined – rape and murder are not unusual. Even soldiers may go out at night only in pairs. Rona has been given a revolver and we are to have shooting lessons in a quarry.

Today I telephoned the head of the Red Crescent in Jerusalem to ask if I might do voluntary work for them. He told me that secretaries are urgently needed by civil and military establishments in Palestine but there are no needs in Rehovoth. 'Even if you have a car I think you should not drive alone, and there is the problem of the curfew . . . If you move nearer to Jerusalem or Haifa let me know and we'll grab you,' he said kindly.

Two little Scots Greys' children – Jane Finlay and Caroline Todd – often invite me to play with them: I have been a bridesmaid at their doll's wedding and a groom in Jane's 'zoo'; she has a donkey foal, a young gazelle and a baby camel.

No one here can understand why regular Army wives and their children may live here and Yeomanry wives are forbidden.

8 March 1940   *Rehovoth, Palestine*

Last night, when Rona and I were about to go to bed, we heard footsteps approaching the bungalow. We stopped talking, turned off the lights and listened. We heard low voices nearby and, peeping through the slats of our shutters, we saw three figures standing a few yards off.

We waited for them to go away but after a while, to our horror, someone began to tug at our sitting-room shutters. As the shutters loosened and a thin beam of moonlight broadened on our floor I felt terrified, fetched my little Colt revolver, unlocked the front door and strode outside. Shaking with fear I kept my finger on the trigger. Rounding the corner of the bungalow I found myself only a few paces away from three tall men. As soon as they moved towards me I fired, but none of them ran away or fell over – and a very English voice said 'Goodness, you are a poor shot.' Then came a burst of laughter.

They walked through our front door and seated themselves on the floor – still laughing – three young Royal Scots Greys' Subalterns we'd never seen before. Rona, ashen from fright, and I could not even raise a smile. Politely we sent them packing after promising not to tell their Colonel about their stupid spree. They did not seem to register how petrified we'd been or that I might have hurt or killed them.

Great excitement – Toby has arrived. She rushed to London after I left and the travel agent got her a visa and an air passage quickly. Nancye Yarborough, Myrtle Kellet, Ann Feversham and a few others are arriving soon, but Toby says no more will come via the travel agent – he'd told her the risk was now too high.

Whitaker in his solar topee and shorts, which have a huge V at the back where he has let in a gusset, is a remarkable sight. His poor face, arms and knees are lobster pink from the sun, but he is wonderfully cheerful. His comments on the Holy Land and its people are very funny and often interesting. He told me that when our troops first arrived they much preferred the Jews because they were easier to converse with, but soon they changed their minds. 'Take the shops,' he said. 'If you go into a Jewish shop and don't buy something the owners are often rude and sometimes swear at you, whereas Arab shop-keepers generally offer coffee and laugh and say, "Maybe next time you come you'll buy something." On the beaches, in swimming clothes, it's difficult to tell Arab from Jew – both have aquiline noses and thick lips. Did you know that the ones with red hair are said to be descendants of the Crusaders?'

Whitaker has been twice to Tel Aviv and his remarks about the long, lank hair and hypnotic outfits of Hebrew sects do not bear repeating.

Dan has bought a Baby Austin car for twenty-five pounds. It has a canvas hood but no radiator cap – just a piece of hose-pipe stuck in the bonnet away from the windscreen so its occupants don't get scalded when it boils. It boils very often, so a can of water must always be on board. Today, in this splendid vehicle, we set off to see Jerusalem.

We drove between orange groves and on across a plain where crops were tall and green. We passed Dan's military camp at Latrun and soon after we were stopped and questioned at a Military Police Check Point. Then we began climbing the steep, twisting road through the mountains. This pass must have been hair-raising in the Troubles: there are a thousand hiding places for brigands amongst the rocks and one edge of the road has a sheer drop. We saw no one except for groups of barefoot Arab children who were selling fat bunches of anemone and dwarf cyclamen on the roadside. We filled the rear of our little car with flowers. We boiled twice before we passed the trenches of the First World War and entered Jerusalem by an untidy street of poor shops and garish advertisements. We found our way to the King David Hotel for lunch. It was crowded with Australians. Philip Parbury and some of the 16th Australian Brigade Group gave us a warm welcome.

Afterwards we went on foot to the Old City where the streets are narrow and dirty and the sun makes open doorways and alleys look dark and mysterious. There was a strange musty smell of grain, food and dust, and sometimes the stench of drains or lack of them. We jostled past pack-asses, goats, beggars with flies swarming on their poor eyes and stumps, and people and priests of many nationalities. We went to the Wailing Wall and the Holy Sepulchre and I thought both revolting, and then we went to the Dome of the Rock, shed our shoes and admired. But it was the little Garden of Gethsemane, with its few ancient olive trees and large dog violets, which touched me most. Here, at least, I could imagine Christ pacing up and down, struggling to muster courage to meet His awful fate.

Tonight, with great sadness, we learned that an Armistice has been signed between Finland and Russia. For so long the Finns have struggled to defend their country with inspired daring and courage. The red claws of Russia and the black shirts of Germany now threaten all Europe. If our turn comes I hope we will be as brave and resolute as the Finns.

13 March 1940   *Rehovoth, Palestine*

The Sherwood Rangers are moving north to Karkur, near Hederah, so Toby, Rona and I hired a car and went in search of somewhere to live. From Hederah there is only a sand track to

Karkur which consists of a few Arab houses, a little Jewish settlement of box-like bungalows, a water tower and a small agricultural school. Except for the view over the plain beyond, where the Yeomanry will camp, it is a dreary place.

The Arab Muktar who met us was most kind but said there was nowhere for us to stay. Just when we were leaving in despair I knocked on the door of one of the Jews' bungalows. A large, untidy woman came out and gave me the customary 'Shalom'. She could only speak German or Hebrew. I asked, in my poor German, if she would let me her bungalow. After a lengthy talk with her husband and discussion with some of her neighbours, she agreed to move into a friend's bungalow and let me hers unfurnished for twelve pounds a month provided her husband could continue to work in their garden. Then and there we drew up an agreement and signed it. While this was going on four of her neighbours offered their bungalows on the same terms to Toby and Rona who jumped at this and signed for all four – one for each of them and the others for Nancye Yarborough and Dotty Morse. Then we emptied the sand from our shoes, shook hands, shalomed and drove away – jubilant.

This evening Toby and I went over to the Rehovoth Agricultural School. We saw cows feeding on oranges. The Director of the School told us Rehovoth is one of the old Pica settlements established by Baron Edmund de Rothschild of Paris. These early Jewish settlers lived on friendly terms with their Arab neighbours.

16 March 1940   *Rehovoth–Karkur*

Today Whitaker and I loaded our luggage and his, and the camp beds, on to the Baby Austin and set off for Karkur. Whitaker clutched our Primus stove on his lap. The little car was so over-loaded it could only go at twenty-five miles an hour. En route we stopped in Tel Aviv where I bought a wooden bed and mattress, four upright canvas garden chairs, and a table to eat off – all for under fifty pounds. Whitaker saw an upright 'honky tonk' piano in the furniture store and went mad and hired it. These will all be delivered tomorrow to Karkur. We stuck twice in the sand track before we reached Karkur and had to get out and push. We found Elsa, my landlady, had cleared and cleaned her bungalow. She asked me if she might clean and cook for me regularly for a little more money and I agreed.

The bungalow has two rooms, a small kitchen, bathroom and loo. Its walls are white, yellow tiles cover the floor and I've bought enough blue sail cloth to make curtains. Whitaker and I lit the bath heater and prepared dinner after we'd driven back to Hederah to buy stores from the NAAFI. We were tired and rather proud of our progress, but when Dan arrived he was too exhausted to notice anything: the Sherwood Rangers had a terrible two days getting here. Now Dan and Whitaker are gone to their tents in camp and I am alone – stitching curtains and listening to the night serenade of frogs and crickets, and the eerie howls of pye dogs.

Dan said it was a fine sight – seeing the Regiment parade by squadrons below Latrun and file away across the plain. Each man carried a forage net, a nose bag, and rations for two days. They rode all morning, plagued by flies and halted at noon for lunch in a narrow lane with a hedge on one side and a line of trees on the other. Dan had dismounted and given his troop the order to take bits out and prepare to water when suddenly, without the slightest warning, two squadrons of horses, which were standing in a rise beyond him, charged down the track at full gallop. Dan flung himself into a ditch. They swept by like an avalanche; some of them crashed headlong into two army trucks which were parked in the lane, others hit the telegraph poles which fell like nine-pins and, as they passed, Dan's troop broke loose and went with them. When the dust cleared Dan saw an incredible scene of destruction – injured men, dead horses and a tangle of equipment lay everywhere and, far away, a moving trail of dust showed the horses were still racing madly on. Doctor Brooke, who had been dressing a soldier's foot in the middle of the lane, had a marvellous escape; when he saw the horses charging down on him he flung himself over his patient and the whole cavalcade passed over him. Neither of them was hurt.

They collected the casualties and then set off on foot to find the horses. It took ages. Some had gone back to Latrun; some are still lost. Dan found his chestnut mare covered with blood – all the skin torn off her shoulders and flanks. She had galloped through a barbed-wire fence. But many other horses were worse and several had to be shot. Gradually the Regiment reassembled and started out again. When evening came they put down horse lines and bivouacked. A special watch was kept in case of more trouble. To add to their anxiety, storks, which are in migration, kept landing on the nearby power cables and burning in blue flames. Dan put his bed two hundred yards from the horse lines and went to sleep. He was woken by the thunder of hooves. It was terrifying – in the dark he could not see which way they were coming till one horse crashed into the cook-house tent and sent it up in flames. The poor cook had both his legs broken.

No one knows what caused these stampedes. Some think there may be a mad horse which is the ring-leader. But the fact is that at some indefinable signal a hundred horses will move as one, and nothing will stop them. The Cheshire Yeomanry, who are right up at Acre in the north, have had the same trouble; some of their horses stampeded and plunged over a cliff into the sea. Whitaker says this is all caused by the Holy Ghost.

26 March 1940   *Karkur, Palestine*

Every week Toby and I bump over the sand-track to buy stores, fruit, vegetables and amaryllis lilies, from the NAAFI in Hederah. Sometimes we go to one or other of the lovely little beaches for a swim. We listen often to radio news – in English from Jerusalem, and French from Beirut. Most of the wives and many of the Yeomanry are reading the Bible – partly for religion and partly as a guide book for Palestine.

I dislike the Jewish habit of touching a small strip fixed on the edge of front doors of houses, shouting 'Shalom' and then walking straight in to all the rooms. Today I was seated on the lavatory when I heard a 'Shalom' and my doors being opened

31

and suddenly the lavatory door was flung wide and a Jewish vendor thrust a tray of boot laces at me. Only when I promised to buy some did he retreat to my bedroom and let me finish my business.

1 April 1940   Karkur, Palestine

We all long for letters from home, but when they arrive they are so often marked with the black slashes of censors. Here we all exchange our news hoping, from each other's fragments, to piece together a picture of how it is in England. Poor Tony Herbert told me today that, in his last letter from home, he learned that the lawns at Wilton have been ploughed up. We write home often but our news must seem frivolous when we can only say we have visited Jerusalem or been swimming on a lovely beach. One good thing: as each Yeomanry is raised from one neighbourhood in England, all ranks can share news with interest.

7 April 1940   Karkur, Palestine

At last we may work. Now wives are allowed to drive in pairs to help in shifts at the Soldiers' Rest Camp on the edge of Haifa. We dole out tea, orangeade and buns. It is hot standing by the big urns. There is a wireless, a small library and a lot of games in the canteen. I have also become part-time secretary to Mrs Pollock, wife of the District Commissioner, who is head of the Red Crescent in this area. She was desperate for secretarial help.

As we drive to and from Haifa, we see Arab women sauntering along with pitchers on their heads – barefoot boys piping music as they watch their flocks – and camels so laden with fresh-cut crops that only their heads and hooves show under their burdens. We see Arabs threshing, clustered around a primitive wheel turned by a blindfold ox – and elders squatting in triangles of shade on street corners, wagging their long beards and tongues. And, so often, we see Arab men riding their donkeys with their poor wives walking behind carrying unbelievable loads. It all looks peaceful and slow but in this small country whose inhabitants look so alike except for their clothes there are opposite approaches to life – two different speeds and two quite different religions. Sooner or later there must be more Troubles between Arabs and Jews. Most of the land seems to belong to Arabs.

10 April 1940   *Karkur, Palestine*

Germany has attacked Norway – suddenly, and surreptitiously. We are stunned by this news. With Finns and Danes already out of the conflict I wonder what the Swedes will do. Surely they can't stay neutral. Our soldiers and sailors will have a difficult task to help the Norwegians whose coast line is so long and jagged and whose land is covered in snow. We are dreadfully worried for Europe.

20 April 1940   *Karkur, Palestine*

From my window I can see the long horse lines of the Sherwood Rangers shimmering in the heat haze and the little figures of our Yeomen hurrying about their work. We all know that there is no place for horse cavalry in modern war and we all hate being useless and far away at such a time, yet morale is extraordinarily high. Perhaps fury rather than fear is keeping us sane. Whitaker says there is not a man in the camp who thinks that Hitler could ever conquer us.

13 May 1940   *Karkur, Palestine*

Dan had three days' leave for Whitsun so we set off for Beirut at the Baby Austin's maximum speed of forty-five miles per hour. We drove northwards along the coast road, through Haifa where white houses are wedged on the side of Mount Carmel, past the domes and minarets of Acre to Ras el Naquora, the frontier post. On and on we crawled through sleepy Syrian villages, past terraced vineyards and lovely beaches where cattle stood, cooling themselves, on the edge of the sea. Over pot-holed roads and cobbled streets we arrived at the St George Hotel and civilisation, tired but excited and happy.

Next morning we explored delightful shops filled with French fashions, patisseries and perfume. In the afternoon we went to the cedar-lined racecourse where Dan backed six winners. The crowd was intriguing: chic French women in hats; fat pashas smoking hookahs in the shade; dapper French officers, sailors, Spahis and Foreign Legion. General Weygand, a tiny man covered in medals, walked over from the Residence on the far side of the course to watch the races.

In the evening, when we were dancing happily on the moon-lit terrace of a night club by the sea, a Frenchman told us that Germany has invaded Holland, Belgium and Luxemburg and that Mr Churchill has taken over from Mr Chamberlain as Prime Minister. Dan thought perhaps he was drunk.

16 May 1940   *Karkur, Palestine*

At first we were sure the Germans could not advance far, that the Allies would counter-attack and drive them back but – in less than a week – after heroic but hopeless resistance, Holland has laid down her arms. Belgium and France, next on Hitler's hideous menu, are now in real trouble and so is our British Army. We listen to the wireless incessantly and each day our hopes are shattered. With dreadful monotony we hear of para-chute landings, air bombardments, refugees, the Germans always advancing . . . The size and speed of the German thrust grows hourly more apparent and horrifying. Standing, sweat-ing, behind the big urns in the Rest Camp Canteen I felt so sorry for the soldiers: no one whistled, laughed or even talked much; the books, games and the gramophone stayed in the cupboard today. On our way home, I wondered how Elsa and our neighbours think; they never comment on the news and, of course, we can't understand their Hebrew and German conver-sations. Toby is so near to tears she can hardly speak – she is so worried for her children. Each day, with shaky hands, we mark and re-mark our maps of Europe.

Winston Churchill, now Prime Minister, has made another broadcast. It gave us a clear understanding of the gravity of the hour and of his absolute belief in the British people – that we will never surrender. His news was petrifying but I felt braver for his words. Whitaker came up to the bungalow. He, too, had taken courage from Mr Churchill. We had a chat before his bath and he looked over the top of his spectacles and said, 'My Lady, the likes of me believe we will win this war, somehow, someday. I think it would help all our "hesprits du corpses" if you and His Lordship gave a Ball in this bungalow – just like they did before Waterloo.' I agreed. When he'd gone back to camp I locked the doors, pulled the curtains and wept till I fell asleep.

The Germans are in Brussels. General Weygand, recalled from the Levant, is now French Commander-in-Chief. It is Whitaker's Birthday.

Whitaker stole time to help me prepare for the 'Ball'. First we killed the scorpions and tarantulas which lurk round our trash-cans at the back door. Then we moved most of our possessions, except for the Upright Piano and set them down on the sand track behind our bungalow. We rigged up a buffet in the small kitchen, a bar in the bathroom and cleared our two rooms. We drove several times to Hederah to buy food and drink, borrow glasses, plates and a few more folding chairs.

The 'Ball' went well: our Colonel and most of the officers came and all 'illegal wives' in their best dresses. Whitaker brought friends to man the buffet, the bar and the band. He is a brilliant 'Honkey Tonk' pianist and he fairly let go with all our favourite tunes from the thirties. Our 'hesprits du corpses' soared and soon the party extended all along the sand tracks of the little settlement with soldiers, Arabs, Jews and pye dogs joining in in their different ways. It was long after midnight when Whitaker played 'God Save the King' and the settlement and the camp went to bed.

The news from France is petrifying. The Belgian Army has capitulated.

At last a few letters have arrived from home. One was from Aunt Puss[1] who wrote from Sussex on May 17th. She is still Lady-in-Waiting to Queen Mary. She must have sent it in the diplomatic bag because its postmark is Jerusalem.

I know what an agony of anxiety you must be going through, far away. Events have indeed moved fast since last I wrote.

Here it is incredibly lovely and it is hard to realise that so near the ghastly struggle is going on. From all accounts our Air Force has performed prodigies – our machines and pilots are immensely superior to the Germans, but our numbers are so small. I lunched with the Household at Buckingham Palace two days ago and met the ADC and Lady-in-Waiting to Queen Wilhelmina – who had just arrived – and heard the story of their departure from Holland, without even a toothbrush. They were in a dug-out during a raid when news came that they must leave The Hague. They started off for a port – I think the Hook – and the convoy of cars was bombed; when they got to the quayside a British destroyer was waiting; it was bombed as they arrived but without damage. The Queen's intention was to go to one of the Islands, but owing to the terrific bombing they decided to come to England. The ADC told me he did not know where his wife and family were.

Here the preparations to meet parachute troops are being hurried on, and the Fifth Column rounded up – I only wish they'd intern alien women as well as men. There must be a great deal of spying here – I don't doubt lots of the refugees were, in a number of cases, women who had been in service or positions of some sort in Holland and knew exactly where important points were. It is quite true some were dropped dressed as nuns. Many of the parachutist men who were wounded proved to be boys of only fourteen and sixteen.

By the time this reaches you much will have happened: pray God the German advance will have stopped. General Carton de Wiart, who was in Norway, said the German organisation

---

[1] Lady Constance Milnes Gaskell, Dan's aunt, for many years Lady-in-Waiting to Queen Mary. Tiny, adored by all of us, we kept in close touch.

and equipment are marvellous but the men inferior to the 1914 German Army. This must tell in a short time . . .[1]

P.S. I saw Lord Hardwicke yesterday, just back from Italy. He said the anti-ally demonstrations are all organised, that the five heads of the great corporations are in German pay – the people loathe the Germans but the strangle-hold of the Fifth Column is terrific. He thinks it fifty-fifty whether Italy comes in or not. He had a horrid experience in a café – was clouted over the head by a bunch of thugs . . . eventually he was released but the Italian who was with him, and tried to defend him, was murdered next day.

3 June 1940   *Karkur, Palestine*

Desperate fighting is going on in France. The French and British Armies are now in terrible danger. In the canteen, in the camp, in our bungalows, in the newspapers and on the wireless one word is holding us spellbound – DUNKIRK. Our prayers, thoughts and talk pivot on this word. And as we wait, aghast, for news through the long hours and days there is not one of us who would not be in England now . . .

4 June 1940   *Karkur, Palestine*

The fourth of June. I woke and thought of Eton, pretty clothes, and strawberries and cream . . .

I hardly dare write this down: it now seems just possible that in spite of appalling danger and difficulty, most of our troops and many Frenchmen, too, are being snatched from the shores of France in ships and small boats and taken to England. But Dunkirk must fall soon – horribly soon.[2]

[1] Despite lurid stories, *no* parachutists were, in fact, dropped as nuns but everyone believed it! And, unfortunately for us, the Germans were by no means inferior to the 1914 Army.

[2] Operation 'Dynamo', the evacuation of Allied troops from Dunkirk, was complete on 3 June – 225,000 British troops and as many French, had been saved.

'The Italians have declared war and we are evacuating
Norway . . .' I switched off my wireless and walked down the
sand track to Toby's bungalow. Elsa's Alsatian snarled as I
passed and I thanked God he is kept on a chain. Big ants and
spiders hurried into the brown grass as I approached and I
kept an eye out for scorpions. I thought of the war in the blue-
green water a few miles away – the Mediterranean which is a
gauntlet now. And my Mother? Switzerland is nearly encircled
by our enemies.

Toby pushed open her fly-netted door and I said, 'Shalom.'
Her floor was covered with maps and her eyes were filled with
tears. Then began the dreadful discussion we've been having
for days: should she stay with Dandy or return to her children?
With difficulty I made myself say I think she should return to
her children. I did not add that this may no longer be possible.

The Germans are in Paris. In a fury I wrote to Monty Moore
Montgomery in New York – reversing his letter to me as well as
I could remember:

> It was perfectly grand hearing from you, Monty, and I am glad
> you are busy equalling your quota of ecstasy as the
> Madhatters might say. But if you are counting on us British to
> ask quarter, or cry surrender, I suspicion you will be
> disappointed. The feeling here is intense against Nazi-ism and
> sentiment has gone overboard. The British, you know, revere
> freedom and all of us think Churchill is the finest man in
> Europe – if not in the world today – and that, with such a
> leader, England will do a lot of unpleasant things to Germany
> as Hitler insists. It would seem foolish to me to stay neutral
> when such a straight fight is going on between good and evil.
> And just so you won't dislike me too much for my views I'd like
> to say I feel damn sorry for all the neutrals who, while others
> face the music, hope they may stay safe. Their turn will come.
> Of course this does not make pleasant reading but I must say
> you Americans need to enjoy a little realism. Our people will

always fight for freedom and never surrender to tyranny. If America does not join our struggle soon I will be both shocked and surprised. Life here is not usual: the new decor is khaki – we've forgotten exotic islands and night clubs – sirens and search-lights are in third speed. And so farewell to politics. After the war we will meet you in the Ritz Bar in Paris, to celebrate the downfall of Hitler and talk of happy things.

25 June 1940   *Karkur, Palestine*

It is difficult to think straight, perhaps it is foolish to try to think at all. In England it seems the majority of our troops are home but their arms and vehicles are left behind. The terrible air battle goes on – so many of our friends are fighter pilots. The French signed an Armistice on June 17th, but plenty of Frenchmen want to fight on. What will become of the French Fleet and their colonies in North Africa? The Mediterranean is now flanked by enemies. To our north, in Syria, there is great confusion. To our south the Italians are poised to attack. Our reinforcements and supplies – even our mail – will now have to come round the Cape. What will be the fate of the thousands of wounded and prisoners now in Hitler's clutches? What will happen to 1 Cav. Div. and its beautiful horses? What can we say to the Yeomen here whose wives and children are in England?

No one has appeared from the camp today, which seems rather odd. Now there is a soldier on the water-tower close by my house. He watches the countryside through binoculars. Before it did not seem to matter but now we're uncomfortably aware that all our neighbours speak German.

29 June 1940   *Karkur, Palestine*

Dandy Wallace arrived in a great hurry – en route to become a Staff Officer in Jerusalem. I helped Toby pack all their things in thirty minutes flat. I shall miss her. Dandy brought me a note from Dan:

A lot of our officers have been sent to the Syrian frontier to welcome, feed and help any French who come over to us.

There is great confusion in Syria because of German propaganda and rumour. No one knows who or what to believe. Some of the French have accepted the Armistice – others have not. The latter are trying to join us in Palestine – the former are trying to stop them. Last night Frenchmen got through at Ras el Naquora – some in the boots of cars, some under piles of straw on lorries, some just walked or rode. Further along the border, near Tiberius, parties of French Foreign Legion, Spahis and Poles are coming over. I may not see you for days . . .

Dan enclosed a note from Philip Parbury who is with the 16th Australian Group at Julis Camp on the Gaza Road:

. . . In Beirut, at the races, Hermione said General Weygand looked rather nice and able – she was very funny about all his medals and said if he got any more he'd have to sew them on his trousers. How wrong she was. Never mind. A lot of us think it is best to know where we stand, even if we stand alone. I hear from home that, since Dunkirk, Australians are joining the AIF in thousands. All our thoughts are centred on England now.

The Germans are attacking Britain with massive daylight raids. An almighty struggle is going on in the air. As radio news reaches us, day after day, we are amazed at the courage of our fighter pilots and the damage they are doing to enemy planes. But we are fearful of this onslaught – for all our people. Meanwhile it is vital we get the French Fleet to join us or destroy it. The Vichy Government has broken off relations with Britain. A Frenchman called de Gaulle is trying to rally the French in England. No letters are reaching us. We are all trying not to show our deep anxiety – we dress well, make up our faces carefully and try to talk cheerfully. But really we are terrified.

9 July 1940   *Karkur, Palestine*

Dan is back in camp. He dashed in to see me and told me that rumour has it that General de Larminat tried to come over to us but General Mittlehauser upheld orders from France and it

40

is thought de Larminat may now be in prison. Here it is whispered that a squadron of Spahis left their regiment on the line of march and galloped fifty kilometres to cross the frontier into Palestine – and that six thousand Poles have come over to us and brought their equipment with them.

Dan told me the Sherwood Rangers are moving north to Haifa and broke it to me gently that the horses are not coming. They are being sent to a Remount Depot where Mouse Townsend, who really cares for horses, will be in charge. The Sherwood Rangers are to man coast guns and eventually become mechanised cavalry.

For a long time we've known that horse cavalry has no place in modern warfare, but now the horses are going away we feel frightful – so many of them are old friends, hunters and part of our families. It is so sad that these lovely animals will never again graze in England's green fields or enjoy a good stable. We feel like traitors to have brought them here and now must leave them behind, and I'm remembering what my father told me about the British horses which were left in Palestine after the First World War and how, through ignorance, they were neglected and ill treated.

This afternoon Dan's little groom came up from camp to see me – in floods of tears. Together we went down to the horse lines so I could say goodbye to Horse Number Nine and Dan's beautiful chestnut mare . . . I stroked all the velvet noses as I walked back along the lines, and I felt sick with sadness. Whitaker returned to the bungalow with me and he was crying too. Wives are not allowed in the camp, but no one scolded me. Whitaker said, 'I've grown to like horses. They are so much better than bicycles.'

Last week we attacked French capital ships at Oran and Mers el Kebir.

12 July 1940   *Karkur – Haifa, Palestine*

Dan's hurriedly scribbled note just said: 'We are awfully busy. Pack up. I'll find you in Haifa through the Red Crescent Office. Take Whitaker with you.'

Whitaker and I stacked our possessions on the Baby Austin. As always, he made me laugh. As we were loading, a young English wife turned up in a ramshackle car – she was looking for somewhere to live as her husband's Yeomanry is moving to our camp site. I asked her how she managed to get to the Middle East and she told me she had gone as a missionary to Beirut and lived in a convent. I arranged with Elsa that she move into our bungalow on the same terms as us and I gave her all our humble furniture. Just as Whitaker and I were ready to drive off Elsa and her German friends ran out of their bungalows to shake hands. I was very touched and rather surprised.

It took ages to reach Haifa and on arrival I called on Mrs Pollock to tell her I could now work full time for the Red Crescent. She asked where I was staying and I told her I was at present on the pavement. She suggested I try to get a room at the German hospice close by the docks. She came to see me off. When she saw our Baby Austin and Whitaker seated on top of our luggage she began to laugh. She sat down on the door-step and for several minutes she went on laughing.

At the German hospice the Mother Superior rented me a nice old-fashioned room overlooking a large walled garden where nuns were strolling amongst cypress trees. It is not expensive. After dumping our luggage I drove Whitaker to Peninsular Barracks on the edge of the sea. It looked horrible. 'Speaking candidly,' said Whitaker cheerfully, 'I consider this to be a dog's life, but almost anywhere must be better than that ghastly Karkur. I really hand it to Your Ladyship that you did not go mad in that Godforsaken place.'

15 July 1940   *Haifa, Palestine*

God has certainly not forsaken the German hospice. Though the floors are stone, the walls bare, the beds like corrugated iron and the food revolting, the nuns, who are very shy, are so kind we can take courage from that. They put fresh fruit and flowers in our room every day, and arrange our mosquito nets like a sacred ritual. There is a peacefulness in the house and

42

garden which is comforting. We get up very early – Dan to go to his troop which is learning gunnery, and me to join Mrs Pollock and her mountain of work. Some time, when we can afford it, we shall drive to the top of Mount Carmel to dine. It is cooler there, and we are told there is an excellent restaurant. At night our blacked-out bedroom is like a Turkish bath.

Great news: Whitaker has become a Bombadier. Last night I went with him to a troops dance at the Barracks and we won a spot-prize dancing 'Boomps a Daisy'. Whitaker says the Barracks are alive with bed bugs.

2 August 1940   Haifa, Palestine

This morning I heard the drone of aeroplanes and ran out into the hospice garden to see them. We seldom see aeroplanes. There were about ten flying high over Mount Carmel coming towards us. They looked lovely against the blue sky. Our wonderful RAF, I thought . . . and waved . . . then I heard a dull thud of explosion, like blasting, and it came again – crump, crump, crump. Enemy planes. Working in the office and worrying about Dan and the Yeomanry all day was a misery. How can the people in England bear it? When he came home Dan told me they were Italian planes and their pilots most likely are A La Littoria airline crews who flew this route regularly till quite recently. The locals call them the Green Mice. Probably they are based on Rhodes. I wonder why the air raid sirens did not go off.

16 August 1940   Haifa, Palestine

The sun has baked the hills a lovely camel colour and the olive trees are now almost silver. Each day our wireless tells us of more and more German planes being shot down by the RAF. But still the ghastly air battle goes on at home.

Today the Green Mice bombed us again. They were aiming at the oil tanks and refinery, and at the docks which are close to the hospice. The noise of their bombs and our guns was terrific. This time our air raid sirens warned in good time. A little old nun chivvied me into the hospice cellar where I found a crowd of terrified Arabs – all calling on Allah – and a floor seething with huge cockroaches which sprinted around my feet and up my skirt. I hurried back into the sunlight and thanked God Dan was up on Mount Carmel manning the 'Listeners'. Now the harbour is full of dead fish from bombs which fell in the water and a great black, billowing plume of smoke is spiralling in the sky where one of the oil tanks is burning. A bomb fell on a small market place nearby, and bits of bodies are spattered all over adjacent buildings – awful.

As Dan was working late I went, after my work, to the Soldier's Rest Camp and, lo and behold, there was Whitaker thumping away on the Upright Piano. 'A pal of mine brought it from Karkur in an Army truck. It stays here and most evenings I come and play to cheer up the chaps,' he said.

I heard today that some Jews have painted Swastikas on the flat roofs of their houses in Haifa.

23 August 1940   *Haifa, Palestine*

Dan telephoned me at the office and told me to meet him for lunch at Spinney's Garden Restaurant by the harbour. He sounded worried. We met under a big sun umbrella and ordered an omelette. Then he showed me an official paper which reached him from Jerusalem Army Headquarters this morning.

> Wives of British soldiers are to be evacuated voluntarily to
> South Africa, but 'illegal' wives, i.e. those who reached the
> Middle East after war was declared and against military orders,
> will be compulsorily evacuated at an early date . . .

While we were discussing this bombshell the Green Mice flew over us and dropped some more. They were unpleasantly close and the noise was appalling. I felt grateful for the sun umbrella over our table. When I got back to the office I told Mrs Pollock our news. She was furious and dictated a strong letter which I typed and she signed: it stated that English-speaking shorthand typists are non-existent in Palestine and she could not replace me. Because of this she asked that I be allowed to stay. She sent this off to GHQ in Jerusalem and gave me a copy.

25 August 1940   *Haifa, Palestine*

Dan and I drove to Jerusalem to see Toby and discuss the evacuation dilemma. I wanted to go to the Headquarters and ask for exemption but Toby persuaded me not to. 'The one-eyed Brigadier who is dealing with this is fanatical on the subject of "illegal" wives. It is useless to ask him,' she said. She advised me to go to Middle East Headquarters in Cairo where the fact that I was a War Office secretary might be fairly considered.[1] She told us she had decided to let herself be sent home because of her children.

Dan and I lunched at Government House with the High Commissioner, Sir Harold MacMichael and his wife. She is President of the Palestine Red Crescent and most kindly gave me a letter stating that I am doing a useful job in Palestine and it would be helpful if I be allowed to stay.

9 September 1940   *Cairo, Egypt*

Dan's Divisional General, George Clark, not only gave me the necessary permit to come to Egypt for forty-eight hours but volunteered a letter to a Colonel McCandlish recommending that I be allowed to stay at my job in Palestine – this because he too has been suffering from the shortage of English-speaking secretaries. I flew by Misr Airways from Lydda to Cairo today. At dinner with Elizabeth Coke[2] – by a miracle – I met a Mrs Creagh, wife of General Creagh[3] who is in the Western Desert. She, like so many other wives, is considered 'legal' because she was here at the outbreak of war. She bombarded me with

[1] Before I went to Australia I had worked at the War Office, first in the typing pool for strict training and afterwards as secretary to four Generals in Pall Mall.

[2] Soon to become Countess of Leicester.

[3] Commander, 7th Armoured Division.

questions: how long had I been a secretary, how did I get out of England – have we a home in England and children . . . I told her everything. She said it was unlikely that Colonel McCandlish – who is 'One-Eye's counterpart here – would see me, but she is seeing him tomorrow and would like to present my case herself. 'This is just because there is such a desperate shortage of secretaries in Middle East Headquarters,' she said.

11 September 1940   *Cairo, Egypt*

I waited all day at the Continental Hotel for Mrs Creagh. Freddie Hoffman, the Swiss hotel manager, lent me his English newspapers: the descriptions of bombing in England are ghastly. Mrs Creagh arrived at the hotel only an hour before my train was due to leave. She told me Colonel McCandlish had refused to consider my case but she had felt so strongly about it that she had gone to see the Commander-in-Chief, Middle East, General Wavell, who had authorised her to write a letter to General Clark in Palestine.

All my life I will remember Mrs Creagh. Twenty-four hours ago I did not know her. Now she arrived, panting, from seeing General Wavell on my behalf. She demanded paper and pen and wrote to General Clark. She left the envelope open so that I could read it in the train. Then she gave me a hug and was gone. I caught the train by a whisker and read the letter:

Continental Hotel, Cairo.
11.9.1940

Dear General Clark,

I saw Sir Archie Wavell about Lady Ranfurly's exemption.

He is willing to grant it if you and the GOC Palestine will say in writing that you are willing for her to stay *on the grounds of her capacity as a trained shorthand typist who has worked for the War Office.* That is not in any sense a precedent or on compassionate grounds – but solely on the grounds of her usefulness in a capacity which is hard to obtain here.

I don't know what it is like with you in Palestine – down here trained and experienced shorthand typists who are English and reliable are almost non-existent.

I took your letter for her to Colonel McCandlish as I was
seeing him anyhow on business. He, quite rightly, said the
General wished no exceptions made, but on the grounds of
Lady Ranfurly's qualifications which I knew at any rate we
badly needed here I took the rather regrettable step of going
straight on to Sir Archie himself.

Forgive me for bothering you about this, (also my writing
which is with a hotel pen and in a hurry.)

Yours, Jean Creagh

12 September 1940   *Haifa, Palestine*

Dan met me at the station. He was delighted with my news. We
took Mrs Creagh's letter straight to General Clark who was
kind and congratulated us. There and then he telephoned
Jerusalem and spoke to AQMG whatever that may be. I could
hear an irate voice booming back at him. 'It is vital', said
General Clark, laying down the receiver, 'that you take this
letter to Jerusalem tomorrow for General Neame to see. I have
made an appointment for you with the AQMG.' He chuckled
and added, 'You must hurry or you will be removed from the
Middle East in chains.' As we were leaving I asked, 'How many
eyes has the AQMG?'

'What an odd question,' he replied. 'As a matter of fact he
has only one.' My heart sank.

London is being terribly bombed. More and more of our
Fighter friends in the RAF have been killed.

14 September 1940   *Haifa, Palestine*

I arrived at GHQ Jerusalem on time for my appointment and
telephoned from the lobby that I was there. I was told to wait in
the hall. I sat there for three hours. At last I found myself
face to face with Brigadier Brunskill, a dark, square-faced man
wearing a black patch over one eye. I handed him Mrs
Creagh's letter and asked for it to be given to General Neame,
the GOC. He refused and stated I could have no exemption.
'You will go', he said, 'on the first evacuation ship, very soon.

47

You may stay in South Africa or proceed to England. You can't expect me to believe that a Countess can type.'

Over and over again I asked him to show the letter to General Neame but he refused. A young officer stood beside his desk – presumably to make sure I would not put out his other eye. For a whole hour 'One-Eye' tried to persuade me that he was reasonable and right. I asked him why Army wives who do not work at all are being allowed to stay – and was he not aware of the shortage of secretaries in the Middle East? Finally, with Mrs Creagh's letter still lying unopened on his desk, I got up, apologised to the young officer who had been kept standing so long and opened the door. As I left I said, 'Brigadier, if I am forced to leave I will return.'

He laughed and snapped, 'You may be sure I shall make it absolutely impossible for you to return to the Middle East Theatre of War.' I closed the door – which I longed to slam – and made the long journey back to Haifa. When I told Dan this dismal news he told me some more: the Italians have advanced in the Desert.[1]

16 September 1940   *Haifa, Palestine*

I've got sandfly fever and my temperature is astonishingly high. Though I feel awful I am pleased about this because the doctor says if my temperature does not come down I will not be fit to travel. Whitaker came to see me today. He brought me a bunch of flowers which must have cost him two weeks' pay. Dan has received a bill for forty pounds from the Army to pay for me to go to South Africa. This is a ludicrous situation: Dan's pay as a Second Lieutenant is tiny, he won't get marriage allowance until he is thirty. My journeys to Cairo and Jerusalem cost a lot – we are now worried about money.

I am not Brigadier 'One-Eye's only victim – all Yeomanry

<hr>

[1.] On 13 September Marshal Graziani, Italian Commander-in-Chief in Libya, advanced into Egypt with five Infantry Divisions, supported by 120 tanks. After entering Sollum, from which the British had withdrawn, the Italian advance stopped at Sidi Barrani, some fifty miles from Sollum. The Italians then began to construct fortifications and went on the defensive.

wives are being forced to leave. Worst of all a radiologist, who is the only person in this country who can do her particular kind of work, is being sent home. Mrs Pollock is frantic – so many of us work for the Red Crescent in one way or another and her work load is heavy. She really does need our help.

Later. The news is bad: The Italians have reached Sidi Barrani and my temperature is going down – now it is only 102.1. My friend the bank manager came to see me. He gave me a letter of introduction to his great friend in Cape Town – a Mr Butler.

People say that the Italians have 300,000 troops in Cyrenaica and we have 30,000. They also say the Italians are better equipped than us. A dreadful time to be sent away.

The Germans are bombing London and other cities at home night after night with devastating ferocity. It takes courage even to read the news – the slaughter and damage is so awful.

21 September 1940   s.s. *The Empress of Britain, Suez*

I kissed all the nuns goodbye and thanked them. Whitaker came to say farewell – he was dreadfully upset. I gave him some of my remaining money to rent the Upright Piano for another three months. Dan was on duty all day on the Listeners on Mount Carmel but somehow he managed to arrive just before the soldiers came to take me away. As always he looked so elegant and charming but this time dreadfully sad . . . I felt almost insane with grief – but managed not to cry. The air raid sirens went off just as I got into the military car . . . Dan and the nuns waved me away.

They took me to Lydda where the evacuation train was due to leave at 11.30 p.m. There were soldiers everywhere, seemingly to make sure none of us escaped. I found an unhappy crowd of women struggling with their luggage in the black-out. Toby, magnificent as ever, was sitting in a corner seat of the train, keeping a place for me. When I sat down she unzipped her canvas overnight bag and revealed a bottle of whisky and another of gin. 'Which will you have?' she asked.

'Both together,' said I.

We trundled slowly south. None of us slept. Our military escort was quiet and civil but it was evident we were 'under guard'. I wondered what they thought we'd done wrong.

Before dawn we reached Kantara. A soldier told us to get out of the train. 'You'll find breakfast in a hut over there,' he said, pointing into the darkness. Toby fell into a slit trench on the way. 'Breakfast' was simply horrible. Afterwards we had to wait three and a half hours for another train to arrive and carry us even further away. There was no hope of escape – the soldiers stayed with us all the time.

We reached Suez about noon and were told to get out of the train and collect our luggage. Toby hauling hers to the quay with her hat askew and her face set with rage was a sight to see. I sat down on my suitcase and laughed. We waited in a tender alongside the quay for several hours. It was intensely hot and we were tired and thirsty. Eventually we were ferried four miles out to sea to where the *Empress of Britain* was lying. The ship was in great disorder having disembarked 4000 troops from England this morning. No one seemed to expect us and it was late when we were allotted cabins and given some food. Toby and I are lucky – we have nice cabins on the sun-deck.

At nine o'clock we listened to the news: 185 German planes were shot down over England last Sunday. Our air defence is inspiring – Hurricanes and Spitfires – and our brilliant fighter pilots.

23 September 1940   s.s. *The Empress of Britain, Suez*

We are still off Suez. I can see the yellow hills of Egypt four miles away. Around us lie all the other ships which will sail with us in convoy. I got a sailor who was going ashore to post my daily letter to Dan. A late arrival on board brought me a letter from Dan who wrote that he has been asked to be ADC to General Neame, VC, in Jerusalem. He is to take up the post immediately . . . I am astonished.

This great, gloomy ship, which has been stripped of all her peace-time trappings, has beds in the ballroom – beds everywhere except in the dining room and main lounge. It is carrying a good many 'undesirables': ourselves; some officers who are considered to be too old; some 'legal' wives who will all get off and stay in Durban; a lot of drunks and, down below in cells, a few criminals. General Legentilhomme, who has been commanding the French in Djibuti, and his Aide are on board – also Lord Yarborough, who is being retired, and his wife. Colonel Jackson, who I sat next to at meals on the *Mohammed Ali El Kebir*, is also here. He says that ship was sunk recently.

24 September 1940   *s.s. The Empress of Britain. At sea*

When I woke this morning I discovered we had started. It will take nearly six weeks for this convoy to reach England. The distance and time which will now separate Dan and me is terrifying.

28 September 1940   *s.s. The Empress of Britain. At sea*

This is Hades. We are clamped down below decks because we are passing enemy territory. The purser told me that the last convoy which came through took a terrible pasting from Italian planes based in Eritrea and Italian Somaliland. For four days we will be in danger. The heat is unbelievable. The swimming pool has been emptied for this perilous period.

At midday, when the bar opens, the rush for it is astonishing. Toby says we're in a floating inebriates' home. The officer commanding troops confided in me today that the lower decks are fast turning into a brothel. He has had to post sentries to try to restore order.

Toby keeps trying to persuade me to go home with her but I am adamant that somehow I will get back to the Middle East. I am reading a lovely book called *Sand, Wind and Stars*, by St Exupéry. He tells a delightful story about flying over the Andes and carrying a bowl of goldfish in his plane so as to be sure which way up he was. Quite a lot of people are 'enjoying the voyage'. The officers and crew of this ship are quite remarkable. They have superb discipline, manners and kindness but

51

they have incessant problems – they are often in danger and they must be worried for their own families in England.

Mrs Chitty, a very senior AT, who has just surfaced after being seasick since Suez, is being sent home to recruit shorthand typists for the Middle East. She has kindly promised to recruit me if I return to England!

8 October 1940   *s.s. The Empress of Britain, Durban*

Today the whole convoy of ships put into Durban from a very rough sea. A lot of South Africans brought their cars to the docks to welcome the ships' crews and their passengers. Those of us who are going on to England may stay on board but the rest, in charge of evacuation officers, have been taken to billets in and around Durban. I fixed it so I could get off or stay on. Before going ashore I was given a message from Brigadier 'One-Eye' Brunskill who has arranged a job for me here – looking after evacuated women. I am glad I am on his conscience.

11 October 1940   *s.s. The Empress of Britain, Cape Town*

Today we steamed into Cape Town. It was exciting – such a spectacular coast. As soon as we were allowed ashore Toby and I raced for Barclays Bank to pick up mail. I found two letters from Dan. He likes working for General Neame. What irony – if this had happened a little earlier the General would have seen Mrs Creagh's letter . . . Dan works in the next office to Brigadier Brunskill.

Toby gave me an excellent lunch of crayfish and then hired a car to drive round Table Mountain. This is far the loveliest coast I've ever seen: high mountains drop sheer to the sea which is intensely blue. Great waves thrash against the rocks so that the surf looks as thick and white as avalanche snow.

When all the others had gone to a dinner-dance organised by South Africans I stayed behind to write letters for Toby to take home, and pack my luggage. I am going back to Dan.

3

Rebellion

12 October 1940   *Cape Town*

I divided my luggage so that I will be mobile – one suitcase and an overnight bag for me – the rest to go home with Toby. I managed to see the Captain and the purser alone – to say goodbye and thank them. And then I said farewell to Toby but nobody else. It was dreadful leaving her – she is so afraid for me. She promised to say my goodbyes to the others and take the rest of my luggage home but she wept at my decision. I'll never have a better friend ...

I went down the gangplank just before it was pulled up. I stood on the quay and waved till I could not see Toby any more and I stayed there till the great ship went over the horizon. She will cross the Atlantic alone[1] and should reach England on November 3rd. The rest of the convoy has not yet reached Cape Town.

I managed to get a small room at the Mount Nelson Hotel which has a nice garden where squirrels play. Suddenly I feel lonely: Dan is thousands of miles away; it will be nearly three weeks before Toby gets safely home; I've got only twenty-eight pounds left.

---

[1] It had been decided that the *Empress* was fast enough to dodge submarines and would go on alone, out of convoy.

This morning I went to Barclays Bank armed with my letter of introduction to Mr Butler, the manager. I found a short, thick-set man sitting behind an immense polished desk. He wore horn-rimmed spectacles and his pocket handkerchief matched his tie. I asked him how I should set about getting work with the Army as a secretary or a driver and told him I want to go north. He said it would be easy to get a job with the Army but I would have to sign on for the duration and it would be a long time before I would get near to the war. 'The lists of drivers and secretaries waiting to go north are long,' he said, and added, 'I see from this letter you brought that you have just been in Palestine. May I enquire why you want to return?'

'Why did your friend who wrote that letter always refer to you as "Battling Butler"?' I countered – trying to make up my mind whether I dared confide in him.

He grinned: 'My friend who gave you this letter always called me that because, so often, we were in trouble together.'

I told him everything, including what Brigadier 'One-Eye' had said about making it impossible for me ever to return to the Middle East. He invited me out to lunch to talk this over. We discussed the problem from every angle and he answered my questions and suggestions rapidly. He assured me it would not be possible to go from Cape to Cairo by taxi. Then he asked me how much money I've got. I told him. There followed a long silence . . .

Suddenly Mr Butler began to laugh. 'I have it,' he said, and went on laughing for several minutes. Then, beaming with smiles, he said, 'You hold all the trump cards – all of them are winners; Brigadier "One-Eye" will learn quite quickly that you did not stay in Durban, that you stayed on the *Empress* destined for England. All those on the *Empress* who know you jumped ship at Cape Town are now unable to communicate with anyone for three weeks. Probably I'm the only person alive who knows exactly where you are and what you're up to. Now, if the Military in the Middle East ask our Government here to make sure no evacuated ladies return to the Middle East, such a request would go to Pretoria where our Government is now sitting. Such a request will not reach Cape Town for ages. Right?' I nodded. 'This means you are left with only two problems – shortage of money and limited time. Now please forget the money – I shall lend you what is needed. But you must apply for a visa from our Cape Town office right now. This should not be a problem. As soon as you get it you must catch the next train to Durban. There you must not be recognised by anybody and you will find grave difficulty: there is a tremendous queue in Durban waiting for planes to go north. You must jump this queue. I shall give you the address and telephone number of my friend, Mr Hapgood, who works for Cook's Travel. Tell him nothing except that you must go on the next plane out of Durban. Trust me – he'll think you are Mata Hari.' Once again he rocked with laughter.

I tried to thank Mr Butler and offered him my engagement ring and brooch as security on a loan. But he waved my offer aside – 'Not on your life,' he said, 'I know you will pay me back, so I need no security. I just love rebels – and romance and adventure.' We shook hands and then I sped off to the Passport Office to ask for a visa for Egypt. They told me to return in a few days.

15 October 1940   *Cape Town*

Tonight I dined with Mrs Benjamin, Mrs Bloemfontein and Mrs Silberbower who are staying at the hotel. The hall porter told me that when they discovered I was a Countess they decided to give a dinner party. Rather disgracefully I accepted, because I felt hungry. I sat next to a Mr Eger who talked about Oslo and fish. I felt rather a misfit because they were all dressed up and their chat was about cocktail parties, hairdressers and Bridge.

Suddenly I am plunged into a peace-time world of lights, luxury and leisure. Everyone I love is in England where bombs are raining down – or in the Middle East which may ignite at any moment – or at sea and at risk like Toby. In Palestine, though there was no fighting, we lived in a war atmosphere of

55

black-outs, permits, the need to improvise – and all ranks were bound together by shared anxiety and discomfort. If one must live through a war it is best to get as near to it as possible and work all the time. Just now I feel a bit mocking at the trivialities of these very kind and nice people who are hardly touched by fear and tragedy. While waiting for my visa so many strangers have been kind to me but I have had to mind my manners all the time and, of course, I can't tell any of them that I can't wait to leave their kindness and this beautiful country behind.

18 October 1940   *In a train to Durban*

Today I walked to the Passport Office in an agony of mind. They gave me my passport marked with a three-month visa for Egypt. It cost two shillings and sixpence. All the way to Barclays Bank I kept looking at it and thinking of Brigadier 'One-Eye'. When I opened Mr Butler's office door – I forgot to knock – he said, 'You don't have to tell me – you've got it.' He seemed as pleased as me. He lent me 125 pounds and gave me a letter of introduction to Mr Hapgood of Thomas Cook and Son in Durban and another covering all his bank associates in Africa. Then we telephoned Mrs Butler and the three of us went out to toast my journey. Afterwards I airmailed a letter to Dan to explain enigmatically what I am trying to do.

By luck the fast train of the week was leaving for Durban at 6.45 p.m. I bought a second-class ticket for six pounds, eleven shillings and three pence and paid an extra three shillings to have a bed made up on my seat. Mr Battling Butler came to the station to see me off. When I tried to thank him he said, 'One day I must meet your Dan – he must be extra special. I've loved our conversations. I shall never forget that you asked me, so seriously, what a taxi would cost from Cape to Cairo. Best of luck. Remember you have not enough money to come back – or be delayed on the way.'

As the train slid out of Cape Town I stood in the corridor and looked back on Table Mountain – dark against the evening sky, like a gigantic full-stop marking the last bit of land till the Antarctic.

56

On the seat opposite me is a red-haired American mission-ary who never stops talking. I am quite sure she will put the natives off God. I watched the moon rise behind the moun-tains as we crossed a high pass with an engine fore and aft. No hope of sleeping – I am too excited. The wheels of the train seem to be chanting: 'You're going north, You're going north . . .'

20 October 1940   *Durban*

Yesterday morning we crossed a great plain which was scattered with high conical hills – like giant ant-heaps. I asked the guard if we would stop at Kimberley and he said, 'Yes, for ten minutes,' so I gave him the old Lezards'[1] telephone number and a tip and asked him to telephone them at the next stop in case they would come to Kimberley station to see me. They were on the platform when the train arrived and they told me their four sons are all in the war and my stepfather-in-law, Lizzie, is with the King's African Rifles in Kenya. It was fun swapping news. Quite a few people left the train at Kimberley and I was able to move into an empty carriage to escape the red-head missionary who was still talking – also she smelt awful.

The train arrived in Durban at 2.30 p.m. I'd asked the guard for the name of a very cheap and unfashionable hotel and took a taxi. Being a Sunday Durban looked duller than ever. I rented a tiny room which costs seven shillings a day for bed and breakfast in this nasty little hotel which has most peculiar guests. Perhaps it is a brothel. I dare not go out lest I meet someone from the *Empress* who might recognise me.

21 October 1940   *Durban*

This morning I telephoned Mr Hapgood at Cook's and asked him to come and see me. He sounded surprised but came when I told him I had a letter from Mr Butler. When he arrived he seemed confounded by the combination of my name and

---

[1] Lizzie Lezard was my stepfather-in-law.

this squalid hotel. I told him I must fly out on the next plane for Cairo. He shook his head and told me that British flying boats are booked solid with priority passengers for the next six weeks – he could not guarantee me a seat for two months or more. My heart sank.

Just as he was leaving Mr Hapgood hesitated and said: 'Mr Butler would not have written that letter to me for nothing. You are a civilian of rank. You are lodged in most unfortunate premises. May I ask what is your mission to Egypt and why is it so important for you to leave immediately for Cairo?'

I told him I could not explain why I was here or why I must go immediately to Cairo – nor had I any papers I could show to him or anyone else. I held out my hand and said, 'Mr Hapgood, my journey is urgent and secret. I can only put myself in your hands. It is vital I fly out of Durban on the next plane for Cairo.' He looked worried and, no doubt, so did I. He said he would telephone me, but I had little hope. As he left he said, 'For Heaven's sake don't go out of doors in this area after dark – it is not safe. But there is a very good film on at the little cinema across the road – called *Rebecca*.' He left and I contemplated my dilemma: if I have to wait for two months the return on my visa will reach Cairo before me and I will not be allowed to enter Egypt. I locked my door, put my little Colt revolver under my pillow and went to sleep.

22 October 1940   *Durban*

Today Mr Hapgood came to see me. I told him I had seen the film *Rebecca* three times. He smiled in his polite way and said, 'I have fixed it but don't ask me how. Tomorrow you must be ready at 4 a.m. Our car will collect you and take you to the flying boat.' He held out a big box of 'Cape to Cairo' cigarettes: 'To wish you luck,' he said. I wondered if he had telephoned Mr Battling Butler. I was so stunned by his news that I had to ask him to tell me all over again. I am allowed to take with me forty-four pounds of luggage – anything more he will send after me by ship. I am to be in the hall of this 'hotel' at 3.45 a.m. tomorrow. The cost of my ticket to Cairo is 115 pounds. I paid him in cash and he pulled my ticket out of his pocket. He shook me warmly by the hand and before I'd hardly thanked him he was gone.

23 October 1940   *Mozambique*

The flying boat took off at 6.30 a.m. We were hardly airborne when I remembered, to my horror, that I'd left my little Colt revolver under the pillow of my bed in that sordid hotel. We flew over hills where circles of mud-coloured villages looked like toadstools in fairy rings. Natives ran out to wave at the plane – tiny Lilliputian figures. Their crops looked beautifully symmetrical. Wads of cloud lay in the deep valleys. Amazing to think that Shelley wrote 'The Cloud' when he had never flown. Soon we were over wilder country with olive-coloured trees. Our shadow chased along beside us. Two children played trains on the floor of the cabin with their parents' shoes.

At 9 a.m. we landed on the water at Lourenço Marques. It took fifteen minutes to refuel the plane. Then we flew over land which looked like rhinoceros hide – flat, brown and pock marked. We crossed the Limpopo river – a great green and brown slash in the ground. Across forests we came down again at Beira and got a glimpse of bougainvillaea in the sun. On and on we flew, now over land, now along the edge of the coast where surf looked like a frill of lace. We saw no house or human for ages, but I counted twenty-four bush fires. Around teatime we passed over miles of scrub plain patched with swamps. A passenger told me we were once offered Portuguese East Africa for four million pounds. Funny to think Dorothy Paget could have bought it.

We landed on a lagoon off Mozambique and spent the night on a comfortable house-boat where I ate dinner with Captain Mountain, our pilot. He told me about the routes he flies. Then, suddenly, he asked me why I was going north – he seemed to know most women were being sent south. I told him the truth – all of it. He was charming and said he would help me all the way to Cairo. He laughed about my revolver, said not to worry – he'd get his office to pick it up and he'd bring it to

59

Cairo on another trip. After listening to the news on radio I felt exhausted and went to bed.

24 October 1940   *Kisumu*

We took off at 4.30 a.m. and flew over an immense wilderness of leafless trees. We landed at Lindi and then at Dar es Salaam to refuel. The skies were bumpy; it was hot and humid in both ports. Captain Mountain invited me to sit upstairs in the co-pilot's seat while we flew over Kenya – hoping there might be a break in the clouds so I could see snow-clad Kilimanjaro. Later he flew low to show me wild animals in the game reserves. The clouds became thicker and the little plane lurched crazily about the sky. I was dreadfully sick. We landed on Lake Victoria and were driven to the Kisumu Hotel. Just before dinner Captain Mountain knocked on my bedroom door: 'Bad news for you,' he said. 'General Dickenson, who commands East African Forces, and the Provost Marshal from Cairo are staying in this hotel and will fly in my plane tomorrow. You had better come and dine with me and my friends, Major and Mrs Galmin who live in three rondavels in a lovely garden just outside Kisumu.' I accepted gratefully.

25 October 1940   *Khartoum*

At five in the morning Lake Victoria was a sheet of blue and gold. Hippopotami were lounging in the water – a lot of them snuggled close together. I felt afraid: of being sick again and of the General and the Provost Marshal who were seated immediately behind me. Just before we took off an Italian prisoner of war was brought on board. He looked frightened and miserable.

We flew fairly low over native villages surrounded by high green hedges. When next we landed – at Rejaf on the Bahr el Jebel – the river looked so narrow I was petrified. In that part of the world natives stand about on one leg gazing into space. I saw lots of them doing this – it seems to be a local custom. From dawn to dusk we have flown fast and well, but still we are a long way from Cairo. I thought a lot about how on earth we can ever recover Europe from Hitler. I watched the prisoner, across the aisle from me, and wondered what he was thinking, poor devil. I got up and gave him a cigarette and lit it for him. When I got back to my seat the Provost Marshal tapped me on the shoulder: 'Two days ago that Italian was strafing our troops,' he said. 'You should not give him a cigarette. He is being taken to Cairo for interrogation.' We landed at Kosti on the White Nile. When the passengers got off the plane to stretch their legs I stayed behind for a moment to talk to the prisoner. He spoke a little French and told me his wife is expecting her first baby this week and he will be posted 'missing'. He produced from his pocket a small, crumpled photo of his young wife and tears rolled down his cheeks. I gave him Mr Hapgood's box of cigarettes and my lighter. As I stepped down into the sun I thought how terrible it must be to be a prisoner.

We landed on the Nile at Khartoum and I was put in the same car as the General and the Provost Marshal. I slipped quickly into the front seat beside the driver. We had hardly started when the Provost Marshal leaned forward and tapped me on my shoulder and began: 'I thought all ladies were going south . . .' I turned and grinned into the back of the car and began to explain that I could not talk much because I had been so terribly airsick – and then I produced a handkerchief and retched and retched into it. There the conversation ceased.

Khartoum was extremely hot. The hotel was crowded. I was given a room in the annexe. There was a big, old-fashioned fan in the ceiling. I could not sleep well because of the heat and my terror of being caught before reaching Cairo.

26 October 1940   *Cairo, Egypt*

We took off early. I smiled at the General and the Provost Marshal and the prisoner but spoke to none of them. Captain Mountain invited me up to the flight deck and told me exactly what to do on arrival in Cairo. He flew low over the ruins at Luxor and told me we were only 317 miles from Cairo. 'Stay brave', he said, 'and you'll make it.' It was exciting flying in over the Pyramids. We landed elegantly on the Nile and little boats came out to meet us. Captain Mountain came ashore with me and told Customs and Immigration officials that I was a special passenger and must be helped in every way possible, and he introduced me to Mr Teague, Head of Imperial Airways, who had come to meet the plane. Mr Teague kindly offered to drive me into Cairo. He dropped me at the Continental Hotel. I dared not go inside but got my friend, Abdul the concierge, to fetch me a Cairo telephone book so I could look up the address of Dan's best man, Pat Hore-Ruthven,[1] and his wife Pam. I then gave Abdul the little money I had left and hailed a taxi.

All the way to their flat in Gezirah I felt frantic: supposing they are away, out for the day, or anti 'illegal' wives . . . I had no money left, not even to pay the taxi. In a crumpled cotton dress, dusty and tired, I stood at their front door and rang the bell.

Pat Hore-Ruthven opened the door and stood for a moment, aghast. Then he began to laugh and I thought he'd never stop. 'Can you possibly pay for my taxi?' I asked. Pam and their guests then came to the door and they laughed too.

'Dan was here last week with his General and he thought you must be on the way to England as you'd not got off the boat at Durban,' they told me and most kindly invited me to stay with them in Pat's dressing room – 'till you are found or forgiven'. They were having tea so I sat down and wrote a note to Dan for their guest, Peter Thynne, who is going to Jerusalem tomorrow, to hand to Dan personally. Pat wrote a note to Dan too – he laughed all the time he was writing it. I asked Dan not to write or telephone me at this flat and suggested he address his letters to Pam at the Continental Hotel where she can pick them up. At dinner we toasted Battling Butler, Mr Hapgood and Captain Mountain.

I have been woken by air raid sirens and cannot get back to

[1] An Officer in the Rifle Brigade, he was the only son of Lord Gowrie, whom Dan had served in Australia. He joined the Special Forces set up for deep raiding in the desert.

sleep. It is 3.30 a.m., time to get up for flying boats. I've put on my dressing gown and, on the fabulous wings of memory, I've retraced my journey: glimpses of places, bougainvillaea in the sun, snatches of talk – 'you should not give him a cigarette' – the sounds and smells and sickness, the dawns and dusks, and the amazing kindness of strangers . . . Now my desperate fear of being caught and not getting into Egypt is gone and I am thankful. Egypt is a neutral country and, however hounded, I doubt I can be sent away. How lucky I am – compared to Toby, still on that great, gloomy ship . . . I can hardly believe I was on the *Empress* just fourteen days ago.

4

Suspense

At breakfast, Pat, Pam and I decided that no one should know where I am. If anyone comes to their flat I must retreat to the dressing room and stay there till they are gone. Pat is on leave from the Desert. Pam works at GHQ. She thinks she may hear if there are repercussions on my return. She is considered to be a legal wife and so is allowed to stay in the Middle East. This because, on her way back from Australia to England in 1939, she stayed for two weeks at Mersa Matruh and can therefore say she was resident in Egypt before war was declared. Pat has been telling me about the fighting in the Desert where the Italians greatly outnumber our forces. At present there is a halt in their advance.

I arrived for breakfast just as Pam was leaving for her office. She turned at the front door, her big, blue eyes very serious and said, 'Thank God you are here.' Then she left. I turned to Pat who was walking up and down the room with his toes turned out as they always are and rifling his hair with his fingers, and asked why Pam had said that. 'The *Empress . . .*' he began, and handed me the newspaper. I poured some coffee and looked at the front page of the *Egyptian Mail*.

Copy from newspaper

EGYPTIAN MAIL
Tuesday, October 29th, 1940

'EMPRESS OF BRITAIN' SUNK
VERY FEW CASUALTIES

London, Monday

The Admiralty regret to announce that the 'Empress of Britain' has been sunk as a result of enemy action. She was attacked by enemy aircraft and set afire and it was necessary to abandon her. Salvage operations were commenced immediately, but whilst in tow the ship blew up and sank.

Some 598 survivors out of a total of 643 aboard have already been landed by British warships. Included in this number were military families and a small number of military personnel. The resolute and efficient handling of the ship's anti-aircraft defences contributed to the high proportion of the total complement saved.

The liner was attacked 700 miles off the coast of Ireland.

GRAPHIC DETAILS

Survivors from the *Empress of Britain* landed at a western port on Sunday, declared the liner was bombed seven hundred miles off Ireland on Saturday morning. The aircraft then disappeared but returned and dropped four more bombs, including incendiaries. A number of people were killed when the bombs exploded and some of the ship's lifeboats caught fire and could not be lowered but, as there was little danger of the ship sinking immediately, there was plenty of time for passengers to take to the lifeboats before the liner was completely ablaze from stem to stern. The last were taken off some six hours after the attack. In the meantime there was no panic, women and children calmly obeying instructions to remain below until the time to leave. The youngest passenger was a baby boy, eleven months old, who was strapped to a sailor's back to go down the ladder to a boat.

Captain Charles Sapsworth, the Commander, stood on the bridge encouraging his gunners as they battled with the raider until all were killed or wounded and the guns out of action. Captain Sapsworth is believed to be among the survivors. The crew made rafts out of cabin doors in case the boats proved insufficient.

A member of the crew declared the raider machine-gunned the passengers after the ship's anti-aircraft guns were put out of action. He praised the women stewards who, he said, behaved marvellously. An RAF man repaired the damaged engine of a lifeboat and this was used to tug the heavy lifeboats from place to place picking up survivors, while a naval officer aboard the liner led a party of men through the flames and smoke to lower a lifeboat which saved many lives. A British flying-boat spotted the blazing liner and brought warships to the rescue.

(Reuter)

31 October 1940   *Cairo, Egypt*

Yesterday Pat met General George Clark who told him he believed I was working happily in South Africa. Air Marshal Longmore visited the Ruthvens and I had to stay in the dressing room. I spent the day wondering about Toby and searching through the Cairo telephone book – making a list of firms who might give me a job. I need to repay Battling Butler quickly and earn money to live. I telephoned Barclays Bank, Socony Oil and Egyptian Radio to no avail but I got an appointment to see a Mr Charvet, head of Shell. Awful that Greece has been invaded by Italy . . .

Today Pam returned from GHQ to lunch in the flat. She was loaded with news: 'Dan is coming with his General to Cairo tomorrow for two nights; the news of your return is out at GHQ and there is much gossip – some think it very funny but the authorities concerned are furious and suspect you must have used someone else's passport as such care had been taken that you should not return. They are determined to "make an example" of you and throw you out again. My girlfriend in the Provost Marshal's office says the Military Police have been told to find you. Apparently all Naval, Military and Air Force units have been told not to give you a job . . .' None of this seems to matter because tomorrow I will see Dan.

I telephoned my good friend Freddie Hoffman at the Continental Hotel and asked him to book a double room and bath for Dan and me, and warned him I have no money at present and will have to pay in instalments. 'Don't you worry,' he said. 'I shall give you our honeymoon suite for two nights as a little present.' And he added, 'You'll have to arrive by the tradesmen's entrance, cross the garden and go up the backstairs or the fire escape. I'll book you in as Mr and Mrs Globe Trotter. Don't worry at all – I'll meet you myself.'

3 November 1940   *Cairo, Egypt*

Two days ago Dan arrived at the Ruthvens' flat. It was wonderfully exciting. Pat got us a gharry and put up the hood and a rather tired little horse clip-clopped us to the tradesmen's entrance of the Continental Hotel. Pat had telephoned Freddie Hoffman who was waiting for us in the small garden and led us up the backstairs to a marvellous set of rooms. He stayed to have a drink with us and suggested we have all meals in the suite. 'The talk in our bar', he laughed, 'is all about how on earth Hermione ever got back, and so quickly. Rumour has it that she travelled some of the way with the Provost Marshal.'

Dan and I forgot the war until the next morning when Dan told me, very gently, that Toby was killed on the *Empress of Britain*. It is not known exactly what happened. Some say she was in the main lounge reading a book when a bomb went right through the sun-deck and hit her – but rumour is that she was so terribly wounded on the upper deck that no one could move her and she had to be left to go down with the ship or burn in the fire. Dan insists she would not have been conscious. Dandy Wallace is going home to Scotland to their two little children . . . It is a frightful, shattering story. Next to my own family I loved Toby more than anyone else.

Around six o'clock on our second evening together, when we were playing backgammon, there came a knock on our door. A short stocky officer came in. He had rather a large head shaped like an ant-hill and quick eyes under a heavy brow. 'Lady Ranfurly,' he said, 'I hope you will forgive me for intruding but I want to see you urgently.' Fear clutched my heart – obviously I had been traced.

'How do you know my name, and who told you I was here?' I began, but he interrupted: 'I know all about your recent journey and that is why I am here. I need your help.' Dan waved him to an armchair and fetched him a drink. He went on talking in a quick deft way, with his head stuck a little forward. There was something compelling about him.

'My name', he said, 'is Wingate, Orde Wingate. I am going south in five days' time. I shall raise a revolt in Abyssinia. First I shall go to Khartoum – the Emperor is there. Then I shall drop behind the lines and stay there till, with the aid of the Abyssinians and my small force, we can overthrow the Italians. Now I want you to come as my secretary – you can type, do shorthand, cope with signals?'

I nodded.

'Can you ride, and speak French?'

I nodded again.

'You might have to be dropped by parachute – you wouldn't mind that?'

'Not if I am supplied with the right kind of underwear,' I laughed.

'Lady Ranfurly, I must have an English secretary. There are none to be found in the Middle East. Will you come and help me? Can you be ready by Tuesday? You will be back in six months.'

'How dangerous would this be?' asked Dan.

'No more dangerous than being in London in the blitz,' he replied. We told him that GHQ authorities were furious about my return – that they have put a ban on me working for any military project. We warned him he would meet great opposition if he asked to take me on. He replied, 'None of that matters. I have been told to take what I need and I must have a secretary. You are exactly the kind of person I need.' Then I asked him how I could be sure that, as GHQ wants to be rid of me, and he needs help outside the Middle East, this was not a ruse to get me out of neutral Egypt. He laughed and said that this was a mean thought and he would not be party to it. He left as suddenly as he came – saying, 'I'll fix it – thanks for the drink.' Dan and I went on playing backgammon. After a bit, Dan looked up, laughed, and said, 'Orde can't be short for Ordinary.'

Dan and his General flew back to Jerusalem this morning and I returned to the Ruthvens' flat via the backstairs. Saying goodbye was ghastly – there is always the awful possibility it might be forever . . .

Orde Wingate telephoned me and asked me to dine with him tonight in his flat. When I arrived he said cheerfully, 'Goodness, you are unpopular.' He explained he got it all taped at GHQ when, just as he was leaving, he was stopped and told there is an order out that no military unit could employ me. He went straight to the Deputy Adjutant General's office where, after an argument, he was told that if he took me to Abyssinia it must be on the understanding that I could not come back to the Middle East.

I explained to Wingate that I'd be foolish to leave neutral territory. He argued that his offer was my only hope of getting a job. I still refused to go but promised that, if I were forced out again, I would join him and try to help but *still* only on the proviso that when his mission had succeeded he'd get me back into the Middle East, by parachute or whatever.

Through dinner we talked of other things – of the Palestine Troubles and what he did at Nablus; of his plans for Abyssinia; and of General Wavell. He spoke well and fast, smattering his conversations with biblical quotations and I was amazed at his vitality and convictions. He described the situations in Ethiopia, Somaliland and Eritrea – the battles and terrain. A fascinating but frightening conversation. I was glad I knew so little of all this when I sailed down the Red Sea on the *Empress of Britain*. I like, and admire, Wingate and feel sure he'll win his little war.[1]

---

[1] Orde Wingate had made a controversial name for himself during the pre-war Palestine Troubles and he continued to be a figure destined to arouse passionate feelings, both admiring and hostile. He was a man of total

This morning Wingate rang up to ask if I'd changed my mind. I said, 'No. But if I get kicked out be sure I'll come and lend you a hand.'

Today I went for my interview with Mr Charvet, Chairman of the Shell Company of the Middle East. Sadly he had no vacancy to offer me. 'Why on earth don't you go to the Navy, Army or Air Force who are quite desperate for secretaries?' he asked. I explained – briefly as possible. There was a long silence and then he lifted his telephone, asked for a number and said to someone, 'I've got just the job for your outfit. Can I send her round to see you right away? I'd be obliged if you could help her.' He put down the telephone, wrote an address on a pad, and handed it to me. 'Go straight there,' he said. 'I'm pretty sure they'll give you a job – and quite well paid, too. If this fails, come back to me and be sure I'll help.'

I went to the address he gave me – a flat on the eighth floor of a modern building in Sharia Kasr El Nil. A small man wearing thick glasses and a Charlie Chaplin moustache opened the door and took me along a passage, past a couple of secretaries, and opened a door to where a tall, grey-haired man was sitting at a huge desk. He asked me a lot of questions and then suggested I start work tomorrow: 'We could pay you £25 a month if you will work from 8.30 a.m. till lunchtime and then from 5 p.m. till 8.30 p.m. This includes Saturdays and Sundays.' I accepted with alacrity. He introduced me to two very nice English secretaries. As I was leaving I asked if this was a spy organisation. 'You'll soon find out,' he laughed. I told him I was prepared to do anything except sleep with people. He said, 'OK.'

---

conviction and of extremely strong personality. His courage was legendary. He was now off to play a part in the liberation of Abyssinia – he was a born guerrilla leader. Later he was to form and lead the Chindits, deep penetration forces, in the Burma campaign. He had a strong vein of fanaticism, could be quarrelsome and suspicious, was a natural thorn in the side of authority. Some people found him paranoiac, egocentric, near mad and, conventionally speaking, disloyal; but he stood out from most men with his energy, faith, originality and strength of purpose. It is a privilege to have known him.

The Provost Marshal found me today at my work and asked to see my passport. He laughed when he found it in good order and well stamped from my journey from the Cape. 'The authorities are making a ludicrous fuss about you,' he said. 'There is no need for you to hide or fear being booted out again. Egypt is a neutral country. Don't forget to renew your visa next month and list yourself as "Civil Servant" instead of "Officer's Wife" which has been stamped all over your passport.'

Practical, kind and obviously amused he added, 'I'd rather like to know if you were really airsick on the plane or if this was part of your cover?' I told him I'd been dreadfully sick the day before but not on the morning he spoke to me. We both laughed. 'Ring me up,' he said, 'next time you're in trouble.' I asked how on earth he had discovered my whereabouts. Amazingly, he said Dan had told him how to reach me.

When I got 'home' that evening I found a letter from Dan. He wrote that when he was at GHQ Cairo with General Neame the Provost Marshal approached him and demanded to know my whereabouts. Dan said he would telephone this from Jerusalem when he got back. On the flight to Jerusalem Dan told his General the whole story and it seemed likely Brunskill had never given him Mrs Creagh's letter, which I took by hand to Jerusalem. Anyway, General Neame was extremely nice to Dan and said he didn't give a damn if I was in Egypt so long as I was happy and being useful. So Dan telephoned my address to the Provost Marshal.

Dan wrote that a Memorial Service will be held in Palestine for Toby, and Padre Hughes will officiate. He also said that General Neame thinks Germany will be at war with Russia soon. Poor Dan ended up his letter, 'I do hope the hue and cry over you will die down soon. What a miracle you got off the *Empress.*'

Tomorrow is my twenty-seventh birthday. I shall buy myself a little present as there is no one else to do this.

I have obtained a new passport. It states my profession as civil servant. It is valid until 25th November, 1945 – for the British Empire, Syria, Palestine, Iraq, Iran, Greece, Transjordan, Sudan, Egypt and Cyprus.

15 November 1940   *Cairo, Egypt*

A letter came today from Dan:

> Brigadier Brunskill has ordered me to arrange for your departure from the Middle East. He has threatened to send me to the North West Frontier of India if you do not leave immediately (I believe there is excellent shooting there!). I have to report to him on what action I have taken re this. My pay has been docked for your fare from Durban to Cape Town. I wonder if the authorities will have the face to demand money from Dandy for Toby's disastrous journey. As the Army does not give marriage allowance until one is thirty years old I am wondering if I should divorce you. The many wives who are still here because their husbands are 'regular army' often ask after you and send you messages.

Last night there was a devastating air raid on Coventry – terrible damage was done.

1 December 1940   *Cairo, Egypt*

Mr Pollock (my boss) showed me a letter he received from the Deputy Adjutant General saying that I am in Egypt without either Military or my husband's consent – that no application for exemption from evacuation has been received on my behalf and if any application was received it would not be accepted. It finished up by stating that it was undesirable that SOE should continue to employ me: 'Lord Ranfurly has been informed by Headquarters that his wife's presence in Egypt may get him into serious trouble.'

Mr Pollock laughed a lot while we discussed the situation but I had to struggle not to cry. Later he went over to see 'A' Branch and explain that I am useful and he has no one to replace me – but they are adamant: I must go. Luckily our work does not come under the authority of GHQ and so I may stay here for a while in spite of GHQ demands. Maybe someone should remind GHQ that there is a war on – and that truth is important. Mr Pollock told me that GHQ has applied to our Embassy to have my passport removed.

My job is interesting but secret.[1] Most of the employees work 'in the field' and all of them use numbers instead of names. They come to this office from Middle East and Balkan lands to collect or send out their personal mail both of which go by diplomatic bag. We keep an arsenal of weapons and ammunition in a special room, and in our safe are stacks of gold bars. This morning one of our people 'in the field' came in to collect his mail. I asked him if he'd had a good trip. He laid both his hands on my desk. The ends of his fingers and thumbs were mutilated. He'd been tortured but had escaped. Sometimes the 'numbers' who come into the office are people I know. That is always a nice surprise. It is touching to see how pleased they all are to find their letters from home.

11 December 1940   *Cairo, Egypt*

Great surprise and excitement here – we have advanced in the Desert. We have captured Sidi Barrani. Wherever I've been in Cairo there is a new optimism, perhaps because we've taken the initiative and a lot of prisoners – Italians – perhaps 130,000 or more.

We are moving our office – quite a palaver – to a lovely flat on the edge of the Nile. Amazing that we live with no blackout – with good restaurants and shops and plenty, while the struggles, dangers and discomforts of the Desert continue nearby. Sadly, wounded or 'on leave' soldiers bring us news of

[1] I was now working for the Cairo office of SOE – Special Operations Executive – which came under Dr Hugh Dalton, Minister responsible for Economic Warfare in London.

more and more friends who are missing or dead. Now, in my lunch hour, I go to one or other of the hospitals to take down letters for soldiers who are too ill to write home themselves. It seems to help them to talk to an English civilian. I take their letters in shorthand and then type and post them. It is exasperating to know that letters now take six weeks to reach England and vice versa.

17 December 1940   *Cairo, Egypt*

Good news is still coming from the Desert. General O'Connor's attack seems to have taken the Italians by surprise. We have captured Sidi Barrani and now Sollum has fallen to us and Fort Capuzzo. We've taken thousands of prisoners.

I lunched at the British Embassy with Sir Miles and Lady Lampson. (She is Italian.) I sat next to the Ambassador who immediately talked about evacuation of wives. He told me GHQ had asked if my passport could be removed. Sir Miles explained to me that to remove a British citizen's passport they must first be proved undesirable, after which they are deported by the Egyptian Government. 'As you do not appear to be a white slave trafficker or involved with drugs, I cannot remove your passport,' he said cheerfully. He went on to say that the evacuation controversy was now right out of proportion: this because there exists a very real shortage of English secretaries in the Middle East and it did not seem sensible to ask South Africa to send up secretaries while sending trained English ones away.

30 December 1940   *Cairo, Egypt*

News keeps coming in of ghastly incendiary air raids on London. We are all distressed and anxious. It will take ages before we hear if our families and friends are all right.

Dan was given a few days' leave for Christmas and we stayed at the Continental Hotel. He brought good news: General Wavell has written to General Neame to ask if he has any objection to me remaining in Cairo and General Neame has replied personally to say he has no objection. So Dan and I did not remain in hiding although, so far, we have had no official communication. We have been out dancing and visiting friends – celebrating two victories: the one in the Desert and our own. At Shepherds Hotel we saw Brigadier 'One-Eye' Brunskill dancing with a fat woman – he was wearing a green paper hat.

4 January 1941   *Cairo, Egypt*

A letter signed by General Wavell, bearing wonderful news, reached me this evening:

> General Headquarters,
> Middle East
> CRME/4770/29/AG la–
> 24 December, 1940
>
> Dear Lady Ranfurly
>
>   I am informed that you have certain valuable qualifications which are of considerable importance in your present work.
>   I have therefore decided, somewhat reluctantly, that you will be permitted to remain in Egypt on giving a written undertaking that you will remain at this work for as long as you are wanted, and that, should you at any time leave the work or become no longer required, you will leave the country at once. On receiving this undertaking I am prepared to grant you exemption.
>
>   Yours truly,
>   (signed) A. P. Wavell
>
> The Countess of Ranfurly,
> c/o The Economic Advisory Committee,
> Flat 43,
> Rue Kasr-el-Nil,
> Cairo.

Embarrassingly, the letter went to our old office address and was dated December 24th, 1940. I replied at once and took my letter to the front door of his house to make sure he would read it himself. Astonishing that, with operations going on in the north, south, east and west of his big theatre of war, he should find time to sign a letter to a typist. I wrote that I had only ever asked that I might stay in a job where I was useful, so now I am deeply grateful to have the chance to prove this.

6 January 1941   *Cairo, Egypt*

Bardia has fallen to us. I hear we have taken 20,000 prisoners. Can this be possible? How can we feed them? And water?

Tony Palmer, of the King's Dragoon Guards, arrived from England via South Africa today. Nice to know reinforcements are getting through. He told me that London has been badly knocked about but that people at home are magnificent. He said that taxi drivers wait on their ranks in air raids as though nothing was happening. His poor mother and father – they have four sons on active service . . .

8 January 1941   *Cairo, Egypt*

From my bedroom window I can see the tops of gum trees – they are yellow with a polleny blossom. I wake to the sounds of trams trundling by in the streets and the lift outside my door clicking up and down. I walk to work – it's quite a long way.

My work is interesting. I have been taken off shorthand and typing and now look after all mail and filing – so I see everything which comes in or goes out of the office and all visitors who come to see my boss. A mass of reports come in to our office from Egypt, the Sudan, East Africa, British Somaliland, Palestine, Iraq, Jordan, Persia, Syria and the Balkans. I have much to learn of the intricate politics of these countries, our own military position and the secret activities of the large organisation I work for.

10 January 1941   *Cairo, Egypt*

Today is the Feast of Bahram, which is a relief to everyone; the Arabs are sleepy and irritable when they are fasting.

A letter came from Dan – he and General Neame have been in Transjordan looking at a defence line. We write to each other every day, and swap news as best we can, often in parables.

There is an article about Wingate in today's newspaper – he is progressing well in Abyssinia.

I had cocktails with Abu Fath who owns an Egyptian newspaper. We discussed the war from the Arab angle. Now the Mediterranean is a battlefield our supply lines depend very much on the goodwill of the Arab world.

31 January 1941   *Cairo, Egypt*

We have captured Derna. The Sherwood Rangers have been made coastal gunners – they are off to man the defences of Tobruk.

I am puzzled. I think there is something rather peculiar about this office. Our activities do not always carry out the directives we get from London and GHQ Middle East. Our own reports tend to cover this up. Some of our actions are quite contrary to the directions and regulations we receive.

A whole precious month has passed since I saw Dan.

7 February 1941   *Cairo, Egypt*

Lord Lloyd has died. In the Middle East he was well loved and respected. I am just one of the many here who feel sad about this news.

Pam Ruthven and I lunched at the British Embassy. Before lunch all guests were arranged in a big semi-circle in front of the fire to be introduced to His Excellency and Bob Menzies who is now Prime Minister of Australia. General Arthur Smith, who is Chief of Staff to General Wavell, limped in late. When he was introduced to me he said loudly, 'I do not want to shake hands with you. You should not be here at all. You have given us a great deal of trouble.' I was very embarrassed.

Bob Menzies sat next to me at lunch and we talked of old

times in Australia. He told me Billy Hughes is going strong in Canberra and switches off his hearing-aid whenever something is said he doesn't agree with. Bob wants to talk to his troops so I suggested that, while he's in Cairo, he pay a visit to the 'Dug Out' night club where most Australian ranks gather at night when on leave in Cairo. We fixed to do this tomorrow evening. Sad that Bob is not more popular in his own country. Perhaps he is so clever the public can't easily understand him.

News from the Desert is splendid: the Australians are in Bengazi where Bob will go later this week. General Dick O'Connor is the hero of the hour.

10 February 1941   *Cairo, Egypt*

The Seventh Armoured Division has made a brilliant spurt and cut off retreating Italians about sixty miles south of Bengazi and captured an immense quantity of prisoners and equipment.

It has been raining in big tropical drops. I enjoyed this, very much. Today I met Bonner Fellers, the US Military Attaché here – an original and delightful person who seems to say exactly what he thinks to everyone regardless of nationality or rank. He has just returned from the Desert and spoke with amusement and admiration of how our attack was kept secret. 'General Wavell told me they were going to do manoeuvres so up I went as an observer, and God dammit – it was the works.'[1]

17 February 1941   *Cairo, Egypt*

Dan and his General flew in unexpectedly. General Neame is taking over command of Cyrenaica from General Jumbo

---

[1] Bonner Fellers did not know that the Germans – and, separately, the Italians – were soon to break the American cipher with which he reported the news he culled from the British Commanders, with whom he was on excellent terms. His telegrams to Washington, for a while, became one of the best sources of Intelligence for Rommel who arrived in Tripoli on 12 February. Ultimately (in 1942) the British, through ULTRA, realised what was happening when they read signals between Rommel and Berlin; and then Bonner Fellers was moved.

Wilson who is going to command our forces in Greece. Dan expects to be in Cairo for a week while his General is being briefed. Poor Whitaker has to travel from Jerusalem to Barce in an open truck with all their gear. There is some consternation in high places that Churchill wants troops to be taken from the Desert to help Greece.[1]

27 February 1941   *Cairo, Egypt*

Dan has left for Barce. We had the most wonderful week together in spite of carrying on with our jobs.

I am now sure there is something wrong with my office. Security is almost non-existent. If you give our office address to a Cairo taxi driver more often than not he'll say 'Oh, you want to go to "secret office".' We spend money on a fabulous scale but it's difficult to trace results. We enable people to enter Egypt to come to our office who are listed as persona non grata by home and ME authorities. Secretary Peggy Wright said laughingly to me in the office today, 'Hermione, sometimes it's difficult to know whose side we are working for – British or German.'

4 March 1941   *Cairo, Egypt*

I get up early, around 6 a.m. Often I breakfast with friends in a garden restaurant nearby. We work hard in the office from 8 a.m. till 1.30 or 2 p.m. If possible I ride in the Desert in the afternoon but must be back at the office by 5 p.m. When lucky the office shuts soon after 8 p.m. Then I go back to my hotel room to have a bath and paint on a clean and hopefully brave face. Nearly always I dine with soldier friends who have 24 hours' leave from the Desert. Usually they want to dance after

[1.] It had been decided in London to send help to the Greeks, who were defending their country against an Italian invasion which it was suspected would soon become, additionally, a German invasion. This led to a change of command in Cyrenaica and put a stop to any idea of continuing General O'Connor's wonderful advance. British Empire troops were diverted to Greece and started to arrive there in early March. The Germans were to declare war on Greece on 7 April.

dinner. The news they tell me is more graphic, and sometimes quite different, from written or spoken news from GHQ. Always they are cheerful and uncomplaining. They trust and admire General Wavell more than anyone else and fully understand his predicament – shortage of everything except courage. Most of them ask me to write home to their parents to say they are in fine order. Sometimes, within days, I learn they have been killed or wounded. I get dreadfully tired because, so often, I get too little sleep. Also, I suppose, anxiety for people at home as well as in the Desert makes one weary. Beneath my paint and polite patter I feel dreadfully sad.

11 March 1941   *Cairo, Egypt*

A Lend Lease Bill has been signed by President Roosevelt. Bonner Fellers telephoned me: 'Now we're getting places,' he said.

Dan wrote from Barce:

> I am amused and interested in our new situation. Our house is comfortable and the garden is full of flowers. We found a little tame gazelle here, and a visitors' book signed by Graziani, Balbo and all our own Generals.
>
> The countryside is entirely green. Pat Ruthven is in the neighbourhood – he is liaison officer between Straffer Gott[1] and the Free French. I see him often. It is bitterly cold and blowing a gale. I pity Whitaker in his open truck in these sandstorms. Please send me some corduroy trousers . . .

15 March 1941   *Cairo, Egypt*

A letter came today from my sister Cynthia,[2] posted in 1940.

> . . . In September the bombing was very bad in London. We slept on mattresses in the passage. We hated going to the

---

[1] General Gott, commander of a mobile force, then an armoured division, then a Corps, was killed in an air attack in August 1942. He had been nominated to command Eighth Army.

[2] Mrs George Laws. She was working for MI5, at Blenheim Palace, Woodstock.

cellar because our flat is over a bakery which is full of cockroaches; only once did we go down there when there was a bomb in the street. It swayed the whole house and that night we slept on an eiderdown with the cockroaches. Our lives are pretty regular – we start work early, get home around 6.30 p.m., raids permitting, and then we have a bath and dinner. Afterwards we sit and knit or read. The bombing starts at about 8.30 p.m., and gets earlier as the evenings grow darker. Then we go to bed. Our guns make a terrific noise, growing louder and louder. It is very frightening when they are right overhead – one never knows – the man has only to press a button . . .

At the end of September our office was evacuated to near Oxford, so we went too. We were not sorry to leave London as the gas was not working – no baths or hot meals – and it was only a matter of time before our telephone, lights and windows went too. I have just heard that our furniture, which we'd put in store, has been hit. There is nothing left. If a German ever arrives in England I shall make it my business to meet him.

I can't tell you anything about my work – it is 'over the top' secret. Nor can I give you my address so write via one of our aunts who'll have my telephone number at least. You never say what your work is, and I wonder if we're in the same boat. It's good to be 'up to the neck' if there must be a war, but it is awful that we are separated by thousands of miles and necessary security. The only definite news one gets of friends and family is when they are killed or missing.

24 March 1941   *Cairo, Egypt*

I spent a hot morning struggling with a mass of filing and mail. At every turn I found evidence that things are not as they should be in this office. I decided to warn Mr Eden[1] who is staying at the British Embassy waiting for news of the crisis in Yugoslavia. At lunchtime I went back to the Continental Hotel and rang up the Embassy and asked to see Mr Eden for five minutes. His secretary demanded to know why I wanted to see

[1] Anthony Eden had become Foreign Secretary in December, when Lord Halifax went as Ambassador to Washington. The 'crisis in Yugoslavia' arose from Yugoslavia's decision on 20 March (soon overturned) to join Germany and Italy in the Tripartite Pact.

him. I said I had important information and they could reach me at the hotel if they wanted it. I could say no more and rang off. In a few minutes the Embassy rang back to say the Foreign Secretary would see me immediately.

I had not met Mr Eden before. He came out of lunch and met me in the hall and asked immediately, 'Is it about Yugoslavia?'

'Sorry, it is not. It's about SOE and it's serious,' I replied. I told him briefly but strongly with great emphasis on security. He said this was not the first time he'd heard of this but SOE came under another Ministry. However, he promised to check up on all I told him and to see if anything can be done. He thanked me – we shook hands and I left.

Soon after I got back to my office, Peter Fleming, whose mission is temporarily attached to us, came into my office and carefully shut the door behind him. 'Just what did you say to Mr Eden?' he asked. I was appalled – I'd told no one what I'd done. There was a long silence. 'I was at lunch at the Embassy when your call came through. Mr Eden thought you must have news about Yugoslavia but I wondered . . .' he began, but mercifully the door opened and Peggy Wright came in. 'Dine with me at Shepherds Hotel at eight-thirty tonight,' said Peter and left. I spent a miserable afternoon and evening wondering if Peter would go straight to my boss and I would be sent straight back to South Africa.

At dinner I told Peter all my anxieties about my office and my fears about security and double-crossing. He told me I was dead right to warn Eden and he insisted I must stay on at my job and stay alert. I was thankful to be able to consult Peter and discuss the situation. Luckily he knew just enough about our set-up to recognise how dangerous the situation is. Afterwards we talked about Greece where he and his mission go tomorrow.

27 March 1941   *Cairo, Egypt*

Revolt has broken out in Yugoslavia . . . the pro-Axis Government has been overthrown.

A note came from Dan dated March 17th from Barce:

> . . . General Dill the CIGS and General Wavell are here. For
> three days we've been motoring in the Desert. Whitaker has
> arrived – very shaken – the 15cwt. truck he was travelling in
> turned over. He's had a difficult time . . .

4 April 1941   *Cairo, Egypt*

The enemy has attacked in the Desert. They have chosen their
time well – we've sent so much of our strength to defend
Greece.

There is a horrid rumour that Germans have arrived in
North Africa. Thank God Dan has a staff job.

We've won a sea battle – seven Italian warships have been
sunk in the Mediterranean. But on land we are retreating . . .

In Iraq the Prime Minister has resigned on being pressed by
the Regent and his Foreign Secretary to break off relations
with Italy. The Italian Legation is a hot-bed of intrigue, and for
months the Germans have been pouring money and propaganda into Iraq. Now Rashid Ali – who is backed by the Axis
and supported by the Iraqi Army which is convinced that Germany will win the war – has proclaimed himself head of a
National Defence Government, advocating absolute neutrality
as opposed to the Anglo-Iraq Treaty. The Regent has left
Baghdad.

6 April 1941   *Cairo, Egypt*

The Germans have invaded Greece and Yugoslavia. We have
evacuated Bengazi.[1] I hope Dan and Pat Ruthven are all right.
The only good news is that Wingate has succeeded in his mission: Addis Ababa has been recaptured – the Emperor will be
reinstated.

---

[1] Rommel's offensive – the first time he made an impact on us – began on 2
April. In six days he had driven the British from Cyrenaica and was poised for
his first attack on Tobruk.

Two days ago I got a high fever. Dr Moore came and gave me a huge white pill to make my temperature go down. He insisted I stay in bed and so I missed the truck going to the Desert. My parcel for Dan which contained whisky, cake, a set of dominoes and a tunic for Whitaker is still in my bedroom. This morning I was writing my letter to Dan – advising him to sleep with his tin hat on and asking if he had received the oil compass I sent him – when there came a knock at my door and in walked Lady MacMichael. She is staying with Lady O'Connor.

She said she hoped I am getting better, talked about the weather, fidgeted around the room and looked out of the window. I longed for her to go away because she is so large she made my room seem overcrowded. Suddenly she turned and came to the end of my bed and said, 'Your Dan is missing. General Neame and General O'Connor are missing too. It is thought they may have been ambushed and taken prisoner, nobody knows . . .' With tears pouring down her cheeks she went on talking but I did not really listen. After a while I thanked her for coming to tell me, gave her a hug and closed the door gently behind her . . .

Jack Dent, General O'Connor's ADC came to see me. He'd just returned from the Desert. He told me that Dan and several Generals had set off in two cars and were last seen heading for a short-cut track behind Derna en route for Tobruk. He said an Australian who had gone that way had doubled back after finding a lot of cars stationary and hearing shouts. It was dark. For two days a big search was made for the Generals, to no avail. He told me Germans are now in the area and he thought it probable that a German commando had captured Dan and the Generals.

My temperature is very high and my spirits very low. Doctor Moore says I have gyppy tummy and chicken pox. He wants to move me to a fever hospital. I felt shy when Lady Wavell and Lady O'Connor came to see me because I look so awful; my spots are painted over with a purple liquid like Deadly Nightshade and I am hollow eyed because I can't sleep. They told me the German wireless has announced they have captured six British Generals. General Carton de Wiart who was coming here from England is also missing. Reuter has this news too.

All day I've been watching the birds in the jacaranda tree outside my window and the gardeners down below who sit to dig, and sleep when no one is about. I am reading *The Importance of Living* which seems to be a sensible thing to do just now. Since Lady MacMichael's visit I've not gone to sleep . . .

The war rumbles on and most of the news is awful; Germans are in Belgrade; in Greece our troops are in action; in the Desert we are still retreating; Tobruk is besieged. In Abyssinia alone we are successful. We are bombing Tripoli and, from Malta, harrying enemy reinforcements for North Africa. If Dan is a prisoner, this is the route he'll be travelling on so he may be in great danger . . .

I have received a very kind handwritten note from General Wavell asking me to stay in his house when I am fit enough to move. Amazing, when he has such a gigantic load, that he should have time to think of me and specially when he has only heard of me as a nuisance.

A telegram arrived today from 2nd Echelon Mid East, dated April 14th: 'Deeply regret inform you 2/Lieut. Earl of Ranfurly reported missing believed prisoner of war.'

A khamsin is blowing and the jacaranda tree is weeping blue

tears. Hawks are doing acrobatics in the wind. It is very hot. Kind Freddie Hoffman has saved me from being sent to a fever hospital. He told Doctor Moore he'd like me to stay in my room and will have it disinfected and repainted when I recover. I am thankful.

I have sent telegrams to the Vatican and to the Red Cross in Geneva begging them to try and get news of Dan. Kind Bonner Fellers has wired the American Legation in Rome asking their help.

Tobruk is far behind enemy lines now. Reports from Greece are confused and worrying. We have sunk three Italian destroyers off Tripoli – this good news worries me lest Dan is being taken to Europe, in which case he'd most likely have to go via Tripoli. We are bombing Tripoli regularly. If Dan is a prisoner he is still in great danger . . .

17 April 1941   *Cairo, Egypt*

A telegram reached me from Alexandria: 'Am in Alex waiting conveyance Cairo. Whitaker.'

Freddie Hoffman, by whose kindness I've been saved from being sent to hospital, came to see me this evening. He told me that Wingate, who was staying in the hotel in the room above mine, has been rushed to hospital because he cut his throat with a razor.

Freddie said, 'My special friends all seem to be in trouble. Wingate lost about a gallon of blood – I wonder it did not come through your ceiling. Apparently he was desperately depressed after some row at GHQ.' He went on to tell me he'd had a struggle to persuade Dr Moore to let me stay on in this hotel. Freddie is a Swiss and a saint.

21 April 1941   *Cairo, Egypt*

There came a tap on my door this morning and Whitaker walked in – fat, panting and heroic. For a moment he did not speak – perhaps he was astonished by my chicken-poxed face. Then, his round face creased with consternation, he began to
86

tell me about the headquarters at Barce – of the retreat, and of Tobruk whence he had come. And, while he told me what Dan was wearing on the day he disappeared, and what kit he had with him, Egyptian porters carried in Dan's familiar luggage and piled it in a pyramid near the door. Last of all they brought in a little dog on a lead which Whitaker had brought back for safety for its owner in Tobruk.

'When His Lordship set off from Barce with the Generals I had to take all their kit to Tobruk along the coast road. I got there all right but it wasn't very funny. The Sherwood Rangers are now in Tobruk which is besieged. Every evening I went to lend a hand in the bar of the Officers' Mess. One night General Wavell came in and he recognised me. You see, I'd looked after him at Barce. When he walked in he came straight up to me, shook my hand and said he was so sorry to hear that His Lordship was missing. He ordered six whiskies, and I thought they were for him and his friends, but he only drank one and said the rest were for us bartenders.'

Whitaker's description of the retreat in the Desert, of dust storms, muddle and hurry was very vivid. He said it was a nightmare because no one really knew what was going on.

After a while we began to unpack so that I could make up a parcel of clothes to send to Dan via Turkey and the Red Cross in Geneva. The smell of Dan's hair brushes made me cry. Whitaker's comments on his journeys made me laugh. He and I and the little dog lunched in my bedroom. Freddie Hoffman sent up a feast.

This evening Lady O'Connor rang up. She has heard through the Vatican that General O'Connor is a prisoner at Sulmona in Italy and is 'enjoying good health'. I don't expect there is much else to enjoy there. Poor Lady O'Connor – her fascinating husband, a brilliant General, greatly loved by all ranks, is a gigantic loss for her and for our Army.

Lady Wavell telephoned to ask if I am getting better and when should she expect me to stay. She was very kind. I told her what Whitaker said about General Wavell in Tobruk.

Just as I was settling down to sleep Lou Sweet-Escott, who works in my office, walked in. She'd just returned from Yugoslavia. She told me of the coup d'état and German invasion, the bombing and refugees – and of her journey back through Athens. A hair-raising story.

23 April 1941   *Cairo, Egypt*

Bonner Fellers lunched with me. He is sad because his friend, Colonel Brower, has been killed while flying an aeroplane up from Takoradi. 'You'll have to stop scolding us Americans for being neutral when my friends are getting killed flying planes up to you British,' he said. Bonner thinks that some of the engines of the American planes which are being shipped across the Atlantic and reassembled at Takoradi are not being fixed properly and so vibrate and shake to bits in the air. He calls this 'periodicity'. A great many American planes are reaching us over the jungle route from West Africa.

Donny Player, now second-in-command of the Sherwood Rangers, came to see me today and brought me a handful of letters from the Regiment. He is back from Tobruk for two days' leave. He told me: 'We are bombed incessantly, live on iron rations but all are cheerful. We can't get out overland but it is still possible to get in and out by sea.' I asked him if Tobruk was a big town and he said, 'It won't be a town at all very soon.'

A sapper called Brigadier Kisch paid me a visit. He'd been at Barce with Dan and told me of the search for the Generals. His men blew up the Derna road early on the morning of April 7th. He sat on the end of my bed and explained what Sappers do – how often they must go first in an advance to deal with mines – and in a retreat they must go last to blow up the roads, rails and bridges. A delightful man – I was very touched he should come and see me when we'd never met before.

Whitaker has found 'digs', and also a few friends. He comes to see me several times each day. We're both so pleased Dan's parcel of food and clothes is on its way. I've asked if he can have a job in my office. Still no news of Dan.

I am up and dressed. Whitaker helped me pack. This morning I am to leave my room, no. 112 at the Continental Hotel. I am very sad – this was the last home I had with Dan. I am going to live with Elizabeth Coke on Gezira. She is a wonderful friend. Freddie Hoffman came to see me off: 'Be sure there will always be a room for you in this hotel,' he said and added: 'Now I'm going to have room 112 fumigated and repainted. Let me know if you get any news of Dan.'

I slept tormented by sandflies after a torpid khamsin day. Bonner Fellers fetched me for lunch. He said, 'We reckon this is one of your worse emergencies – the whole Mediterranean is threatened. America must declare war soon.' Then he talked about the German 88-millimetre gun which he says is excellent. He grumbled because the US War Department and our War Office turned this gun down before the war as it has only a small shield to protect the crew and both thought it would prove too costly in men. As it outranges most other weapons and is very mobile, Bonner thinks this was a grave mistake. 'Anyway,' he said, 'the Germans now have it in the Desert where it is deadly.' The Germans also have a very good Fifth Column.

The Desert war continues. We have bombed Barce. Poor little tame gazelle. This evening I took Whitaker and his friend McCall to a movie – we saw *Congo Maisie*, 'a tropical love tangle with allure and alligators'. I got home in time to hear Mr Churchill's broadcast. He made a long and very honest statement.

A telegram arrived to say Dan's Grandmother has died. Poor old 'Eighty but Active'. What a sad time to die when everything she loved is at risk. I shall miss her. She was inspiringly brave.

Today I lunched with Lady O'Connor who tried to persuade me to go home to England. I explained I couldn't do this: I'd fought hard to be in the same theatre of war as Dan, and I couldn't run away now – I must work doubly hard so as to contribute for us both.

Bonner Fellers rang up at bed-time to say he had just got a message from the US Legation in Rome. 'General O'Connor says Ranfurly captured. Last seen in good health.'

2 May 1941   *Cairo, Egypt*

I've come to stay with the Wavells. Lady Wavell has a delightful vague air as if she had lost or forgotten something. 'Hello,' she said, fluttering her eyelids, 'now let me see . . . oh yes, Nannie will show you your room.' Nannie gave me a big hug. 'You poor child,' she said, 'I know all about you.'

I felt very shy of meeting General Wavell but when he came in this evening, he thanked me for the letter I wrote him about my exemption from evacuation and added, 'In the last war my wife followed me right across Russia. For sheer obstinacy there is not much to choose between you.' He told me not to worry if I do not get news of Dan for some time – being a Lieutenant he would be taken overland to Tripoli and thence to Europe by boat, whereas the Generals would be flown to Italy or Germany . . . He spoke so kindly I had a struggle not to cry.

General Wavell is thick-set and not tall. His face is much creased and his blind eye gives it a puckered look. Unhurried and quite slow in movement and speech, he exudes serenity – as if he knew trouble well and had often stared it in the face and now was not afraid of it any more. I thought, to myself, if I ever saw him ruffled I would be terrified. He talks very little, but listens to everyone carefully and when his daughters came home and talked of their jobs you might have thought they were as important as his. I felt sure he'd only signed the letter on my exemption – that someone else drafted it. General Wavell is not the sort of person who would use the word 'reluctant'.

While we were having tea General Jumbo Wilson arrived

from Greece.[1] I made to move but General Wavell bade me stay. General Wilson sat on the sofa, which he filled. He talked of our three Divisions and the Germans' twelve. He said our soldiers were the better fighters. He spoke of shepherds, Ministers, caiques and wild flowers and how, when our troops drove out of Athens on their way to be evacuated, the Athenians threw flowers and shouted, 'Come back soon.' He told us about the ammunition ship that blew up in Piraeus harbour and shook the city – and of our great needs: aeroplanes and gear.

General Wilson has a twinkle in his eyes. He is so large that he looks silly holding a cup and saucer. He puffs when he sits down and he puffs when he gets up again. I wondered, as I listened, if our gesture to help Greece was right or wrong. Perhaps that we have taken the pressure off England is the best part of it and that our casualties are low. But now we have two retreats . . .

3 May 1941   *Cairo, Egypt*

I looked out of my window at six this morning and saw General Wavell setting out on his morning ride round the racecourse. I am not allowed to work yet and find idleness is hell.

In Iraq Rashid Ali's rebels have invaded Habbanyeh which was held by a small garrison of Iraq levies and RAF personnel – mostly ground staff. In Baghdad our Embassy is completely cut off and our Ambassador, Sir Kinahan Cornwallis, and some 350 British men and women, are virtually prisoners. Axis aircraft operating from Vichy-controlled Syria are assisting the rebels.

After dinner I played backgammon with General Wavell. He said cheerfully, 'You seem to be the only enemy I can be sure of defeating these days.'

---

[1] British and Imperial troops had all been evacuated from Greece by 1 May.

I sat in the garden this morning and listened to the swish of the Arab gardener watering flowers. Nannie came down from the nursery and gave me a sprig of frangipani. 'Don't get depressed,' she said, 'soon your doctor will let you go back to work.'

Today General Wavell asked me about my work. I told him how worried I am about it and explained why. And I told him that, if I had not promised him to leave Egypt should I leave my job, I would have resigned weeks ago. He asked me many questions and then said he knew something of all this already, but as SOE does not come under the War Office he cannot rectify the situation but only take precautions over their information and operations. Above all he is worried over their lack of proper security. He asked me to stay at my work, make copies of any documents I thought worrying and take these direct to his Chief of Staff, General Arthur Smith. 'Could you do this?' he asked. I told him I locked up the office at night and could get there first in the morning – so I could remove papers in the evening, type copies in the night and return the originals first thing in the morning. But I'd need help from his Chief of Staff to accept and return my envelopes quickly as I'd have to deliver them to him by hand and would have little time to do so. He said, 'Fine, I'll fix it.'

Late this evening Lady O'Connor telephoned to say that a message had come through the Red Cross that Dan is a prisoner and will shortly be taken to Sulmona Camp in Italy. I am wildly happy that Dan is alive. Amazing to be pleased to hear that one's husband is a prisoner. But I am. I've been so dreadfully afraid that he might be dead.

This morning I started work again. Whitaker, who now mans the switchboard in my office, was so excited about the good news of Dan that he got wrong numbers for everyone all morning.

Peter Fleming, just returned from Greece, came to see me. The boat he was escaping on was bombed. One of his men was killed and he was wounded.

On my way home from work I called on Peter and Bill Stirling whose flat is close by our Embassy. I wanted to give them my news of Dan. Mo, their Sudanese Sofragi, opened their door furiously brandishing a dustpan. Apparently the Stirlings went to a party last night, lost all their money at cards and rode home on a 'borrowed' donkey which they inveigled up to their third-floor flat. Mo found it in their drawing room when he arrived in the early morning. Since then it had refused to go downstairs and had thoroughly manured the carpet. Mo, erupting with rage, said to me, 'I give notice many times to Mr Stirling but he only laugh. First they scramble eggs in my tarboosh; next they hire one damn bad cook who chase me with chopper; and now they catchit one donkey who sheet everywhere. It's too heavy to carry downstairs... Last week they sit in drawing room and practise their revolvers at wall and bullets come through wall into dining room where I lay table and I have to leave in hurry on stomach...' I suggested he find a safer job, which made him more angry: 'You know they give me awful times but you forget they are my very best friends and I never, ever, work for nobody else.' I patted his shoulder and he began to laugh: 'No ever any dull times,' he said and wandered off to the kitchen.

Bill Stirling, who works for SOE, appeared and told me he is so disgusted with our office that he has walked out and won't return. 'Their latest folly is to use the small craft we use for fixing limpets on enemy ships for bringing illegal Jewish immigrants from the Balkans to Palestine,' he said.

Dinner with the Wavells was fun. It was the General's birthday. I gave him a sponge and *This Man is Dangerous* by Peter Cheyney. After dinner a courier arrived from Habbanyeh where our little garrison is still holding the seven-mile perimeter. General Wavell gave him a drink while he read the messages and asked questions about the fighting.

Though he must be very anxious about the Desert war, Crete, Iraq and so on, General Wavell is quite unruffled. He deals personally with an incredible amount of things in a huge arena and at all levels. At first, to stay in his house one might think he is doing little or is, perhaps, lazy, as how can he find time to ride every morning and often be back for lunch or dinner or both? Yet it emerges – never from him, but from his officers and other ranks and household staff, and even Nannie – what he has been up to: quick but important flights to all over his huge theatre; visits to workshops to thank, encourage and hurry repairers of tanks and equipment of all kinds; visits to hospitals, endless meetings, personal kindnesses and serious talks with high and low under his command. And when he returns home he seems unworried, unhurried, and always good humoured. His mileage is prodigious and his attention to detail remarkable and it is all accomplished without fanfare or fuss.

6 May 1941   *Cairo, Egypt*

A khamsin is blowing. It is almost unbearably hot. The desert must be a furnace. I lunched at our Embassy and met a lot of refugees from Greece. Philip Parbury, of the 6th Australian Division, said that the ships which brought them away from Greece were dive-bombed continuously. 'Every available Bren gun was brought up on deck – it is amazing how morale rises when one has some chance of hitting back,' he said. Each new arrival from Greece tells us of the marvellous way our navy handled the evacuation – our soldiers were taken off the beaches in pitch darkness and the overcrowded ships had to get beyond the enemy's bombing range by daylight through waters sown with mines.

I helped Lady Wavell with her work party, making swabs and bandages, till it was time to go back to the office. Tonight I am going with her to the dance she organises each week for the soldiers and nurses. It is called the Lonely Hearts Ball.

I have left the kind Wavell family and returned to stay with Elizabeth Coke.

Someone rushed into my office this afternoon and said, 'Hess has landed in England by parachute – it's on the radio.' Peter Fleming, who had come in to collect some papers, looked up: 'For a moment I thought she was joking,' he said. 'You see, I wrote a book about that not long ago – it is called *The Flying Visit.*'

11–31 May 1941   *Cairo, Egypt*

A small mechanised force under command of General George Clark, together with Colonel Glubb and his Arab Legion, have left Palestine to relieve Habbanyeh. They had to cross 500 miles of desert. A few Blenheim aircraft, just back from Greece, went to support them – their wings still riddled with bullet holes from Greece.

We are all talking about Hess who has flown himself from Germany and crash-landed in Scotland. None of us knows why.

On 19th May the Duke of Aosta surrendered at Amba Alagi. The Emperor Haile Selassie was reinstated in Addis Ababa on May 5th. I sent a signal to Orde Wingate: 'Congratulations to you and Gideon.[1] Ranfurlys.'

On 20th May Germans descended on Crete in parachutes and were followed soon after by many more Germans in commandeered caiques. British, Australian, New Zealand and Greek soldiers under General Freyberg, supported by our Navy, tried heroically to hold the island but after ghastly fighting and dive bombing, with heavy casualties on both sides and dreadful losses of our ships we had to evacuate it. Many of our troops got left behind, including two batteries of Notts Sherwood Rangers. Bob Laycock and some of his Commandos got out and King George of Greece fled to Egypt. The loss of Crete is going to make life more dangerous in Alexandria and

[1] Wingate had named his force in Abyssinia 'Gideon Force'.

Malta. I got ticked off in the office for spelling Suda Bay 'Pseudo Bay' in a despatch.

Thank God reinforcements of troops have arrived from England recently – but even so, Wavell is short of everything but courage. In the midst of all this he wrote to tell me that Sir Harold MacMichael, High Commissioner in Palestine, needs an assistant private secretary and he (Wavell) wanted to know if I would like the job when I can be released from my present post and under-cover work. I accepted thankfully.

The Chief of Staff, General Arthur Smith, sent for Bill Stirling and me and asked a great many questions about our office. He became increasingly anxious as we answered his queries. General Arthur Smith wants to make up a dossier of evidence for the Minister of State who is due to arrive in Cairo very soon. Once the Minister has extracted any information I may have I shall be allowed to go to my new job in Palestine. General Arthur Smith is very righteous and behaves as if he is a close friend of God and me an infidel. He has a small Bible stuffed in his hip pocket.

Good news – we've sunk the *Bismarck*. About 2000 men went down with her. And I write 'Good news'. Oh, the madness of War.

1 June 1941   *Cairo, Egypt*

The Iraqi rebels have sued for peace. The Regent will be reinstated.

5 June 1941   *Cairo, Egypt*

Mine is a horrible job. Every day I arrive first at my office and replace the papers I 'borrowed' the night before. Then I settle down to my ordinary work. I feel terrible betraying these people who have been so kind to me and Whitaker. I leave the office last and lock up the safes and filing cabinets, hide key papers in my bra and depart, slamming the front door which is fastened by only a Yale lock. I walk across Garden City to the Stirlings' flat where I type copies of the papers I brought. As I
96

can rarely leave our office till eight-thirty and it takes ages to type the papers, I get tired. I must be back at the office well before 8.30 a.m., after collecting the original papers en route. Bill Stirling takes the copies I've typed to General Arthur Smith each morning.

A telegram has come for me from Sir Harold MacMichael in Jerusalem via our Ambassador in Cairo: he will keep his job for me till I am released.

8 June 1941   *Cairo, Egypt*

Amazing! General Arthur Smith invited me to lunch. When I arrived at his office he was sitting in his shirt sleeves with a towel round his neck while his ADC, Captain Noel, cut his hair. I sat down at the lunch table before he said Grace – otherwise we got on well. I asked him about the little Bible in his hip pocket. He said he'd always worn this because in the last war it stopped a stray bullet from wounding him – he took it out and showed me the hole in it. He said he would write to Sir Harold MacMichael to say I can go to Jerusalem as soon as the Minister of State has cross-examined me. 'But first you must finish your horrible job,' he said. I think we are destined to be friends after all. He is amazed at the papers I've sent him.

Our troops have gone into Syria and are fighting the Vichy French.

22 June 1941   *Cairo, Egypt*

Germany has attacked Russia. The general opinion here is that Russia will be beaten in a few months – that she is ill equipped and without military leaders. Bonner Fellers is the only person I have met who thinks the Russians will survive – he has been to Russia fairly recently and says the Germans have bitten off more than they can chew.

I received a letter today which cheered me very much. It was from an RASC Captain McClure in Alexandria:

I was listening in to Radio Vatican yesterday at about 19.40

hours. The announcer was calling out a list of prisoners of war. He spoke in English with a Scottish accent and gave out the regimental numbers in Italian. I heard him send one message as follows: 'Lord Ranfurly sends his love to his wife Countess Ranfurly, the Continental Hotel, Cairo.' All messages were repeated twice and it was only after hearing the Continental Hotel, Cairo, mentioned I took notice. The majority of messages sent kind regards or wished to be remembered. Yours was the only one in which love was sent. I am taking the liberty to write to you in case you did not receive the above message. I have the honour to remain, Madam, Your Ladyship's obedient servant J. K. McClure (Captain R.A.S.C.)

Bill Stirling and I went to Heliopolis Hospital to see his brother David who has injured his back making a parachute jump. I asked David what he would do when he is better and he told me that he belongs to Bob Laycock's Commandos but they are being disbanded shortly. 'When I have got my legs to function again I have a scheme to put to Headquarters,' he said in his quiet voice. 'It may be difficult to get them to accept it, but it is vital they do.'

28 June 1941   *Cairo, Egypt*

Around midday I found an important-looking envelope lying on my desk. It was addressed to me but had already been opened. I read it. It was a copy of a letter from General Arthur Smith to Sir Harold MacMichael in Jerusalem. I read it three times to try and figure out how many cats it let out of the bag. It was hard to know. Fear crept all over me. When I stopped shaking I picked up the letter and walked along the corridor and knocked on Mr Pollock's door. I asked him if he had read my letter. He shook his head. But I could not be sure. I told him I'd been asked to go and work for the High Commissioner in Palestine quite soon and I wanted to go. I thanked him for all his kindness to me and asked one more favour: would he waive my notice and allow me to leave this evening. He agreed to this and thanked me for doing a good job. 'Lucky High

Commissioner,' he said. We shook hands and I returned to my office and then I began shaking again. It was impossible to find out who had opened my letter – if anyone had read it through and, if so, what they made of it. At 8.30 p.m. I said goodbye to everyone, handed over my keys and departed. I asked Whitaker to come and see me at the hotel after his work. On my way I stopped at the Stirlings' flat to ask Bill to let General Arthur Smith know what had happened and scold him for getting me in such a hideous position. Bill thought it all very funny and roared with laughter but I felt uneasy and said so.

Whitaker sat on my bed and I told him that everyone wanted me to go back and work in Jerusalem. He was horrified. 'My Lady, you will be miserable there – it is an unhappy place. Centuries of quarrels still continue there. And you'll be bored, too, in that Government House and we will be separated all over again. I wish absolutely that you don't go. I hated living there.'

3 July 1941   *Cairo, Egypt*

Today I went to say goodbye to the Wavells who are going to India. General Archie's departure is a real blow to all ranks and particularly to my generation. He is one of the very few senior soldiers who back young methods of war and enterprises like the Long Range Desert Group and Wingate's operation in Abyssinia. Tough luck on David Stirling that he must operate without such a leader. How they would have enjoyed each other. I found Lady Wavell and Nannie packing in their petticoats. I felt as if my own family were leaving. I tried to thank General Archie for all his help to me. He didn't seem to listen very well but he said, 'Don't forget you can always join us – as a guest – or I'd be proud to give you a job . . .'

Later in July 1941   *Cairo, Egypt*

This morning I was sent for by Oliver Lyttelton,[1] the newly arrived Minister of State. We sat in the British Embassy garden

[1] Minister Resident in the Middle East. Later, Viscount Chandos.

and for a while talked of New South Wales where we last met. As always he was great fun and we laughed a lot. Then he asked me about my late job. He held in his hand the file of papers I had collected and typed.

10 July 1941   *Cairo, Egypt*

Today I received a letter signed by the Deputy Adjutant General saying that he understood I had left my job and he wished to remind me of my promise to leave the country if such circumstances arose. I replied that my change of job had been arranged with the full knowledge and consent of the Commander-in-Chief and I was sorry he had not been informed.

15 July 1941   *In the train*

When I crossed the canal at Kantara and heard the frogs croaking I felt, suddenly, desolate. Palestine will be different this time: Dan is in prison in Italy; Toby is dead; the Sherwood Rangers are besieged in Tobruk; and Whitaker is left behind in Cairo ... As the train puffed its way north I felt increasingly afraid lest, from panic over my job in Cairo, I'd made a huge mistake.

5

Civil Servant

A lovely welcome from all at Government House made me feel a little ashamed of my apprehension about returning to Palestine.[1]

After tea Sir Harold told me the terms of my appointment as Assistant Private Secretary: four hundred pounds a year; a first-class passage to England after eighteen months' service or longer; the job can be terminated by a month's notice on either side. He emphasised that leave is a privilege and not a right. I am to work under his Private Secretary, Donald MacGillivry, who will show me the files and combination of the safe. My hours are 8.30 a.m. to 7.30 p.m., with a lunch break, seven days a week.

Sir Harold works in his study at Government House and seldom goes to the Secretariat in Jerusalem which is headed by John MacPherson, a charming man. This household consists of His Excellency, Lady MacMichael who is head of the Red

---

[1.] Palestine was a British Mandate since the end of the First World War and the downfall of the Turkish Empire. The 'Arab revolt' against British Administration in the Thirties was the clash against the idea of Palestine becoming the National Home of the Jews. Nazi persecution of Jews in Germany sharpened this situation as so many fled to Palestine. Now there was still tension and unrest in Palestine.

Crescent, their daughters, Araminta who is twenty-one and works in a hospital and Priscilla who is fifteen and does lessons at home. Major Nicholl, the ADC, is about fifty. Mardell, the English butler, is charming and very efficient. Arab, Jewish and Sudanese servants, a donkey, a dog, tortoises and pigeons complete the outfit. Donald MacGillivry and his wife live in a flat in the house.

I have a comfy and pretty bedroom next to a bathroom; a desk has been set up for me in the billiard room – at the opposite end of the ground floor from the Secretary's office. I am to type, file, cipher and decipher and work along with MacGillivry. This latter may not be easy – he has already announced I must knock at his office door before entering and my first attempt to obey this order was depressing – it took him fifteen minutes to say 'Come in'. He showed me the files and the combination of the safe and then told me to read the introductory chapters of the Report of the Royal Commission of 1937. 'They sketch the historical, political and economic backgrounds to the problems of present-day Palestine, of which a knowledge is clearly an indispensible prerequisite to any intelligent discussion of the subject and particularly for anyone taking up an official position in the country,' he said, and added, 'Don't come back for three days.'

Early this morning I ran down the black marble staircase and out into the garden. Government House is built on a hill and from one side of the garden, across a deep valley, one can see the walls of the old city of Jerusalem and the blue dome of the Mosque of Omah. Further up the garden, from the highest peak of the hill, one can see the Dead Sea. On a sundial there, on a bronze plaque, are carved the distances to Mecca, Cairo and Beirut.

The views from this garden are superb and the garden itself is delightful with lavender hedges and lawns bordered with beds of delphinium and poppies and other herbaceous flowers. The fig trees are bent with the weight of their fruit. The grounds are encircled by a high double wire fence erected because of the Troubles. As I walked back to the great white house I watched an Arab on its roof hoisting the Union Jack.

At the front door the Arab kavass, Said, bade me a very good morning. It was 8.30 a.m. and time to start work.

For comfort and beauty few places can equal this – but I am wondering, all over again, if, when Dan is a prisoner and all our friends are in the Desert or besieged in Tobruk, or being bombed in England, I should be so sheltered. My only hope is to work extremely hard . . .

22 July 1941   *Jerusalem*

Each day I am driven in a van to the King David Hotel which is divided between the Government Secretariat, Army Head-quarters and an hotel. The dingy back bedrooms where the Secretariat is situated make a poor contrast to the Jewish Agency nearby. I spend the morning learning and practising Colonial Office ciphers and then return to Government House for lunch. After that I work for HE till 7 p.m. Signals which need deciphering generally arrive in the middle of the night. I do these in my dressing gown. I am still rather slow with these but am getting faster.

To drive along the streets of Jerusalem is never boring – one sees Jewish men in flat, fur-edged hats with their uncut hair falling over their shoulders; Arab women in tall, almost medi-eval headdresses; Greek priests with buns and stove-pipe hats; officers of the Transjordan Frontier Force with high black fur headgear slashed with scarlet to match their belts; Arab Legion, Abyssinian clergy, Palestine police, Americans, Bed-ouin, and British uniforms – it is quite a fashion show.

General Jumbo Wilson, who commands this area, came to see Sir Harold this evening. His ADC, Mark Chapman Walker, told me that the General had received a letter from Cairo GHQ, asking that I be sent back immediately and quoting the old evacuation order. The General replied that as my husband had been in enemy hands for some months he considered the initial reason for my evacuation extinct and furthermore I'd been sent to Palestine with the consent of General Wavell. He concluded, 'This lady has outmanoeuvred every General in the Middle East and I do not myself intend to enter the arena.'

I've still not had a letter from Dan since he was taken prisoner in the first week in April. I send parcels to him – they go via Turkey and Switzerland but sadly I may only send one every three months. I am permanently worried for him . . . Letters from England take ages to reach us and the news they bring is frightening.

12 August 1941   *Jerusalem*

I've received a letter from the Chief Secretary's office laying down the terms of my new job at Government House. I've agreed to it all in writing.

Oliver Lyttelton and General Arthur Smith have been staying here on their way to Syria. Oliver told me that a large number of the senior staff in SOE could be court-martialled. The Department is now being cleaned up. General Arthur Smith brought the good news that I will hear no more about evacuation.

A letter came from David Stirling saying he's won his battle with GHQ Cairo and is now training his small force at Kabrit in the Delta. He wrote, 'My parachute unit is now training but we've very little visible means of support. However, we raid neighbouring units at night and return in the small hours with tents and other movable goods necessary for the establishment of this camp.'

16 August 1941   *Jerusalem*

It hadn't dawned on me till lately that when I left Cairo I was moving from a military into a civilian world. Now I miss knowing first-hand what is happening in the Desert – what the 'grown ups' (GHQ) and the Desert Rats are saying (always so different). Conversations here are quite unlike those in Egypt and so are the jokes. I listen to the radio news at night – signals permitting – but otherwise I am quite out of touch with the struggle against Rommel, though even up here people sing and whistle 'Lili Marlene'. But I do know that reinforcements are still arriving in Egypt via the Cape – that Churchill and

Roosevelt have met on a ship in the Atlantic and signed the Atlantic Charter – and that the Germans have thrust far into Russia. It is a very dark hour for us whichever way one looks. I'm going to send all the news cuttings on the Atlantic Charter to Dan. If the Nazi censors hold them up it will still do them good to read them.

24 August 1941   *Jerusalem*

I am beginning to understand why one feels unhappy and apprehensive in Jerusalem. Wherever you go, for work or fun, there is an unspoken mental undertow of suspicion. No one asks, but everyone wants to find out, which side you are on – Arab or Jew. Slightly to His Excellency's disapproval I accept social invitations from Jews and from Arabs. I enjoy dining with Jews who entertain lavishly with often brilliant conversation, and with Arabs whose clever and kind talk and lovely manners are a pleasure. I realise I am often invited because of my job and that I must be careful what I say – but even so I appreciate both their kindnesses and hospitality and their laughter. But sooner or later I discover how they think, and, as I can do nothing about it, it makes me sad.

The Jews think His Excellency and his Government are pro-Arab and the Arabs think His Excellency and his Government are pro-Jew. And I, who work for Sir Harold, type his despatches, see his signals and keep his files have not the slightest clue as to where his sympathies lie. His conversation, behaviour and his writings are so strictly neutral it is impossible to know whose side he is on. While we British hold a mandate over Palestine and must referee the endless problems which inevitably arise – these Jewish and Arab criticisms bear good proof of our honourable impartiality. Today, after carrying papers to his desk, I dared to ask the unforgivable question, 'Your Excellency, what do you really think about the situation here? Who is the main cause of controversy and conflict?' He looked up and said, 'You are not here to ask questions and we are not here as judges. Just remember that Palestine is a very

105

small country and no one can get a pint into a half-pint pot.' I retreated and hoped I'd not annoyed him.

British and Russian troops have entered Persia where the Germans have been infiltrating technicians and agents and trying to gain control of radio and press. The German, Count von Ettel, and members of the German, Italian, Hungarian, Roumanian and Bulgarian Legations are all involved in this. Considering how short we are of men and materials it is astounding how we manage to deploy and maintain troops over such an immense Theatre.

General Auchinleck, now Commander-in-Chief Middle East, and General Blamey are staying with us. We have heard some inspiring stories of how our Navy steals in and out of Tobruk. Not only has it managed to maintain the garrison there which is bombed incessantly, but they have moved huge numbers of our troops in and out of it. An Australian Division has recently been relieved from there by a Polish Brigade and two British Brigades.

The General's Aides told me the Long Range Desert Group, which so recently crossed the Great Sand Sea to raid Kufra Oasis and Mursuk and linked up with Colonel Leclerc's Free French Forces in Chad, is still operating deep into enemy territory raiding landing grounds and ammunition dumps. Often they are hundreds of miles ahead, and wide, of our forces.

2 September 1941   *Jerusalem*

Sir Kinahan and Lady Cornwallis have been staying with us. Their description of how they were besieged in the Embassy in Baghdad, with all communications cut, was fun to listen to but must have been a terrifying experience. Freya Stark, who was on her way to Tehran, had to turn back and take refuge with them. They said she made a cheerful and amusing companion.

Today Colonel Glubb, who commands the Arab Legion, paid us a visit. Few people have such knowledge of the Arabs as he. They call him Abu Henaik. He looks rather dull but if you can get him to talk he isn't. Quite the reverse. He kept me riveted throughout lunch.

5 September 1941   *Jerusalem*

From the Arctic to the Black Sea the Germans are attacking Russia. Marshal Voroshilov is defending Leningrad heroically – in a most ghastly battle. Casualties on both sides must be horrendous.

10 September 1941   *Jerusalem*

At last a letter has come from Dan. It is dated April 11th and is written on a scrap of paper torn from a notebook. He wrote: 'We were ambushed by Germans. I do not know where we are going. The Generals were taken away by air. None of us were wounded. We do not know what has happened – whether Egypt is seriously threatened. I do hope Whitaker got back. I am desperately worried about you . . .' It was wonderful to see his handwriting. I read it over and over again. It has taken five months to reach me.

12 September 1941   *Jerusalem*

Mr Stonehewer Bird, our Minister in Jedda, and family lunched with us. They are on leave. The conversation went roughly like this: 'Tell us about Jedda – do you play much tennis?'

Reply: 'We can't – no tennis balls.'

'Probably you swim a lot?'

Reply: 'We can't because of the sharks.'

'How about riding?'

Reply: 'We don't ride.'

'Maybe you dance in the evenings?'

Reply: 'We can't, there is no band and gramophone records curl up in the heat.'

'Perhaps you bicycle for exercise?'

Reply: 'It's far too hot to pedal.' Old Nick came to our rescue and began a long rigmarole about Christmas in Bethlehem. Mr Stonehewer Bird has a very deep voice and pronounces Jedda with great emphasis on the last syllable – like comedians pronounce Poona.

Two young Sherwood Rangers, Michael Parish and Miles Hilliard, who were captured on Crete, have arrived here clad in Turkish civilian clothes. They escaped, on foot, via Turkey and Syria. Michael has a damaged arm and eye because one night he fell over a precipice. We gave them a great welcome.

16 September 1941   *Ramallah, Palestine*[1]

Sir Harold is easy to work for: he works fast and never forgets detail. His private and personal despatches to the Secretary of State in London are brilliant. It is sad they must remain private as they are such good evidence of his complete impartiality as far as Arabs and Jews are concerned.

19 September 1941   *Ramallah, Palestine*

It is quite difficult to work and live in the bosom of a family. Sooner or later one becomes the confidant of all age groups and gets to know everyone's virtues, faults, stories, jokes, little feuds and jealousies. In these small and rather uncomfortable quarters tact and loyalty are of paramount importance. We live cheek by jowl and work and play tend to get entangled.

HE, who is always charming to everyone, stays mostly in his study, happy with his work and books and safe from the domestic arena. Lady MacMichael, forever kind and great fun, is apt to overwork. Then she gets easily upset and needs to pour out her problems repetitively to someone and the someone is generally me. Araminta, pretty, petulant and pleased with herself, keeps up a vendetta with her mother. Aged twenty-one, with the longest feet I've seen on a female, she is endearingly

---

[1] While Government House was being springcleaned and domestic staff given holidays the High Commissioner and family moved into an empty school at Ramallah.

naive. Priscilla, much younger, lives for her animals and specially her donkey. She, too, is pretty but doesn't know it.

Nick, the ADC, looks and works well in public and appears to be a kindly old man but basically he is hyper-critical and bitchy about all and sundry and particularly the MacMichaels. His remarks on them are very funny but unfair and unforgivable. Donald MacGillivry is a small man in every respect and difficult to work with. He has a charming wife whom no one could envy. Mardell, the butler, is a major contributor to all our comfort and happiness – intelligent, able and kind, he takes good care of all ranks and age groups. The dedication and kindness of the lesser staff is something to think about and remember – apart from their attractive uniforms they have so little and give so much, always with smiles.

27 September 1941   *Jerusalem*

General Wavell and General Auchinleck are in Baghdad discussing co-operation between India and the Middle East in connection with the anti-Axis 'front' now established from Syria, through Iraq and Iran – to the flank of the Russian armies. The Germans have attacked the Crimea. This concerns us.

8 October 1941   *Jerusalem*

Though we are so busy, almost overworked, the days seem to drag. I think this is because all of us are waiting: for letters; for the outcome of the battles in Russia where casualties on both sides are appalling; for the Desert war to start again; for news of Tobruk; for news from everywhere; for the war to end . . .

I feel dreadfully restless. Except for dinner occasionally, I seldom leave Government House and must be on hand always for coded messages which I decipher in the billiard room – often at night. Each day, after tea, Sir Harold goes out in the garden to chop wood. When I can find time I walk round the big garden inside the high wire fence. The MacMichaels are very kind to me; my work is interesting; I live in great comfort; and yet I am unhappy and long to go away. It seems to me sometimes that there is a curse on Jerusalem – I so seldom meet anyone who is happy here. There is a tense atmosphere, not only over religions but as if the turmoils of centuries are still alive. Perhaps these thoughts stem from my own sadness yet I suspect Jerusalem may remain, forever, a place of conflict.

17 October 1941   *Jerusalem*

The other day His Highness the Amir Abdullah[1] of Transjordan came to lunch. Dressed in a silk robe with a gold dagger in his belt and a white cloak over his shoulders he is an impressive figure. He has thick eyebrows, wide, placid eyes and a short black beard. Round his head he wore a white Keffiyeh held in place by a gold aggal – a double twist of silk cord which, in olden days, the Arabs used at night to hobble their camels. His Highness was in great spirits, ate his lunch with relish and joked in Arabic with little Priscilla about her donkey. I sat next to Mr Kirkbride, British Resident in Amman. He told me the Amir rarely uses his Palace except for entertaining – but prefers to live in tents on a hillside nearby. In the winter he moves to a camp in the Jordan valley. The Amir is a strict Moslem and is apt to arrest his subjects if their wives walk about his capital in too transparent veils. He enjoys playing games, backgammon, etc., and has a schoolboy love of weapons. He has four wives, two sons, a daughter and a good sense of humour.

19 October 1941   *Jerusalem*

Today, Donald MacGillivry told me he is leaving Government House to go to a District. Ronald Fleming, who was in Greece till recently and has since been working in the Secretariat in Jerusalem, is coming in his place.

David Stirling and his small unit are doing well in the Desert. When the moon is down they are dropped behind enemy lines near landing grounds and dumps. They sneak past enemy sen-

[1] Later, King Abdullah of Jordan

tries and patrols, fix their bombs on aeroplanes and then make for home. Sometimes they are picked up by the Long Range Desert Group which they call 'Carter Paterson'. Considering that David's unit consists of only four officers and sixteen other ranks, the number of enemy planes they've destroyed is quite remarkable.

29 October 1941   *Jerusalem*

The Germans are crossing the Perekop Isthmus into the Crimea. Danger for us.

A whole batch of letters, written in June and July, arrived from Dan at Sulmona prison camp in Italy. '. . . The bombshell of war between Germany and Russia burst on us last night . . . Six officers arrived today. I sent you a message by Vatican Radio yesterday; with great pomp and ceremony we were visited by the Papal Nuncio – a Cardinal. He gave the camp a present of money from the Pope as well as forms for radio messages . . .'

Jerusalem is full of soldiers on leave from the Desert who've come to cool off. Today Lady MacMichael gave a tea party for convalescent soldiers from our two hospitals and her convalescent home in the town. Ronald Fleming has taken over from Donald MacGillivry – he does not require me to knock on his office door!

10 November 1941   *Jerusalem*

Freya Stark arrived to stay with us for a week on her way back to Baghdad where she works for the Ministry of Information. She is very small and rather ugly. She wears eccentric clothes and has her hair looped down on one side to hide something. It is said she fell on to, or in front of, a mowing machine when she was young and lost an ear. Her voice is curiously pitched – like no other, and her laughter is catching. She is a fascinating and kind person – interested in everything and everybody – a very brave lady with an iron will hidden under the hypnotic hats she wears more often than not. Woe betide those who stand in her way – they will be defeated with a dexterity and force which will surprise the most stubborn opponent. I like her very much.

Today she and I went for a walk in the hills. She hurried over the rocky ground like a sturdy little pony and stopped whenever we met an Arab to pass the time of day. She told me all about her work. In 1940, when she was in Aden, she invented and launched the Brotherhood of Freedom whose aim is to counteract German and Fascist rumours and to train young Arabs in the actual principles and working of democratic institutions. This is done by personal influence, from friend to friend, and kept centralised by a weekly bulletin which Freya and a small committee produce. Soon after she began in Aden she was moved to Cairo where she started again, this time with the help of two students. That was a year ago – now there are twenty thousand members of the Brotherhood in Egypt and the numbers are steadily increasing. She is on her way to Baghdad to start there and has left a Mr Fay to continue in Cairo.

13 November 1941   *Jerusalem*

Today is my twenty-eighth birthday. Everyone spoilt me. Old Nick gave me a photograph frame; Sir Harold a lovely silver box; and Priscilla three goldfish in a bowl. Lady MacMichael gave me a dinner party and a cake with candles and allowed me to ask three friends. As there were too few girls I dressed up Priscilla in one of my frocks and painted her face. When she arrived with other guests Sir Harold did not recognise her. She is only fifteen but looked stunning. I was very touched – Mardell and all the servants gave me a huge bunch of flowers.

16 November 1941   *Jerusalem*

Sir Walter Monckton and Mr Steinhardt, US Ambassador to Russia, arrived last night from Moscow – both very tired. Mr Steinhardt told me he found it very trying to be perpetually watched in Russia, with servants planted in his Embassy to report, and never being sure that microphones were not hidden in the walls. He said that on the way here Mr and Mme Litvinoff, who were on the same plane, would not get up in the morning and came downstairs too late to allow enough flying time to cross the Caucasus. After several days of this Sir Walter and Mr Steinhardt left the Russians behind in bed and now a furious telegraphic row is raging because the Russians say they've been insulted.

Peter Stirling is in Jerusalem on leave from our Embassy in Cairo. He brought me all the Cairo and Desert news and as always was most amusing and very well informed. It is amazing how different official, GHQ, news of the Desert war is from news and views of my contemporaries in the field. I find the latter more accurate than the former. Maybe military high-ups don't talk and listen enough to the young. This is where General Wavell was so good – he talked and listened to all ranks and age groups.

18 November 1941   *Jerusalem*

We have attacked in the Desert.[1] Ironic to be fighting for territory we captured last year. I hate to think of so many friends struggling down there in the dust.

21 November 1941   *Jerusalem*

Bob Laycock's Commandos have raided Rommel's headquarters and it is rumoured that Geoffrey Keyes was killed and Bob is missing. By ill luck Rommel was away and so escaped capture or worse. Other news from the Desert is good so far. It must be a thrilling moment for the garrison in Tobruk.

Cables keep coming from anxious wives and mothers in England asking for news of their men, but, of course, we know little about individuals. In Cairo I was better informed. It's difficult to find time and money to cope with these sad enquiries – telegrams are so expensive.

[1] This was Operation Crusader which was intended to raise the German siege of Tobruk and did.

A letter has come from Dan dated May 10th, written two days after he arrived at Sulmona POW camp in southern Italy. He wrote they had a terrible journey back across North Africa to Tripoli. Nearly all the prisoners had dysentery. He found my telegram waiting for him at Sulmona – forwarded by the Red Cross in Geneva. He wants cigarettes, chocolate, books, tinned butter and a shaving brush. He may only send one letter of eighteen lines each week . . . My poor Dan . . .

Dan's stepfather, Lizzie Lezard, has arrived in Jerusalem from Kenya where he was serving with the King's African Rifles. He is joining the Eighth Army where most of his friends are. He is rather old to be on active service anyway, but with his usual enthusiasm and great sense of humour he is determined to be a hero. He told me he was staying with Lord Erroll on the night he was murdered and was a witness at the trial of Sir Delves Broughton in Nairobi. He regaled me with every detail of this strange and dreadful story and ended up in his cheerful way: 'The murderer's weapon was never found, which goes to show how large Africa really is.'

6 December 1941   *Jerusalem*

A big tank battle is raging in the Desert near Sidi Rezegh. I think the Sherwood Rangers may be involved. Perhaps, after all, I am lucky that Dan is a prisoner and not in the midst of this turmoil.

I am afraid we are not yet as well armed as the Germans – their Mark 3 and 4 guns are excellent and they have the awful 88mm gun.

8 December 1941   *Jerusalem*

Old Nick burst into the billiard room this morning – his face pink with excitement. 'You've been across the Pacific,' he said. 'Just where is Pearl Harbor – it's not marked in my Atlas?'

'Go away,' I said. 'I am struggling with a cipher signal.'

'To hell with that,' he said, 'the Japs have bombed Pearl Harbor, destroyed a lot of American ships and the USA are coming into the war.' We danced round and round the billiard table.

10 December 1941   *Jerusalem*

Wonderful news: we've advanced in the Desert and raised the siege of Tobruk. For us in the Middle East this is wildly exciting. Through the dark days of 1941 the defenders of that shattered town have been an inspiration to us all, except perhaps for dear Lady MacMichael who announced at lunch she could not find Tobruk on her map of Russia.

18 December 1941   *Jerusalem*

Japanese troops have landed on Hong Kong. North, south, east and west of us war goes on and spreads. Nothing seems to improve – except our geography.

24 December 1941   *Jerusalem*

A letter arrived from Dan which cheered me a little. He is being moved to a prison in Florence where Generals Neame and O'Connor are held. He says my letters take five weeks to reach him. It seems forever since I saw him . . .

Christmas Day, 1941   *Jerusalem*

This must be a specially sad day for many millions of people.

29 December 1941   *Jerusalem*

The MacMichaels have gone on holiday to Syria and I have been granted two weeks' leave. I am tired and glad of a rest. When I get back I think I should ask for a half day off each week.

Sim Feversham, who was going to Cairo, gave me a lift in his

115

car. We started early and drove via Beersheba across the Sinai Desert. Mostly we talked about prisons because, before the war, Sim had spent much of his spare time on planning improvements for both prisoners and warders. Sim is a very kind man.

The sun was setting when we reached Ismaelia. We drove through the dusk into heavy traffic and arrived in the seething streets of Cairo, and went on to Gezirah island where Michael[1] and Esther Wright's nice house is situated. There was just time for me to wash and change my clothes and go with them to dine at the Mohammed Ali Club. I sat next to Randolph Churchill, who talked of his *World Press Review* which is a good newspaper. At dinner I learned that Bob Laycock,[2] who has been missing for many weeks, has turned up after walking for over forty days across the desert to our lines. He lived on berries and, amazingly, is not much the worse. I shall go and see him at the Lytteltons' house in Mena. I nearly fell asleep at dinner – it's been a long day.

1 January 1942   *Cairo, Egypt*

Last night soldiers on leave in Cairo saw the New Year in with a vengeance. They behaved disgracefully but were so funny and happy no one seemed to mind. They swung from the chandeliers in Shepherds Hotel and turned on the fire hoses; they rode gharry horses after donning their drivers' tarbooshes and galabeyas and placing them in their underclothes on their carriage seats; they 'borrowed' trucks and buses and raced around the streets letting off fireworks and singing. Amazingly no one got hurt. Whitaker and I hired a gharry and drove round and saw chariot races in Kasr el Nil, bank notes fluttering on the pavements, and military police convulsed with laughter, hopelessly trying to restore order.

[1.] He was serving at our Embassy.
[2.] Later, General Sir Robert Laycock, Chief of Combined Operations and subsequently Governor of Malta. He was the son of our host at Torridon in August 1939 and commanded the raid on what was thought to be Rommel's headquarters.

I visited Bonner Fellers in his office and looked at his fascinating maps and photographs while he finished dictating in his colourful, downright way. He drove me to lunch in his 'hearse' as he calls it – a camouflaged van which has a bunk in the back, which he uses when he goes up to the Desert. We talked about the Russian Army which he is still convinced will hold the Germans – and about the Palestine problem: 'You British should give the Jews a kind of Vatican City which would solve the whole goddam problem,' he said. And he told me, 'I'm getting unpopular here. Not so much with your people as with the US Embassy in Cairo and in Washington; they think I am a defeatist but that's not going to stop me saying what I think about the military situation, which is my job to do. The trouble is your top brass are overconfident which they've no right to be: your gear is still inferior to the enemy's, and you are less well led – too many senior officers are sitting on their arses at GHQ. If I get levered out I shall join MacArthur – he's the best soldier we have.'

As I was leaving he said, 'Remember one thing: we've got a helluva lot to learn – your country and mine. I reckon if we don't stop worrying about our different customs and snobberies then Russia will take the lead in tomorrow's world. You people are so busy with tradition and mine so stuck on making money that I guess it will serve us right if they do.' A grin and he was gone.

As I was leaving Shepherds Hotel, a tall, gaunt, scruffy figure climbed out of a taxi and asked me to pay the fare. It was David Stirling – just back from the Desert. Considering the length of his beard he must have been there for a long time. 'How many men have you got now, and what's the score?' I asked.

'Four officers and fourteen men, and around ninety enemy planes destroyed on the ground,' he said and added he now only had one idea in his head – a bath. Before I had time to congratulate him on his Honour[1] he hurried away saying, 'Meet me here for dinner.' I did.

[1] The DSO – Distinguished Service Order.

I spent the morning exploring shops and the Musqi. I saw lovely things and many were not expensive: French scent; American make-up and clothes; leather shoes, handbags; rugs and materials made in Egypt and Turkey.

I went to the Lytteltons' house at Mena to see Bob Laycock. He was sitting up in bed looking thin and drawn. He had sinus and toothache. He was cheerful and generously told me of his escape. I suggested I should take it down in shorthand so he could send it home and he was pleased.

A party of nine officers and fifty-six other ranks left Alexandria on November 10th in two submarines to go to Chesm el Chlb which is near Appolonia, between Derna and Bengazi. Their operation was timed to coincide with the Eighth Army's attack; its object was to cause maximum damage and interruption to German installations and communications and, incidentally, to raid a house at Sidi Rafa where Rommel was known to stay frequently with the head German 'Q' General. This house and German headquarters are eighteen miles inland from Chesm el Chlb and about two hundred miles behind the enemy's front at Sollum.

They surfaced off Chesm el Chlb at 6.30 p.m. on 14th November. The first submarine closed the beach and trimmed down to allow the raiding party to bring their rubber dinghies up through the hatch. These were pumped up on the casing with a foot pump. A strong swell was running and, instead of taking the calculated hour to land, the first party took five: this caused anxiety because the submarines had to go to sea at least two hours before dawn so as to charge their batteries before submerging again at daylight. By midnight, when the second submarine began launching their party, the weather had worsened considerably; many of the rubber dinghies were washed overboard and others capsized in the water. Only Bob and nine other ranks managed to get ashore. They were met on the beach by Haseldon of the Long Range Desert Group who had signalled them where to land with a torch; he was dressed as an Arab and had walked fifty miles to meet them. The whole party lay up in a wadi for the remainder of that night and all the next day. Because of the bad weather their numbers were reduced to six officers and twenty-seven other ranks, and their dinghies had to be hidden in caves instead of being returned to the submarines on a grass line.

On the following night Keyes despatched some of his men to bust the electric light plant and others to cover the hotel, guard tent and car park. Then he, Campbell and Sergeant Terry crept up to the house. They could not get in by the back or side doors, or by the windows, so Campbell, who speaks perfect German, banged on the front door and shouted to the inmates to let him in. A sentry opened the door and was promptly shot. Two men came down the stairs but fled back again. No one came out of the hotel or guard tent but two Germans carrying lights hurried towards them. They were shot. Cautiously Keyes, Campbell and Terry entered the first room. It was empty. They had heard voices in the room beyond but now all was silent. The door was shut. Keyes went forward and flung it open. Inside was complete darkness. Shots rang out and Keyes fell; he had been silhouetted against the light. Campbell and Terry machine-gunned the room and threw in hand grenades. They entered the room and found they had killed several high German officers but Rommel was not there. They learned afterwards that he had gone to a birthday party in Rome.

They dragged poor Keyes out. He died almost at once. Then a stray bullet hit Campbell and broke his leg.[1] In the darkness and confusion the Germans had begun to fire at each other. Campbell knew he could not make the eighteen-mile dash over rough ground to the coast so he ordered Sergeant Terry to leave him and take the men back. At 5 p.m. on the eighteenth they joined Bob at the rendezvous. He led the exhausted remnants of the expedition down to the beach but when they reached the cave where they had hidden their boats they found them gone. Soon after dusk they sighted the submarine. Bob signalled for life jackets. The reply came, 'It is too rough

---

[1] Captain R. F. Campbell. His leg was amputated in an Italian prison camp.

to make the attempt tonight: food and water will be floated ashore; we will return tomorrow night.' Bob and his party waited in terrible suspense, taking turns to keep watch . . .

Towards midday on the nineteenth they heard shots and soon Germans began to appear. Slowly they closed in. When they were within two hundred yards of Bob's perimeter he ordered his men to scatter in twos and threes and make for the east. For the first half mile they ran across the open under continual fire. A few were hit. The rest hid in high scrub and watched the enemy searching for them. Bob and Sergeant Terry moved into the wadis the Germans had already searched. This went on for days. After a week most of the party had been captured and there was no longer a chance of the submarine picking them up. Bob and Terry had four tins of iron rations, two tins of bully and a packet of sweets. It rained incessantly which had one advantage – they had enough to drink. They wandered and wandered, trying to avoid the Arabs who trail every track and are paid by the Italians for information. When their food ran out they lived on berries. So they waited – desperately hoping that our army would advance and find them before they died of hunger or were captured by the enemy.

After forty-one days, on Christmas Eve, Bob sighted some soldiers through his field glasses; they were on a rise a few miles away. At first he thought they were Italians, they were so dusky, then he saw they were Indians. 'You can imagine how I felt when I found myself eating Christmas dinner at Eighth Army Headquarters. Sergeant Terry ate a whole pot of marmalade at one go,' he said.

5 January 1942   *Cairo, Egypt*

A year ago in Cairo I met a Syrian called George Antonius who impressed me by his sparkling, humorous conversation and his good command of English. Today, by chance, I met him again. He invited me to go to the zoo. 'Said the Hippo is far the nicest person in Cairo,' he said. So we spent a pleasant afternoon feeding animals. Of medium height and build, lithe and deliberate in movement, George has an arresting face – fine, dark and sensitive. His eyes match his conversation, now smouldering with purpose, now swimming with laughter, or again, darting with wit and questions. I asked him so many questions that he told me his life story.

He was educated at Victoria College, Alexandria, and at Cambridge and has since travelled in Europe, Asia and America. When he left Cambridge, during the last war, he worked in the censorship office in Alexandria and eventually became head of it. In 1921 he joined the Palestine Government in the Department of Education and from that time often journeyed with his friend General Clayton, who was then High Commissioner in Iraq, to India, the Yemen and Arabia. Once they went on a six months' tour to make the Treaties with Ibn Saud – George acted as interpreter.

I asked why he had left the Palestine Government. He explained that while he was on one of these official trips with General Clayton an Englishman was appointed as Assistant Director of Education over him. 'Till then I had been working happily with the Director who was a friend of mine. I was angry at being superseded. You realise, I suppose, that your Government never allows a "foreigner" to get to the top of a Department? Well, I rebelled against this and appealed to the Colonial Office, but all to no avail. I was transferred to the Secretariat; I liked the work there but saw no chance of ever getting far. So I left. In 1930 I joined Charles Crane.'

'Who is he?' I asked.

'An American millionaire. He is dead now,' George continued. 'Twice an Ambassador in the days of Wilson, he visited Russia nine times and later became crazy on A-raabs. He knew Ibn Saud and all the Kings of Arabia, sent them gifts and produced books ... do you remember the King-Crane Commission in 1919 when they went to Syria to decide the Plebiscite? No? Well, anyway, when I left the Palestine Government I joined the Institute of Current World Affairs which Crane had formed, launched and financed in USA, to teach the Americans about other parts of the world. I became their Middle East man. Later I dedicated *The Arab Awakening* to him because it was largely due to his interest and assistance that I was able to travel about collecting material for it. He and I both wanted to present the Arab Movement to the rest of the world.'

George told me that he had lectured all over America and Canada and described many amusing things that happened to him during that time. *The Arab Awakening* was published just before the White Paper Conference in 1939. He went to London and became Secretary General to the Arab Delegation. 'But the White Paper was turned down. Hitler walked into Prague and Middle Eastern problems were eclipsed by the troubles looming in Europe. I returned to Cairo and since have been suffering from forced inactivity; I cannot send my reports on Arab social reforms, politics and literature back to the Institute in America because of censorship, and His Majesty's Government have not yet offered me a job.'

I dined with Peter Stirling at his flat. David was there and told me of his raids on Jalo and Gailo beyond Misurata. As usual he and his men were dropped by parachute and after destroying enemy planes on the ground they were picked up by the Long Range Desert Group. His score of enemy planes destroyed in this way behind enemy lines is now fantastic. David hates talking about his nocturnal raids so I felt honoured to hear a detailed account. Mo, with the dignity of an English butler, served dinner and handed round captured Italian wine, murmuring, 'Mussolini, Sir?'

9 January 1942   *Cairo, Egypt*

This morning I went with Michael and Esther Wright to Mena where we met Freya Stark, Sir Walter Monckton and some more. We mounted donkeys and set off with a picnic lunch for Sakara. My donkey was called Telephone and trotted along well, but some of the others were less amiable and progressed by fits and starts. Freya Stark, dressed in a hideous sporting jacket, spun on her own mills in Italy, and snake gaiters topped by a large double-brimmed felt hat, was a sight for the gods, and her running commentary to her donkey made Walter Monckton laugh so much he nearly fell off his mount.

This evening I went to the Scottish Hospital to visit the

wounded. It was tragically full. I found it difficult not to flinch at some of the sights and had to struggle to appear cheerful and smiling.

I heard tonight we have taken Sollum. Japan has declared war on the Dutch East Indies.

17 January 1942   *Cairo, Egypt*

I am sitting up in a train trundling north through the night to Palestine. Today is Dan's and my third wedding anniversary. I am trying not to look back on that wonderful day in London – or look forward to returning to the Holy Land whose turbulent past and uneasy present makes it an unhappy place to be. I am trying not to think at all . . .

On my return I found a letter from Dan, dated October 3rd:

> Imagine an old castle restored in the worst Victorian style,
> grey and featureless with enormous battlements and a tower
> in one corner. It has a minute garden with ornamental yew
> hedges and the whole is surrounded by a high, thick wall
> which one can only see over from the upper windows. The
> castle is three storeys high. General Neame does needlework
> most of the time; General Gambier-Parry plays poker
> extraordinarily badly and we all win his money. General Carton
> de Wiart is a delightful character and must hold the world
> record for bad language . . .

Dan's address is Campo Concentramento, P.C. No. 12., P.M. 3200, Italy.

HE and Lady MacMichael seemed pleased to see me. They'd enjoyed their holiday and visit with General Catroux who keeps a whole tribe of Siamese cats in his house. His Aides, secretly, refer to Madame Catroux as 'The Mad Cat'. She is a rather formidable lady.

22 January 1942   *Jerusalem*

The MacMichaels have decided to keep chickens in the garden here, and sheep from Transjordan. Nick is outraged and keeps

123

muttering, 'Common people. Suburban habits. Nitwit economy.' I am kept very busy in the office by day and often at night, too, when most of the cables come in. Now I have little time to write letters to my family at home, or keep my Diary – but I still manage to post a note to Dan every day. Each morning I paint on a brave face and all day I manage to look and be cheerful. Only when I close my bedroom door at night can I unleash my terrible sorrow.

Good news: From England – the RAF is making giant bombing raids on Germany and France; Mr Churchill and President Roosevelt have had successful talks and more help may now come to us; the Russians have launched new offensives in the Ukraine and Crimea; Araminta has stopped using my hanging cupboard as her chief hiding place from her Mother.

Bad news: Rommel has counter-attacked at Agheila; Malta is being heavily and continuously bombed; the Japanese are advancing in SE Asia and it is likely they will take Singapore and Malaya. Now we are worried for Australia. Most of their troops have had to leave the Middle East to defend their own country. An awful jungle war is going on in Burma. It looks as if we'll have trouble here ere long because of the 'illegal immigrants' who keep sailing to our shore from Europe, scuppering their boats and wading ashore.

It is becoming more and more difficult to follow war news. A multitude of events on land, sea and air are happening fast and furiously in every hour all around the world. The tragedy and suffering of all races is now beyond reckoning. In this lovely house filled with flowers and food, and in spite of my interesting work, I feel embarrassed and rather ashamed to be so lucky. I am restless and know I must leave soon to work closer to the war and my contemporaries.

1 March 1942   *Jerusalem*

A letter came from Dan:

> Yesterday was Christmas Day. Somehow ordinary days are easy
> to bear and it is only on days like yesterday that one really

feels what it is like to be a prisoner . . . Luckily I was fairly busy preparing our rather ersatzy celebrations and didn't have time to think too much. I didn't win the watch the Pope had given us, but the tea and dinner paraphernalia, all of which I arranged, went with a swing and I think the Generals enjoyed themselves . . . The MacMichaels' wire to General O'Connor arrived on Christmas Eve . . . The YMCA has sent us a magnificent lot of games, musical instruments, etc., and two complete badminton sets so I'm hoping some of them will play and give me some exercise which I long for. The Red Cross as usual did not send our Christmas parcels off till much too late . . . So many people write to us in all seriousness and say, 'How nice for you to see the art galleries, etc., in Florence.' Are we indignant! I've only seen Florence from the railway station. This *is* a prison . . .

Here the grass is turning brown and spring flowers are over. The skies are cloudless, and, across the valley from Government House, Jerusalem looks like an alabaster city under the midday sun. The tortoises in the sunken garden by the front door are busy mating – they find this hard work because of their shells.

16 March 1942   *Jerusalem*

Trouble. A ship called *Struma* was scuttled off the coast of Palestine and the illegal immigrants who waded ashore were all interned. Jewish feelings ran high and there have been protests to and from London. Jewish extremists made attempts on the lives of our Inspector General of Police and his Deputy. The latter was killed. One of the assassins was caught and it was discovered that, as well as tying bombs to the back of these officials' cars and putting sticks of gelignite in their gardens (I think seventy were found in the Inspector General's garden), it emerged that they had also sown the Jerusalem cemetery with mines, hoping to kill most of the Palestine Government who would attend such high officials' funerals. A bomb was also placed in the fence which encircles Government House. It went off while we were at dinner – made a terrific bang but did no damage.

A big mail has arrived – many of the letters are nine weeks old. My sister Daphne wrote from London: '. . . I am twenty now, so stop writing to me as if I were still at school. I am determined to join you, so no use warning me of the perils of submarines . . .'

My old Nannie wrote from Washington: 'We left England – the family were posted to America. We saw a whale and a submarine on the way over. All the children were seasick – they are better behaved than you were, but I don't laugh so much. You'd be surprised by the servants here – they are black . . .'

Peter Fleming wrote: 'I'm on my way to join General Archie and, I hope, the lands of pink palaces further east . . .' General Wavell's ADC wrote from India: 'So sorry. I forgot to post the General's letter to you. I put it in my pocket when we left India to go to SE Asia, and it's remained there ever since and now we are flying back to Delhi. You are lucky the Japs didn't get it – we only just got out in time. General Archie is well and unperturbed as always . . .'

Lady Gowrie wrote from Canberra Government House: 'Now it's our turn. The Japanese are uncomfortably near and we are thankful to get our troops back from the Middle East . . .'

Mummy wrote from Switzerland: 'The Swiss are so good to me but we are all horribly aware that this little country is now encircled by the enemy and, of course, we do not know if its neutrality will be honoured . . .'

26 March 1942   *Jerusalem*

King George of Greece and his Master of the Household, Colonel Levides, are staying with us. The latter has had no news of his wife and baby in Athens and is terribly anxious for them. The King's news of Greece, and his present situation, are awful. He told me that thousands of Greeks starved last winter. Men, women and children died in such quantities that vanloads of dead had to be collected each day from houses and streets.

The MacMichaels are going away for Easter – Sir Harold to

Haifa and Lady M to the Lebanon so that Priscilla can learn to ski. Our Mountain Warfare School is training there and the snow is still good. Because of this the MacMichaels have arranged for the Greeks to go to the King David Hotel for Easter. Some of us are worried because the hotel is like a cattle market in Holy Week, with people sleeping on the floors up and downstairs. Nick, Araminta, Mardell (whose wife is Greek) and I are unhappy about this. I felt strongly that the poor exiles should stay here in peace and quiet, so I went to HE's study and said so. I got a very thick ear! Perhaps there is some rule of protocol to justify this, but HE was so annoyed I did not stay to enquire.

During Easter, Araminta and I invited the King and Colonel Levides to lunch several times, and once we dined with them at the hotel, which was bedlam. We took them some lovely books instead of Easter eggs and stayed with them until they left for the Patriarchate for the Service of the Resurrection.

7 April 1942   *Jerusalem*

A year ago today Dan was taken prisoner. It seems more like ten years. Ghastly to know we can never recapture that year of our lives.

Sir Harold has flown to England via Lagos for talks with our Government. In his absence I am working for the Acting High Commissioner, John MacPherson. I sit in a small room at the Secretariat with his secretary, Molly MacQueen – a kind and amusing person whose knowledge of the Palestine situation and Government surprises me almost as much as my ignorance surprises her. She was here in the Troubles, and sometimes she tells me hideous stories of what went on then.

Today I confided in Lady MacMichael that I feel I should be doing war work rather than be in this interesting and luxurious civil job. I was afraid she might think me ungrateful but marvellously she understood and said: 'I can quite see that all your generation are living dangerously and uncomfortably. The only trouble is that we really do need you here.' We agreed I should talk to HE when he returns but I assured her I would stay for my promised year anyway.

Malta has been awarded the George Cross. We are all tremendously pleased about this.

This morning one tall and one short stranger walked into our office and announced they were checking up on security. Both looked suspicious and were wearing civilian clothes so I demanded brusquely to see their papers. Amid bursts of laughter they produced these. 'At last! At last!' they chortled and went on laughing. It emerged that the short one was Sir John Dashwood, and the tall one a Scotland Yard detective whom Sir John referred to as 'Killer'. When they stopped laughing they explained that their job was to check security in offices throughout the Middle East but, so far, until today, they had never been asked for their credentials: 'We've been to the most important and secret offices in Egypt but no one ever checked up on who on earth we are. We might have been Hitler and Mussolini for all they knew.' Molly and I took them out to a hilarious lunch.

I dined with George Antonius who'd come to Jerusalem to see his wife, Katy. They are separated but obviously he adores her. He wore a smart brown suit and flung his mackintosh over the back of his chair. 'It's easy to see', he said cheerfully, 'which are the Fifth Column in the King David Hotel – they are always so badly dressed.' After that he grumbled good-naturedly about the Palestine Government's disapproval of him. I suggested this could be because of his close friendship with the Mufti. He told me the Mufti was a boyhood friend of his and he'd always admired him. I asked him to tell me about the Mufti.

'The Mufti is a great patriot – but remember – a patriot for the Arab world. He was forced into being an enemy of Britain because he was convinced that British policy as regards Zionists represented a very real threat to the Arab world. Haj Amin is not personally anti-British but he is an intelligent man. He came of a leading Jerusalem family whose members held important religious and civil positions in the Ottoman days. Educated in Jerusalem and at the Moslem University in Cairo, and later in a French Catholic School, as a young man he served as an officer in the Ottoman Army and attended Staff College in Constantinople. In 1917, when the British occupied Jerusalem, he offered his services to the British and became assistant to Haddad Pasha, a Syrian Christian who held a high post in the military administration. Among other things he recruited Palestine Arabs for Feisal's army which was then fighting on Allenby's flank. But a year later his troubles began: he saw that British policy as regards Zionism might end in disaster. Being a man of character and loyalty he resigned his post and joined Feisal's army. This was before the Balfour Declaration. From then on his quarrel with England grew, not from antipathy to your people – indeed he has always seen the importance of Anglo-Arab co-operation – but because British policy continued the way it did. Later he became Secretary of the Executive Committee of the first Palestinian Arab Congress. During the disturbances of 1920 an order was issued for his arrest. He fled to Transjordan and Syria. Eventually he was amnestied and returned to Palestine. On the death of his half-brother he was appointed Mufti. You must know the rest of his history if you have read the Peel Report.'

'Why did he go over to the Germans?' I asked.

'Where else could he go?' said George. 'He was wanted dead or alive by the British who are spread all over the Middle East, and Turkey refused to let him go and live there.' Then we talked of Amal Atrash, a lovely Jebel Druze Princess whose green eyes and black hair have caused a sensation here.

It is always fun and interesting to talk with George Antonius. You can ask him anything and he answers quickly and directly. He is intelligent, well informed, travelled and has a great sense of humour. He is an outstanding Arab.

As I drove him home I thought how sad it is that he and Katy are separated; together they'd be a valuable and attractive couple to represent Arabs anywhere. And I thought, too, that it is a pity that George and Sir Harold can't, won't or don't ever meet and talk together. They would have brilliant conversations – it would be fun for both, and perhaps useful.

8 May 1942   Jerusalem

A letter arrived from Dan, dated March 13th – the quickest so far. He wrote: 'Great excitement here – four new arrivals today. They were taken prisoner in Libya last November. Two are New Zealanders – Brigadiers Miles and Hargest . . .' I think this may help Dan a bit as they will have news of the Desert war even if it is not very new or cheerful. Also because of Dan's connection with New Zealand[1] there will be something new to talk about – fishing on Lake Taupo, the Ranfurly Shield Rugger Trophy and the Countess of Ranfurly's Own Regiment, etc . . . I am to send General Neame a mosquito net.

22 May 1942   Jerusalem

Yesterday I heard that George Antonius was ill so I went to Katy's house and took flowers. Katy and I sat and talked but George did not come downstairs. 'He feels rotten,' Katy said, 'but in a few days he'll be fine.' This morning she telephoned me: 'George is dead. It would help if you come to the funeral.' Her voice broke and she hung up. What a terrific shock for Katy – no one knew George was dangerously ill.

Ronald Fleming and I went to the funeral in the Russian Cathedral. No one used pews or chairs but stood around the altar and the coffin. Someone put a lighted candle in my hand and priests began to chant. Suddenly two bearers appeared and, to my astonishment, lifted the lid off the coffin and there lay George Antonius in his smart brown suit. Ronald nudged me and whispered, 'Your mouth is wide open.' It was a touching service – distinguished Arabs and Oustoz Sakakini, a Greek poet, spoke and then we all filed out into the sunshine. George is a very great loss to the Arabs and, maybe, also to the Jews. If

[1] Dan's grandfather was Governor of New Zealand from 1897 to 1904, and for his last year Dan's father acted as his ADC. Dan and I had visited New Zealand.

ever honest and sensible talks take place to find a solution to the Palestine problem many will regret that George is dead. On our way home, Ronald told me that at Greek Orthodox funerals coffins are nearly always uncovered, the idea being that everyone should see who the dead person really is.

26 May 1942   *Jerusalem*

Rommel has attacked in the Desert.[1] Rumour has it that we are better armed this time.

Several letters have arrived from Dan – some only five weeks old. He wrote:

> Six letters and a photo arrived from you on our wedding anniversary. It's been too cold to do anything these last few weeks except walk. Our tiny garden has been dug up and planted with vegetables. I saw and chop wood for our fire which is good exercise but I long for spring when we'll be able to play badminton and deck tennis . . . It made us laugh that you sent General Carton a parcel because he gets twice as many parcels as anyone else. I am endlessly amused by him. He is a really nice person – superbly outspoken. He reads a lot and so will enjoy your books . . .

My poor Dan – how ghastly to be a prisoner. But I suppose I am lucky that he is not in the Western Desert now when all hell has been let loose.

We had an official dinner for HRH The Duke of Gloucester who is staying with us. He is visiting troops ail over the Middle East and next month he is going to India. His itinerary is enough to give anyone a stroke. At dinner there was a discussion about the rubber shortage and, stupidly, I chipped in and said I thought this news was worse for women than for men. HRH fixed me with an amused eye and demanded that I explain exactly what I meant. I said it may become difficult to obtain elastic girdles and that bras are very dependent on elastic, but I dodged mentioning needs further south.

[1] This was the beginning of the battle of Gazala, Rommel's most resounding victory.

After dinner, when HRH moved around the big drawing room talking to everybody, I got tired from standing up but discovered the advantage of wearing a long evening dress is that by perching one's behind against a table or armchair one can still look quite erect in front. Poor Nick was less fortunate – said his varicose veins were standing out like the Dolomites. He and I talked to Howard Kerr, the Duke's Equerry, who told us about our giant air raids over Germany; and what spring was like in England. He laughed when I absently asked if he had a large wife and children.

28 May 1942   Jerusalem

The Desert War has started again with a vengeance. It is terrifying to think that nearly all our friends are down there fighting in the dust and smoke. We read the newspapers carefully, watch Reuter's reports, and listen to the nine o'clock broadcast from London, but we don't learn much – and it is not yet possible to know which way the battle is turning. Our lives go quietly on: each morning an Arab gardener arranges flowers in the cool arched rooms; the red leather boxes go back and forth to the Secretariat; important visitors come and go; Lady MacMichael and I visit hospitals, grumble about her temperamental cook, and inspect her pigs and sheep. Letters from home are rare nowadays and devoured when they arrive, but they, too, don't tell us much because of the censor. The evening sun turns the hills gilt colour – at dusk Jerusalem looks like a drop scene in a play. We change for dinner and afterwards, if there are no visitors, we all read. Around ten o'clock we take ourselves and our anxieties to bed.

31 May 1942   Jerusalem

News has reached us of a gigantic RAF raid on Cologne last night when some three thousand tons of bombs were dropped. How wonderful and how terrible. This raid was bigger than any Luftwaffe raid on England and must be a hideous warning to Hitler and all Germans of what they may expect. The odd

132

thing here is that none of us hate. We think of such raids as unpleasant necessities but still feel so sorry for those we are hurting, and especially for children.

11 June 1942   *Jerusalem*

General Koenig and his men have put the *Tricolore* back where it belongs. At Bir Hakeim the Free French were attacked by Rommel's full striking force. Outnumbered, blitzed by Stukas, and stormed by 88mm guns, they suffered hideous casualties but still held on. Over and over it was thought they were lost but they refused to surrender. Only when they were ordered back did they move. Then, what was left of them fought their way out with rifles and bayonets. General Koenig and his men will long be remembered.

14 June 1942   *Jerusalem*

The Desert seems to be one long ghastly battle now. Conflicting news and rumours keep coming in – that our Gazala line is broken, that Rommel is retreating . . . The only thing we know for certain is that casualties are appalling on both sides. Dreadful to think of all the women at home with their hearts and minds straining on the Desert. Poor Lady Halifax has three sons down there.

16 June 1942   *Jerusalem*

Today I lunched with Princess Peter of Greece who has a flat in the Greek Patriarchate. There I met Cecil Beaton who was busy photographing the Greek Patriarch, a fine-looking old man with a white beard. When I got back to Government House I found Whitaker waiting for me. He has been sent up to work in the Jerusalem branch of my old office. He said that when he left Cairo the news from the Desert was not good: 'There has been a big battle at a place called Belgravia – and we lost it.' He must mean Knightsbridge.

The Germans have taken Tobruk. No news has shocked us more since Dunkirk. The retreat must be worse than last time. Tragic that Churchill could not understand Wavell and moved him. Now our leadership is not so inspired. At present, we have superb troops but no great leader.[1]

Wounded are pouring into Palestine because the hospitals in Egypt are overflowing. Each day between one and five I go down to a hospital in Jerusalem to help in the wards. I have no training so I do all the odd jobs such as washing soldiers, making beds and emptying things. Today I washed four heads which were full of sand. I am learning a lot about pain and courage and getting used to smells and sights. The soldiers make fun of everything and, even in the long ward where the serious cases are, no one ever grumbles. I cannot describe the courage of these men. Only when they ask me to help them to write home do I glimpse their real misery: some of them are so afraid their families will not want them back now they are changed. They call me 'Sugar'.

[1.] Rommel, attacking on 26 May, had led a great mass of armoured and mechanised forces, both German and Italian, round Bir Hacheim, which was the southern end of the British mined and fortified line of positions and was valiantly held by the Free French until the night of 10 June. The fortunes of war had alternated, with what seemed at one point the opportunity to cut off Rommel's advance, isolate it from its supplies and win the battle. But Rommel smashed the British defences in the centre which enabled him to be reinforced and supplied: and defeated British attempts to counter attack in the area known as the Cauldron. After a confused battle between the Knightsbridge 'box' and El Adem on 12 June, Rommel had concentrated his armour and held the initiative. By 14 June the British were in retreat towards the Egyptian frontier and Tobruk was again surrounded. On 20 June, the Tobruk garrison surrendered. The fall of Tobruk and the rapid retreat of the British and Imperial troops to Egypt marked the high point of German success in the North African campaign. Rommel was made a Field Marshal. But when the Germans reached the desert immediately west of the Nile Delta, the country running south from Alamein to the Qatara Depression, the tide began to turn.

We can no longer hide our anxiety. Down in the Desert the battle, now only about four hundred miles away, has reached a terrible intensity. Reuter reports: 'The noise and heat are terrific – it cannot go on much longer . . .'

Last night I dined with Pat Hore-Ruthven. He left for the Desert this morning. We sat under a full moon, which must be very unpopular in the Desert, and ate chicken soup, fish and savoury. It was a meatless day. Pat was pleased and excited to be going to do some fighting and my heart felt like a gallstone as he chattered about the battle and joked about saying 'shalom', the Jewish greeting, in Germany if he were taken prisoner. He gave me messages to send to Pam and his mother, and spoke of his little son Grey,[1] who keeps two photographs on his nursery mantelpiece – one of Old King Cole, the other of 'Old Queen Mary'.

It is always the same. These young men come on leave or courses to Cairo or Palestine, or for a while they are on the staff. They take you out to dinner and talk of their families and what they are going to do after the war; they laugh and wisecrack and spend all their money in the short time they can be sure they are alive. Then they go down to the Desert leaving their letters, photographs and presents to be posted home. So often they never come back. When people write from England saying, 'You must be having a whale of a time in the Middle East,' I have not the heart to reply that so many parties are farewell parties in the truest sense of the word.

4 July 1942   *Jerusalem*

The Germans are only seventy-five miles from Alexandria. Rommel has made himself very vulnerable; his supply line is stretched like taut elastic; if only we could cut it. Lady Mac-Michael and I have been writing cheerful letters home. Rather stupid, really – people in England will know one way or the

---

[1.] Now Earl of Gowrie.

other before our letters reach them. I have told my family to keep sending good news of me to Dan even if things get worse. Poor Dan, it must be hell reading Italian newspapers now.

General Jumbo Wilson is staying with us on his way back to Beirut. He has been in the Sinai Desert preparing a line from Mitla Pass to Wadi El Arish in case the Germans break through at El Alamein. He is also turning all the box defences in the Lebanon and Syria which were built against invasion from the north.

6 July 1942   *Jerusalem*

We are full of hope because we have held our line all this week.

Jerusalem is crowded with evacuees from Cairo: people of all nationalities who have helped us and would get hell if the Germans caught them. A great many women and children have come too. We only had twenty-four hours' notice of their arrival so Lady MacMichael and her Red Crescent had a frantic time collecting the bare necessities for them. They arrive by train at night. Already the hotels and pensions are overflowing: people are sleeping on the floors in the passages of the King David Hotel.

Said, the fat kavass, who looks like a gigantic beetle in his baggy blue trousers, waddled in to consult me this morning: he is worried over the war news and asked me whether he should take his donkey and his two wives (he obviously prefers them in that order) and hide them. He is a dear old man and dreadfully lazy – we suspect that he sleeps standing up by the front door.

9 July 1942   *Jerusalem*

News from Egypt seems a little more reassuring. In Jerusalem emergency preparations are being hurried on. Civilians drill on the golf course.

Lady MacMichael went over to tea with some of the evacuees from Cairo. They are billeted in two convents in Bethlehem – two thousand of them.

136

1. *Dan Ranfurly*

2. *On my way
to St George's,
Hanover Square*

3. *Dan and me leaving the church*

4. *We went riding after learning that, like all yeomanry wives,
I would not be allowed to go overseas*

5. *Gerald Grosvenor and me at Brocklesby station, where I said goodbye to Dan, waiting for horses and men to be loaded on the train for overseas service*

6. *Whitaker in Bethlehem, 1940*

7. *Whenever he could, Dan rode up to see me at our little house in Karkur*

8. *Toby Wallace, Lord Yarborough, Dan and me admiring our new car*

9. Mr and Mrs 'Battling Butler' came to Cape Town station to see me off to Cairo He said, 'Remember you've not enough money to be delayed on the way or to come back.'

10. Dan and I gave dinner to Captain Mountain who had flown me up from Durban

*11. All our thoughts and
conversations centred on
the Western Desert*

*12. David, the youngest of the
Stirling brothers, arrived in Cairo
determined to form a unit
of his own. It became the SAS*

13. Whitaker sightseeing in Egypt

14. Freya Stark came to stay and told us all about her travels

15. Abercrombie gave me the playing card that he had made me hit while teaching me to shoot

16. Coco, my beautiful green parrot, from the grain shop in Baghdad, who came with me everywhere, and was probably the only parrot to be given a visa to the USA

After my work I went down to the King David Hotel to see Robin Stuart French who has arrived recently from England. He came on the *Queen Mary* via the Cape in twenty-eight days which is probably a record. There were ten thousand troops on board. In spite of the cramped accommodation, the terrific heat and their unattractive destination, Robin says none of the soldiers grumbled. Cairo, which is now so near the front line, is still fairly serene. Many people have been evacuated to the south and more will come up here. The British Embassy and GHQ have been burning official documents and there is some anxiety that there will be a rush on the banks but, apart from that, life goes on as usual: the night clubs are full – boabs still sleep in rows outside the flats in Garden City. Robin said that when things looked bad he bought a bicycle.

While we were talking several people joined us and soon an argument began as to whether we can hold the Germans in Egypt and what will happen if we don't. There was talk of evacuation which I still find rather a sore subject. 'Lord Byron said women and cows should never run,' I said.

A little man who was standing nearby turned round – he had a red, rather belligerent face: 'And what use would you be?' he asked.

Robin came to my rescue: 'She would fight with the rest of us,' he said. 'Can you shoot?' the stranger asked me.

I shook my head – I was beginning to feel foolish.

Red Face glared: 'Well,' he said, 'I like that bit about Lord Byron. I'll teach you to shoot. Be at the police station on the Jaffa Road at six tomorrow.' He stumped off before I could ask his name.

This evening I went straight from the hospital to the police station on the Jaffa Road. Red Face was waiting for me in a bare Arab room. I asked his name. 'Call me Abercrombie,' he said, 'it's as good as any other. Now, sit down,' he continued, 'I shall

137

tell you all I know. I was taught in America by "G" men and I am a bloody fine shot. Make the gun part of your arm. You must get so accustomed to it that when you point at anything you damn well hit it. What do you do when you eat? You put your fork in your mouth, not in your cheek. See? When you wipe your nose, you find it first shot. So it is with shooting. It must be. Now. Take this gun. Don't be afraid of it; it won't bite.' He showed me how to hold it easily in my hand, how to cock it and recock it without moving anything but my fingers and wrist. 'Never pull the trigger,' he said. 'Your gun is like an orange in the palm of your hand. You must squeeze that orange.' He strode up and down the small room jerking out his directions, telling me to think of my gun as a pencil with which I must learn to write, neatly and indelibly, in bullets.

He took me over to his range. It was dark inside and after the stark Palestinian sun I could not see. 'There are six dummy men in here,' he said, 'Stay where you are and use your eyes. Kill them.' He was unsparing. I shot with my right hand, with my left hand, and with both hands. I hated the noise and blinked my eyes. My wrist wobbled; my mind wobbled. He made me go on. Sometimes I shot in the dark. Sometimes he turned on the light. He bawled. I shot. 'One, two. One, two. Now left. Now right. Now both together. Squeeze that orange. Keep your eyes open.' Sweating and shy I plugged on, standing close to and then far from his life-size dummies. After an hour he told me to return at the same time tomorrow.

16 July 1942   *Jerusalem*

Ronald Fleming told me today that he is leaving. I am to carry on with the two jobs, his and mine. I am sorry Ronald is going – he is a delightful person and easy to work with. I hope I shall not have to give up my hospital work.

A magnificent parcel, covered in tape and seals, arrived for me from India. Inside were two pairs of old-fashioned corsets with bones and laces. They were sent by HRH The Duke of Gloucester. Nick and I had an argument as to how one should thank one of the Royal Family for a present of corsets. Which-

ever way we put it looked disrespectful. Finally we sent a telegram saying: 'Reinforcements received. Positions now held.
Most grateful thanks.'

This evening 'Abercrombie' lent me his 'Silver Lady', a
special Smith and Wesson with a light trigger. It is perfectly
balanced. 'There are twenty-five dummies in the chain of cel-
lars below us,' he said, pointing with his thumb at the floor.
'They are hidden all over the place. Go ahead and don't forget
to reload.' At the bottom of some steep steps I opened a door
as he had taught me: with my gun arm against the door itself. I
saw three dummies and fired. Another ran across the room on
a wire and then another sat up on a bed in the corner. They
were hidden in every conceivable place, behind the doors and
pillars. They jerked down from the ceiling on strings. Once I
forgot to load before entering a new room. 'You bloody fool,'
growled a voice behind me. 'You deserve to be dead.' When I
had finished we counted the bullet holes. I had hit seventeen
out of twenty-five dummies. Then we went through it again
with a tommy gun. The noise was terrific.

20 July 1942   *Jerusalem*

Down between the Qatara Depression and the sea the two
great armies face each other. The situation is still pretty
dangerous but that we have held on as long as this makes us
hopeful. Each day we expect to hear that the battle has begun
again. In Jerusalem everything is calm: the local attitude is that
the crisis is over.

Ronald Fleming has gone so I am pretty busy doing both
jobs. Sir Harold has been very kind and allowed me to go on
with my hospital work, but today he rang for me and said I will
have to give it up if I get absent minded. He showed me a long
despatch I had typed: I had ended it, 'Sir, You have the Honour
to be my humble and obedient Servant.'

'On purpose?' he asked.

'Yes, your Excellency,' I replied.

'Then retype' he said brusquely. Before I closed the door I
turned and saw he was shaking with laughter.

Today I had my last lesson with 'Abercrombie'. I shot with his Smith and Wesson, a Browning, a Mauser pistol and a tommy gun at dummies, playing-cards and oranges on trees. At last he said, 'You'll do. If the Germans break through at Alamein I reckon you'll make your contribution, you and Lord Byron.'

3 August 1942   Jerusalem

General Jumbo is staying with us on his way back from Cairo. He brought news of Pat Ruthven: apparently when General Auchinleck was up in the Desert he heard an unusual volley of oaths coming from under a truck and after a while Pat crawled out. According to the description Pat is still the worst-dressed man in the Desert.

I have been given a rise: I now earn five hundred and twenty pounds a year.

31 August 1942   Jerusalem

All through August I have been too busy to keep my Diary. One day, in mid-August, we asked General Jumbo about General Montgomery. He said, 'He is a very good soldier.' He'd better be.

We saw General Archie Wavell on his way back from Cairo to India. He rang up from Lydda and we all drove down and spent twenty minutes with him on the aerodrome while his plane was being refuelled. He told us about his time in Russia – he dined with Stalin and picked raspberries in the Kremlin garden. He asked me whom I was sharing a hat with these days: it always amused him that Elizabeth Coke and I could never go together to formal lunches in Cairo because we only had one hat between us. General Archie took two photographs of me to send Dan and then kissed Lady MacMichael and me goodbye – I don't know which of us was the most surprised.

Today the whole family went to the Duke of Kent's Memorial Service at the Cathedral.[1]

---

[1] The Duke of Kent had been killed in a flying accident in Scotland.

Last night, on my way to dine with Robin Stuart French and Peter Wilson, who commands the Transjordan Frontier Force, I drove into the back of Czech General Gak's car which was parked on the side of the road without any lights. My brake handle ran into my knee and levered it up, so I drove to the Jerusalem hospital where an Arab doctor gave me a strong anti-tetanus injection and sewed me up – ten stitches but no anaesthetic.

When I reached the King David Hotel Robin and Peter were talking about General Glubb, who commands the Arab Legion. Dinner was 'off' but we managed to get sandwiches. I told Robin how surprised I was when I first saw General Glubb – except for his medals and his chin (which has earned him the name of Abu Henaik – the Father of a Chin), he is insignificant looking. I had imagined a hefty, awe-inspiring man . . . Peter, who has known and worked with Glubb for a long time, said, 'There are few men I admire so much. I believe we owe it to him more than any other man that the Arabs have not come into the war on the German side. Glubb's influence is unique; he knows every tribal chief from the Tigris to the Nile, he is liked and respected in Iraq, Transjordan, Eastern Syria and Northern Arabia. His knowledge of Arab history, poetry and song, which are like the Bible to them, is unprecedented.' Peter told us how Glubb gained his position with the Arabs without money – just by sheer character. Then he went on: 'He is unassuming, dislikes any form of publicity; he is not easy to work with but once you get to know him he is a staunch friend; a great stickler for dress, he does not mind how dirty his men are provided they are correctly turned out for the occasion. His house in Amman is filled with gold and silver swords which the tribal chiefs have given him as marks of friendship and esteem; when there is any trouble about, their messengers come and go in an unending stream, keeping him informed . . .' Peter was so interesting that I forgot about my leg. Today it is very stiff and it hurts.

Air Marshal Coningham, who commands the Desert Air Force, has been staying with us. He cheered us up a lot: at last we are going to have air superiority.

Mr Wendell Willkie, Mr Barnes and Mr Coles arrived today. They are flying round the world studying global war. Mr Willkie shakes hands heartily and says, 'Delighted to meet you. Delighted to meet you.' The handshake and the phrase are not simultaneous so it looks very comic – as if he were talking to himself. As we talked our way round the world I decided their trip was no joy ride. When one comes to think of it the situation is rather depressing: the Japs hold such strong positions in the Pacific, the Burma road is cut, it will be a miracle if the Russians manage to hold Stalingrad[1] and another miracle if we can beat the Germans back from Alamein. Malta and England are still being bombed, occupied Europe faces another winter . . . However, Mr Wendell Willkie seemed cheerful. We liked him. He told me that *Mrs Miniver* is one of the best films he has ever seen.

Lady MacMichael has gone to the sea for two weeks and Sir Harold to Transjordan for the weekend so I have two whole days off. This morning I went to Lydda aerodrome and cadged a lift to Cairo. There were twenty-seven people in the plane; we all sat on mailbags. It was very bumpy and soon after we started the man next to me unfolded his *Palestine Post* and was sick in it. Then he folded it up again. I shut my eyes and tried not to follow suit. When we circled Heliopolis I saw hundreds of aircraft – more than I have ever seen before.

I got a lift to Cairo in a truck. At the Continental Hotel Freddie Hoffman welcome me with a lovely bunch of tuber roses and zinnias: 'From the bad management,' he laughed. I could not go shopping because it was a Jewish holiday, an Arab

---

[1.] The German summer offensive, led by Paulus's Sixth Army, had reached Stalingrad on the Volga.

Sunday and a Christian Saturday afternoon, so I went round to the Stirlings' flat where I found Peter Stirling and Mark Chapman Walker. They told me that General Jumbo's new job – he has been made Commander-in-Chief of Persia and Iraq – will be very important if the Germans break through at Stalingrad. Apparently Mr Churchill's visit to the Desert was a tremendous success; he went dressed in a dark blue boiler suit, a flat-topped topee and carried a pale blue umbrella. General Alexander, the new Commander-in-Chief, is here and very well thought of . . . Straffer Gott's death is a great loss . . . David Stirling is operating far behind the German lines . . . While we were talking I began to swell. I had been warned that this might happen because of my anti-tetanus injection. I hoped the others would not notice but of course Peter did. 'Either I am drunk or you look like the fat boy of Peckham,' he said. They took me to dine on the Continental Roof which was well lit in spite of Rommel being in the neighbourhood. Cairo's 'blue-out' is bright compared to the Stygian darkness we keep in Palestine. We watched a superb cabaret – some child acrobats Freddie found in the slums. A weird little snake-charmy tune kept the rhythm for them. By eleven my face and legs were so swollen I had to go to bed. The others went off to gamble which is now the rage in Cairo.

16 September 1942   *Jerusalem*

A wounded officer, who apologised profusely for taking so long about it, brought me this letter from Pat Ruthven. It was written at Alamein soon after his birthday which is 31 August.

> My birthday was very hectic. About 2 a.m. Gilbert, my second in command, called me with the news that Rommel had started his advance, so we leaped to horse and away to our battle positions by moonlight. It was Gilbert's birthday too, his twenty-first, so we didn't forget to wish each other compliments before driving off into action. It was rather stirring that drive through the moonlight to our battle stations, with all the tanks and guns on the move at the same time, like some long-forgotten border ride to the clank of

143

modern armour. Callum's boys made contact first and we spent the day listening to the reports of the battle. Then about five p.m. my little lady tanks made contact and for the next hour it was like listening to the Grand National with a lot of money to win or lose. If it hadn't been so desperately important it would have been very amusing. On they came with Dick Wintour hanging on to them and 'picking out the colours' of who was up and who was down, like forty Bob Lyles. Nearly all the time he was under fire. Eventually the Hun hit fair into our line of battle as was intended and hell's delight broke loose among us. Our tanks were well concealed and did a great execution as they came on. It was terribly thrilling. I was sitting in the middle of Sandy's Regiment who were in the centre of the line and took the brunt of the first charge. Several tanks were hit quite close to me and blew up but fortunately not before the crews got out. The noise was terrific and one couldn't believe that anyone else was left alive. Fortunately I was so busy bawling orders down the wireless that there was no time to be afraid and anyhow tanks were much too busy shooting at each other to worry about my miserable little car which was dug down in a deep hole out of which I peered cautiously from time to time. Then, just when all seemed lost and I had lost communication with my right, down through the haze of sun-bloodied dust came the Greys. It was a grand sight seeing them go into action. The sun was behind them from me and they ground their way on through the smoke and came into line on the right. This turned the day. The Hun gave up and withdrew out of range, leaving a lot of dead tanks behind him and all the scattered disarray of broken armour. We then began to count up our own losses which on the whole were very slight. My right-hand platoon had been run over and had disappeared completely from the face of the earth. We had lost some guns too, and the squadron behind whom I had been sitting was almost non-existent. Later some of my right-hand platoon made good their escape in the dusk but unfortunately without their officer, who, we think, is a prisoner. So ended the first day with the situation still rather in the air but with our own forces more or less intact.

I spent a fairly busy night running round and seeing people and reinforcing wherever I could: borrowing things, lending things, mending things, carrying things, dropping things and swallowing things – in fact the sort of night one expects to spend after such a contest. In the morning the Hun came in

144

again, this time from the left, but in much less strength than on the night before. I was taking some more weapons up to my left-hand platoon and arrived at a moment when our tanks were swopping shots with theirs at very close range. I managed to pick up the crew of one of our tanks which had been hit: most of them were all right but they took rather a long time getting away and insisted on diving inside their tank for their belongings – cigarettes, matches, packs and rations and all the other essential paraphernalia of war. They tried my temper considerably as there was quite a lot flying through the air at the time. Fortunately it was mostly solid which, providing it doesn't hit you, doesn't do much harm. The noise was terrible again and in the clear morning light the shooting by both sides was pretty good. The enemy again withdrew but we were not allowed to be up and after him; it was known that he had brought up a lot of guns behind his tanks and was expecting us to pursue. He then shelled us fairly angrily for the rest of the day but with the anger of frustration rather than the anger of desire. Our own guns replied to some purpose.

After this my recollections become rather hazy. There followed a series of night patrols, of day patrols by my own little babies, 'to observe and report', and of skirmishes between our light squadrons and his guns, always beautifully sighted – for them. In one of these poor Dick Wintour was severely wounded; he may lose a leg. The tempo diminished and the Hun started to fall back through the minefields to wipe the blood off his nose. The Air Boys were after him all the time and did great work throughout the battle; they never missed a chance of catching him badly dispersed or on the run. I feel, rightly or wrongly, that the two hours on my birthday evening were the turning point in the battle for Egypt.

From now on we are getting stronger all the time. The Germans lost so much. The ebb tide left some pretty grim relics behind it; monsters stranded and incapable as on the bed of some prehistoric ocean after the flood has receded. Armoured horrors in their death agonies are not beautiful. It is all so impersonal when tank encounters tank that human fear and courage play little part. It is the mighty machines which overawe us, and all the splendid and squalid which pertain to humanity are entirely dominated as by some unknown power which has mastered the world. Man has created something in the devil's own image and now must bow before it as he can no longer control it. It rises like the Phoenix from the ashes of an industrial age. God give us power to control what we have created and let it serve, not master us, lest like the Phoenix it will destroy its creator . . .

17 September 1942 *Jerusalem*

Dick[1] and Maie Casey are staying with us. He has succeeded Oliver Lyttelton as Minister of State in Cairo. I last saw them at the Melbourne Cup in 1937. They brought news of Australia, America and England whence they have just come. They told me that Emily, their Emu, is still alive and kicking. That horrible bird used to chase me round the garden in Canberra, making a noise like a dinner gong. Lord Forbes[2] came with the Caseys – he pilots their plane; a fat, intelligent young man. He called me a bluestocking.

20 September 1942 *Jerusalem – Beirut*

Yesterday Sir Harold joined Lady MacMichael at the sea and I was given two more days off. I got a lift to Syria in a Public Relations car; the back was stacked with bales of propaganda printed in French and Arabic. We drove through Nablus and Jenin, crossed the Plain of Esdraelon – striped brown and yellow with plough and stubble and dotted over with new aerodromes – and skirted the Haifa Refinery which the Green Mice never hit. From Ras el Naquora to Beirut the road has changed; now a railway runs beside the sea and there are little graves from the Syrian Campaign.

Beirut, like Cairo, has altered a great deal since I was here. The pleasant atmosphere of a sleepy French garrison town is gone – now it is crowded, tawdry and expensive. The bottle of Guerlain scent I coveted in Mr Krikorian's chemist shop this morning did not change hands: it was priced at one hundred pounds sterling.

---

[1] Later Lord Casey, and from 1965 Governor-General of Australia.
[2] Son of the Earl of Granard, whom he succeeded in 1948, he was 'Air Adviser' to the Minister of State.

I wanted to loaf, but my host, John Hamilton, who is one of those people who are so kind they are almost selfish, had organised every hour of the day. We bathed before breakfast, went shopping immediately afterwards, lunched with Lady Spears, hurried back to a cocktail party and finally entertained a Greek Admiral for dinner. Of all these, Lady Spears was the best. An American, she writes under the name of Mary Borden; her husband is British Minister here. She is small, has direct, rather lidded eyes, a snub nose and a large, humorous mouth. Her voice is high and she speaks very slowly but one never gets impatient because she is so interesting. Her description of the Desert, where her mobile hospital is attached to the French (she keeps it as close to the Front as she can), made me feel I had lived there for months. Sitting on her terrace which looks down over rough hills to Beirut, I could have listened to her forever. In three phrases she paints a man, in two more she gives the background, and then, with her kind crackly laugh she sets them in motion, they talk, gesticulate and move about. This afternoon I met Colonel Koenig, General Catroux and General de Gaulle whom I have never seen – they came and went on her high thin voice and so did the mobile hospital, the smell of blood and burning tyres, the chatter of girl drivers and nurses. Lady Spears has a lot of courage – that sticks out a mile.

22 September 1942   *Jerusalem*

Up and down our long, silver-laden dining-room table float so many interesting and deadly conversations. Sometimes I wish I had six ears, sometimes I wonder if one can really die of boredom. If only we had a dictaphone so that we could piece together all those conversations – they would make a fascinating kaleidoscope of the war. This evening there was talk of Russia – the Germans are fighting in the streets of Stalingrad – three quarters of a million men are fighting on that front . . . my neighbour went booming on about the early Greeks but I was trying to listen to Sir Harold and General Alexander, the new Commander-in-Chief, Middle

East,[1] arguing about art. If he were not so immaculately dressed, General Alexander might be an Irish horse coper.

Short, athletic and charming, he has a slight smile which never quite leaves his face even when it is still. With his chin in the air and his head tilted he always seems to be listening to something outside the room. He and Sir Harold disagreed about painters all the way down the ages and finally came to a halt at Epstein. Then I tried to listen to Boomer again.

25 September 1942   *Jerusalem*

I met General Adler of the United States Air Force. We talked plumbing and politics. Americans expect greater comfort than we do on their aerodromes: they want to fix pipes and plugs where we just have trenches. I told him there was a great deal to be said for our arrangements, they are cheaper and they are temporary – we do not want to be here forever. Quite apart from this there are no pipes. General Adler offered me a trip in his new Liberator. I have never seen one and would have loved it. Alas, I cannot get away.

30 September 1942   *Jerusalem*

After weeks of deliberation I have made up my mind to leave. This morning I sent a note, in true civil servant style, to Sir Harold giving a month's notice and thanking him for having entrusted me with his interesting job. He buzzed back on the house telephone: 'No bones broken, I hope?' he said. I explained it as my old restlessness. He was very nice and next time Said brought a red box out of his room it contained this note:

> I have your letter of today telling me that you have decided to leave and giving one month's notice.
> I shall greatly regret your departure both on personal and

[1.] Later Field Marshal, and later still Earl Alexander of Tunis, he had taken over from General Auchinleck in August, when General Montgomery took over command of Eighth Army.

official grounds and owe you a deep debt of gratitude for all your most willing and efficient assistance. I will let the Chief Secretary know so that 'relief' arrangements may be made before November 1st.

10 October 1942   *Jerusalem*

It is getting cold; there are fat clouds in the sky again and in the morning the lawn is soaked in dew. Now there is a fire in the big sitting room and I have a blanket on my bed.

The battle of Stalingrad still goes on and the lull in the Desert continues; if the Germans get through in the north or the south we shall be in a sorry plight.

Though there are ATs, WAAFs and WRNs here now, English secretaries are still rare birds in the Middle East. I have been inundated with offers of interesting jobs. Freya Stark needs an assistant in Baghdad; she writes there is a vacancy on her establishment at five hundred pounds a year. General Jumbo Wilson, also in Baghdad, needs a Private Secretary; he has offered me the job but says I am to think it over carefully because the climate there is so bad. General Wavell has sent me a kind message: 'I can fix you up with a job in my head-quarters if you feel like coming to India.' Mrs Casey has written from Cairo saying that she has something she very much wants me to do and I am not to fix myself up till I have seen her. She wants me to go straight to Cairo and stay with her when I leave here.

23 October 1942   *Jerusalem*

The Desert is on fire again at Alamein.[1] The battle for Egypt has begun. Practically all our friends are down there fighting – it is dreadful to think that whatever happens so many of them will be killed or wounded. Thank God Dan is not there.

Nine of Lady MacMichael's chickens have died of cold.

[1] On 23 October the British Eighth Army, under Montgomery, attacked and attacked at Alamein; and by 4 November Rommel's Panzer Armee was in full retreat.

25 October 1942 Jerusalem

It looks as if the tide is turning in the Desert.

My relief, John Montgomery, has arrived from Cyprus. I am busy handing over and packing up. Whitaker has been recalled to Cairo. We plan to meet if Rommel breaks through.

1 November 1942 Cairo, Egypt

Yesterday I said goodbye to the MacMichaels. They were awfully nice to me, invited me to return for Christmas and loaded me with presents: Sir Harold gave me a generous reference and Lady MacMichael, very appropriately, a travelling clock with an alarm bell.

I am staying in the Caseys' flat in Garden City. They live at Mena and use their flat for staff and entertaining. At the moment the only other occupant is Mrs Chitty, Head of the ATS. I travelled with her on the *Empress of Britain* – she was on it when it went down. At first I thought her stuffy but we've become good friends.

Maie Casey says that General Alexander may want a secretary: she has told him of me so I am to wait until I hear from him before I decide on any job. He is in the Desert now. It looks as if he is going westwards on the road that leads to Rome and Dan – so it would be a lovely job. Rommel is retreating.

8 November 1942 Cairo, Egypt

Each morning Mrs Chitty and I breakfast on a balcony overlooking the Nile and gloat over the news: Alexander's soldiers are pressing the Germans back ... American and British Forces have landed in French North Africa. Surely this must be the beginning of the end of war in North Africa ...

So the days begin – on peaks of optimism. But as the hours wear on and I visit the Cairo hospitals I sink back into chasms of gloom. The price of this news is so terrible: you see it in the leg wards where some of the tallest are the shortest now – poor Richard Wood has lost both his legs; you see it in the long ward

150

where the burn cases lie so still – sometimes even their eyes are bandaged; it glares at you from screened-off beds where people are dying. You put on your gayest frock, paint your face, collect sweets and magazines and determine to be cheerful. Then at the hospital, the smell of rotting flesh meets you in the long, dark corridors and you begin thinking again. You owe them so much but there is nothing you can do except try not to talk of things they will never do again. Today when I took down letters in shorthand for those that cannot write I sat with my back to them so they should not see my eyes . . . They all wrote of victory; not one of them mentioned the price.

10 November 1942   *Alexandria, Egypt*

For a week I have had such bad sinus that I could hardly see. The doctor who gives me electric treatment ordered me to the sea so yesterday I came to Alexandria which is not so dusty as Cairo. Maie Casey has promised to telephone me when General Alexander returns from the Desert.

Today I lunched with Tony de Cosson who is in the RNVR. While we sat on the Yacht Club terrace overlooking the harbour, he pointed out his own ship which is a Chinese river gunboat called *Aphis*. She has an unusual camouflage of pink, yellow, green and two shades of blue. Tony told me that *Aphis* was built in 1915 and after the last war was towed out to China as she was considered unseaworthy in open sea. However, in 1940, she sailed under her own steam from the Yangtze River to the Mediterranean, since when she has had many adventures. She carries two 6-inch guns, which is the same as a modern cruiser, and some Italian 20mm guns; she is 625 tons; her draught is five feet and her freeboard three. At the beginning of the war the range of her guns was about five miles; since then she has been refitted and has a range of twelve miles. She carries seventy-five ratings and four officers.

'In a heavy sea *Aphis* is hell to sail in,' Tony told me. 'The waves break right over the decks where the galley is, so eating is impossible, and often the living quarters below are awash. There is always danger of her back breaking, and if we turn

151

and run before the sea we sometimes cannot get back; once, when we were sailing from Tobruk, we couldn't make the corner into Alexandria and had to go on to Port Said. We live in the central superstructure and when off duty the watch lie all over the place around the bridge and guns. We can only fire on the beam as, besides having only one gun to bear on any other bearing, we buckle the deck if we fire anywhere else.' Tony told me that *Aphis*'s main task is bombardment but during the Wavell advance she supplied the army with water at Sollum. During the siege of Tobruk she used to lie in Tobruk harbour during the daytime, pretending to be one of the many wrecks. At dusk she weighed anchor and bombarded targets outside the perimeter, always returning to her wreck anchorage before dawn. Once she steamed right into Bardia harbour by daylight and fired off all her guns for twenty minutes and then steamed out again unscathed. Several times she has been attacked by enemy aircraft who mistook her for a U-boat. During the first Commando raid in the summer of 1941 she was attacked by enemy aircraft for two hours and accounted for eight enemy planes.

After lunch *Aphis*'s motor sampan came to the Yacht Club jetty and I went to have a closer look at her. This evening I am going to meet Captain Frank Bethell who commands her, and the ship's doctor.

14 November 1942   *Cairo, Egypt*

Last night when I arrived at Mena to stay with the Caseys they told me that General Alexander is lunching with them on the Sunday when my fate will be decided. 'General Alexander has been shown the file about your evacuation,' teased Dick. 'It is the size of the London telephone book and so your chances are zero.'

I spent today with Pat Ruthven who told me he is now with David Stirling's unit. 'David is the greatest soldier I have ever met,' said Pat. 'He is a born leader; we would follow him anywhere.' Then he told me fascinating stories of raids on enemy communications, lagers and dumps. If I had not known Pat well I would not have believed them.

I dined with Lord Moyne (a Guinness) who is Deputy Minister of State. A quiet little man, wearing a bow tie and an aertex shirt, he is interested in most things, wild flowers and animals, Colonial administration, New Guinea, yachting... At the moment his main interests are Abyssinia and Palestine – the former is in a sorry state because our administration there is rotten, the latter seems to be arming and preparing itself for revolution.

16 November 1942   *Cairo, Egypt*

Today the Caseys gave a big lunch party. I sat next to Dick Casey who told me how difficult the English are to know. He has worked in England three times and on each occasion thought he had got to know and understand us but when he returned found he had to start all over again.

After lunch I sat in the garden with Dick and General Alexander; they talked like schoolboys about revolvers and a Fiesler Storch aeroplane which we have captured in the Desert. The Germans use these little planes for observation. They fly low and slowly and land in a very short space; they have immense springs and plop down very comfortably.

When the guests had gone Maie told me that General Alexander had left me a message – as he was going to be in the Desert for some time he does not want to employ a woman. He suggested that I should go to work for General Jumbo Wilson and he will let me know in three months' time if he wants a female secretary. Funny of him not to tell me so himself.

This evening I sent a wire to General Jumbo saying I shall be delighted to go to Baghdad if he still needs a secretary. Whitaker is appalled by this – he associates Baghdad entirely with the Forty Thieves.

6

Soldier Servant

I got up at 3.30 a.m. after a chequered night, having been
disturbed by the man in the next room quarrelling with his
wife, or somebody else's; every time I knocked on the wall he
called, 'Come in.' I was collected from the hotel by a lorry,
climbed into the back of it with my suitcase and typewriter and
drove with a lot of soldiers to the aerodrome. It was dark but
peasants were already driving their overloaded donkeys into
the markets; they made a soft cloppety noise as they passed.

We flew off before daybreak – twenty passengers packed on
narrow steel benches; we had to sit bolt upright because of the
joints in the fuselage. When the sun came up over the Sinai
Desert, Lord Moyne, who was sitting opposite me, fished some
gadgets out of his pocket and began calculating our height and
speed; from time to time he compared notes with the pilot. We
landed at Lydda to refuel so I got out to stretch my legs. It had
been raining and the earth smelt good. 'Wonderful thing, air
travel,' said my neighbour; 'from Cairo to Palestine in a couple
of hours – it took Moses forty years.' Flying over the long
stretch of desert to Habbanyeh I began fussing about my new
job; will I ever learn military terms and initials? Will my shorthand be fast enough? Where shall I live? So many people

warned me that Baghdad is a horrible place – famous only for boils . . .

Mark Chapman Walker, now Military Assistant to General Jumbo, met me at Habbanyeh. As we drove into Baghdad he explained the situation in Persia-Iraq Command: 'Our position depends on the Russians; if they defeat the Germans on the Stalingrad front the chances of war in this Theatre will diminish; if they fail and the Germans come through the Caucasus we shall have a hard time holding them on the Paytak Pass which we have fortified. We have only two Corps, one British and one Indian, and it would take time to get reinforcements from India or Middle East; we cannot ask for them till we really need them – manpower is short and shipping not available. If a disaster happened and the Germans forced our Paytak Line we have planned to 'scorch earth' Abadan . . . At the moment,' continued Mark, 'our main task is to guard and develop the routes by which Allied aid is being sent from the Persian Gulf to Russia. This is not easy: Jap submarines are thought to be operating in the Persian Gulf; pro-Axis elements are trying to stir up trouble amongst the tribes in Persia where there is already a good deal of unrest owing to inflation and a serious wheat shortage. Incidentally, the wheat belt is in the Russian zone.'

Mark told me that 116,000 Poles have arrived in this Theatre from concentration camps in Russia; they are part of the 1,600,000 Poles who were taken from Poland to Russia in 1939. They have had a ghastly time: about forty per cent of that original number are already dead and these men, women and children who have arrived here are in an awful condition – riddled with malaria and typhoid. Some 10,000 are being sent to England where they will join our Navy and Air Force; the rest are being formed into an army – the Polish Army in the east, under General Anders. We have tried, and are still trying, to get more Poles out of Russian prisons but it looks pretty hopeless.

As we drove through the outskirts of a poor little town I interrupted Mark to ask its name. 'Baghdad,' he said. Soon afterwards we drew up at a small villa surrounded by a sea of mud: our Headquarters. Mark introduced me to the ADC, Francis Dorrien Smith, and the orderlies. They all came to show me my office which they have taken immense trouble over. It is a small room with a coconut matting floor; the windows overlook a muddy car park; in the door connecting with General Jumbo's room is a peep hole – 'So that we don't barge in when he is busy or asleep,' said Francis. A typewriter on a thin table, a safe filled with secrets in shaggy paper folders; a stationery cupboard stacked with foolscap and quarto flimsy and glossy white top sheets, a couple of chairs, a map of the Caucasus and a tooth glass full of flowers – I am delighted with my office.

General Jumbo was sitting at his desk with his tin spectacles on the end of his nose; he held a fly swotter in one hand. Tall, immensely fat, with kind little twinkly eyes, he looks exactly like an elephant – an elephant standing on its hind legs. He outlined my job and told me that I have been invited to stay with Sir Kinahan and Lady Cornwallis at the Embassy till I can find a room. From time to time he paused to swipe at a fly; though they are sleepy now he nearly always missed and uttered, 'Winged it'.

After I had seen the General, Mark showed me a telegram which had just come from General Alexander:

To P.A.I.C. <u>Personal for Wilson from Alexander</u> From M.E.

Ranfurly left for you today. I have the honour to take your place as the only General in the Middle East who has not been outmanoeuvred.

Scrawled on the bottom in General Jumbo's handwriting was: Reply: 'Better to have Ranfurly in the bag than Rommel on the loose.'

Then I settled down to study the files:

Letters: Chief of Imperial General Staff
                    Commander-in-Chief, Middle East
                    Commander-in-Chief, India

Aid to Russia

Persia:	Pro-German elements: Defence; Inflation; Wheat
Poles:	Refugees; Formation of 'Polish Army in the East'
Abadan:	Defence; Demolition
Iraq Army Rashid Ali:	The Golden Square – (Pro-German Iraqi Generals).
Jask Lights:	Jap Submarines in Persian gulf.
Quashquai: etc.	Tribes

Under a leaden sky Baghdad has a dismal appearance; the one-storeyed houses that straggle along both sides of the Tigris are brown as the river itself; the narrow streets are lined with shabby shops – some of them mere hovels; and the land is flat. The Embassy stands on the edge of the Tigris. This evening a dead camel floated past the windows. Save for my lacquered fingernails and the General's red tabs, there seems to be no colour here.

9 December 1942   *Baghdad*

General Jumbo, his son who is delicate, General Baillon, the Chief of Staff, General Selby, Chief Administrative Officer, Mark and Francis all live in a villa not far from Headquarters. Their Mess is run by Corporal Trayler, a quiet little man who is the proud owner of a saluki dog. The General has two cars, a box body, a jeep and a couple of horses.

I have to get to the office first to unlock the safe and desk drawers and type out the day's programme. Soon after eight-thirty General Jumbo arrives – I always know when he is coming because the sentry on the front door stamps to attention. Then our day begins: orderlies in heavy boots clatter along the stone passages; telephones peal unceasingly – Francis draws wild fowl on his blotting paper while he answers them; Iraqi, Polish, Indian and British visitors arrive and salute – salute and depart. The General's bell keeps ringing for Mark

157

who drafts all his telegrams; sometimes the buzzer calls for me to take down letters. General Jumbo dictates slowly and spells out the long Iraqi and Persian names that are strange to me. He is very kind.

12 December 1942   *Baghdad*

Two days ago I came to live with Freya Stark in her bungalow on the outskirts of Baghdad where she works hard for her Brothers and Sisters of Freedom. She has turned one room into an office. When I arrived Nigel Clive, Freya's other lodger, led me aside: 'Be careful of Jasim,' he said. 'He will tell you he is the butler but that is an understatement; he is the Master of the Household. If he likes you there are hot baths, second helpings and roses in your room; if he does not he will see that you arrive late at the office, that your clothes get lost at the laundry, that you starve and wash in cold water.' Jasim has a swarthy face, fierce moustache, and a voice like thunder. He wears his turban, which looks suspiciously like a pair of pyjama legs, at an angle of forty-five degrees. I arrived in Baghdad with only a tiny suitcase; the rest of my luggage was to have followed in a freight plane but is now reported 'lost – somewhere between Cairo and India'. One can buy very little here and anyway Baghdad prices are fantastic. I earn forty pounds a month but have to pay Freya thirty pounds a month for my board and lodging – there is no hope of replenishing my wardrobe. If Jasim 'loses' my clothes I shall have to stay in bed.

15 December 1942   *Baghdad*

At first I thought Baghdad a dreary place but I have learned to love this town which has a mulled beauty all of its own. King-fishers live in the river banks; painted boats lie beneath the latticed windows that overhang the river; there are parrots in the grain shop near the bridge. Each day I ride. Generally I go down before breakfast to the racecourse where sleek stallions from the Royal Stud, scraggy steeds from the poor backyards, gaily rugged polo ponies and donkeys stand about in the thin

158

winter mist while their grooms argue the latest form. Now and then a rider detaches himself for a gallop or yells his way over the little jumps in the centre of the course. When I am too lazy to ride early I gobble my lunch and go over to the remount stable on the far side of the town. Then I ride out into the desert or canter along the bund under silver gum trees to cross the Tigris by the Bridge of Boats and explore the streets of Mu'addham where brass door knockers, fashioned like Fatima's hand with elegant cuffs, gleam on the old doors.

We work again from five till eight and then, sometimes, I dine in the town – at the Sinbad hotel, the Tigris Palace or the Zia where Uncle Elie plies you with walnuts, and Jesus, the barman, mixes cocktails called Desert Dreams – and afterwards I go to one of the antiquated cinemas where you sit in little red plush boxes, or to the Opera House where the Poles give brilliant performances of ballet and folk dance. They make their own clothes and scenery out of odds and ends of sacking and material from the bazaars. The streets are crowded with Indian, Iraqi, Polish and British troops.

17 December 1942   *Baghdad*

This morning a tall, angular young man dressed in a kilt arrived in my office; he brought me a letter of introduction from David Stirling:

> This is to introduce Fitzroy Maclean who is going to Paiforce to recruit and raise an SAS Regiment which will be held in readiness for operations behind enemy lines if the Germans break through the Caucasus. Help him if you can – he will need men and equipment. When the war broke out Fitzroy was in the Foreign Office but he managed to extricate himself by being elected a Member of Parliament. He then enlisted in the Cameron Highlanders and eventually joined me. He has done well on our raids. Don't be taken in by his rather pompous manner or his slow way of speaking – he is OK.

Fitzroy told me that he is on his way to Persia where Zahidi, the Persian General commanding the Isfahan area, is plotting an armed rising against us, to be combined with a German parachute landing and a rising of the tribes in Southern Persia. 'I have been allotted a platoon of Seaforth Highlanders and instructed to kidnap Zahidi,' said Fitzroy sedately, as if 'snatching' had been his hobby for years.

'How will you do it?' I asked.

'I expect Sergeant Duncan will think of a method,' said Fitzroy. 'By the way, he says he is an old friend of yours – he is outside in my jeep.' Sure enough it was the tall, handsome Scotsman who used to work for Bill Stirling. We all drove round to lunch with Freya and on the way Fitzroy told me David's news: 'His attempt to cut Rommel's supply line during the Alamein crisis was doomed to failure from the start; GHQ Cairo issued hundreds of orders, all of which were quite useless. You can only run that kind of operation on the spot,' said Fitzroy. We all like Fitzroy very much.

26 December 1942   *Baghdad*

Yesterday was Christmas Day. When I woke I found that Freya had given me a stocking; it was filled with the few things one can get in Baghdad – poker dice, odorono, garters, a swansdown powder puff and soap in the toe. After we had waded through mud to the English church Mark, Francis and I gave a party for the orderlies and clerks in the office. I gave them all shaving brushes – the only male presents I could afford.

Today Freya and I drove to the Palace to pay our respects to the Queen Mother. We were shown into an ornately furnished room – one seldom sees upholstered chairs or sofas in these parts because they are uncomfortable in hot weather. I had expected to meet an old lady and was surprised when the Queen walked into the room; she is about the same age as me, slight and pretty; she dresses in semi-European clothes. Freya talked to her in Arabic which I cannot understand so I sat there laughing when they laughed and shaking my head and clicking my tongue when they shook their heads or clicked their tongues. Once Freya turned to me – 'She is telling me about her son, little King Feisal, who is learning English. He is only eight,' she said. I feel sorry for this charming girl who has to lead a secluded, widow's life and wear nothing but black. Her husband was killed in a motor accident a few years ago; she is not allowed to marry again.

Afterwards we drove to another villa to see the King's aunts. When we arrived they were playing 'The White Horse Inn' on the gramophone. Both wore red polka-dotted frocks. They were friendly and full of questions and fun.

Freya's bungalow is very pretty inside. Her sitting room has pale blue walls, primrose chair covers and is gay with books and Persian ashtrays. Nothing is boring here – there are so many surprises. Freya has a magic all of her own; she gets on well with high and low – old and young – and with all nationalities. She works very hard at all projects and getting her own way. Her reminiscences of her travels and her comments on each day's activities here are hilarious, and always sudden and short. She is reading her *Letters from Syria* which have just arrived from England. She gave her publisher *carte blanche* to edit them and now is startled by their directness. She is priceless; when I asked her what I should pay for board and lodging she just said, 'Whatever you earn I'd like three quarters of it.' It was said so charmingly I agreed and now I'm rather short.

Tonight Nigel Clive watched me while we ate dinner. His face twitched with suppressed laughter. Next time Freya left the room he said: 'I loved your "Look out stomach – here it comes," expression. Most of the meat Jasim cooks is camel but sometimes it's cat or wild dog. The puddings aren't bad when they're not made with goat's milk . . .' Freya returned and he changed the conversation.

2 January 1943   *Baghdad – Khaniqin*

General Jumbo had to go and inspect the base area at Basra and Abadan and would be away for a week and so he suggested I might like to drive to Tehran in the car which carries the military bag to Persia.

Dunbar, the General's second driver, a delightful Scot, and I left Baghdad at midday and drove off across the desert. The road is just baked earth, wide and corrugated. For ages, we saw nothing except for a few silent villages of mud huts and an enormous drove of sheep, black, white and tan, trotting along before their own cloud of dust and watched over by one solitary figure and two shaggy dogs. Where the road and the railway meet we crossed a river by a single span bridge, bumping over sleepers with little room to spare on either side and horribly close to the open edges. As the sun sank we came to low hills where shadows were deep blue and the earth looked golden. Soon after we passed a huge camp filled with Poles recently arrived from concentration camps in Russia. Twisting from one little valley to the next we came to Khaniqin, where the smell of oil permeates everything. Just before the town we drew up at the bungalow of the Anglo-Iranian oil manager who, with his pretty wife, gave me tea beside a fire. Mr and Mrs Dix have lived here for eleven years. Their house is air-conditioned, with electric light, a bathroom to each bedroom, plenty of flowers, books and nice furniture. At six o'clock they took me to see a movie in a shed crowded with employees and fifteen officers from a nearby camp. Afterwards there was a buffet dinner. When they all went off to dance at the local club I went to bed after being warned it was hopeless to try and reach Tehran next day because the road is so bad and after dark there is a risk of brigands.

3 January 1943   *Khaniqin – Hamadan*

We drove out of the gates of the compound at five-thirty in the dark and turned on to the main road which is about two cars wide and has a surface of shingle. After a time the first grey-green light of dawn slid a few outlines out of the darkness and slowly, miles away, a line of blue mountains appeared. The sun came up from behind the hills so suddenly that I said, 'Good morning, Dunbar'. We were on a vast sloping plain with small erect trees on either side of the road. Through a sleeping frontier village we drove into Persia. All that cold and silent morning we sped on towards the distant range of mountains. After a while we saw Kurds going to work on the road – they

162

carried long rakes. Their job is to keep the gravel on the surface of the road. They all wore coster caps, baggy 'Blue Beard' trousers and sheepskin coats flung over their shoulders. These small men all seemed to have Charlie Chaplin moustaches. They waved as we passed.

From the foothills the road spiralled up the steep, well-fortified Paytak Pass in a series of hairpin bends. Each curve unfolded a new valley or mountain torrent. I was astonished by the size and beauty of the range. On the plain beyond, framed by snow mountains, lay Kermanshah. We drove down its wide main street where shops were crammed with Kurdish gloves, donkey trappings and bottles of brightly coloured sweets. A few miles out of town we filled up with petrol and changed yet another tyre. Soon after this the inner and outer tubes of a front wheel burst, and we swerved off the road. 'Flints,' said Dunbar. As we changed the wheel a great convoy of trucks, all covered with tarpaulins, passed us. This was aid to Russia trundling north.

Across wide valleys and high mountains we drove on but we had to stop often to blow up tyres with slow punctures. We had piled a quantity of spare tyres on the back seat of the car when we started but all of them were now damaged and no wonder – the roads are so rough. Once, when I sat on the running board and Dunbar pumped up a tyre an old road mender came and talked to me. He leaned his rake against the car, picked up a handful of snow and said one word over and over again. 'Snow,' I said, and he was delighted and repeated, 'Snaw, snaw, snaw.' I gave him a cigarette and as we drove away he went on 'Snaw, snaw, snawing'. I watched him through the rear window – he looked a lonely little figure against the giant landscape. Occasionally we passed an overturned truck or a couple of them buckled together – probably their drivers had fallen asleep on their long trek over the empty road to Russia. We drove in bottom gear up the corkscrew road, edging the precipice and crunching through the deep snow of the Shah Pass. The sun was low when we reached the valley below. Half-wild woolly dogs barked as we passed. The cold was intense and I shivered in my sheepskin coat. We arrived in Hamadan in the dusk and set about replacing our tyres. Then we went to the oil company guest house where a cheerful little Persian servant lit fires and brought a steaming chicken dinner. But still the cold was overwhelming and I went to bed in most of my clothes with my sheepskin coat on top.

4 January 1943   *Hamadan – Tehran*

We were off again at seven. The sun was already hitting the high peaks behind the nice old town. Over the plain ahead of us a convoy, like a string of black beads, moved towards us. I counted thirty trucks. We drove through a white wilderness seeing no sign of life till Kazvin in the Russian zone where we were halted at their check post. I fell asleep and was woken by Dunbar saying, 'Tarmac.' Sure enough we were on a fine blue surface. I ate some chocolate, fixed my face, and quite soon we were driving down the wide boulevards of Tehran. We delivered the military bag to the Town Major and went to stay in the Legation Compound with the British Consul and his wife. He told me about the wheat crisis and said more riots were imminent. No one knew the extent of the wheat harvest but an immense quantity was being hoarded. He thought if a thorough search were made and anything up to a hundred arrests in high places it might be possible to control the food situation. The Russians, who occupy the main wheat belt, seem to be playing a long-term game and he felt we could not make things worse by showing strength. He added that, from the military point of view, even if the Germans did not come through the Caucasus their agents could make havoc with the vulnerable internal situation in Persia if we did not do something soon.

After lunch I went to see Sir Reader Bullard in the rather gloomy Legation. He told me that wheat was an age-old racket in Persia. 'It generally ends', he said, 'by the mob baking one of the millers in his own bread oven. Then it peters out for a while only to begin again later. The Persians are used to the wheat problem – they are bred on it,' he said, smiling at his pun. 'If supplies were brought in from outside it would make

164

no difference – that would be hoarded too. If the ring leaders were rounded up another gang would take over immediately.' He talked for a while about the history and manners of Persia and then I left him among his books. A charming, scholarly man. He was so nice to me.

5 January 1943 Tehran

Down in the town I found shop windows full of merchandise but often behind the windows there was only a miserable little room and no stock. Luxuries like ham, smoked salmon, French silk and English tweed could be bought at prodigious prices. Antique shop windows glittered with gold trinkets and icons; dark stores were crammed with Persian rugs and pictures; corset shops flaunted stays of every imaginable shape and colour. In the streets an astonishing variety of uniforms mingled with the crowds, Persian, Indian, Polish and British ... Near the market a disgruntled crowd milled aimlessly. It was easy to see they were hungry. Long tunnels of little stores and workshops lit by candle-light criss-crossed the native quarter. The filth on the floor was indescribable.

This evening I went to a party given in honour of the Minister of State from Cairo, who never arrived. I heard many different slants on the wheat situation and decided it would need a strong man to clean it up. One per cent of the population is extremely rich; five per cent are tradesmen; and the rest are poor peasants who are not politically minded and who, because of the country's geographical position and oil, tend to be exploited rather than helped. I talked with some Russians at the party. I can only say 'I love you' in Russian, but it seemed to help.

6 January 1943 Tehran

Today I rode up the bare slopes above Tehran on a pony from the Legation stables. I galloped up a twisting track hidden between hills where Persian jockeys train their horses. Away in the distance the peak of snow-capped Demavend towered at

165

18,600 feet. I rode back into the city on the edge of a broad tarmac avenue and saw the Shah driving himself in a big shiny Mercedes. The làte Shah tried to modernise Tehran and built banks, hotels, a fine station and roads but though these look impressive the town is still very primitive: taps do not work, nor plugs pull; tarmac roads turn to shingle not far out of Tehran; and drains run down the gutters from the rich quarter to the poor quarter further down the hill.

8 January 1943   *Tehran – Baghdad*

Yesterday Dunbar and I left Tehran at 6 a.m. Fitzroy Maclean followed us in his jeep. He has been rounding up Quashquai bandits who have been holding up our trucks and stealing the supplies we are sending from the Persian Gulf to Russia. His jeep had three punctures before we reached Hamadan. This did not worry Fitzroy, who liked admiring the view and was always hungry and wanting to stop to eat. But it made Dunbar and me anxious as we had only left minimum time to reach Baghdad so as to be there before our General returns. It was dark when we reached the filling station outside Kermanshah and Fitzroy and I had an argument about staying there for the night. It was mad, he said, to fuss about being late at the office in the morning. Dunbar and I had hardly left Kermanshah when we missed the jeep and so we turned back. We found the jeep would not move. We wondered if the Persian at the petrol pump had filled its tank with water. Dunbar and I could hardly conceal our mirth. Fitzroy climbed into the back of our car. We stopped in Kermanshah to send help to the unfortunate jeep driver, and then Dunbar and I drove in shifts through the night and reached Baghdad at dawn today. We'd done 800 miles over bad roads.

In the office we staff swapped news. I heard that the American Persian Gulf Service under General Connelly is going to take over our base headquarters at Basra; we will continue to be responsible for the internal security of Persia and Iraq, but the Americans will take over the transport of aid to Russia. Bombers are being flown direct to the Stalingrad front. They are often in action eight days after being unloaded at Basra. Fighters, tanks and other equipment will go by the arterial road from Khorramashar and Bandashabir to Tabriz. We have built a bridge across the Shat-el-Arab river. Originally we wanted to build a drawbridge but owing to the swampy ground we have had to build an underwater bridge; the roadway of the bridge can be dropped under water to allow ships to sail over it.

We had a busy morning in the office getting papers ready for General Jumbo to take to Cairo this afternoon. He is flying down for a Joint Planning Staff's Meeting.

19 January 1943   *Baghdad*

The siege of Stalingrad has been raised.[1] We are thrilled. At dinner in the Mess I suggested we celebrate this wonderful news. 'This is the City of A Thousand and One Nights,' I said. 'There must be a theatre or night club hidden away somewhere.' Everyone assured me I was wrong but as I would not believe them we set out in jeeps to explore the town. We asked at all the bars and hotels but the answer was always the same: 'There is nothing like that in Baghdad.' We hurried up narrow streets and alleys, crossed and recrossed the river, listening for music, searching for lights. Presently, in a poor quarter of the town, over an open doorway, we saw a red light. 'A brothel,' said the Aides, but we climbed out and woke the drowsy Arab on the door who mechanically gave us tickets. We swung open the inner doors and found ourselves in a huge room. It was a theatre. Iraqis were crammed in boxes and stalls, lolling from the balconies and leaning up against the pillars. We stood

[1] The German Sixth Army, under General Paulus, had advanced in Southern Russia and reached Stalingrad, as the spearhead of an enormous venture aimed at the capture of the Causasus, the oilfields, and at producing a general collapse of the southern part of the Red Army front. Then, in November 1942, the Russians counter-attacked and soon Paulus's army was itself isolated in the city and suburbs of Stalingrad. Stalingrad had never completely fallen to the Germans and now they, themselves, were surrounded and besieged. The German losses in Stalingrad were enormous and eventually Paulus surrendered with the remaining 200,000 men of the Sixth Army on 3 February.

by the door and looked around. Suddenly the music stopped and there was complete silence while everyone turned round and stared at us. We stood and stared back. Then one of the dancers on the stage shouted something in Arabic. Perhaps she said, 'Give them seats.' In a few seconds we were seated in a box and the show went on and we were offered nuts, cigarettes and stuff to chew. Some offered us their hookahs and indicated the spitoons on the floor. Then a little play began. It was the story of a pasha who discovered he was going to have a baby. The audience roared with laughter and interrupted and were almost as funny as the performers. Afterwards dancers came on and were really good. We all stamped and clapped to their rhythm. It was great fun.

After the performance we were invited to the stage door. At the top of some rickety stairs the actors received us. We drank araq. An Iraqi, who understood a little English, translated for us. The actors said that we were very welcome and they hoped we would come every night. They explained that no woman had ever come to watch them before and this was the joke of the evening. We asked them what was the name of their Theatre. They told us 'Hilayla Felayla', which we suspected meant 'A Thousand and One Nights'.

24 January 1943   *Baghdad*

When news reached us that the Eighth Army had entered Tripoli I could hardly believe it. As soon as I could escape the office I took a pony and rode out into the desert to think.

Memories slid through my head like a newsreel: the long, awful struggle in the Western Desert; the advances and retreats; Army, Navy and Air Force miracles and disasters; the amazing courage and laughter of all ranks; the dead, the wounded, the 'missing' and the prisoners . . .

I thought of General Wavell and how tragic it was that Mr Churchill could never like or understand him – what a combination they would have been; of Auckinleck, so handsome and charming but not quite able to cope with the intricate Desert war; and of Monty whom few of us like or admire – who did not go into action until he was reinforced beyond Wavell's wildest dreams. And I thought of Rommel who, in spite of being our enemy, gained our admiration and respect – almost our affection.

I remembered all the friends I'll never see again; the shattered lives of the seriously wounded; and the small gazelle at Barce; the valiant little Chinese river gun-boat – *Aphis* – with only three-foot clearance; of David Stirling's cool and fantastic courage; and the multitude of heroes who have made it possible for us to reach Tripoli . . . Most of all I thought of Dan, still incarcerated in an Italian castle – now nearer to our Forces but still so far away . . .

As I cantered on tears ran down my face but I did not know if they were from joy or sorrow.

28 January 1943   *Baghdad*

Of all the people who come to Freya's house, His Excellency Nuri Pasha Said, Prime Minister of Iraq, is the most fun. He has a very pretty wife and a son called Saba who is in the Air Force. I suspect that Nuri Pasha finds his son nearly as large a responsibility as Iraq because Saba is one of those people who enjoys every second of his life and is always having adventures. Not long ago Saba asked his father to go to a certain bridge in Baghdad where, he assured him, he would see something very surprising. At the appointed hour Nuri Pasha waited. Before long an aeroplane appeared and flew under the bridge with only inches to spare. It was Saba. During the early days of the war Saba made a stout effort to join the RAF in England. It was when our flying losses were very high. Saba attached himself to a party of British pilots who were being sent back to England. He told no one of his plan and got as far as West Africa. By ill luck he was delayed and a telegram demanding his immediate return caught up with him and he was forced to return to Iraq. When Nuri Pasha comes to see us it is always interesting.

Mark returned from Cairo with General Jumbo, full of news. The Casablanca meeting between Mr Churchill and Mr Roosevelt went well. General Jumbo accompanied the Prime Minister to the Adana Conference and very nearly got stuck climbing out of the narrow hatch of the Halifax plane he was travelling in. We are sending a great deal of equipment to the Turks who are also being supplied with armaments from Germany. Last, but not least, General Jumbo is going to be Commander-in-Chief, Middle East, based in Cairo.

General Jumbo has presented little King Feisal with a miniature model tank for him to ride in. It was made by our Tank Corps. It is a beautiful toy, perfect in every respect. We all played with it in our office. The Aides reported that, though the little King was polite and seemed pleased with it, afterwards he burst into tears and said to his nurse, 'I never wanted a tank – I only wanted a jeep.'

It was announced on the wireless today that General Jumbo is to be Commander-in-Chief, Middle East. Now we can all talk about it. The General asked me this morning if I will go with him and added that he thought it really funny that, after all the fuss over my evacuation, I should become Secretary to the Commander-in-Chief. 'No orchids for McCandlish, eh, Hermione,' he chuckled. I chuckled too.

I am glad we shall miss the hot weather here. I have heard plenty about summer in Baghdad when the temperature averages around 120 degrees or more for weeks at a time.

And I am glad to be going nearer to Dan.

Freya has flown to India where she will work for three months on propaganda.

General Anders came to our office today. He commands the Polish Army in the East. He has a fine, handsome but rather sad face and great charm. His soldiers are steadily recovering from their terrible time in Russia: when they first arrived they were riddled with disease and practically starving. It is appalling to think that there are still thousands of Polish prisoners in Russia and nothing we can do can get them out. The rate of their mortality is beyond belief or forgiveness.

7

No Orchids for McCandlish

16 February 1943   *Cairo*

I left Baghdad before dawn and drove in a van to Habbanyeh.
The Indian driver went at snail's pace and refused to be
hurried: 'Slowly is orders,' he said and kept the needle on
twenty-five miles an hour. The flying boat came from India and
the pilot was my good friend Captain Mountain. I sat in the co-
pilot's seat and we swapped news. After a snatched lunch on
the Dead Sea we flew off again and reached Cairo at teatime. I
went straight to GHQ to fix up our new office. We have three
rooms – the General's office which opens on one side to the
Aides' room and on the other to mine. Beyond mine is the Map
Room – an Aladdin's cave of immense interest if only one had
time to devour all its information.

When, at last, I got to the Continental Hotel I found Whitaker waiting for me in the cool, old-fashioned bedroom which
is to be my new home. His kind, fat face was set and serious and
he pulled a newspaper out of his pocket: 'I hate to tell you, my
Lady, I have bad news . . . His Lordship's best friend and best
man at your wedding is dead.' On the front page I read that
Pat Hore-Ruthven had died of wounds in an Italian hospital on
Christmas Eve. I rang for a little supper for two to come up to
my room and a couple of whiskys. After a while Whitaker,

obviously miserable, announced he had more bad news: David Stirling and his brother-in-law, Simon Ramsay,[1] are both missing. If I must learn such ghastly things I was thankful to have Whitaker with me. We stayed up late – talking of Pat, David and Simon. When Whitaker departed to go to his digs he said, 'My Lady, you'll have to write and tell all this to His Lordship. I don't envy you writing the letter or him reading it. Please tell him we're going to win this war and that you and I will stick together until it ends – come what may. Tell him that the likes of me will never surrender.'

17 February 1943   *Cairo*

When General Jumbo and Mark arrived from Baghdad yesterday we spent a busy evening going through our predecessors' files. It seemed to me his Staff had put everything under 'Miscellaneous'.

Mark brought with him one of the green parrots from the grain shop in Baghdad and gave him to me as a souvenir. The parrot is beautiful. His name is Coco. Poor little bird – he is still nervous from the journey but already he will sit on my shoulder and feed from my hand.

Cairo is cool and sunny and far emptier than when I was last here. Now it feels a long way from the war. This afternoon I went with General Jumbo, his son, Patrick, and Mark to the zoo to see Said the Hippo who is an old friend of the General. The two outsize personages seemed pleased to renew their friendship. We went in a smart new Lincoln Zephir car which had just arrived for the General. We had wired home for a new one because his old one was worn out but there were none available in England. Queen Wilhelmina heard of this and very kindly sent us her own car.

[1] Now the Earl of Dalhousie.

When Coco arrived from Baghdad he had a very small cage so today I went in search of something better. In a slum shop filled with snakes, pigeons, guinea-pigs and finches I found one and after much bargaining bought it. The shopkeeper gave me a present: a white mouse with pink eyes called Fuad, which he put in my pocket. At GHQ the orderlies are delighted with Fuad and are going to make him a little house from a cigar box. Lovely that Coco now has a stately home.

Later. When people come to see General Jumbo and Fuad is running about the floor some say, 'Oh, is that your mascot?' Others see him but don't comment; we suspect they think he is part of a Cairo hangover.

18 March 1943   *Cairo*

Today General Jumbo interviewed Sergeant Seekins and I was asked to take down the whole conversation in shorthand. The General sat before a big map of North Africa and a marker was on a road just west of Misurata. Sergeant Seekins said:

It was on the night of 20th December. There was Captain Hore-Ruthven and myself and three other men. We had mined the road about forty-six kilometres outside of Misurata. We had a couple of jeeps. Soon after we had finished we came across six enemy vehicles and three tanks parked on the side of the road. We went in to do a reconnaissance and found they were guarded and that there was a tent full of soldiers. The night before we had found a heavy concentration of vehicles which had been too large to attack, so tonight Captain Hore-Ruthven said we must have a go at these. Three nights before we had destroyed twenty trucks and mined the road about three miles further down. That had been a very successful raid but now all the Italians were on the alert. Well, we found they were guarded. About forty yards from the trucks we were challenged. Captain Hore-Ruthven dashed straight in and got his two bombs on a truck (they take about twenty minutes to go off). There were two explosions round the trucks. The sentries shouted and fired their revolvers. Captain Hore-Ruthven came round the end of

another truck and by a dug-out which was filled with Italians.
I shouted to him to run. I threw in a hand-grenade. Our men
were getting very excited. He shouted to me, 'I have got it.'
Then I realised he had got it. He doubled up. I grabbed his
right arm but he screamed, 'That's where I'm hit.'

I managed to help him get to a big sandhill about fifty yards
away. The fire was terrific. I tried to persuade him to crawl
but he could not move. He told me to get out of it. He passed
out. So I crawled out and after about a hundred yards I
heard shouts as if they had found him. Firing started afresh.
I dropped down. It appeared to me that a figure ran for
about thirty yards. Tracer was all around him. He dropped
down. The Italians fired many rounds from their pistols at
something on the ground.

General Jumbo also asked me to copy out this statement made
by Dr Ceciarelle of Hospital Civile Leonello Mariani, Misurata:

I am sorry that I cannot remember exactly the dates, but the
incident happened between the 20th and 30th December,
1942. During the night an Italian armoured car took by
surprise an English officer who was attempting to mine the
Balbia road near Tauorga. As he essayed to take flight he was
fired on with a burst of machine gun fire which struck him in
the thorax and right arm. The medical officer of the nearby
airfield came immediately and treated him, and the
following morning he was taken by motor ambulance to
the Civil Hospital in Misurata. Here there was also at this
time a military surgical section under the command of an
excellent surgeon. On arrival Captain Hore was still wearing
clothes which, by reason of his long sojourn in the desert,
were much worn, whilst his hair and beard were unkempt
and full of sand. Immediately after treatment he was dressed
in clean linen and his hair and beard attended to.

The day following his arrival he was given the postcard
which the Italian Government provides for all prisoners of
war, to allow them to send news to their families. Seeing that
he could not write I myself offered to fill up the postcard for
him. He asked me if the wound was very serious and I assured
him that he had reason to hope for his eventual cure. During
subsequent days I paid him frequent visits, in order to keep
him company a little. I can assure you that he was cared for

in the best possible manner but bronchial pneumonia occasioned by the wound supervened, and this proved fatal.

The coffin, covered with the English flag, as was our custom with deceased prisoners of war, was carried down to the Cemetery of Misurata Marina on a military vehicle. Captain Hore's remains were accompanied by the Lieut. Chaplain and escorted by a platoon of soldiers under the command of an Officer.

With great sadness I typed this out for the General to send to Lord Gowrie in Canberra. I can't make up my mind if I should send a copy to Dan. It is such a dreadful story. Whitaker says, 'Don't', but Dan will want the truth.

13 April 1943   *Aleppo*

Yesterday General Jumbo, his son Patrick, Mark, Brigadier Davy and I flew from Heliopolis to St Jean aerodrome near Haifa in a violent storm. Then we drove along the coast road to Beirut. The fields were a strange sour green under a livid sky. We are going to Ankara to discuss the military situation if Turkey should come into the war on our side.

This morning we bumped over the cobbled streets of Beirut and out on to the Aleppo road which winds between the sea and rough cedar-coated hills. We stopped to look at the Nah-relkelb, a great rock wall on which, for centuries, the con-querors of Syria have carved their names: Assyrians, Babylonians, Crusaders, Turks, French, British and Alexander the Great. We passed near Biblis, the village where Venus and Adonis are supposed to have lived. We left the coast at Tripoli and drove through mountains where, Patrick told me, a wild tribal chief rules today; he covers himself with phosphorescent paint and does cheap conjuring tricks to convince his followers and his seventeen wives that he is a Prophet of God. We glimpsed the Crusader castle, Craq de Chevalier, away on our left and sped on through Homs, the great weaving centre, to Hama where we stopped to look at the water wheels in the Orontes river. Crossing the rich plain before Aleppo I saw villages where the houses were shaped like beehives, not unlike those mud-coloured native huts I saw in Africa.

This evening we listened to our very secret trip being announced from London by the BBC. So much for security.

14 April 1943   *On the Taurus Express*

Early this morning I walked with General Jumbo through Aleppo's sukh where the sun slants through iron gridded roofs on to brilliantly coloured merchandise. There are many miles of covered-in bazaars. The way in is just car wide. We saw a T model Ford squeezing along through the crowds. We made our way to the citadel which is moated and has an immensely high wall. The arched gateway is slitted in the ceiling: the defenders poured boiling oil on uninvited guests. The General puffed up the steep path to the ramparts and told me the fortress was many times besieged but never taken except by treachery. It commands the whole fertile plain between the Euphrates and Orontes rivers. This is supposed to be an old camping ground of Abraham; outside the gate is an old stone trough which, it is said, he used to have filled with milk for the poor.

At eleven o'clock we climbed into our special coach on the Taurus Express which snorted and simmered in the little station. As soon as the train started my four companions changed into civilian clothes. They looked like gangsters in their hurriedly made Cairo suits. All day we travelled through fawn-coloured foothills. Peasants in dark, tight-legged trousers work in the wide drab fields. After an excellent dinner, towards midnight, we reached Adana. I went along the platform to see the engine. It was German. The driver hauled me up into his cabin and showed me with pride an English-Turkish book from which he was learning.

We have a big sitting room with a table down the centre and three sleeping compartments; Mark and Patrick have wagon-lits further up the train. Ours is the last coach; it has a little platform at the back where we stand and watch the single track lines slide away and the big horizons change. The Taurus

Express is temperamental and sometimes goes so slowly that we get out and pick flowers beside the line.

15 April 1943   *Ankara*

Arriving last for breakfast I found the others struggling with nearly raw eggs. Pointing to my watch with four fingers I tried to explain to the waiter that I wanted mine cooked for four minutes. He returned immediately with four uncooked eggs in their shells. At this moment a dapper Turkish officer arrived and saved the situation. He had been sent by Marshal Cakmak to meet us. From now on we have to speak French. When the General had exhausted his fat, schoolboy phrases he retreated to a corner and read a detective novel and we staff played poker and backgammon with the Turkish officer.

At teatime, hours late, we arrived at Ankara, a great modern station. A crowd of officials met the General. I was told to remain in our coach for fear the Turks mistook me for a harem. I was fished out by Dorothy Arnold, wife of the Military Attaché, with whom I am staying. We drove fast down wide, well-lit streets, past the Vichy and Italian Embassies and Von Papen's[1] house where, not long ago, a patriotic English clerk climbed on the roof at night, pulled down the German flag and hoisted the Union Jack in its place.

We dined at the Embassy with Sir Hughe Knatchbull Hugesson and talked of German reactions to our visit, of our prisoner-of-war parcel organisation in Turkey, and of chrome. They told us that after George Carlisle,[2] representing United Kingdom Corporation, had successfully concluded the chrome deal for Britain the Turks invited representatives of all the nations concerned to a dinner party. Knowing that the National Anthems of the winner and runner-up countries would be played at the end of dinner to announce the result, George arranged with the band to play 'God Save the King'

[1.] Franz Von Papen, for a short while Chancellor of Germany, then Vice Chancellor to Hitler, and now German Ambassador to Turkey.
[2.] Earl of Carlisle.

first – as we'd won – and then, instead of 'Deutschland Über Alles' for the runner-up, Germany, they should play, 'I can't give you anything but love, baby.'

Champagne and central heating made me sleepy and I was glad when we drove home through the snow.

16 April 1943   *Ankara*

This morning the conference began. Brigadier Davy was to take the minutes which I shall type afterwards so I had a free morning. I went down to the town. The shops are full of expensive wirelesses, cameras, cosmetics, and pre-war luxury goods. Blue hyacinths, slender red tulips, violets and dwarf daffodils blazed from the flower stalls. In the Ankara Palace Hotel, where Germans and British live side by side, I found an old friend, Leigh Ashton, who is Press Councillor here. We sat in the long bar amongst our enemies while he told me of his press work and Istanbul. On the way home we passed a bookstall piled with magazines of every nation. *Parade*, our Middle East pictorial with a picture of General Alexander on the cover lay alongside *Signal*, the famous Nazi paper, printed in English, German and Turkish. Leigh touched my arm – 'There is Claudius's[1] secretary,' he said, indicating a blonde civilian across the road. It was the first time I had seen my opposite number in the war. What secrets we could swap.

After lunch I worked in a small room at the Embassy. It seemed to me, tapping out the great list of what Turkey would need should they come into the war on our side, that it would be a colossal task to equip her, and seeing that our shipping and air resources are needed elsewhere it would be nearly impossible to bring it all in over their poor land lines of communication.

I worked late and missed an official cocktail party. Mark, Patrick and I took the Arnolds to dine at the night club under the Ankara Palace Hotel. The Germans at the next table watched us with curiosity. Alan Arnold told me that last week a

[1] I cannot remember which German Top Person we codenamed 'Claudius'.

Turk was dancing here with a pretty Hungarian girl when an American airman, interned on parole, came and tapped her on the shoulder saying, 'Pardon me, may I cut in?' The Turk was left on the edge of the floor to figure it out. Presently he went up to the girl, tapped her shoulder and said, 'Pardon me, may I cut in?' whereupon the American socked him and a brawl began. Turks, Germans, English, Hungarians and French joined the fray. The American Consul, hoping to intervene, had both his eyes blacked. Finally when the police arrived order was restored. An amiable Turkish Minister asked them to make no arrests because he said, 'It was only a friendly argument.'

We drank vodka and ate an excellent dinner while we watched the cabaret. A Russian soldier came up to our table and said, 'Hello, English,' and joined us for a drink. I looked around. The women are very ugly, and I remembered Shevky Pasha, the Turkish Ambassador in Cairo, telling me that he had joined his country's foreign service because there were eight million plain women in Turkey.

17 April 1943   *Ankara*

On the floor below my office, when searching for somewhere to wash, I encountered a white-haired old man sitting in a little cold room writing letters. 'Who the devil are you?' he asked cheerfully. He was Admiral Sir Howard Kelly who was sent here by Mr Churchill in 1940. I took a great liking to him; he combines beautiful manners with the most astonishing directness. The Turks like him enormously. I asked him if Turkey was coming into the war and if it would help if she did. 'It would be a diplomatic victory but might also prove a military disaster,' he said. After growling that I ought to know this already, he explained that neutral Turkey served as a protecting bastion to our Middle East front. He added that Turkey had helped us in many ways 'far surpassing the bounds of the most benevolent non-belligerency' and particularly with regard to shipping, prisoners of war and the supply of chrome. 'If Turkey came into the war what will be the advantage to her or to us?' he
180

asked with a vehemence that made me jump. 'The opening of the Straits would be small assistance when the Germans hold the Aegean and the Russians already have naval superiority in the Black Sea. Air bases might have helped us at one time but then we did not have enough aircraft to carry out offensive operations and accord Turkey air defences as well. Besides this, Turkey would have to defeat the Bulgarian army before she held down a single German soldier. That is exactly what the Germans have been angling for her to do for years.'

Our Ambassador gave a big dinner party for General Jumbo and the heads of the Turkish Government and Army. All the women wore dinner dresses. M. Saraciojlu asked whether I had seen the column in this morning's paper about myself, and then he turned to General Jumbo and asked how long I am to stay. General Jumbo replied laughingly, 'That depends on whether you come into the war or not.'

'We shall declare war instantly,' said Saraciojlu. The Turks are very simple and love talking nonsense and though they try hard to pretend they are sophisticated their attractive naivety keeps creeping through. After dinner we were shown a Walt Disney film. Then all the Turkish veneer came off. They were thrilled by Donald Duck. Menemoglu, the Foreign Secretary, is far the cleverest Turk I met. He talks brilliantly.

18 April 1943   *Ankara*

George Carlisle, Air Vice Marshal George and I drove down the valley to the riding school. Through an arched gateway we came into a large yard surrounded by low stables. A crowd of Germans and English were waiting for their horses to be saddled. The horses were about fifteen one hands, raw-boned shaggy animals showing no trace of Arab or English strain. I watched a good-looking German showing off, turning and twisting round the square in immaculate riding clothes, a handsome slightly ludicrous figure and an amusing contrast to George Carlisle who was dressed in very old riding clothes. We rode up the valley past old Ankara where the houses are small and primitive compared to the great modern buildings on the other side of the town. We cantered up the plains to the hills; villages are wedged like hutches in the rocks and there seemed to be a lamentable lack of drains. We rode down a valley by a mountain torrent which overflowed through orchards of cherry trees, and then we turned back along the main road to cross the plain to Ankara. I asked George about the chrome. He told me that during the first two years of the war we took practically the whole of chrome from Turkey. Largely through our own fault we did not continue with this. The Germans used every means in their power to obtain it and finally, after a struggle, the chrome was divided into two equal shares. The Germans got one half and we the other. Now it is splendid that we've collared it all.

19 April 1943   *Ankara*

I finished my work at lunchtime, clipped together the fat minutes of the military conference and distributed them around. In the early afternoon I drove with Admiral Kelly to the Barrage where a big lake is dammed up in the hills to supply Ankara with water. We stood in the garden beside the great waterfall and had to yell to hear each other. Later I went down to the town to see whether I could buy anything to take away with me but everything was so expensive I gave up. The price of a bar of chocolate is fifteen shillings.

20 April 1943   *Taurus*

I am sitting in my berth with my typewriter on my knees. Outside the sun is shining on the Taurus mountains which rise on either side of the railway from pebbled slopes to lovely snow-covered peaks. Soon we shall be passing the Cicilian Gates, the most exciting part of our journey. It is difficult to type, the train goes awkwardly, jerking up the hills and bolting down them. Against the blue sky hover great eagles, the only sign of life we have seen for many hours.

Later. We chugged round steep bends and through tunnels and crowded on our little observation car to see the splendid

182

scenery. The rail track, a highway and the river criss-crossed each other through the bare mountains. No country for tanks. General Jumbo is tired and has slept in his corner most of the day with his big head nodding on his chest. I played poker, wrote my diary and ate figs. Some time in the early morning we shall reach Aleppo and the coaches will be slipped in a siding till it is time to get up.

21 April 1943   *Aleppo*

I left the train before the others and went over to the hotel to get a bath and then had a lovely breakfast of fried eggs and thick Syrian honey. At nine-thirty our convoy of cars started south. The grass on either side was thick with flowers, stretches of blue periwinkle, soft pink clover, and yellow daisies. Almost at once we got a puncture. I was delighted because I could pick flowers and watch the dragonflies. We bumped on towards the sudden hills ahead and twisted slowly up the hairpin way. Soon our American car boiled over. I sat on a warm bank and looked back over the plain; snow mountains merged with clouds in the distance. Above me, towering from the summit of the hills stood Craq de Chevalier. We drove on and in half an hour we were at the foot of the castle.

We crossed the moat, went through a gateway and walked up a roofed ramp that curled into the outer castle, for Craq is built like two fortresses one within the other. It was cold away from the sunlight. We came to courtyards and a vast hall which once stabled four thousand horses. It was well ventilated from the roof. We walked round the huge battlements and then ate a picnic lunch beside a water tank where water was stored in case of siege. Afterwards we climbed another cobbled ramp into the inner castle and explored the great banqueting rooms and kitchens. Outside a little chapel were the green mounds of Crusaders' graves. I wandered up broad slabbed steps to cloisters and towers and marvelled at the size and beauty of the building.

The Master's Tower has well proportioned graceful rooms looking out over the plain. I sat in a high arched window and thought of the old Count of Toulouse who, with his wife and baby, rode from the South of France, across the wild Dalmatian coast, through Turkey and the Taurus mountains, 'Those damnable mountains', on the first great Crusade. Nine centuries ago he lived here with his Knights and his hounds and his hawks and commanded the country below as far as one's eyes could see.

22 April 1943   *Beirut – Cairo*

We stayed the night in Beirut. This morning the General drove to Haifa to inspect troops. I flew by Misr Airways to Cairo and went straight to the office to sort out the mass of papers that had accumulated in our absence. I stole five minutes to go to the Map Room: the First and Eighth Armies are steadily closing in on the enemy.[1]

28 April 1943   *Cairo*

For three days a khamsin has blown; nine hours in an office in this heat makes one's temper brittle. We all drink buckets of water, but none of it ever appears again. Yesterday I rode. The burning wind caught the red dust from my pony's hooves and chased it along ahead of me. Little whirlwinds of grit stung my face and arms like pins and needles. General Jumbo seems unmoved by the great heat and wades steadily through the immense amount of work and visitors that pass through our office.

Whitaker telephoned me today from my room at the Continental Hotel and said he was cleaning out Coco's cage and that there was a bad smell in the room. 'It must be you, Whitaker,' I said.

'No,' he grumbled, 'it's this filthy thing, your parrot. May I put eau-de-cologne on it?'

[1.] On 12 May, when all German and Italian forces in Tunisia finally surrendered – over 100,000 Germans and 90,000 Italians were taken prisoner – they were under the command of General von Arnim.

Very Important People are arriving from far and wide for the Middle East War Council: General Platt from East Africa, General Pownall from Persia-Iraq Command, Lord Gort from Malta, and Ambassadors and Governers from all the Middle East countries.

The daily life of the personal staff is made up of a vast assortment of things. Like the waiters at a great banquet we hurry from the kitchen to the hall serving up the complicated dishes, listening to the comments of guests and cooks alike and keeping, as Whitaker would say, our traps shut. Cars, horses, aeroplanes, rations and the press; the General's dentist, tailor, hairdresser and shopping are all part of our job. As we file away the intricate political and military papers, Americans, French, Greeks, Poles, Czechs and Egyptians pass through our office and we must remember their names. We censor the orderlies' letters; get dragged into the synthetic social whirl of Cairo, run errands for the great, and 'fix' things for the young. We keep the big military plans and decisions in our safe along with our tin of toffee. We read the war news on the walls of the Map Room, which spoils our morning newspapers. We know the petty quarrels of those above us and below us. Our enemy is time, our friend the waste paper basket.

Last week all Axis forces in Tunisia surrendered. The struggle for North Africa is ended. It will not be long now before we invade Hitler's fortress, Europe. Bill Stirling and I dined together and drank to all prisoners of war; this news must be most precious to them *if* they learn of it.

The RAF have made a thrilling raid on the Mohne and Eder Dams in Germany.

Today is Whitaker's birthday. He came up to the office and we all drank his health in Syrian champagne and gave him a little present.

Later Pauley, our Sergeant, came into my office; he was obviously very upset. I thought perhaps he had bad news of his wife. He stood awkwardly, looking very downcast and then he began, 'I have bad news . . .' but he could not get any further, he just opened his large hand and held it out and there, flat as a little sporran, was Fuad. They had been moving my safe at lunchtime and it had fallen on him.

For months Fuad had lived in my office, locked up at night with the secrets, wandering all day among the files and telephones and exploring the long tunnels of rolled up maps. He had become a Very Important Person. Lord Gort was fond of him and when he was in Cairo would always stop for a moment and watch him. General Monty had faced him fearlessly and he had even met General Smuts who smiled at him as he passed into the Map Room. At eleven each morning Pauley always took him to the orderlies' room where he had tea and doughnuts with them, and then he would be brought back to curl up on my desk and go sound asleep. Pauley and I are going to miss Fuad. In a war animals and birds help one very much. Pauley wore a black garter on his arm and looked really sad all day.

General Sikorski, Commander-in-Chief of the Poles, has arrived with his daughter and Victor Cazalet. He has come to see our old friends the Polish army in the East who are now in Palestine. All three are charming.

I dined at the Embassy, and sat between Admiral Kelly who has come from Ankara, and the Ambassador. They talked of their time in China where they met Edda Ciano who once took them to a night club. Their conversation was ludicrous and very enjoyable.

General Jumbo has just returned from the Gulf of Aqaba where he has been watching the full-scale dress rehearsal for the landing in Sicily. Aqaba was chosen because of its remoteness. Mark, who went with him, told me that the rehearsal did not go very well: the troops took too long getting ashore. All day I have been typing out long signals and letters to the CIGS and General Montgomery about this.

I lunched with Peter Fleming who is on his way back from England to India. He told me a little about the tough proposition we are up against on the Burma front.

I dined with Padre Hughes who, at the beginning of the war, was Padre to the Sherwood Rangers Yeomanry. Now he is Chaplain to the Eighth Army. He told me of his great admiration for General Montgomery who, he said, has greatly improved the transport facilities for Padres. Now they can get round to see the men more easily and be with them when they are most needed. He also told me that he had been much criticised during his leave in Cairo for going to night clubs, etc.! 'It is not much use me spending time in respectable places,' he told me. 'I belong where people look like getting into trouble.' I gave him a little white ivory mouse as a mascot. He told me he would take it in his pocket to Berlin.

Cairo was crowded with people back on leave from the two thousand mile advance to Cape Bon. They told us how General Freyberg and his New Zealanders turned the battle at Mareth and how well the German Ninetieth Light Division fought. They brought us sad news too. Many of our friends have been killed and wounded, among them the Colonel and Second in Command of Dan's Regiment, and Francis Dorrien Smith who was General Jumbo's ADC in Baghdad, and Gilbert Talbot who succeeded him. They were all so young and attractive, and so brave . . . I feel dreadfully sad.

A large party of ENSA stars arrived from England. I met

Dorothy Dickson, Vivien Leigh and Leslie Henson who has such a croaky voice that I expected a thorn to shoot out of his mouth like the witch in the fairy tale. I was mistaken for Josephine Baker from behind; though hers is probably black I was very pleased. Bea Lillie stole the show. The troops adored her.

I get too little news of Dan. His letters sometimes take five months to reach me. Daphne is still trying to join me from England.

Yesterday I came to Alexandria for four days' rest. I have a huge carbuncle on my leg. I came by the desert road in a jeep; the dust and heat were awful but my good friend the jeep driver shared his water bottle with me. I was interested to see this road which, a year ago, might well have been the last lap of Rommel's advance on Cairo. We passed minefields and wire entanglements which had been laid hastily to delay the Germans if they broke through at Alamein. I am staying at Sidi Bish with Babe Moseley who does liaison between the army and the navy.

6 July 1943   *Alexandria*

Ghastly: I read in the papers this morning that Sikorski's plane crashed at Gibraltar; he and his daughter and Victor Cazalet were killed. Probably the plane was overloaded and did not get off the short runway in time. Or – was it sabotaged?

I spent the morning lying on the beach under a huge umbrella watching large native women in heliotrope petticoats paddling with their children. At lunch Babe and the sailors who share his house announced that they were going to take me sailing in the harbour. Having come all this way for peace and solitude I said I would rather lie on the beach and read a book. However, they were quite determined so we drove along the coast to Alexandria.

When I reached the terrace of the Yacht Club I understood why my friends had brought me sailing today. The harbour was crowded with ships and overhead the sky was dotted with balloons. A good breeze took us out towards the ships while Babe explained to me the vast organisation of loading and
188

scheduling the departures from Alexandria and all the other ports along the North African coast. 'You watch,' he said, 'they are leaving at four-minute intervals.' We sailed round the harbour looking at Liberty ships, hospital ships and liners. Gear was piled high on their decks, on one a railway engine and landing craft; on another a lot of trucks . . . In the lazy sunshine on this lovely day it seemed fantastic that I was watching the launching of the invasion of Europe. 'Will you come with us?' shouted the soldiers hanging over the sides. 'Good luck,' we shouted back. Out on the horizon in single file they went. It was thrilling but desperately sad.[1]

21 July 1943   *Cairo*

Two days ago my friend 'Abercrombie' telephoned my office out of the blue and said, 'I'm opening a street-fighting school in Cairo in a couple of days and have invited all the top brass. I've billed you as my Exhibit A, so don't fail me – be on time and shoot straight.'

'You devil,' I said, 'I've not used a gun for months and anyway it is difficult ever to leave my office.' He gave me the time and place and hung up after saying I'd ruin him if I didn't turn up.

Today, shivering with fright, I arrived at a crowded hall filled with officers. I told 'Abercrombie' I'd only permission to stay a very short time. He grinned. 'You and Lord Byron can kick off right now,' he said, handing me the 'Silver Lady', his Smith and Wesson, and shoving me into the target area. 'Shoot the pips out of all the playing cards you see, and kill anything else which pops up while you are here – except, of course, the officers,' he boomed.

Though it was a hot day I felt frozen with shyness. '*Now,*' he shouted and off I went. 'Right hand. Left hand. Both hands together,' he bawled. By the grace of God I missed nothing. He handed me the bullet riddled playing cards after showing

[1.] This was 'Operation Husky', the invasion of Sicily, which began 10 July 1943.

them to the audience, thumped me on the back and said, 'I know you have to go back at once to run the war, so thank you and goodbye.' As his other pupils moved into the target area I fled back to the office.

25 July 1943   Cairo

When I woke this morning the fierce sun was already slanting through my windows. Coco was grumbling to himself under his green baize cover. I slithered out of bed and turned on a cold bath and then fished the newspaper from under my door. Printed in huge letters across the top was 'Mussolini Resigns'. The first rift in the Axis has come. Italy must be in a turmoil. So am I.

Today I got my 200th letter from Dan. It had taken three and a half months to reach me. Large strips of it were blacked out; somewhere there is an Axis Struwwelpeter who daubs his ink greedily over the poor little twenty-six line letter-cards that prisoners are allowed to write.

18 August 1943   Cairo

Sicily is now in our hands. It seems almost certain that Italy is coming out of the war. I am ricocheting from high hope that Dan will be set free, or manage to escape, to deep anxiety lest he be taken to Germany or caught in a revolution. I am exhausted with waiting and wishing and guessing. Everyday life in Cairo seems a farce now.

3 September 1943   Cairo

We have landed on the toe of Italy. I am in a fever of excitement – perhaps I shall see Dan this week.

Today Whitaker, who now works for the NAAFI, came to tell me he has been made a sergeant; he was wearing three of the largest stripes I ever saw.

For two weeks I have been in bed with dysentery.

Our troops have landed at Salerno. The Italians have asked for an armistice.

This morning I heard that General Carton de Wiart who was in prison with Dan in Florence has arrived in London. It seems that the Italians sent him to Portugal as a good-faith exhibit when they asked us for an armistice. I have written to him asking for news of Dan, whom he must have seen less than a month ago. General Jumbo has very kindly wired to General Eisenhower in Algiers asking if there is any news of the Generals in Florence.

Last night I went to a dinner party given by Air Marshal Sholto Douglas. There I met the King of Egypt, the Caseys, Noël Coward and all the Service Chiefs. After a buffet dinner we saw a film called *Arsenic and Old Lace*, and then Noël Coward sang.

King Farouk wears European clothes, a tarboosh and a beard. He is twenty-three years old and speaks good English. I found him a cheerful, friendly person. He told me how much he enjoyed Sholto's informal parties and that he is learning to fly. At the beginning of the war he was said to be pro-Italian and no doubt our officials who had dealings with him found this difficult. But during the last three years the King has been given very little opportunity of getting to know and understand English people better. Except for Sholto and a handful of others who have gone out of their way to know him, he has met very few English and practically none of his own generation. I have heard him much criticised for his wild parties, fast cars and selfish behaviour, but these are only the faults of youth and do not warrant our unfriendliness. Egypt, by its geographical position alone, is of great importance to us and it is a grave mistake that we have let an opportunity slide of making friends with the King. I enjoyed talking with him and we laughed a lot.

Each day I expect to hear that Dan is free. I have had a yellow fever inoculation so that I can fly to meet him when he gets out.

The Italian fleet coming over to us caused great excitement here: many of their ships are now in Alexandria. All this week we have been anxious about Salerno but today the news is better. The great Russian advance continues; we are bombing Germany on a tremendous scale; the Balkans are rustling with rebellion; surely this must be the last winter of the war.

I dined with General and Lady Freyberg and spent a pleasant evening talking of fishing in Lake Taupo and of Pelorous Jack, the famous dolphin which used to meet ships at Auckland. The New Zealand Division is now at Maadi, resting after their long campaign in North Africa.

28 September 1943   *Cairo*

Field Marshal Smuts came through my room on his way to a meeting and stopped to chat. He is always nice to staff. There is something very impressive about this small Edwardian figure. We all admire him.

At first when my telephone rang I did not answer it. I was reading the thrilling Intelligence Report on Mussolini's escape: German commandos landed a Fiesler Storch on a mountain ledge, overpowered the Italian guards and flew Il Duce off to Germany. When I picked up the receiver a small voice, which sounded a very long way off, said, 'It's me, Daphne.'

'Daphne who?' I enquired politely.

'Half wit, your sister,' said the voice.

'Are you speaking from London?' I asked, much impressed.

'No, from Cairo, Egypt,' came the triumphant reply. Half an hour later we met on the steps of the Continental. We had not seen each other for three and a half years. She was at school when I left England. She flew via Lisbon and Castel Benito in a bomber and has come to work for SOE at my old office in

Garden City. Like me, she is a civilian. We talked far into the night – we were far too happy to go to bed. Daphne is twenty-one years old.

29 September 1943   Cairo

I dined in General Jumbo's Mess where he was giving a dinner party for the Maiskys.[1] Madame Maisky was smartly dressed in American clothes; her expensive handbag was filled with luxury compactums and cosmetics. She wore her hair in the style of Madam Butterfly with a red zinnia in it. Monsieur Maisky wore a white shirt, red tie and shorts. They both speak English. At dinner they laid down the law a good deal and asked, amongst other things, when are we going to get rid of our 'useless' House of Lords. After dinner Madame Maisky expressed surprise that an English Countess should be working as a secretary. I told her that, like a great many other people in England, I had earned my own living since the age of seventeen. I refrained with difficulty from adding that I thought it a good deal more surprising that she should live like a capitalist and talk communism.

7 October 1943   Cairo

Daphne is feeling the heat very much. Sunday was the hottest day in Cairo for forty-six years. Worse still, she has found bugs in her room. We had a battle to get her another room: Freddie is away ill and Samy Bey, the assistant manager of the Continental, kept saying, 'Believe me, ladies, hotel is full.' Only when we told him that we never believed him did he give in. 'Oh, oh, I have my pride as an Egyptian,' he cried. 'Another room you shall have at once.' Daphne knows no one here so I take her everywhere with me.

South African General Klopper, who has escaped from a prison camp in Italy, came to the office today. He told me that a great many prisoners are wandering about in the mountains

[1.] Soviet Ambassador to London.

in Italy but it is very difficult for them to escape because our line is so far to the south and because of the Fascisti.

We see a good deal of the King of Yugoslavia and the Yugoslav Government who are now living in Cairo. The King has been to America lately which he enjoyed very much. He talks with a strong American accent. He told me that there is always a big Opposition Party in Yugoslavia; his people are divided racially as well as politically. It is awful to think that this young man's father and grandfather were both assassinated.

The Germans have taken Kos.

13 October 1943   Cairo

This morning I got up at 3.45 and went down to the flying-boat anchorage to meet Sir Archie Wavell, now Viceroy Designate, and his family. The Nile looked like liquid metal under a full moon. It was fun watching them land. They came ashore in what the Americans please to call a 'gasoline gig'.

After lunch at Maadi with General Jumbo, the Wavell family, Mr Eden and General Pug Ismay (these last two are on their way to Moscow for the Foreign Secretaries' Meeting), Daphne and I escaped to the stables. We cantered the full length of the cultivation. Dragonflies were darting over the shallow ditches and white storklike birds were stepping elegantly in the soggy brown fields. We came back across the Desert. Through the shimmery heat haze the citadel looked like a drop scene in a play.

18 October 1943   Cairo

Lord Gort, or 'The Fat Boy' as his contemporaries call him, paid me a visit today. He said, 'I have come to ask after your dear little mouse.' I told him that Fuad had been killed in action and he offered me his condolences.

There was a big meeting in the Map Room today: Mr Oliver Stanley, Secretary of State for the Colonies, is here, and General Monty. While they were at the meeting we tried on the famous beret. It was too big for me. We gummed the lining of

194

it with sticking paste and felt very sad that we will not be there the next time Monty doffs it. Amongst all the VIPs we take care of we find him the least attractive.

The Wavell family and their staff have left. General Archie was the same as ever – charming and unruffled.

General Carton de Wiart arrived from England this evening and dined with Daphne and me. He is tall, slim and elegant – very direct and amusing.

He told me that on the evening of 18th August Italians arrived at Vincialata and told him to prepare to leave for Rome in the morning. They did not tell him why. That was when he last saw Dan. Two smart cars came to collect him; one was for luggage, which amused him as he had only an attaché case. He was taken to a palace in Rome and given lobster mayonnaise and champagne for lunch. Then an Italian General arrived and said they wanted him to go to Lisbon to talk of exchange of prisoners, which in reality meant he was to be a good-faith exhibit for their peace overtures. He was told he must wear civilian clothes. He replied that they must be properly made – he would not wear one of their 'bloody gigolo suits'. A tailor was waiting outside. After he was measured he was taken on a drive round Rome. The streets were full of Germans. Before he left he sent a message back to Vincialata to send his books, which was code for 'I am on something to do with an Armistice'. He was then flown to Lisbon.

General Carton was extremely kind; he told us all he could of Dan, that he was fit and well when he last saw him and that there was a good chance of his escape though it might take a long time because they are so far north. He described their previous attempts to escape: on one occasion they dug a tunnel for many yards under the chapel and battlements of the castle. That was when Miles and Hargest got away. Dan was not allowed to make that attempt because he ran their Mess and stores and his absence would have been noticed immediately by the Italians.

General Carton is on his way to Chunking where he will be the Prime Minister's Special Representative to China.

Mr Eden and party arrived from Moscow today and with them came Dan's cousin, Charles Milnes Gaskell. He told me that the Moscow Conference had been a great success. Mr Eden has been in conference with Turks nearly all day, discussing possible action by Turkey.

Yesterday Tony de Cosson arrived from Port Said where *Aphis* is getting a long overdue refit. She has had many adventures since I saw her a year ago: after following the Eighth Army advance all the way to Tunis she took part in the Pantelleria, Sicily and Italy landings. She has done all sorts of odd jobs, mine-sweeping, salvaging stranded steamers, towing lighters and giving bombardment support. She has had no casualties but her guns are worn and she can only do five knots now. Except for a week at Malta before the Sicily campaign her crew have had no shore leave for eight months.

Last night we went to a Charity Ball at the Auberge des Pyramides. The courtyard was roofed over with rugs and in the immense space below were dining tables, bars, two band-stands and dance floors, and a quantity of stalls and sideshows. Upstairs in the main building there were gambling rooms. The scene was like a Metro Goldwyn Mayer banquet: overdressed and overfed people seething against a background of oriental carpets with great jewels and blancmanges gleaming in every direction. It seemed as if all the harems in Egypt had come – ladies of every shape and size in fabulous frocks and furs. Every class and nationality were present; I saw three Kings and scores of Generals, merchants, book-makers, diplomats and even Mary who runs the best brothel in Alexandria. After dinner we watched an excellent cabaret of Greek, Spanish and Negro dances.

This afternoon I watched the New Zealand v. South Africa rugger match. Several Maoris were playing; they are short, broad and very fast. I stood with a group of wounded prisoners of war who have just been repatriated from Germany. A one-legged Australian told me that the Germans are terrified of the Russians and that our air raids on Germany are staggering; he said he had read a book for two hours by the light of Kassel burning twenty miles away. These prisoners came out via France and Spain.

Mr Eden has been in conference all day with the Turkish Foreign Minister. I think they are discussing air bases.

11 November 1943   *Cairo*

Armistice Day! The French in Syria have seized and thrown into prison the Lebanese President, Prime Minister and all members of the Lebanese Parliament.

The Russians are only twenty-five miles from the Polish border.

12 November 1943   *Cairo*

At seven o'clock this morning the Germans attacked Leros. There is much speculation here as to whether we can hold it.

I lunched with Admiral Kelly who has come from Ankara. There is a story that he and his brother once had a quarrel and shortly afterwards met in Bond Street. They passed each other silently with their noses in the air but one of them came back, tapped the other on the shoulder and said, 'Excuse me, but am I right in thinking that your Father married my Mother?'

Tomorrow is my birthday. I shall be thirty.

16 November 1943   *Cairo*

The situation in Leros is now very serious. Brigadier Tilney who is commanding wired today, 'Fighting exhaustion not superior numbers'. Our Force has been bombed continuously; the Germans have air superiority in the Aegean. Our Navy are doing all they can but Leros is five hundred miles from Alexandria and without air cover it is very difficult. There are no facilities for wounded on the island. Casualties are high.

Last night King Farouk had a head-on collision with one of our Army trucks in the Canal Area. The King was driving very fast – the skid marks are fifty yards long. I telephoned the Military Hospital for General Jumbo and was told that the King is not badly hurt though he is bruised in some peculiar places. His fat saved him.

The Germans are attacking the Yugoslav islands. No doubt the Partisans will just withdraw and start again later.

17 November 1943   *Cairo*

After five days of non-stop air bombardment the Germans have retaken Leros. Strange how much the British and Germans wanted this twelve-mile island, a stepping stone in the Iron Ring of the Aegean. I am anxious about George Jellicoe who was there with his Boat Squadron.

This evening a rocket came from Churchill about the delay in settling the Lebanese row. The President, Prime Minister and Ministers are all still in prison.

In the evening papers and down the corridors of GHQ people have started blaming General Jumbo for Leros. This makes me angry because no one here is in a position to judge. I saw all the telegrams that passed between Mr Churchill and General Jumbo but even so I know only half the story. These days the Chiefs of Staff and Planners in London run the war, Theatre Commanders only carry out orders. Perhaps General Jumbo should have emphasised the risk, for we had a very thin margin of ships and troops and inadequate air cover, but the people in London knew that as well as we did. Perhaps the Leros operation was a feint to force the Germans to keep more troops in the Aegean. Perhaps a lot of things. This is a global war and planes and ships and men are dispersed where they are most needed.[1] At the moment the North African

---

[1.] The Aegean Islands, recently garrisoned by the Italians, were proving a problem for the Allies. Churchill had pressed for British garrisons to be installed and the British Chiefs of Staff had conceded the point, against their better judgement for the Germans held Rhodes and from it could dominate the air situation and supply to the islands.

Theatre and probably Burma and the Pacific have priority over Middle East demands. We could only do our best with what we had and Brigadier Tilney certainly did that. Public opinion in a war must of necessity be ignorant so fame is a phoney. Wavell may be counted a failure today, and Monty a success but when it is known what they both had to fight their battles with then their positions may well be reversed. And rightly so.

19 November 1943   *Cairo*

Arrangements are being hurried on for the big conference at Mena. The main conference is to be held at the Mena House Hotel; Mr Churchill will stay at the Caseys' villa, Mr Roosevelt and Generalissimo and Madame Chiang Kai Chek will have two villas nearby and so will the Chiefs of Staff. Many houses along the Mena road are being requisitioned for the enormous staffs that are coming. A wire fence has been put up round the conference zone and precautions against land and air attack have been taken. Security arrangements are endless; visitors will be stopped and asked to show their passes at several check posts, however important they are. Food and furnishing arrangements are vast. We have an extra ADC to help us during the conference; his name is Tom Bird. Mr Churchill is delayed at Malta with a bad cold.

The newspapers say: 'Riots in Grenoble. Fierce Fighting in Bosnia, Partisans Retreat. Hurricanes Raid Crete. Bombs on the Solomons. Sir Oswald and Lady Mosley are going to be let out of gaol.' To think I used to have time to read the agony column in *The Times*.

I went to the Map Room to get the latest news. In Italy our troops are fighting their way slowly north through rain and snow. We are bombing Germany with more and more aircraft. Yesterday it was Ludwigshaven. In Europe the Occupied countries seethe below the surface. In New Guinea the grim struggle goes on. The Russian advance is so fast that the Map Room Sergeant quite resents it; 'I never stop moving them pins,' he said. He showed me a picture he has painted from memory of his wife. It was a very large water colour of a completely nude brunette.

I went to bed early. Coco ate two bananas; he is an incredibly greedy bird. I am really tired. We're almost overwhelmed with work at the office.

21 November 1943   *Cairo*

The conference is assembling. Mr Churchill and his daughter, Sarah, are here and Sir John Dill from America and all the British Staff. Generalissimo Chiang Kai Chek arrived early and unheralded so no one was on the aerodrome to meet him. Lord Louis Mountbatten and General Carton de Wiart came with him. There has been a scare that the Germans know of the conference and may try to break it up. Further precautions have been taken specially with regard to parachutists.

This evening General Jumbo went to dine with the Caseys to see Mr Churchill and I went with the Aides to Mena House Hotel. The big dining room was filled with sailors, soldiers and airmen, civil servants, interpreters, planners and staff of all kinds. The food and drink were superb. I was delighted to see Bob Laycock who is on Combined Operations. I was told there is an ack-ack gun on the top of the Pyramids but I don't believe it.

22 November 1943   *Cairo*

Mr Roosevelt has arrived. The first Three Power Conference has begun. In the office we are horribly busy and the telephones never cease ringing. This morning General Carton de Wiart came in to ask for news of Dan. He told me how much he likes the Chiang Kai Cheks. Churchill and Roosevelt are lunching together.

Great news: The Lebanese Government have been let out of gaol. M. Helleu, the French Minister, has been recalled.

Mr Churchill and President Roosevelt are going to meet Marshal Stalin in Tehran after the Cairo Conference. This evening General Selby flew in from Baghdad to be briefed about the arrangements. We were pleased to see him; he was General Jumbo's Administrative Officer in Paiforce. We thought ourselves lucky to leave the office at nine-fifteen this evening. Thank Heavens it is not hot any longer. We are incredibly busy.

24 November 1943   *Cairo*

Air Marshal Tedder brought me good news this morning. He is almost certain that Dan and the Generals are hiding in the mountains in North Italy. He thinks they are comparatively safe but that it may take some time for them to escape, specially when the snow comes.

This morning I was alone in the office as the Aides were all out on jobs; Tom Bird went to Cassacine to ask after King Farouk who is recovering from his accident; Jack was at Mena looking after some Generals; and Mark went with General Jumbo to see Mr Churchill at the Caseys' villa. Having two cars to organise and four telephones to cope with is a terrible fate. Signals kept coming in from Syria and from Fitzroy Maclean who is held up by bad weather at Bari – he is trying to bring Tito's Delegation from Yugoslavia for the conference.

I lunched with the King of Greece and Colonel Donovan.[1] The latter seems to have been round the world several times since I last saw him in Cairo in 1941. We talked of Generalissimo Chiang Kai Chek. 'A tiny little chap but very impressive,' they said.

When I got back to the office I found George Jellicoe and an Italian, both dressed in Turkish civilian clothes. They have escaped from Leros. George told me that he and his men were on the wrong side of the island and on the 17th November he walked up to HQ to find out the situation. He found Germans in possession and was taken prisoner. He told them that his men would fight to the last man unless he himself told them to surrender, so he was set free. He managed to escape with sixty men in a small boat. We are awfully pleased to see him.

Daphne and I dined with General Carton de Wiart at the

[1.] 'Wild Bill Donovan' was head of the American equivalent of SOE.

Mohammed Ali Club which was filled with people from the conference. There are going to be great changes in Command and the ADC world is humming with gossip.

The story goes that Randolph Churchill woke his father yesterday morning saying, 'Twinkle, twinkle little star, how I wonder where you are.' Anyhow the Prime Minister suddenly demanded to know why some of our soldiers were not wearing the Desert Star Medal. Churchill had taken trouble over this medal: the yellow on it is for sand, the blue for sea, and so on. Few have yet been issued – hence the dilemma. Now all the ribbon in existence has been made up and any desert soldier who sees Churchill will wear it but will have to return it at the gate on departure for others to wear.

Jimmy Gault, now English Aide to General Eisenhower, invited me to dine last night at the Mohammed Ali Club to meet the General and his staff. Being the only outside guest I was placed at dinner next to the General. There were about sixteen people there – all Americans except for Jimmy, Kay Somersby, the General's very nice English Secretary who sat on his right, and myself. A superb dinner was served. For the first two courses the General sat with his back turned to me and only spoke to his Secretary and I began to run out of conversation with a shy young American on my left. Opposite me was Elliot Roosevelt who kept putting his arms round the WAC sitting next to him and trying to kiss her with his mouth full of food. (Elliot is the image of his Mother!) When the sweet was served and the General had to turn a little in my direction I asked him if he knew Bonner Fellers, the American Attaché we all liked who was here during some of the Desert war. Eisenhower replied tersely: 'Any friend of Bonner Fellers is no friend of mine,' and smartly turned his back on me again to talk to Kay. Soon after dinner I thanked Jimmy, shook hands with everybody and departed.

Early this morning Jimmy Gault telephoned me to say General Eisenhower thought he'd been rude to me last night and would be pleased if I would dine with him tonight. I asked Jimmy to thank the General for his invitation and say I was sorry I have a previous engagement. An awful lie: I have no date tonight.

27 November 1943   *Cairo*

Mr Churchill and President Roosevelt and their staffs flew to Tehran today to meet Stalin. Generalissimo Chiang Kai Chek, Lord Louis Mountbatten and General Carton de Wiart will leave for India and China tonight. After lunch at the Yugoslav Legation Daphne and I went to the Musqi to buy silk for General Carton as he is running out of pyjamas. He'll get them made up in India.

2 December 1943   *Cairo*

Today the newspapers reported the conference in Cairo and the decision that 'Japan will be stripped of all her possessions after defeat'.

General Jumbo arrived at the office wearing a new uniform made of New Zealand material. He is delighted with it and turned round very slowly to show it to me, keeping his feet in a V like a small boy at dancing class. He looked like a giant teddy bear. He told me they had a record duck shoot with Sir Miles Lampson yesterday and killed 2300 duck. Peter Stirling shot 400.

When General Jumbo left the office early to meet Mr Churchill and General Brooke who are flying in from the Tehran Conference I thought I'd catch up with the work piled on my desk, but Arthur Forbes wandered in exuding news and gossip and greedy for more. 'When Eisenhower moves over to Europe who will become Supreme Commander of the Mediterranean Theatre?' he asked.

'Me,' I replied and asked him to buzz off as I had work to do.

'It must be Alexander or Jumbo,' he went on. 'I hear the Americans and Brookie want Jumbo – but Winston wants Alexander.' He proceeded to talk his way round the world in his intelligent and amusing way and I got hooked and learned a lot, particularly of our bombing of Germany which is exciting but horrifying. Now our incessant air raids, especially those on Berlin, bring us hope of victory but the carnage is appalling.

Land, sea and air news from everywhere bring tales of incredible human valour which we all discuss briefly and then, as more news pours in, get forgotten. New inventions for destruction keep being produced – each more terrible than the last. We did not start this war but now we have to win it. Our target is peace on earth but we must do most ghastly things to achieve this. We are rightly proud of our efforts but, when we get time to think – which is not very often – we are appalled by the misery and suffering we must receive and inflict. Now I can understand why my Mother so often said – after World War I – 'I can never, ever, forgive the Germans.' Now, once again, we have all become murderers – in one way or another.

2 December 1943   Cairo

Fitzroy Maclean arrived with his delegation of Partisans from Yugoslavia. He brought photographs with him – tragic pictures of burned out villages and Partisans dead and alive.

General Jumbo went to see Mr Roosevelt this afternoon and had a long session with Mr Churchill this evening. I've sent off all my Christmas presents for our families at home.

7 December 1943   Cairo

At lunchtime, outside my hotel, I found a big crowd. The road was lined with Egyptian soldiers standing as stiff as the plane trees above them. A band was playing in the Ezbekir Gardens. I pushed my way into the hotel, collected Daphne and went out on to a balcony. Two Americans were already there. They told us, 'It's for that Fat Jerk, the King.' They said that from the station to Abdin Palace the pavements and terraces were crammed with Egyptians. Soon five outriders drove by, followed by a big green car and then the King appeared, standing and waving in a huge open Packard. The Egyptians held their children high and waved and shouted – 'Welcome back, King Farouk, from Cassacine and the motor accident.' Three scarlet and black cars followed the King and the excitement was over. A Red Cross matron who had joined us on the balcony said, 'Two of my nurses are still attending the King, although he is quite recovered. Still they will get a medal, whatever it's for.' I did not like to enquire what she meant.

I had a talk with Col Zigantes who recently parachuted on to Samos having never had a jump before. A very gallant old man. He leads the Greek Sacred Squadron. He introduced me to his charming wife. I've managed to get small Xmas presents for our orderlies, drivers, grooms, Jumbo and household, Aides, King of Greece, Fitzroy, Tony de Cosson, Freddie Hoffman, our dressmaker, and Daphne. Am now bankrupt.

11 December 1943   Cairo

This morning my office was bedlam. First Fitzroy came in and talked about Yugoslavia. He told me that our Ambassador, Mr Stevenson, has now told the Yugoslav Prime Minister that we are no longer supporting Mihailovitch on account of his supposed dealings with the Germans. Several of our Mission to Mihailovitch are still at his Headquarters. If we are not careful the news will break before they have time to get out and they will be murdered. We were joined by David Wallace who works for our Ambassador to Greece, Mr Leeper. He told me that he got ticked off at dinner last night by Mr Churchill for arguing about the Greek Monarchy. Billy Maclean joined us. He is with our mission to Albania and began to talk about Hoxha.

14 December 1943   Cairo

General Patton of the US Army and his nice Aide, Colonel Codman, have come to stay at General Jumbo's Mess. The General is tall, with a rugged face and manner. He wears battle-dress with boots and gaiters. It is said that recently when visiting a hospital in North Africa he hit an American soldier and called him a coward. None of us knows the rights and wrongs

205

of this but the American press have made much of the supposed incident and it seems probable that the General has come here to let the story die down.

Yesterday I was asked to take General Patton shopping as he wanted to buy presents for his family in America. On our return for lunch he asked me to find someone to show him the antiquities of Cairo, 'I'll need an expert – someone who knows exactly what he is talking about,' he said. I telephoned Sir Robert Gregg and asked him as a favour to show the General round but unfortunately he was busy. However he kindly arranged for a Professor to meet the General at nine this morning on the terrace at Shepherds Hotel. Jack Wintour, our Aide, would accompany the General, the Professor and Colonel Codman on the tour in one of our cars.

Jack returned to our office after lunch and regaled us, with much laughter, of the expedition. The General arrived very late at Shepherds Hotel and after introductions the General asked the Professor what he was going to show him. 'First we will visit the mosques . . .' began the Professor – but he got no further.

'Now, Professor,' roared the General, 'NO, NO, NO. I don't want to see any of your Goddam mosques. I've seen enough of the darn things in Tunisia to last my lifetime. I guess we'd best go see the Sphinx.' There was an agonising silence and then the Professor announced he knew nothing of the Sphinx. He was angry, but so was the General. 'Waal, Professor, then I guess you'd best go home,' he said and, turning to Jack said in a loud whisper, 'Should I pay the little old guy off?' Jack, suffocating with laughter, shook his head and turned to the Professor who made a prolonged fart, turned on his heel and departed. Jack hurried the guests into our car and made for Mena where, fortunately, the General wished to go to the lavatory, giving Jack just time to ring our office and tell me to telephone the Professor and grovel – 'Smother him with apologies,' said Jack and rang off.

I rang the Professor who was furious. I could hardly deliver our apologies and for all of twenty minutes he unleashed his opinion of what he thought of the inhabitants of the United

States of America. Then he slammed down the telephone. I asked Jack what he had told the General about the Pyramids and the Sphinx. 'While the General was in the lavatory and I'd spoken to you,' said Jack, 'I bought a guide book in the hotel and read out bits to the General and it went fine.'

16 December 1943   *Cairo*

At dinner General Patton told me he had had a marvellous day and invited me to fly down to Luxor tomorrow to see more 'reylics'. I explained I can't get away. I wrote a nice note to the Professor and asked Jack to deliver it with a bunch of flowers. Jack did this and returned to say, 'I got him a big bunch of forget-me-nots.' I like General Patton very much and Colonel Codman – both are very direct and great fun.

21 December 1943   *Cairo*

Last night I was woken by the telephone; it was Mark to say that the signal had just come in from Italy: Generals Neame and O'Connor and Air Marshal Boyd have reached our lines. Mark said Dan was sure to be with them. I could not believe my ears and made Mark repeat this over again. Then I got up and started to pack. I hardly slept at all and rushed to the office early.

I found the telegram and read it over and over again. It was true, the Generals are out and they are safe and well. Just as I was going into General Jumbo's room to ask for leave to join Dan, he came into mine with a telegram in his hand. He gave it to me. It read, 'Philip Neame tells me personally that Dan is safe and well in hiding. We hope to see him soon. Signed Alexander.' I was too crushed to say anything. As I typed through the morning I kept thinking of all the dreadful things that could still happen to Dan, he might get recaptured or shot or drowned or meet a Mona Lisa. Oh, bloody hell.

We now know for certain that General Jumbo will succeed General Eisenhower as Supreme Allied Commander, Mediterranean Theatre.

General Jumbo gave a large official dinner party last night and Daphne and I went to help. There were twenty-four guests and they sat at three long tables. I was between General Royce and Dick Casey who told me he is going to be Governor of Bengal. With the fish course came a signal and after the guests had gone General Jumbo told me he is going to Tunis and then on to Algiers[1] and London. He asked me to stay and look after the home front. He and Mark flew off in the first light today to join Mr Churchill at Tunis; the two old men will spend Christmas together at Carthage. Jack and I spent the morning cancelling appointments and struggling with a mass of papers which Mark had not had time to hand over to us. After lunch I went into the town to buy Christmas presents. I dined with the King of Greece, Crown Prince Paul and Natasha Bagration. We had a very pleasant dinner but I think we all felt rather exiled. This is my third Christmas away from Dan and my fourth away from home. Today I got a lovely pair of silk stockings from General Patton.

An urgent signal has come from Tunis asking for penicillin and a doctor who knows how to use it. Mr Churchill must be ill again.

Tonight Daphne, Whitaker and I drank a solemn toast – that we shall see Dan in 1944.

[1] Allied Supreme Headquarters Mediterranean had been set up in Algiers.

8

Westward Ho

13 January 1944   *Cairo*

We have said goodbye to all our friends in Cairo, the Sofragis,
baggage men, our Italian dressmaker and her fat pug, the King
of Greece in his villa on the Nile, etc. Daphne[1] and I are
packed and ready to go to Algiers. For years I have lived close
to the Desert but never seen it. Tomorrow I shall see the stage
of all those adventures, tragedies, retreats, sieges and victories.
The land where all those people I knew, and listened to, lived
and fought and perhaps died.

14 January 1944

It was cold on the aerodrome this morning. We looked a comic
party: Daphne in her white sheepskin coat with a bundle of
coathangers under her arm; Arthur Forbes, round as the Michelin tyre man in two overcoats, carrying a couple of dead turkeys; Patrick Wilson, muffled to the ears and already green
with anticipation of flying; myself in my new battledress,[2] holding Coco in his cage. Corporal Robins and Sergeant Clark, the

---

[1] As Daphne was to be secretary to Dudley Clarke in Algiers, General Jumbo
kindly said she could come in his aeroplane with his staff.
[2] I'd had a khaki battledress made for special occasions.

chef, handed a vast assortment of luggage into the Dakota while Achmed, the General's Sudanese servant, explained with immense dignity to the American crew, 'Me no Sambo. Me Achmed.' When Mark and George Davy arrived we said good-bye to the drivers who were not coming with us, took airsick pills and flew down the Delta.

Everyone craned at the windows. Coco wandered about my chair, grumbling to himself. Soon we were over the Western Desert, not far from Alamein. I saw old tanks and trucks and scrap strewn about. Wheel tracks were so distinct the battle might have been yesterday. I saw Halfaya Pass and the railway which only goes to Mersa Matruh; scrub and wadis; black blobs of burnt vehicles; the road to Tripoli. Tobruk looked like a village. Wrecks in the harbour showed clearly through the green water . . .

The land below seemed drab and flat as the map on my knees, yet all day I stared out of the window. Old stories and phrases darted through my mind. Each place had some special significance for me. 'The noise and the heat of the battle at Alamein are terrific. It cannot last much longer.'

'These siege operations around Bardia are getting mono-tonous. We are longing to be on the move again.'

'In Tobruk we are all cheerful and we shall fight to the last man. You would be amused if you could see the assortment of guns we are using.'

'For two days we searched for the Generals. There is a rough track south of Derna and we think they were ambushed there. My men blew up the road in the early morning.'

'The garden at Barce is full of flowers. We found a little tame gazelle and a visitors' book signed by Graziani, Balbo and all our Generals.'

'David Stirling is operating far behind the enemy lines. They use the Long Range Desert Group as Carter Paterson.'

'It appeared to me that a figure ran for about thirty yards. Tracer was all around him. He dropped down . . .'

The Germans are gone from North Africa and there is no trace of the battles save for a few old wrecks on the edge of the sea and twisted tanks on the land and those wheel marks on the sand. Flash Kellett, Pat Ruthven, Brigadier Kisch and many more are dead. Dan and David and thousands of others are still missing or prisoners. For once I saw the war in perspective and I did not like it at all.

We landed to refuel at Tripoli. Hangars were torn and spotty with bullet holes. Aeroplane wrecks were stacked high on one side. I played backgammon with Daphne to try and forget that Corporal Robins was being desperately sick just behind me. We landed at Tunis in the dusk and drove up narrow streets to a village called Sidi Busaid. We had to reverse to turn the steep corners. We are staying in a Moorish villa which General Eisenhower used as a guest house. The rooms are tiled and well furnished; each bedroom has a bathroom adjoining but alas no hot water. After dinner Arthur and I visited General Mast who commands Tunis. In spite of the shortage of everything Madame Mast has decorated her house very gaily. The walls are lined with books she had bound herself in brilliant Moroccan leather.

15 January 1944   *Tunis – Algiers*

This morning I washed furtively in cold water and went out to watch the sun come up. I walked through courtyards to the paved garden which is planted with orange and lemon trees. I looked down over Tunis and Cape Bon and then walked round to the back of the house where the land falls steeply to the sea.

We took off at nine and flew through clouds. It was very bumpy. For a while Coco whistled on his perch but presently he fluffed out his feathers and closed his eyes. Finally he opened his beak wide and was sick. He looked dreadfully funny.

When the clouds cleared we saw below us steep wooded mountains running down to a rugged coast line. White torrents showed clear against the deep green. After three and a half hours we came to a great plain dotted over with big farmhouses. Shortly afterwards we landed on Maison Blanche Aerodrome. Away on the edge of the field was another hideous pile of wrecks and parked in long lines all around us were aeroplanes and gliders. We were met by our new American Aide, Logan Schultz. He seemed hypnotised by the strange cargo that was being unloaded from our Dakota. He told us that General Jumbo was landing on the other side of the field from Gibraltar.

The Supreme Allied Commander's house stands high above Algiers in a lovely garden. At lunch General Jumbo told us his news, of Christmas at Tunis with the Prime Minister, of the conference at Marakesh and of London. He asked us countless questions about Cairo. Then we drove down to the old white hotel where Headquarters are situated and found our way to our office on the first floor. It is well carpeted and furnished, much more comfortable than any office we have had before. The General's room has two doors, one into the ADC's room where Mark, Jack and Logan Schultz have desks, the other into my room where I am to keep the files. Beyond is a Map Room and rooms for the typists and orderlies. On the wall facing my desk is a huge map of the Mediterranean Theatre – stretching as far north as the Alps, south to the Atlas mountains, east to the Middle East and west to Gibraltar.

All through the afternoon visitors streamed in to see General Jumbo while we unpacked office gear and studied lists of the integrated staff. After work I walked up a narrow footpath to the cottage where Daphne and I are to live. It is very dirty and lined with a frightful wallpaper but has a bath and a wonderful view over the roofs of Algiers to the harbour which is crowded with warships, tugs and a submarine. We dined with the General who is delighted with his luxurious house. Very kindly he has asked us to dine with him till we can get some help. We talked about the battle for Italy and of General Eisenhower who was well loved by both Americans and English when he was here. Then we walked back to work on our cottage. Coco is very subdued after his journey.

19 January 1944   *Algiers*

Being new is exhausting: we must learn the names of a huge staff, study all files, discover who lives here – specially the

French élite – explore the food situation, go and see where the horses are kept and check they are all right, make friends with Army, Navy and Air Force heads and their staffs, and find out about shops and supplies. A lot of things, like the distribution of papers and some courtesies, seem to be different from those we are used to. American military police – called Snowdrops because of their white helmets – ask to see our passes incessantly. Now General Jumbo's car flies three little flags from its bonnet – the Union Jack, the Stars and Stripes and the Tricolour. Americans can use our NAAFI and we their Post Exchange. We are busy, too, preparing the offices for General Jumbo's American Deputy, General Devers, who is due to arrive. I am delighted to hear his Secretary is also a civilian. Daphne and I get stared at and whistled at wherever we go.

Later today General Jumbo flew to Italy and took Mark and Sergeant Trayler with him. The General will watch the Anzio landing from a destroyer.[1]

23 January 1944   *Algiers*

Whitaker and some of our luggage arrived from Cairo this morning. He'd enjoyed his first flight. Already he is cultivating an American drawl and greeted me with 'I sure am happy to know you'.

I drove out to the farm we have inherited from General Eisenhower – it lies eight miles west of Algiers close by the sea. I found Sergeant Higgins installed in rather uncomfortable quarters but cheerful as ever. General Jumbo's marvellous Arab had arrived safely (present of Saudi Arabia) and I rode him in a snaffle. Sergeant Higgins took a pony I'd not seen before and we cantered down an avenue of eucalyptus trees, skirted a little chateau and under a tunnel of pink and white blossom entered the forest where wide rides had been cut through the pine trees. Through gaps in the forest we saw two

[1] The Allied landing at Anzio – Operation Shingle – with a force under the American General Lucas took place 22 January.

large convoys slinking off the coast – on their way to Italy. Mimosa trees looked brilliant against the sea. We passed a troop of French soldiers who sang as they marched. We returned to the stables along the edge of the sea. Never have I seen such a galaxy of wild flowers. For a whole hour I forgot about the war. Jumbo's Arab is a marvellous ride and exceptionally good looking.

On my way to dinner I went with Arthur Forbes to visit M. and Mme. Schneider of Air France who live in two tiny rooms and are short of food. Algiers is so overcrowded that the French have difficulty in getting accommodation and stores, yet the Schneiders, a gay and intelligent couple, make the best of what they have and were great fun. Afterwards I dined with Dudley Clarke at the Cercle Interallie where we sat on cushions on the floor of a bare room and drank cocktails and then dined in a bare hall which used to be stables. Now I know why Arthur brought two turkeys with him to Algiers.

Dudley Clarke is one of our favourite people: quite small, brilliantly clever and imaginative and always on the edge of laughter. It is he who thinks up all the misleading things for our enemies, like the drowned British officer who was washed up on enemy shores with Top Secret papers in his uniform, all of which were clever fakes pointing in the wrong directions. Fake tanks and guns, probably made of cardboard, were one of his 'jokes' in the Western Desert, designed to mislead enemy reconnaissance planes. As always he made me laugh this evening. He has taken on Daphne as his secretary – she will not have a dull moment.

1 February 1944   *Algiers*

General Giraud came to see General Jumbo this morning. We watched his arrival from the flat roof outside our window. General Jumbo went down to the garden to meet him. A guard of honour was lined up and the band played the 'Marseillaise', 'The Star Spangled Banner' and 'God Save the King'. General Giraud reminded me of the photographs of French Generals in the last war. I was interested to see this old man. He and his family have suffered a great deal in the war. He was captured by the Germans in May 1940 and escaped in April 1942. His wife is still in German hands. His married daughter and her tiny children were taken prisoner by the Germans when they left Tunis and have not been heard of since. His youngest daughter is still in France.

Daphne and I dined with M. and Mme. Offroy – he is secretary of the Committee of National French Liberation. We met the de Lesseps there and a one-legged Frenchman who had escaped from France. We all sat down to dinner in our overcoats because they have no heating. We had an excellent dinner of sweet wine and fish for which they apologised profusely. The French cannot obtain spirits, meat or eggs here. When it was time to go home they refused to allow Daphne and me to walk up the lane alone to our cottage. They told us lurid stories of rape and robbery in Algiers.

4 February 1944   *Algiers*

I walked to the office in a fine drizzle and slithered down the steep road in my crêpe rubbersoles. Army vehicles roared by in an unending stream. French and Americans drive dangerously fast – I had to leap into the hedge several times to avoid being knocked down. In the office telegrams were coming in from Italy. The Germans are counter-attacking hard at Anzio and shelling the beaches. Casualties must be enormous. Virginia Cowles came into the office. She told us that she is trying to go to Yugoslavia and having a great deal of difficulty in getting there. She was wearing an American mackintosh over civilian clothes. She is not pretty but very attractive and has an awfully nice voice. We all liked her. Later General Anders, whose Polish Army is now in Italy, paid us a visit. He brought me a silver Polish badge with an eagle on it, the same as the one he wears himself.

I went riding in the forest with General Jumbo. He rode General Eisenhower's chestnut barb stallion. The General enjoyed himself – he talked about Gloucestershire and occasionally made hunting noises. Whenever we came to cross paths he asked which way I thought it best to go. If I said left, he went right. After a bit I got wise to this and so we both had our own way.

I dined with Captain Sanderson, Mr Duff Cooper's ADC, and met Eve Curie whom I last saw in Jerusalem on her way to Russia. She is shorter than me, very pretty and rather serious. She is extremely intelligent and speaks many languages. She told me in perfect English of her great journey from America, across Africa, Asia, India and China. She said that after she had written her book *Journey Amongst Warriors* she joined the ATS and worked her way up from the bottom. Now she is a Lieutenant in the French Army and does liaison work. We compared notes on whether it was best to be in uniform or civilian clothes in a war and agreed that there was little difference as the drawback of being a woman is always the same. I told her that Mary Alice, General Devers's American secretary, and I mind very much that we are nearly always left behind while the Aides take turns to go on trips. Our masters visit Italy very often and go to London and other places for conferences but though we keep the same hours as the Aides and do most of the spade work in the office we are generally left behind. No doubt poor Virginia Cowles suffers from the same disadvantage.

Today, after dropping leaflets warning Italian civilians to evacuate, we have blitzed the old Benedictine Monastery at Monte Cassino. It stands high above the town of Cassino and the Germans installed there can see every movement on the plain below and rake our advance with terrible fire.[1]

---

[1] In fact, as was later discovered, there were no Germans in the monastery at Cassino before it was bombed.

The weather is so bad that General Jumbo could not fly to Italy this morning. He dictated personal letters thanking his friends for their congratulations on his new job. Robert Harris and Margaretta Scott who are touring with an ENSA show called *Quiet Weekend* paid me a visit this evening. They told me their lodgings are very uncomfortable.

23 February 1944   *Algiers*

The weather seems dead against us. At Cassino and at Anzio we fight stubbornly on. The Germans show remarkable resistance.

Eve Curie gave a dinner party at a tiny restaurant called the Varsovie. We tapped on a door in a backstreet and found ourselves in a small room with half a dozen tables and a bar. An old Madame cooked dinner on the fire and served the food and drinks herself. We were crammed at two little tables covered with blue paper instead of cloths: Duff and Diana Cooper, Daphne, Mark, Eve, the American Counsellor and M. Palewski[1] who is on de Gaulle's personal staff. The food and drink were excellent but the conversation was rather precarious – there are so many fragile matters between the French, Americans and British these days particularly as regards the de Gaulle–Giraud controversy. Eve is a very adroit hostess. I sat next to Duff Cooper who occasionally slung a remark across the table where they were talking politics. After dinner Madame took two pictures off the wall and very shyly presented them to Diana and Eve. They were paintings of the German Embassy in Algiers and quite hideous but they were all she had to give. It was very touching but I had a struggle not to laugh. Where can Eve hang her picture of the German Embassy? After dinner Palewski dated me up. Interesting to see which he is after, me or General Jumbo. Behind his clever talk and charm there is a ruthlessness.

[1.] Gaston Palewski, half Polish and later de Gaulle's *chef de cabinet*. There had been great acrimony and rivalry between Giraud, a very senior general who had escaped from German captivity, and de Gaulle, a brilliantly political figure, for leadership of the French outside France. De Gaulle won.

We are now bombing targets in Germany from England and Italy. The weather is abominable. Fighting conditions at Cassino and Anzio must be appalling. People coming from Italy tell grim stories of mud, cold and casualties.

I lunched with General Catroux[1] who lives in an attractive white house just above our cottage. His Spahi guards wear blue uniforms, red cloaks and white headdresses. The General is short and slight and his face is remarkably wrinkled; he has such lines under his eyes that he looks dreadfully tired. We talked of Indo-China and Brazil where his son is going shortly. We were waited on by Indo-Chinese servants. After lunch the General took me upstairs to show me his family of Siamese cats. There were three generations of them, the kittens were still pure white. Then he took me across his garden to the stables to see the white Arab horses of his guards. He told me I could ride them whenever I like. General Catroux impressed me with his charm and shrewdness – I should think he is a brilliant diplomat.

This morning I typed an immensely long letter for General Jumbo to the CIGS – it is all about Cassino and Anzio, the Commanders, weather and green troops. He also wrote of the intricate political set-up here. It looks as if General Giraud is going to be levered out by General de Gaulle. The intrigue is so involved that it is hard for us British to get the rights and wrongs of it.

I lunched with the Schneiders who gave a big party considering the size of their room. I sat between General Clark and M. Massigli, French Foreign Secretary, who wears very thick glasses and speaks good English. We talked about Turkey. John de Salis upset his plate of soup in his lap. When everyone had left I stayed behind to talk to St Exupéry. He is short and broad

---

[1] Member of the French Committee of National Liberation.

and looks rather like a frog because of his prominent eyes. His conversation was very funny and very clever. I asked him about his air crew who carried goldfish in their plane to know which way up they were. After a while Mme. Schneider persuaded him to do his card tricks for which he is famous. He told me to choose a card and shuffle. Then he took the whole pack from me and without looking at it threw it into the air. The card I choose was the only one that fell face upwards on the floor. Again he told me to choose a card and shuffle. This time I had to place the whole pack on the table. He did not touch the cards. Then he told me how many cards I must count to reach the one I chose. He was always right. He did many tricks and they were fascinating. Either he hypnotises you or he is a magician.

10 March 1944   *Algiers*

Rain soaked the hills and flooded the valleys all through February. Now the winter is over and dwarf cyclamen, iris and violets are growing in the woods. In the fields there are cobalt blue lupins, red 'bacon and eggs', fat white daisies and a mass of other wild flowers. In the orchards and gardens fruit blossom, bougainvillaea, rambler roses and cascades of wistaria are in bloom. Dozens of silver balloons float lazily over the harbour under a high blue sky. It is hard to believe that over the water in Italy the slow struggles at Cassino and Anzio are still going on.

An amusing letter has come from Commander Butcher, Aide to General Eisenhower. He wrote that he was returning to us a collection of pictures which he took from the walls of the Supreme Allied Commander's house in Algiers and shipped home to the United States as souvenirs. He wrote that 'Ike' had found out that he had them and told him to return them at once. 'He gave me billy hell, and to think I wanted to take the fountain on the patio and could not get a packing case large enough. Just too bad.'

General Jumbo gave a big official dinner party. I sat between General Catroux and Mr Duff Cooper. I met Air Marshal Sir

John Slessor and Lady Maud Baillie head of the ATS. She wore a khaki tunic over a kilt. After dinner General Catroux wisely slipped away to work. The rest of us sat through an extraordinarily bad film. This new fashion of having a film after a dinner party is ghastly; most of them are duds but no one likes to walk out.

6 April 1944   *Algiers*

General Juin arrived today. He is a great soldier and unlike most of his countrymen manages to keep out of politics. The French row is breaking. De Gaulle has offered Giraud the post of Inspector General and Giraud has refused it. Really I think Giraud would prefer to retire and live in England but it seems that he cannot become reconciled to de Gaulle being Commander-in-Chief of the French Forces. Meanwhile, in the Middle East, trouble is looming amongst the Greeks in connection with the lack of co-operation between the Greek Government in Egypt and the guerrillas in Greece. The King of Greece is in London and will no doubt have to fly out to Cairo again. We are discussing whether or not to take Elba and also whether to move this vast Headquarters to Italy.

John Lascelles is coming over from Cairo as head of our new Joint Inter Services Secretariat. Liaison between military and political matters is badly needed. The machinery of this integrated Headquarters is complicated, specially as the Commanders-in-Chief move about a great deal. Admiral Cunningham has to be in Naples very often, and Air Marshal Slessor in Caserta where General Eaker's[1] Advance Headquarters are. Also a great deal of our work is connected with Mr Macmillan, British Resident Minister in North Africa, and Duff Cooper our Ambassador to the French, not to mention Mr Murphy the United States Ambassador and Roosevelt's special representative, and M. Bogomolof the Russian Ambassador. Apart from this, transport and supply, and ammunition and questions concerning the French and Polish

[1.] Commander Allied Air Forces, Mediterranean.

armies, our Mission to Yugoslavia and the Italians, who are now co-belligerents, concern both the military and political departments and badly need co-ordinating.

9 April 1944   *Algiers*

Telegrams are coming in from Egypt reporting the Greek mutiny. The crew of the Greek destroyer *Pindus* have thrown their Commander and all their officers overboard in Alexandria harbour.

Fitzroy Maclean arrived from Yugoslavia. He came up to my house for a bath, his first for many months. He told me that Tito is still living in a cave and spends a lot of his time in the bushes because of German air raids. Randolph Churchill lives in a house with six Croat girls and a pig. He has a beard. Tito is delighted with the jeep that General Jumbo has sent him. Yugoslavia is a cauldron of hate – the tribes all loathe each other.

Last night Eve Curie asked me to dine and brought all her guests up to drink in our cottage before dinner. She arrived with Virginia Cowles, Douglas Fairbanks Junior, Jock Whitney, Hervé Alphond, a French officer of Spahis and Mark. Hervé Alphond told me my drink was disgusting. I told him the alternative was milk. He refused it. Next he told me that our wallpaper was vile, that it was obvious I had chosen it myself. We all drove to a café near the sea for dinner and dined on prawns and politics. Somehow it was an uncomfortable evening. Hervé was rude to Virginia and to me but I got to like him. He has a brilliant and beastly façade and behind it a deal of kindness. I sat between the French officer who told me he had motor-cycled from Casablanca to Cairo before the war, and Jock Whitney who got hiccoughs. I enjoyed talking to them and we three avoided a heated political argument.

Lord Gort arrived this morning. He always remembers the orderlies, drivers and staff. He was charming to me. He enquired after Fuad again and then remembered he was dead.

I lunched with Douglas Fairbanks Junior at the American Naval Mess. We ate pork with jam and hot chocolate! Afterwards we sat in the sun and talked of California and films, politics and the war. He introduced me to Commander Cramer, an expert on explosives and mines. He had dull brown eyes, a thin sharp nose and never smiled. He reminded me of Buster Keaton. He had just returned from a trip to Washington, New Guinea and London where he gave expert advice on mines. He described his journey and his job in the most amusing way, an entertaining and doubtless a very brave man. Douglas took me over to his office and for a while we talked to the orderlies. He had a fine selection of maps and books and lent me *The History of the World*, a fascinating book printed in America which gave in alphabetical order a brief historical, geographical and political summary of every place in the world. Douglas Fairbanks seemed interested in everything, particularly the Navy, politics and the war. He speaks good French and was not in the least like a film star.

I dined with the Duff Coopers. Sir Noel Charles, our Ambassador to Italy, Fitzroy Maclean, Virginia Cowles and I had a great argument as to whether, if one could choose, one would prefer to be given the Victoria Cross or ten thousand pounds. I chose the ten thousand pounds which shocked everybody. I do not think one can judge bravery, seeing that you cannot tell how frightened people are. I am frightened of so many things; the sea, flying, reptiles, skyscrapers, making speeches, roller-coasters, caves, dentists etc. – I should have got a VC long ago.

27 April 1944   *Algiers*

Yesterday I had a day off. I took Coco down to the Casba to introduce him to an old grey parrot in the bird shop. Coco whistled in the jeep but when he saw the other parrot he became very silent. He looked most disconcerted. Perhaps he had thought he was the only parrot in the world.

Eve Curie and I drove out to General de Lattre de Tassigny's villa in the country for lunch. In the garden a lot of young French officers were sitting at trestle tables listening to a lecture: General de Lattre's Cadet School. The General came into the room after everyone else and his staff simply leapt to attention. He is dark, dapper, middling tall and exudes energy. I sat next to him and we talked in French about nothing in particular. I was grateful to be spared politics for once. He was very excited because he had just heard that his wife has escaped from France.

Since I arrived in Algiers I have been able to see for myself something of the predicament of people whose countries are overrun by Germans, a predicament we English can never quite understand. The French, Poles, Greeks and other nationalities I have met in the Mediterranean Theatre are nearly always cheerful. We meet them at work and at dinner parties but rarely discover the tragedies behind their façades. Nearly every week people manage to reach Algiers from occupied France. All too often I discover that these escapees are close relations to people I have met almost daily and who never mentioned their anxiety. No escapees talk of their adventures or their grim journey – it is kept quiet for fear of jeopardising the chances of thousands of others who are trying to get out. So often we have judged people as flippant – too often we have judged them as carefree. The French have taught me that behind the gayest faces lie the deepest tragedies. I admire them very much. Recently General Giraud's daughter, aged seventeen, travelled across France to leave her grandmother in a safe place. She then set out alone to walk across the Pyrenees and Spain. Somehow she reached Gibraltar from where she was flown to Algiers. In the war people seldom see each other working. They only meet at official functions and parties and in lobbies and judge each other on that. I think of all the nations the English are worst at judging others.

This evening Mark and Fitzroy and I rode in the forest.

Green lizards basked on the edge of the paths. The trees are at their best now; the acacias are frilly white and there are wild flowers everywhere. I hate to trample on them. Fitzroy has a bad liver so we tried to cure it by riding for miles across hills and valleys, jumping ditches and crawling through thick bramble hedges.

I dined with Admiral Troubridge who talked about Berlin before the war. He is always interesting and amusing. After dinner we sat on his terrace and listened to the nightingales. Flowers and trees, birds and animals are important to us all in wartime – they remind us of peace, gardens and happy days when we would be sure of tomorrows. I found myself thinking of the little dog Whitaker brought out of besieged Tobruk, of General Jumbo's great affection for his beautiful horse, and Coco who never fails to welcome me when I return from work. These silent allies are very precious.

Field Marshal Smuts has arrived to stay on his way to the Dominion Conference in London. He has a slight cold and was given a hot toddy before he went to bed. The Aides laced it with whisky and are now worried lest he wake up with a hangover. Field Marshal Smuts is a teetotaller.

30 April 1944   *Algiers*

There was great activity, and laughter, in our office this morning. General Jumbo was leaving at lunchtime for England to discuss the situation in Italy and the possibility of invading the South of France – the operation we call 'Anvil'. Mark was briefing Jackie[1] whose turn it is to accompany the General, and handing over wads of top secret papers. Jackie, wildly excited to be going home and appalled by his responsibilities, seemed unable to concentrate and kept dropping the papers and talking about his mother. Fitzroy, who was going with them, wandered about asking questions without waiting for the answers. All ranks were scribbling notes to their families for

[1] Jackie Wintour, General Jumbo's second ADC. There were two, Mark Chapman Walker being the senior.

Jackie to take home. Generals came in and out. Orderlies came in and out. Telephones pealed. News from everywhere poured in. Luggage appeared. To add to the turmoil there was a spare seat in the aeroplane and much talk of who should fill it. The General kindly offered it to me but though I long to see England again I am going to wait until Dan escapes.

When the General and Jack drove off there was a mountain of work to do: appointments to cancel, files and papers to retrieve and visitors to be seen and placate.

5 May 1944   *Algiers*

Daphne and I had a day off. We left for the farm at seven and rode out for two hours along the tracks and trails behind Guyoteville. There were convolvulus, deep blue pimpernels and regiments of thistles everywhere. Sergeant Higgins gave us breakfast in the farmyard and afterwards we changed in the saddle room and drove west along the coast road. We stopped at Trapaza to look at the Roman ruins in the hotel garden and then drove on through pleasant vineyards and hills. We met a gigantic swarm of locusts. They hit the car and fell in hundreds on the road behind us; one of them landed on Driver Olroyd's neck which horrified him. We reached Cherchell at lunch-time, a little old walled town with a fine gateway. In the centre of the town the trees are so old that their gnarled roots stand out of the pavements like elephants' feet. We lunched in an hotel which was really a French Officers' Mess and were offered fresh mackerel, an omelette or meat. Afterwards we swam in the little harbour and walked round the town. Cherchell has an air of a small garrison town in France; every officer had a wife or girlfriend with him. The war seemed very far away. On the way home we caught up with the locusts – they had travelled many miles towards Algiers. Farmers were hitting cans and tins in their fields to try and frighten them away from their carefully grown crops.

Late today General Jumbo arrived back from London. Jack Wintour came up to my cottage to tell me about the trip. He brought me some bluebells from Scotland. He said, 'It was the greatest week of my life . . . Mr Churchill was busy with the Dominions' Prime Ministers. General Jumbo saw the King and the Secretary of State for War and General Eisenhower who was in great heart . . . We have brought some sherry and bananas from Gibraltar. The tulips in St James's Park were wonderful. Everyone is working tremendously hard on the Second Front. We may get a few more landing craft and be able to put on a modified "Anvil".'

Jack exploded about Lady Wilson. He said, 'Mark warned me she is difficult but that's an understatement – she is impossible. Poor Jumbo is petrified of her. There were some ugly scenes when I was there – mostly about Patrick whom, she insists, we all neglect. I was very embarrassed several times and longed to crawl under a table. I regretted I'd left my tin hat behind.'

I didn't know much about Lady W. General Jumbo never speaks of her. But I have guessed she is rather peculiar because of the parcels of underclothes she sends Patrick in the diplomatic bag and the priceless instructions which come with them about where and when he should use them. None of us knows what is the matter with Patrick – only that he is 'delicate'. He is tall, stoops, has crestfallen hair, wears tin spectacles perched on a long, thin nose and is very moody. We take him along to parties to please the General and because he has no friends of his own. He belongs to the Rifle Brigade but lives with the General and has a small job at GHQ.

Today a sirocco bustled the trees in the garden. Algiers was hazy with dust. This wind is famous for its ill-tempered effect on people – it is said that Arabs murder their wives on the third day of it. Even parrots are silent.

General Jumbo is easy to work for. He gives short, clear orders and expects us to carry them out quickly and exactly. Always smiling and good-tempered he has a great sense of humour. He works very hard. He relies greatly on Mark who drafts most of his despatches and signals and organises his journeys and meetings. He is devoted to the Rifle Brigade from which he draws most of his staff. In spite of his size he gets around quickly.

9 May 1944   *Algiers*

Every minute of our day and evening is full. Early each morning Daphne and I walk down to the Headquarters, along the path we call Bond Street because the long grass sparkles with dew – like diamonds. I straighten up the office – say hello to the orderlies – sort out signals and despatches for the General, file papers, list priorities, organise visits, cars, visitors and stores, and arrange a few flowers. If there's time I go to the Map Room to see how things are going on in the rest of the world, specially the Far East. Problems are endless – this week: Should Rome be declared an Open City? Should compassionate postings be made easier? What is to be done about increasing desertions? And how about Italian prisoners of war – it seems wrong they are working side by side with Italians who are fighting for us? Shipping is forever a big problem: day-to-day maintenance is vital – supplies for Allied Armies in Italy for coming battles are top priority, and requirements for a possible 'Anvil' are too. And there are many other problems.

We hurry from early morning till late evening and then, if there is no official dinner, we dine in our cottage and usually invite Allied guests because we can get food which they can't. Even bully beef stew is welcome these days. Often we are asked out by our generous Allies. Our bath is in constant use by all ranks who bring their own towels. We can get soap from the NAAFI. Meanwhile we must write letters to people at home, wash and iron our clothes, get shoes cleaned and mended, wash our hair and visit the wounded. Visitors, on leave, are incessant at our cottage: as we have no spare beds friends arrive with sleeping bags and ask for space on our sitting room and passage floors. Most of them want a cooked breakfast which we leave them to make after we have gone to work.

227

Laughter and improvisation help us along. It's difficult to refuse to help in a war. Meanwhile news from the Front – of casualties and deaths – keeps arriving and sadness is never far away. None of us gets enough sleep.

13 May 1944   *Algiers*

Yesterday Daphne and I sang all the way down 'Bond Street' – it was such a beautiful, sparkling morning.

When I opened the door of my office I saw a signal lying on my desk and after tidying up a few things I sat down to read it. I heard the General arrive in his office but I just sat and reread the signal:

EYES ONLY   ALLIED FORCE HEADQUARTERS   SECRET

INCOMING MESSAGE

Dates 1 1 1925 May 1944.
Received 1 1 s036B.

From: Allied Armies in Italy

For: General Wilson's Eyes Only from General Alexander

Brigadier COMBE, Brigadier TODHUNTER and DAN RAN-FURLY arrived here this afternoon. They leave for ALGIERS tomorrow, 12th May, on Flight 328. Estimated time of arrival MAISON BLANCHE 17.20 hours. I know you will help COMBE and TODHUNTER to get home quickly.

Distribution:
1. Supreme Allied Commander (action)
2. Deputy Supreme Allied Commander
3. Chief of Staff
4. Lady Ranfurly

General Jumbo's bell rang but for the first time ever I did not leap to my feet and answer it. I just read the signal all over again. The General came into my office: 'It's been a long time, Hermione . . .' he began. And then he saw my face. 'You'd better go home,' he said, and patted my shoulder. 'You look as
228

if you've seen a vision.' He smiled so kindly and I suddenly realised I'd not stood up when he came in. I began to apologise but he shook his head, waved me away and quietly closed his door.

I ran all the way up 'Bond Street' and in at the door of the cottage to tell Whitaker. He burst into tears. We rang up Daphne and then started unpacking Dan's clothes which we'd brought from Cairo. We pressed and polished everything and laid them on my bed for Dan to see. He might have been away for a weekend. We forgot lunch but I rang the office to apologise for my absence. Mark promised me a car to meet Dan and said that he would collect Combe and Todhunter and take them to the General's house.

At five o'clock I was on the airfield. Overhead planes were circling, waiting for their turn to land. Most of them were Dakotas. One by one they landed. Some officers from headquarters came over: 'Meeting a VIP?' they asked. 'Yes,' I said, 'I am meeting a VIP.' They wandered off.

Dakota 328 made a perfect landing, blew clouds of dust and came to a standstill. I'd waited three years and one month for this arrival.

The doors were opened. Steps were run up. People began to walk down into the sunshine. I stood there transfixed and seconds turned into hours. Ted Todhunter and John Combe emerged and Mark welcomed them and drove them away to the General's house. I waved. I stood and waited but I began to sway and my eyes misted up. I did not see Dan getting out of the plane but, suddenly, his arms were around me . . . Heaven – is being together.

9

What Next?

When Dan arrived he looked thin and drawn. Only a few
things he does clue me how, for months, he has been living: he
smokes his cigarettes down to the tiniest stubs so they nearly
burn his finger-nails; he spreads his butter on bread or toast so
that you can hardly see it; and when we switch on the radio for
news he leaps up automatically to turn it down. So many things
we have grown used to are a surprise to him – jeeps and so on.
When we talk there is much he does not know about and
cannot easily follow. For two and half years he got only the
news we wrote in parables, or Italian propaganda. And for
the last ten months he has been out of touch with the war and
the world – hiding in the mountains under terrible conditions.

Yesterday we went to the General's house to say goodbye
to John Combe and Ted Todhunter who were being flown to
England. Then we went to the NAAFI to buy socks and shoes
and other kit for Dan. When he arrived his clothes were almost
rags. Even in rags Dan looks elegant.

Today I returned to the office and felt surprised to find the
war is still going on. General Jumbo was very kind. He said that
I could have indefinite leave to go to England with Dan and

that I could come back to my job afterwards. General George Clark wrote a paper to this effect:

> The Countess of Ranfurly, PA to the Supreme Allied Commander, Mediterranean Theatre of Operations, accompanied by her husband, The Earl of Ranfurly, a recently escaped Prisoner of War from Italy, is visiting the United Kingdom on leave. It is requested that she may, with her husband, be accorded facilities to return to AFHQ, BNAF, on conclusion of her leave.
>
> (Sd) J. G. W. CLARK, Lt. Gen.
> Chief Administrative Officer. AFHG.

We dined with the General and toasted the French and General Juin who have cut the Gustav Line in Italy. General Jumbo leaves for Caserta tomorrow. I am to hand over to Jean Thompson of the ATS who will do my work while I am away.

16 May 1944   *Algiers*

After dinner Dan told me how he got captured.[1] Whitaker came and sat with us to listen to the story:

> When General Neame took over command of Cyrenaica you'll remember that the Abyssinian war was still going on and that General Jumbo was taking an Expeditionary Force to Greece. We were left to hold Cyrenaica with the 9th Australian Division, an Indian Motor Brigade and part of General Gambier-Parry's Armoured Division. We were short of everything. General Neame always thought the enemy would attack and that this time there might be Germans to reckon with. I think I wrote and told you that General Wavell and General Dill, then CIGS, flew up to discuss this in March.
>
> On the 1st April the enemy launched an attack on our slender forces at Agheila. By April 6th we had fallen back. The Australian Division was holding a defensive position on the escarpment east of Barce and the Armoured Division were swinging back on the El Abiar–Mekili Axis before

---

[1] I wrote down Dan's story in shorthand then typed it out later for his Mother.

German armoured thrusts in the south. The Indian Motor Brigade was at Mekili. At our Operational Headquarters at Maraua it was exceedingly difficult to keep abreast with the situation as we only had one wireless set, so on the morning of April 6th General Neame and I went over to the 9th Australian Headquarters to see General Morshead. Later we looked for General Gambier-Parry but he was on the move and we failed to find him. It was very hot and our car boiled incessantly. At six-thirty we arrived back at Maraua where General Dick O'Connor and Brigadier John Combe were waiting anxiously. We tried again to telephone our Rear Headquarters at Derna Aerodrome and to get the Armoured Division on the wireless but they were both moving and we failed to contact them. While we were eating bully, General Morshead came in with a bottle of whisky; he was cheerful as ever and said his Division was packed up and ready to move.

At eight-thirty that night we left Maraua and set out for Temimi. General Neame drove his car and took General O'Connor, Brigadier Combe and a driver with him. I followed with two soldiers and all the kit in a Ford Mercury van. I had to drive like hell to keep up with the General. We were stopped many times by traffic blocks on the road and it took two hours to reach Giovanni Berta. A Military Policeman directed us off the main road on to a desert track which bypasses Derna. The dust was awful and there was an immense amount of traffic. After an hour, when we were held up for several minutes, I got out of the van and walked forward to the General's car. John Combe climbed out to talk to me and just as we met we heard a man shouting. It was very dark and we could see nothing. Suddenly a figure loomed out of the blackness and the next thing I knew was that he had stuck a tommy gun at my middle. He shouted something incomprehensible and then more figures appeared. They were Germans. I heard John Combe whispering to the Generals in the car to get down on the floor and take their badges of rank off. More Germans came and ordered the others out of the car. They herded us all into a nearby hollow. We found a lot more British there. We were surrounded by machine guns on fixed lines and guarded by sentries armed with tommy guns. When anyone moved tracer bullets sprayed in every direction; it was impossible to escape.

All through the night we stayed there praying that the Australian Division, which was behind us, would come along. When dawn came we saw that we had been ambushed by a

17. Dudley Clarke. A genius of deception, his job was to confuse the enemy.
He did. My sister Daphne was his secretary

18. His Majesty King George VI gave Winston Churchill the Crusader's Sword
to present to Stalin at the Tehran Conference in 1943
after the Russians successfully defended Stalingrad

19. *Jumbo, the Supreme Allied Commander, loved to ride in the forests around Algiers on his beautiful horse, the present from Saudi Arabia*

20. *General Sir Adrian Carton de Wiart VC, a prisoner with Dan, was let out first as proof of Italy's wish for an Armistice*

21 and 22.
After months of hazard,
Dan, with Brigadiers
Combe and Todhunter,
reached our lines

23. *Sometimes, the staff worried lest Jumbo get stuck getting in and out of planes*

24. *Dan flew off to Yugoslavia to join Fitzroy Maclean's mission in late 1944*

25. *His Majesty King George VI with General Alexander inspecting Allied Forces in Italy, 1944*

26. *We returned to Athens very soon after the Germans retreated in 1944*

27. *The top brass, American and English – (from left) Admiral Hewitt,
General Eaker, Air Marshal Slessor, General Alexander, General Cannon,
General Jumbo, Admiral John Cunningham – the gods we served*

28. *Dining at the US Air Force Mess at Caserta. On my left is General Cannon and
General Eaker is at the head of the table. Hearing the news was always inspiring
but often sad – every day there were new triumphs and tragedies*

29. *General Jumbo and General Alexander swapping news just before General Alexander became Supreme Allied Commander when General Jumbo went to Washington*

30. *A miracle – Dan gets a wonderful job in the City*

31. *We lived happily ever after in England, and with a spell of service in the Bahamas*

32. *Now like Dan's granny – eighty but active*

small German column with a few tanks, armoured cars and half-track vehicles and several hundred men. For three nights we stayed in that hollow. On the third day we were taken in trucks to Derna and handed over to the Italians. When the Generals' identities were discovered they were told that they would be flown to Europe at once. That night we plotted to take the plane over in mid-air. General O'Connor would take an airman as ADC and General Neame would take me. We reckoned that if the whole party went in one plane there would not be room for more than four guards and that once we had disposed of them we could force the pilot to hand over the controls. We rehearsed our plan from all angles taking into consideration every possible seating arrangement on the plane. We had one revolver which was strapped to a very private part of General O'Connor's anatomy. My job was to knock out one of the guards. It was exciting waiting.

When the dawn came an Italian officer told us that only the Generals would go by air. Our plan had failed. The Generals went off that morning and the rest of us were put in trucks, twenty in each, and taken to Bengazi. We remained there a week in appalling conditions. Forty or fifty officers were crowded into each small hut and not allowed out for anything. There were no washing arrangements and we were given a dog biscuit and a tin of bully between two of us a day. We were terribly thirsty as they gave us practically no drinking water. We all got dysentery. The Italians would do nothing for us unless the Germans were around. At the end of a week we were put into rows and rows of Fiat lorries. Nigel Strutt, who had lost an eye and was lame, came with me. We drove for five days and were not allowed off the trucks for anything, except at night when we drew up and lay down on the ground. We became quite numb from being jolted and cramped and from getting so little to eat and drink. We were taken to Subrato, twenty miles beyond Tripoli, and put in prisoner of war cages. We were given two plates of soup a day and became very weak. The Italians treated us abominably; they even stole things off the prisoners. I reported this and was sent to the orderly room. The Camp Commandant gave the thieves six months and me two packets of cigarettes; he delivered the sentence lying in bed.

After ten days at Subrato we were put on a train and taken to Tripoli. Our men were locked in trucks with the windows clamped down – forty in each truck. It was terribly hot. We were marched five miles from Tripoli to the docks and put on a ship. Much to our surprise we were given first-class cabins and good food and were allowed on deck for exercise. A German officer came every day, clicked his heels, and offered us cigarettes. In three days we reached Naples. We were taken across the town in buses. I became ill on the slow train journey north and had the utmost difficulty in marching five miles from the station to Sulmona prison camp. That was the bloodiest month I ever spent.

Whitaker and I stared at each other in horror as Dan talked in his straight, unostentatious way.

19 May 1944   *s.s. Arundel Castle*

Great news: we have captured Cassino. The Poles took Monastery Hill. How marvellous and how brave. It must have been a hideous struggle. I hope General Anders is all right.

Today Dan and I drove down the steep twisting road to the docks and threaded our way past iron derricks and great wharfs to the Master of the Port's hut where a launch lay alongside. We chugged out past a French destroyer and a hospital ship to the *Arundel Castle*. Nearby lay the *Altmark*, a Swedish ship just back from Marseilles carrying some 850 British wounded prisoners of war who are being repatriated.

From the boat deck we saw many ships lying inside the submarine net, their balloons straining lazily on their cables. The white houses of Algiers rise steeply above the harbour and we picked out our cottage high on the hill. It looked the size of a cigarette box. After boat drill in life-belts and a quick lunch we stayed on deck and watched Algiers and the forest disappear. Out at sea we joined twelve large liners and a destroyer escort.

This ship is crowded with a great many Italian prisoners who are being taken to England to work as a Pioneer Corps: some survivors from a ship which was sunk off Algiers recently; British soldiers going home on leave or being retired; two murderers who are returning to do 'life'; and a considerable and very nice crew. The Captain told us it will take about a week to reach England – he is making a great detour in the

Atlantic for reasons he explained. I am anxious to reach home in time for the great day but can't share this impatience with anyone.

Dan and I spend most of our time in our tiny single cabin which has two bunks and only enough floor space for one to stand at a time. Everywhere else on the boat is overcrowded and noisy – the Italians sing and play their mouth organs all the time, poor devils. At night when the ship is blacked out it is incredibly hot but Dan and I are sublimely happy. I try not to think about the Atlantic, the *Empress of Britain* and Toby . . . Our Steward advised us to sleep in our clothes.

Today Dan told me of his escape and I wrote it in shorthand and then typed it out on my portable typewriter to show his Mother:

On the evening of 8th September 1943 we were playing bridge when the Italian Commandant came into the castle and told us that an Armistice had been made with the Allies. We were all terribly excited. Early next morning General Neame saw the prison Commandant and demanded that the sentries be taken off the walls and the gates opened. The Commandant refused to do this but after an argument consented to face them outwards in case the Germans should come; he also agreed to get in touch with the Commanding General in Florence at once. By this time we had fetched money from our secret hiding places and collected all the stores and civilian clothes we could muster. Later in the day the Commandant returned to say that the Commanding General had ordered that we should remain in the camp but we were on no account to fall into German hands. We at once made plans with the Commandant so that we could block the main entrance if the Germans came and escape by a ladder which was placed against the battlements. At dusk Ted Todhunter and I pushed our way out of the camp, past the sentries and listened to the BBC news in the guard room – the first time we had heard it for years. That night we hardly slept at all, the suspense was devastating and the Italian sentries reported movements of big convoys of vehicles through Florence and the valley below us. We watched from the tower of the castle.

On the 10th the Commanding General in Florence sent

two lorries to take us to his Headquarters. We wore our
British uniforms; our haversacks were filled with escape
rations and our few civilian clothes. As we came into
Florence people crowded the streets and cheered us. Perhaps
they thought we were the vanguard of the British Army.
German Officers were driving about in their staff cars. We still
had a guard, an armed Italian Officer and a Sergeant in each
lorry. On arrival at Italian Headquarters Italian Officers and
German liaison Officers craned out of the windows to see us.
The General said that he had been given orders that we were
not to fall into German hands and that he was to defend
Florence against the Germans. As he had no troops, arms or
ammunition and there were two German columns within
half an hour of the city the only thing he could do was to send
us south by train. He asked if we had any money or civilian
clothes and was astounded that we had both: he had searched
the castle so regularly for them.

We drove to the station, dumped our kit on the platform
and began to change into our civilian clothes. The Italians
on the station thought this was a great joke. They locked the
gates in case the Germans should arrive and swopped our
uniforms for some of their clothes. Cigarettes and chocolates
were bartered for caps and coats. I got an old tweed coat and
a ticket collector's cap for a hundred cigarettes. By the time
we had finished we looked an extraordinary sight. The train
took two hours to arrive. Waiting was terrible.

Our first stop was Arezzo where the Italian Commander had
been given orders to meet us. He told us that the Germans
had cut the railway line at Chiusi a few miles to the south and
we could go no further by train. We asked him to find billets
for us in neighbouring farms but he piled every difficulty in
the way. The Germans were so close his one idea was to be rid of
us. After an hour or more of useless argument an officer
rushed into the room and said that the Prefect of Fascist
Police was outside. The Commandant nearly died of fright.
Before any of us could do anything the Prefect came in. He
said he knew who we were. There was an uncomfortable
silence and then he said he had come to help us. He was
immensely practical and in a few minutes he had made a plan.
He said we must hide till dusk when he would send transport
to take us to a monastery in the mountains. The monks would
hide and feed us. We walked out through the streets of Arezzo
in small parties. Three miles down the main road we turned
off into the fields which, at that time, were high with Indian

corn. We spent an uneasy afternoon wondering whether the Fascist would betray us.

At seven o'clock we cautiously approached the rendezvous and were all surprised to find trucks waiting for us. We piled in and started off along the main road from Arezzo to Bibbiena where we branched off into the mountains. At the Monastery of Camaldoli we were given a genuine welcome by white Benedictine monks who had prepared us a huge meal, and comfortable rooms. Though the monastery was high up in the mountains it was easily accessible from two directions so General Neame arranged a system of watches from positions where traffic could be spotted some minutes before it arrived. Nighttime was, of course, the most dangerous and I for one felt very uneasy all the time we were at Camaldoli. Ted Todhunter discovered a Dutch Baron who lived with his English wife about three miles down the road and he and Dick O'Connor went every day to listen to the news on their wireless. Soon we realised that the Allies were not advancing as fast as we had been led to expect by the BBC. Meanwhile more and more German convoys moved along the valley below the monastery. We decided to go further into the Appennines, away from roads and communications.

On September 14th four Generals went to the Monastery of Eremo further up the mountain to keep some contact with the outer world. The rest of us walked over the watershed and down into Romagna. A monk called Don Leone, who had a flowing beard and twinkling eyes and carried in his haversack a flask of the strongest wine, guided our party over precipitous barren country to some poor farms on a windy ridge. We all slept in a tiny schoolhouse. It was a terrible climb for Brigadier Armstrong who has a game leg. There was not enough food for our large party to live in that miserable village so we dispersed in small parties and stayed in rich farms over a district of ten miles. The Generals from Eremo joined us. Someone had betrayed them and they only just escaped from the monastery before the Germans arrived. The news they brought was dismal. The Germans were strongly reinforcing Italy, the possibility of the country falling into Allied hands quickly was gone. We must prepare ourselves to make our way south on foot. Somehow we must keep out of German hands until we could get more concrete news of the military situation.

General Neame and I went to live in a village called Segatina which was typical of most of these mountain villages. A jumble of grey broken down houses lay along a bare ridge below steep wooded mountains. Each house was one storey high and the ground floor was divided between the kitchen and cowsheds. To our English way of thinking the houses were filthy. There were no sanitary arrangements of any kind. A nearby path on a steep slope had for centuries been used as a rubbish dump and local lavatory. Flies abounded. Several families lived in each house, all of them worked on the land. Every inch of the hillside was ploughed and terraced. Most families owned two oxen and in the village street were some chestnut trees which were highly valued. Our hosts, the Rossis, owned some beehives and so were richer than the other villagers. Their house had a large kitchen with a deep fireplace over which hung a copper pot on a long chain. The fire was kept smouldering by putting one end of the branch of a tree in it, the other end stuck out into the room. The furniture was home made; the food was either soup with macaroni or spaghetti. On Sundays and Feast Days we sometimes had a rabbit or even a chicken. General Neame and I were often hungry. In the house where Air Marshal Boyd lived they had polenta frequently – this is made from the flour of Indian corn. It was poured on to the table and a few odds and ends such as tomato and scraps of meat were spread on top of it. Then the whole family sat round with a fork apiece and ate their way to the middle.

When our village learned that the Germans were at Eremo they became frightened so we moved out into the woods where we built two huts of fir branches. Eight of us slept in each hut. During the day we went to the village to get meals. On the 29th September, when we had just sat down to eat, villagers reported that lorries had arrived on the timber road a mile away. We left hurriedly, and climbed the path on the opposite face of the hill to the road and lay down and waited. We watched a party of men crossing the flooded stream in the valley. When they reached the path below us we saw they were Germans. It was pouring with rain. They squelched heavily through the mud loaded with packs and carrying light automatics. We crept back into the woods and before we had gone far we heard machine guns in the village. When night fell some villagers arrived with food for us. They told us we had been betrayed but the Germans had shot no one, they had only fired at some young men who ran away.

It was no longer safe for us to remain at Segatina so once more we set out in search of shelter. We decided to remain in the same district because we had got in touch with an agent who had recently come from the British lines, and with a political organisation of anti-Fascists who supplied us with money, clothes and boots and had a clandestine wireless. We had hardly reached Rio Salso when a message arrived saying an agent had come to help the Generals escape. He had a rendezvous with a submarine on the Adriatic coast seventy miles away in three days' time. The three most senior officers, General Neame, General O'Connor and Air Marshal Boyd set off at once to make the attempt on foot and by bicycle after making hurried plans for the rest of us to remain where we were till the agent came back for us.

For the next four months I stayed at Rio Salso. Sometimes I slept in a barn belonging to Nereo Bertazzoni who lived with his family and niece Theresa in the 'Palace', otherwise I slept in the house of a poor widowed woman who lived opposite to Nereo. The Bertazzoni family were wonderfully kind to me. They always fed me. When food was short Theresa gave me a double helping because she said I was twice as large as they. Often there was nothing to eat. On one occasion she killed the cat which we ate with considerable pleasure. Its skin was sold for one hundred lire. Once a week the family went to market some eight miles away over the mountains. They always bought some little luxury for me such as a packet of cigarettes. My life became bound up in the pattern of the village. We breakfasted off bread, and coffee made from acorns or barley. The morning was whiled away talking to the villagers or helping with baking or washing. There was always a rumour to discuss which had gained fantasy as it travelled round the mountains. We lunched off soup and bread and then I would walk over to one of the neighbouring farms to discuss plans with the Generals. At dusk we supped off bread and sometimes a bit of rabbit. On the 5th November we were told the agent had come back for us and we walked for fourteen miles over the mountains only to find it was a false alarm. Imperceptibly we found ourselves in the grip of winter. Snow came and it was no longer possible to cross the mountain passes. We settled down to wait for the spring. Time seemed to stand still.

A band of Partisans had formed in the neighbourhood. They were of all nationalities, Italians, Poles, Yugoslavs, a few German deserters and some fifty escaped Russian prisoners. They roamed the mountains, looting the peasants' dwindling stocks of food, stealing their beasts and making

raids on the towns in the valleys and plains. They murdered
Fascist garrisons and officials. No quarter was asked or given
on either side. They spent most of their time looting. The
Russians, though professed Communists, always refused to
share their loot. At the end of January the Anzio landing
took place and the Germans brought their troops into Italy
from Greece. On their way to Anzio one battalion was
detrained at Forli to deal with our particular band of
Partisans. Someone warned the Partisans to clear out of the
district, but no one warned us. On the night of 29th January I
was asleep in the widow's house when she woke me saying
there was a crowd of people outside her door. I got out of bed,
dressed and tiptoed downstairs. German officers were in the
kitchen, their maps spread out on the table. I crept to the back
door; Germans were smoking on the step. I went back to my
room and opened the window. More Germans were lolling
against the wall beneath. I was terrified for the widow and
her three daughters. If I was found I would be retaken
prisoner but they would be shot. There was nowhere to hide
so I got back into bed where my tallness would be less noticed.

The women were wonderfully brave. They talked to the
Germans and every now and then one of them came upstairs
to tell me what was happening. After what seemed an eternity
I heard sharp German words of command, the shuffle of
soldiers' feet and the metallic clanking of equipment and
weapons. I lay stiff wondering whether they would come
upstairs. They went out into the street and started to move off
in single file. There were about three hundred of them and
by the time the last one had left it was too late for me to warn
the other farmhouses. All night we watched and waited.
When dawn came Rudolph Vaughan and I filled our pockets
with bread and climbed to a ridge where there was plenty of
cover so that we could watch the neighbouring valleys. We saw
squads of Germans moving about in single file. Shouts echoed
up and down the valley with occasional bursts of light
automatic. All day we watched. When night came we
returned to Rio Salso. As we approached the village we saw the
German column winding up the valley towards us. We hid in
thick scrub. To our relief they did not halt at the village but
pushed on over the pass out of the valley. The German
expedition had been unsuccessful; no one had been killed
and only two British soldiers taken prisoner. Some of the
Generals spent an unpleasant day with Germans in their
houses; John Combe had been fired at but escaped. For the

next two or three weeks I stayed in a lonely barn on the hillside two miles away. The nights seemed very long, and were exceedingly uncomfortable until Nereo managed to buy me some poison to kill the rats and mice that swarmed there.

All our plans waited on the weather. It was not until the beginning of March when the thaw came that Rudolph Vaughan, John Combe, Ted Todhunter, Guy Ruggles-Brise and myself set out on our long trek south. Two young officers who had been with the Partisans during the last few months came with us; they were John Kerin, a big burly Irish Sapper, and Jack Reiter, an American air force officer who had baled out of his plane over Foggia and dislocated both his thighs on landing. Before his legs had properly mended he escaped from an Italian prison hospital because there was talk of his being moved to Germany. He had managed to get fairly fit but his thighs were still partly dislocated. We left Rio Salso on the 5th March in a snowstorm. We got held up at Santa Sofia for a whole week because the snow was so deep. On March 12th we started again. We had to walk 250 miles across high mountains before the 18th March to keep our rendezvous with the agents on the coast. We made very slow progress: there were main roads and rivers to cross and poor Rudolph Vaughan fell every few hundred yards, his game leg went through the snow like a snow-plough. He and Jack Reiter were an inspiration to us all. On the first day we covered the best part of twenty-eight miles as the crow flies. That night I slept on a stone floor and slept well. Next morning Rudolph was so stiff we doubted if we could get him going. We were in the High Appennies and the snow had a hard crust which one stepped through sometimes up to one's thighs. On the third morning we split up into a fit party and an unfit party, hoping that the former would be able to contact the agents and get them to wait for the others. I went with the unfit party. With my long legs I could eliminate many delays by going forward to find out the lie of the land. It was a point of honour that we should arrive not far behind the others. I will pass briefly over the next four days. We had a terrible journey; Jack and Rudolph were completely exhausted. Suffice to say that on one day we walked thirty-three miles and on the eighteenth we arrived at the rendezvous two hours before the fit ones.

Our troubles were not at an end. We were told we must go another thirty-two miles by the next evening. We managed to hire a pony and trap to take Rudolph and Jack the first ten miles. We started at four in the morning. We were now in the foothills of the mountains and had to keep to secondary roads to avoid trouble. This time my little party failed. We slept that night in a cowstall and caught the others up at the rendezvous in the morning. A lorry was waiting for us and we climbed in and lay down on the floor. We drove to the Tenna valley from where we were to make our final attempt to get through the lines by submarine or MTB. Passing through villages we felt painfully obvious to the people who hung out of upper windows. However no comments were made: the Italian people had become used to the underground business long ago.

During the next six weeks, in the dark periods of the moon, we made eight or nine rendezvous on the beach. Italian Partisans who had wireless sets in the mountains informed us when to go. We went in single file through fields to the coast eight miles away. We had to cross the main road and the railway which ran along the edge of the sea. At night the road was crowded with German transport and the railway was patrolled. We would lie down on the narrow strip between the railway and the sea while one of the agents went forward to do the necessary signalling. Sometimes we heard the powerful engines of an MTB but they never seemed to see our signals. Sometimes when we least wanted illuminating the RAF dropped flares by the Tenna bridge which seemed to be one of their particular objectives at that time. We whistled the German song 'Lili Marlene' to recognise each other in the dark. Each time we were disappointed and had to make the whole risky journey back again. About this time we were joined by Roger Cagnazzo, a Jew, and one of the most gallant men I ever met. He told us that after many adventures he had succeeded in getting General Neame, General O'Connor and Air Marshal Boyd through the lines. Now he had come back to help us. In consultation with him we decided to purchase or steal a sailing boat. Fishing had been abandoned because of Allied air attacks and for six months or more all the boats were in dry dock or laid up on the sand. We had a hard time to find one and to get a mast, rudder and sails for it. We moved down to a house by the Tenna bridge where lived the old Count and Countess of Salvadore. The Countess had already spent two years in a concentration camp for her pro-Allied sympathies but, nothing daunted, she had us all to stay while we were getting the boat ready.

On the evening of May 10th we slipped across the road and

collected various pieces for the ship. Jack Reiter and I took the mast. We passed under the railway by a culvert to the shore. The moon had not yet risen but we felt remarkably conspicuous standing there a couple of hundred yards away from the German convoys which rolled unceasingly up and down the road. We put the mast in place and the rudder. But when we came to move the boat it would not budge. For half an hour we sweated and pulled and pushed. Gradually the moon began to rise. Slowly inch by inch we managed to shift it. Finally we got it into the sea. It floated. We got the sails up and were caught before a stiff breeze but then we discovered the boat was as waterproof as a sieve. If one put one's foot on the bottom it went through. We began to bale. The wind freshened and blew hard. Everyone began to be sick. Water crept up above our ankles. We worked like demons to bale it out. Then the mast broke and went over the side. After half an hour of sweating and cursing we hauled it back. British night-fighters zoomed over like pale ghosts. We continued on our way. So we sailed and baled through the night. When dawn came we saw the tops of the Miella mountains above the horizon and knew we had travelled about seventy miles. The wind dropped when we were exactly off the end of the front line and we were becalmed. We got oars out and rowed. All the time we baled. Flights of RAF came over. Two Kittyhawks roared down to investigate us. We waved our shirts and prayed they would not strafe us. After circling three or four times at water level they left us alone. All through the day we rowed. We could see the shells falling on either side of the line. It seemed endless. In the early afternoon we saw some fishing boats and made towards them. By now we were almost waterlogged. One of them took us in tow. Somehow we reached Ortona harbour. It was wonderful to go ashore and feel safe.

30 May 1944   *On the train to London*

After being away from England for four and a quarter years it was exciting to sail up the Firth of Clyde on a fine summer evening. We passed Ailsa Craig. Seagulls escorted us home. A fleet of warships passed us – sailing out to sea: mine-sweepers, eight destroyers, four frigates, two cruisers and an aircraft carrier. The Italians chattered louder than ever and Dan, who understands Italian, said they were astounded to see these ships when they'd been told so often that the British Navy had been sunk. Ahead of us other liners in our convoy began dropping their anchors and then came the rattle of our own anchor being lowered. It was nearly dark. There were no lights on the shores. We are home, we are safe – we are together . . .

We woke early and found the ship in pandemonium. After seeing Immigration and Customs officers we hauled our luggage along the decks and over the gangway down to a dirty quay. No porter, no taxis – only groups of dock-hands slouching about in their lunch break with hands in pockets, caps tilted over their eyes and tired, discontented expressions on their faces. We asked a group of them if taxis came to the docks but none of them answered and one spat at us. Maybe they thought we'd been on a Mediterranean cruise. We moved away and sat down on our baggage and waited – happy as grigs. After a long wait a small car arrived driven by a cheerful, pretty woman, who said she was doing taxi work. She drove us to the station where we discovered we must wait for the night train to London. By a miracle we met Bill Stirling on the platform and he insisted he drive us to his house, Keir, near Dunblane, to see Susan and their newly born daughter, Hannah. Their garden, with great banks of azaleas, rhododendrons and a galaxy of other shrubs and flowers, was a feast for us. Perhaps, in the long time we've been away, we only remembered the lovely things at home – lawns, herbaceous borders, and fields thick with buttercups and daisies where cows cluster for shade under wonderful trees.

31 May 1944   *London*

Early this morning we reached London and went straight to Claridge's Hotel. The concierge, the hall porter and the liftman gave us a marvellous welcome; we were surprised they should remember us. We have a lovely room on the eighth floor from where we can see plenty of sky, which is going to be important. After a bath and breakfast we sped off to Oxford to see Cynthia [my sister] who is dangerously ill from TB of the lining of her tummy for which there is no sure cure. Her appearance stunned us: she is skeleton thin and her teeth jut out of her emaciated face like a corpse. I prayed she did not see my tears. Brave as always, she talked and laughed with us but we were not allowed to stay long. All round her pretty, peaceful cottage Spitfires were half-hidden under the trees. The countryside was as beautiful as ever, though much land has been ploughed up and alongside most roads are ammunition dumps. London seems smaller. Perhaps this is because there is much less traffic. Petrol rationing, food rationing, clothes rationing, the black-out and air-raid alarms have changed everything – even the way we think and behave.

2 June 1944   *London*

Yesterday we went by train to Melton Mowbray to see Hilda [Dan's Mother] who is pretty and cheerful as ever. Now she has no one to help with her house and garden but still she finds time to do war work. She took us out to lunch in a pony cart and we had roast beef and gooseberry pie. We'd forgotten both – long ago. I gave her my typed copies of Dan's capture and escape.

Today we went to the Pantechnicon where all our possessions are stored: furniture, china, glass, silver, clothes – and wedding presents, many of which were still in their gift wrappings with cards attached. We'd forgotten most things. We took away a few clothes but left everything else to stay stored till the war ends – hoping the Pantechnicon won't be bombed.

6 June 1944   *London*

Last night we set our alarm to wake us before dawn. This morning it was dark when we climbed out of bed, drew back the curtains and leaned out on the smutty ledge of our windowsill. Quite soon it seemed as if the whole vault of heaven was vibrating with the roar of aeroplanes. As it grew light we began to see them – great formations of bombers heading for Europe. It was a magnificent and moving sight and we watched

– fascinated – with thoughts flashing through our heads: how terrible what they must do; pray God they may return safely; can this be the beginning of the end of the war; so Overlord has started, it's not a secret any more; when the sun comes up every plane will be a target; in a few minutes they'll be over enemy territory . . .

At eight o'clock the waiter wheeled in our breakfast. 'Kippers for breakfast and the Invasion's on,' he said, and gently closed the door. When we went downstairs nothing and nobody seemed different: the lift-man was arguing with a bell hop about football; the hall porter was booking theatre tickets; the concierge at the front door said, 'It looks like rain.' Only in the evening, when we waited in a huge queue to buy an evening paper, did we see that Londoners were aware of the Invasion and anxious to know how the battle for Europe was going.

14 June 1944   *London*

Our leave is going too quickly. We've been rather overwhelmed by visits from friends and relations – many of these 'drop in' at cocktail time. Now Dan and I invent dinner dates and leave the hotel at 7.45, walk round the block, and then return to the hotel at 8 p.m. to dine alone.

Lately: We lunched with Bill Astor who was in a fuss because it is being said that his mother, Nancy, is responsible for having all the brothels in Cairo closed. Surely this must be a joke?

My Aunt Mary came to see us with a bruise on her forehead. She told us she heard a noise in the night, crept to her bedroom window, peered out – and bumped heads with a burglar coming up a ladder. The burglar slid down and ran away.

Hervé Alphond came for a drink and told us of the French crisis – it seems that de Gaulle and the French Prime Minister have quarrelled.

We dined with the Woodruffs and Evelyn Waugh who, like Bill Stirling, has received a 'bowler hat'. A hilarious evening: Evelyn criticised nearly all VIPs except God.

Stephen [Dan's half-brother] came from Harrow School to

see us and we gave him lunch and afterwards took him to see a film, *The Way Ahead*. He insisted on having tea at the Piccadilly Hotel to hear a 'hot' band, an ear-splitting session.

We paid a short visit to General Neame and his wife in their pretty house in Kent and Dan and he talked of their escapes. They have two stuffed tigers in their sitting room. Their house is close by an aerodrome and it was difficult to talk because planes kept returning from bombing France. We lunched with little Aunt Puss and Alan Lascelles – both so well informed and interesting. Aunt Puss is still in waiting to Queen Mary and so spends a lot of time at Badminton. I rang up Whitaker's brother, Nin, in Sunderland and gave him news. Poor Dan has paid several visits to the dentist.

17 June 1944   *London*

Last night we went to stay with Terence Hone, Dan's farmer friend, who had offered to take us to the Derby at Newmarket. Today we set off early in a lorry loaded with sand. There was little traffic on the way but as we drew near Newmarket hundreds of people were walking, bicycling and hitch-hiking to the races. Soon the back of our lorry, the running boards, the roof of our cab and even the bonnet were festooned with bodies. We had a splendid day and saw a lot of friends. Ocean Swell won the Derby.

Back in London a note was brought to us by a pilot from Algiers – it was from Mark and Jack:

In Italy we're fighting in the Alban Hills. The Appian Way over the Ponteen Marshes is practically undamaged but in the Liri Valley on Highway 6 the road and railway have been demolished. We've taken Rome which is hardly damaged – the water supply is working and hotels are open. Germans raided Tito's headquarters and he had a narrow escape. 'Monty' has been staying in your cottage. Whitaker and Coco are well. We all miss you.

P.S. Look out. Lady Wilson is bombarding Jumbo with vitriolic letters against you. She seems determined to make Jumbo sack you. As she doesn't even know you this is

247

ludicrous but her avalanche of letters upset Jumbo and today he said, 'Hermione is invaluable – but I must get some peace . . .' Lady W says you are a terrible character and bad for Patrick to know!

A new kind of German aircraft is bombing London; it is unmanned, very noisy and rather alarming.[1]

25 June 1944 *London*

When Dan arranged with Fitzroy Maclean to join the Mission to Yugoslavia I was appalled because the situation there is so complicated and dangerous, and because such ghastly atrocities are rife there. Our difficulty is that if he stays in Europe we won't meet again till the end of the war – and God alone knows when that may be. We are not allowed to serve in the same country, so that rules out Algeria and probably Italy. In a way it is clever of Dan to decide on Yugoslavia because Allied HQ are in constant touch with our forces there and certainly we see Fitzroy often. Dan is happy about this decision and says he had good training for mountain warfare while escaping – but I am not happy because I know too much about the hideous things which go on in Yugoslavia. The fact that soon we must be separated all over again is heartbreaking.

27 June 1944 *London*

I went to say goodbye to Cynthia. Because of children being taken away from London and the buzz-bombs the train was alarmingly full – I stood in the corridor pressed tight against other people. I found Cynthia a bit better but not out of danger. She is very brave. Saying goodbye was awful. On my way back, at Oxford, I watched wounded being unloaded from a train – they'd been flown from France this morning. So sad.

Our leave in England has been wonderful because we are together. But it has also been rather a sad time. The courage of

[1.] The VI.

248

the people in England is amazing but so many look weary and sorrowful. We saw most of our family and a lot of friends. Nearly all of them spoke mainly of their elderly relations who have died since we went away – or of younger ones who have been killed in the war, or wounded, taken prisoner or are missing. So many of our friends in Dan's Yeomanry are dead. Most people seemed to be looking backwards rather than forwards, but what can they look forward to except peace and that is still far away and the price of reaching it will surely be devastating? Lovely to see English countryside in June: fun to go shopping even with the few coupons I'm allowed; nice to eat good food again even if it is rationed; great to get a rest from working under pressure and to sleep in comfortable beds; but, with the clock ticking always nearer to another separation and so many farewells being likely to be forever, our holiday has not been carefree.

28 June 1944   *London – The Sky*

I was woken by air-raid sirens. The sound of a buzz-bomb approaching at roof level came nearer and nearer till it seemed to fill our room. I put my head under the pillow. I thought, 'This cannot happen to us – not before breakfast – not on our last day in London . . .' Dan stirred but stayed asleep. I put my other pillow over his head and dived back under mine.

Things on the dressing table began to rattle. A window slammed. Dan woke up. Now the noise was deafening – I couldn't hear what he said. When it passed over us I counted up to eighteen and then it exploded. 'That must have hit Oxford Street,' I thought complacently and got up and was violently sick in the loo. Ten minutes later another drone started. I wondered if they sent them over in pairs on the same course. Without drawing the curtains I knew it was a rainy day because in fine weather most of them get shot down nearer the coast.

This was the worst day. All morning they came over. At lunch at Claridge's the waiters pulled the curtains – 'We don't want you to get glass in your food,' they said. The manager came over and told us he is moving us down from the eighth floor. 'It's too dangerous up there,' he explained. 'We've moved everyone down but most people have left the hotel.' After lunch we went to a movie called *Cover Girl* to hear the song 'Long Ago and Far Away'. Returning in a taxi I looked carefully at the buses, the policemen, shop windows and people on pavements – wondering when I may see them again. Our taxi driver remarked: 'Cheek, I call it – that Hitler trying them buzzers on us at this stage in the war.' We began to pack and soon the great evening symphony began: bombers setting off for Europe. 'If the weather is good enough for them it must be good enough for us,' said Dan, and sure enough Barney, General Gammell's Aide, telephoned: 'Tonight at nine.'

Tex McCrary collected us in a big American car. Driving out of London we saw several places where buzz-bombs had exploded and wrecked houses. We took off from Bovingdon airfield at 10.45 p.m. in General Eaker's silver Flying Fortress which is called 'Star Duster', a very comfortable plane which has four beds and two bunk seats and, in the adjoining compartment, tables and chairs. General Gammell, who had offered us this lift back to Algiers, had been in London for a conference, and to see the King and Chiefs of Staff. He arrived with Harold Macmillan and Aides and immediately we flew off through the slatting rain. Just before all lights were switched off a smart little fox-terrier ran out of the pilot's cabin, stopped to look at us and then walked sedately down to the tail. 'The co-pilot presumably,' said Dan. It emerged it was Bebe Daniels's dog, being taken away from buzz-bombs.

29 June 1944   *Algiers*

A rude awakening – I rolled off the seat I shared with Dan and thumped on to the floor. A chink of daylight was coming through the curtains so I sat up and painted on a clean face. Then I looked out of the windows; the sun was a red ball. Through a rift in the clouds I could see the mountains of Spain and Africa – we were approaching the Straits of Gibraltar. I
250

woke Dan and we looked down on the Rock. In a few seconds we were back in the Mediterranean Theatre.

When Smithy the pilot came with coffee and sandwiches he asked Dan and me to go and sit up front with him. We looked at his fine array of dials. Through a trapdoor in the floor we saw Tex asleep in what might be the bomb bay. Below us was a large convoy with destroyers fanning round it like sheepdogs. I sat in the co-pilot's seat and the fox-terrier climbed on my knee. Like me he does not like flying. Soon cloud wisps were left behind and we flew between two sheets of blue – the water and the sky. It grew hot and we shed our coats. Before long we began to recognise the North African coast – the walls of Cherchell, the mountains of the Tarpaza, the forest of Bahren. We counted the warships in Algiers harbour and raced up the runway at Maison Blanche. The door opened, the high-ups got out and Jack and a hot wind met us. 'Dinner at Claridge's, breakfast in Algiers – you lucky devils,' he laughed. It was ten o'clock.

I went straight to the office. The General and Mark brought me up to date. I thanked the charming AT who'd been doing my job and she departed. Whitaker was full of news. Several of the General's guests had stayed in the cottage when I was away. 'Some queer types,' said Whitaker and showed me a photo of Monty.

'Was he nice to you?' I asked.

'He's a phoney,' declared Whitaker with distaste, 'no more General Montgomery than Ginger Rogers.' Afterwards Mark explained that it was Monty's double – he was part of a deception plan for Overlord.

We are definitely going to invade the south coast of France. General Alexander is flying home at once to discuss how this will affect his operations in Italy as regards manpower and equipment. The whole of this Headquarters is to be moved to Caserta, north of Naples. A vast amount of work lies ahead.

1 July 1944   *Algiers*

Today Dan and Jack Wintour left for Vis – an island off Yugoslavia where Tito and his staff are living and Fitzroy has his
Headquarters. It was awful saying goodbye to Dan. We are all
very fond of Jackie so this was horrid too. I felt quite ill with
misery to see them go.

5 July 1944   *Algiers*

At the Supreme Allied Commanders' Conference today they
discussed General Alexander's objectives after the Pisa–Rimini
line. It looks as if Ravenna–Bologna–Ancona, and then across
the Po to Venice, Padua and Verona may be decided on. The
French have captured Siena.

I dined with General Jumbo and then went on to the Macmillans' dance. I taught American Admiral Hewitt 'Boomps a
Daisy'.

10 July 1944   *Algiers – Caserta*

Today I flew to Italy with General Jumbo who has arranged to
meet Tito at Caserta. We went in 'Freedom', General Jumbo's
Dakota which is very comfortable. It is insulated for sound
and has two bunks, four comfortable armchairs with wireless
earphones attached to them, a kitchen and electric fans. The
curtains and carpet are blue. I have learnt to sleep whenever
possible so I remember nothing of our trip till Sergeant Trayler
woke me. He gave me a cup of tea and some chocolate biscuits
and told me we were approaching Sardinia. The mountains of
Sardinia looked bare and wild; there was little green to be seen
and only a few small roads or tracks and villages. The beaches
were lovely and quite deserted. We flew over a corner of Cagli-
ari which is a fair size, and crossed the plain beyond to the sea.
We flew over Ischia and Capri which looks like a leg of mutton
from the air. In Naples harbour there were literally thousands
of ships. On Vesuvius were dark marks where streams of lava
had run down its slopes last spring. Italy was a patchwork of

brown and green. We landed fast at Marchianese in a cross-wind. A transport plane came in just behind us and burst a tyre on landing. It veered dangerously off the runway but did not turn over.

We drove up a fine avenue to Caserta Palace which is going to be our Headquarters. It is a magnificent building. We drove through an archway and two courtyards to a great terraced park which slopes up the hill with a lake in the middle and trees on either side. The road was lined with statues. At the top is a cascade which runs into a large fountain. We turned off into the woods and twisted up a steep lane to the hunting lodge where General Jumbo stays. The old King of Naples is supposed to have kept two mistresses and forty greyhounds there. The Aides insist on reversing these figures. It is a modest little house with only a few rooms. After dinner I went down to our office which is on the first floor of Caserta Palace. There was a lot of work to be done. It was late when I climbed the gloomy staircase of the palace to the fourth floor where a camp bed has been made up for me in a large musty-smelling, empty room.

12 July 1944   *Caserta*

Getting up is a high art. I must walk down four floors to General Jumbo's vast office where there is a bathroom and a lavatory. Occasionally the water is hot but my ablutions must of necessity be rapid lest the General should come into his office early and imprison me in the bathroom all the morning. I would not dare meet the Supreme Allied Commander in my dressing gown. After my bath I return through the orderlies' room to my attic to dress. Then I descend again to my own office, where the orderlies sleep. I eat breakfast on my desk. At eight my work begins.

Yesterday there was a great bustle in the office because Marshal Tito failed to keep his appointment with General Jumbo. To add to the confusion Mr Stevenson, our Ambassador to Yugoslavia, arrived from London with the Yugoslav Prime Minister, and members of our Yugoslav Mission flew in from Bari.

Today Mark was sent to Vis to find out what was going on. He arrived back in a thunderstorm with Dan and Fitzroy. Dan told me that Tito was adamant: he is not coming. He said that Vis is covered with minefields (ours) and the wrecks of bombers which have crashed on their way back from bombing Ploesti.

This evening Daphne arrived from Algiers. We had great difficulty in finding her a bed. She joined Dan and me in the attic. When I grumbled about our accommodation to Dan, saying that I always woke choked with dust; he told me that it was the Ritz compared to some of the places he had slept in when he was escaping. I am getting tired; we are working eleven hours a day.

15 July 1944   *Caserta – Algiers*

This morning the office was bedlam. The King of England is arriving shortly and arrangements must be made. Fifteen Yugoslavs are to leave at once for London. General Sosonowski, Commander-in-Chief of all Polish Forces, arrived and had to be flown up to see General Alexander. Mrs Ernest Hemingway wanted to contact General de Lattre. Madame Magazina, a Yugoslav secretary, must go to London with the Yugoslav Crown Jewels. Dan, Fitzroy, Randolph and Daphne had to go at once to Bari. We struggled with the jigsaw of planes, cars and food. Ten of us lunched in the office around my desk.

I stole five minutes to look at the war news. We have been too busy to think of it lately. In France we are still in the Caen area. The Russians are only a few miles from East Prussia. In Italy our new offensive has slowed up. The retreating Germans are leaving booby traps everywhere, even on dead bodies. In the Pacific the long struggle goes on. The Japs are killing Allied pilots when they bale out. Far fewer buzz-bombs reach London now – we are shooting them down over the Channel.

The great American naval victories at the Coral Sea and Midway in the spring and summer of 1942 put the Japanese on the defensive but the struggle goes on. In Burma, which we nearly lost in 1942, after some of the hardest fighting in the war till now, the Japanese are nearly defeated. Terribly sad that poor Wingate was killed in a flying incident in March. He and the Chindits fought so brilliantly. General Slim has done wonderfully well in ghastly territory.

21 July 1944   *Back in Algiers*

Yesterday General Jumbo gave a farewell party. Our Indo-Chinese servants were greatly surprised by the British Councillor's wife who is over six feet tall. Today we are leaving Africa. Allied Forces Headquarters, comprising some 25,000 men, is being moved by sea and air from Algiers to Caserta and Naples. We are flying over with a skeleton staff and equipment. Our cars, safes, bulk files, General Jumbo's horses, Purple Kiss and the rest, are coming by ship. Our maps have been taken off the walls, the files and stationery boxes are packed. Whitaker and I have cleaned out the cottage and put the furniture back where we found it. We have said goodbye to all the friends who are not coming with us.

Later: Coco and I flew with General Jumbo to Caserta. Mr Macmillan and Lady Dorothy Macmillan came with us. The plane was so full of luggage that I was afraid we might not be able to take off. A transport plane followed us. It was filled with the rest of the staff and luggage, the Macmillans' kitten and some chickens. One of them laid an egg on the way over. I am back in my attic room – it is terribly hot.

Rescued

22 July 1944   *Caserta*

We are extremely busy because, apart from normal work and the move, we are arranging with the Navy, Army and Air Force the programme for the King's visit to Italy. His Majesty will arrive at Naples tomorrow and stay with Admiral Cunningham at Villa Emma where Nelson used to visit Lady Hamilton. The King will see naval installations and the Port on the morning of the 24th and then fly to Caserta for a lunch party in the palace. In our office we are fixing the lunch party. There will be eighty-six guests, all Major Generals and over. The three Services of British, American, French and Poles are to be present. Apart from contacting these people and making sure they come, there is much to do. Catering officers want the menu approved; waiters have to be briefed; Military Police want to check security; drivers want their instructions. Flowers, carpets and chairs must be found for the two great banqueting rooms. Invitations and passes have to be written out. They are sent by signal and despatch riders. The King's visit is a secret.

Today Mark and Roger Makin fixed the table list – it was most involved. Ellen, the ADC's American stenographer, typed out a list of people who will meet the King. I telephoned Generals all over Italy warning them that dress will be informal

– they are to wear shirtsleeves. Our telephones are not working very well yet and the echo in these high-arched rooms with bare stone floors makes it hard to hear or to be heard on long distance lines. In the next room General Jumbo sat ploughing his way through reports and telegrams.

Soon we shall invade the south coast of France. Outside the windows great convoys of trucks rolled by carrying men and equipment to be loaded on to ships in Naples harbour.

We lunched on our desks and worked late after dinner. We talked of the attack that has been made on Hitler. It seems that a German General[1] left a suitcase with a bomb in it in Hitler's conference room. It exploded and killed several people. The Führer was wounded.

24 July 1944   *Caserta*

Last night the King arrived punctually in his York and was taken to stay at Villa Emma. For two days I have been telephoning up and down the country trying to contact General Juin who should attend the lunch today. He is driving about somewhere in the north, no one knows where. We have even had to ask the Military Police to watch the road for him. Today the four telephones in our office have rung ceaselessly. Our rooms are crowded with visitors.

At eleven I went across the palace to have a last look at the arrangements. In the first room a hugh cherry-coloured carpet was laid on the floor. There was a fine picture of Nelson on a stand. Big bucketfuls of red and white gladioli stood in the windows. I removed some ugly fern from round them, to the fury of the Italian flower man. The cooks had prepared a wonderful cold lunch. In the dining room long tables were arranged in three sides of a square. Sergeant Trayler was regimenting eighty-six plum-coloured velvet chairs. Whitaker was helping. Places were marked all right. The band arrived. Everything was in order.

At midday Daphne and I went across from my office to the

---

[1] Colonel Count Claus von Stauffenberg.

main staircase of the palace which leads to the banqueting rooms. The staircase is made of single slabs of Sicilian marble. A fine pair of lions guard the landing halfway up and behind them a little staircase leads to the roof. At the top of the first flight is a horse statue where we could hide and watch unseen. Presently General Jumbo and General Devers[1] arrived. They waited at the foot of the stairs. All the guests were already in the reception room. Viennese waltz music drifted up to us – it sounded thrilling in those great bare halls. Some soldiers joined us. They did not know what we were waiting for but they stood to see. There was scarcely room for all our heads at the little window. The horse's head got in our way.

The King arrived and walked between the two Generals up the shallow steps below us. He looked very small next to General Jumbo. They walked slowly, talking and laughing. We three lunched in my office on my desk. Afterwards we hung out of the windows to see the King drive away in an open car. News travels fast and there was a crowd of soldiers waiting to see him. American outriders on their high-powered motorcycles roared and revved their engines while they waited, each with one foot on the ground. The King came and the soldiers cheered and threw their caps in the air. It looked very gay in the sunshine. From Marchianese the King flew up to General Alexander's Headquarters.

On the way back to my room I found Scottie, our American girl driver, having a heated argument with Sergeant Pell and Fusilier O'Connor. 'All that goddam fuss about a King,' she said. 'Americans can be rude about anything of ours except the King,' replied Fusilier O'Connor stoutly. For once Scottie, who is a great favourite of ours, was firmly suppressed. There was an immense amount of work to do. Mines have had to be removed from a special track at Monte Cassino so that General Alexander can show the King how that battle was fought and won. Bales of gladioli from the lunch party must go to hospitals and Messes. Papers had to be prepared for a Supreme Allied Commanders' meeting where they will discuss Balkan Air

[1.] US Deputy to General Wilson, SACMED.

Force operations and Turkey . . . We worked very late. It was past midnight when I crept through the orderlies' room on my way to bed. They were all asleep under mosquito nets but Whitaker's bed was empty. I stood there wondering where he was when suddenly I saw a pair of round eyes watching me through the Arab screen we brought from Algiers. 'Don't look, My Lady. I am naked,' said Whitaker. On a table nearby lay his spectacles and his teeth. I climbed wearily up the long flights of stairs and wondered what life would be like without Whitaker.

27 July 1944   *Naples*

Yesterday Mark, Sergeant Trayler and I spent the morning at Villa Rivalta, General Jumbo's house in Naples, which must be got ready for the Prime Minister's visit next month. We shifted the furniture around, made lists of things that are needed, saw about security, hot water, mosquito nets and Italian charladies. When we got back to Caserta I thought the heat was unbearable. No one else seemed to notice it so I took my temperature. It was 103.2.

Today I was moved from my attic to Villa Rivalta. I am in the room Mr Churchill will have. There is a wonderful view over the harbour. The bed is very nobbly.

31 July 1944   *Bari*

Yesterday I was given three days' sick leave so I drove over to stay with Dan who is working at Fitzroy's Headquarters in Bari. The journey took seven hours. From Caserta the road winds through mountains. In the little towns and villages, which are perched on the summits, peasant women sat in the streets in front of vine-trellised houses watching their children play in the gutter. In the valleys the corn was golden. Great white oxen pulling high-wheeled carts, and ponies in gaily painted floats, moved along the roads. The only signs of war were the bridges which had all been blown up. Temporary Bailey bridges spanned the streams and rivers. Towards evening I reached the coastal plain and saw one of Mussolini's greatest achievements: collective farming. The farmhouses are all built on the same pattern. The farms all have the same acreage. I saw hundreds of them.

Today Dan and I went to see Evelyn Waugh and Randolph Churchill in hospital. The plane that was taking them to Yugoslavia crashed on landing and nearly all the passengers were killed. Randolph did not seem in the least subdued by the accident and was busy distributing propaganda posters round the hospital. Periodically he and Evelyn had arguments about nothing in particular and shouted at each other. They are very funny.

3 August 1944   *Caserta*

Great news. I am to leave my dusty attic and live in a tiny cottage in Naples which will be used as an auxiliary guest house. It is called Villa Pina and stands in a garden on the edge of a precipice with pine trees on either side. From the French windows there is a magnificent view: Naples curves away to the left, Vesuvius is opposite – to the right, in the distance, is Capri. Below is a Lilliput world: cars and trams on the coast road look like beetles – scores of silver balloons, the size of ping-pong balls, stand sentinel over the mass of shipping in the harbour.

General Sosonowski came to see General Jumbo this morning. His Aide, Count Lubienski, told me that the Russians are treating the Poles just as badly as the Germans did. His descriptions of the Red Army's advance on Warsaw made me feel very sad.

I dined with the Macmillans at their villa in Naples. It must have been owned by a very nautical gentleman. The bannisters are made of rope, the floor tiles are covered with fish and sea flowers – there are anchors, brass bells, funnels and model boats everywhere. Harold Macmillan talked about General Eisenhower and how brilliantly he ran the Allied Headquarters at Algiers. He said he was a delightful person to work with and always impartial. They told me that when our King was staying at Villa Emma he saw some police in a patrol launch having a fierce argument with a couple in a fishing boat. Later he enquired what it was all about and was informed that when the security police ordered the little old man and his large lady to fish further afield the couple refused to budge. After protesting vehemently in Italian the lady pulled out of her pocket an immense visiting card on which was written 'The King and Queen of Italy'. After that they were left to fish in peace.

5 August 1944   Caserta

Marshal Tito has at last agreed to come to Caserta.

Today I interviewed a maid called Italia. She spoke a few words of French and English. I asked her how much money she wanted. She replied, 'That is for you to say.' At the end of our talk a broad smile came over her face and she said, 'When they asked me to work for you I expected to see a very large Madame.' She departed promising to be a faithful servant.

9 August 1944   Caserta

I was given a day off so I took my luggage and Coco to Villa Pina and spent the morning cleaning out the house and shoving the furniture around to make it more comfortable. Keith,[1] our new ADC, telephoned me at lunchtime: 'Marshal Tito has a free afternoon and we do not know what to do with him, so we are bringing him down to tea with you.' My heart sank. 'There will be fourteen of us,' he said. Then I exploded. I told him I had only been in the house for three hours, there were not enough chairs or tea cups – I had no food and the place was chaotic . . . He rang back to say that it had all been arranged: tea would be sent up from the Villa Rivalta with two waiters. The party would arrive at four o'clock. This was typical of my job, I thought, as I dusted angrily. Apart from office work you might be sent anywhere at any moment, be asked to meet aeroplanes, do hostess at official dinner parties, comfort lonely

---

[1] Keith Egleston, Rifle Brigade.

officers, give tea to Partisan dictators when you don't even own a teapot . . .

At four o'clock sharp, outriders roared up to my little house. Five staff cars exuded Yugoslavs. Marshal Tito, resplendent in a blue and silver uniform and surrounded by five ferocious-looking guards with tommy guns, walked in. He was short and stocky and dressed to kill. With him came his secretary, Olga Humo, Fitzroy Maclean, Keith and some Yugoslav staff officers. They crowded on to my small verandah.

It was a struggle to get them all talking but they stayed till seven and by that time we were all chattering in various languages. Tito spoke practically no English but enough German to match mine. We talked of Vis and of his boots which were magnificent. He told me in German they went many 'wursts' and laughed when I explained to him that *wurst* means sausage in German and he had given away his Russian tendency. We had tea and then Tito drank beer, carefully covered by tommy guns which his guards would not put away at any price. Coco crawled on to the Marshal's knee while I wondered nervously whether he would be shot if he pecked my guest or dirtied his elegant uniform. The Yugoslavs lost a little of their shyness when I showed them my Mauser pistol which they carefully took to bits and put together again. I walked them round the garden and showed them Capri through the haze. We caught a field mouse. I told them how, when Vesuvius erupted last spring, the ashes that fell on Pomigliano aerodrome had rendered useless seventy planes. They asked about the shipping lying below us like an Armada, and told me of their desperate need for hospitals and medicine.

I liked Olga very much. She spoke good English. We talked about the Dalmatian Coast and then the Second Front and they invited me to visit them on Vis. Then, with tommy guns before and behind, they climbed into their cars and drove off and I returned to my dusting.

General Jumbo had a conference with Tito today regarding rations for the Yugoslavs, and seven thousand beds for their sick and wounded. Tito demanded to take his five thugs and their tommy guns to the meeting which caused a delay and much amusement among us. This note came for me from Olga Humo:

Dear Hermione,

It was very kind of you to send my cap down. Marshal Tito enjoyed himself very much yesterday afternoon and so did we all.

How is the mouse? I hope you didn't give it to Coco in the end. I hope you are settled down comfortably by today in your very pleasant little house. I too hope we shall be able to meet soon. It will be lovely if you really come to Vis.

Yours sincerely,
Olga.

At seven forty-five each morning, Lonj, Italia and old Raphaeli see me off to work. They stand at the gate and wave till I am out of sight. Hours later they welcome me back in the same way. None of them stands higher than my shoulder and all of them speak different languages but we understand each other very well.

Raphaeli, the gardener, is seventy-two and very crippled from work. He belongs to the house. I pay him two thousand lire a month, which is about five pounds, and provide his food. Each day he gets up at five-thirty and works till night falls. He sings a funny little jerky song as he waters the flowers. He wears a white American sailor hat on the back of his head. He has a bedroom at the back of the house but he only keeps his canaries there and a lot of junk. He prefers to sleep in the potting shed because he is afraid of air raids.

Italia, the maid, has a thin oval face and large eyes. When we were bombing Naples in 1943 her husband moved her and her children down to the Sorrento Peninsula. He visited them every week with provisions and money. One day he set out in a

263

boat to cross the bay with his basket of food and was picked up by a German patrol boat. He has never been seen or heard of since. Italia thinks that he was press-ganged and taken to Germany to work. She is very unhappy. Her three children are all under seven and she has great difficulty in getting enough food for them. At least I can help over this.

Lonj is one of the Indo-Chinese boys from General Jumbo's villa. He has been lent me to help with the house. He is very shy and quiet and works hard. During the war he has learnt French. I get Alexander Dumas novels for him to read.

Coco has learnt to call 'Raphaeli' which is a great success.

12 August 1944   *Corsica*

Yesterday Mr Churchill arrived in his York. Though he had had a strenuous day, the Aides said he was in great form at dinner at Villa Rivalta and talked till 2 a.m. All the telegrams are being relayed from London to Caserta and after my work I have to take them to Naples. The congestion on the roads is fantastic. We ran over a dog. I felt very sorry. I reached home at nine and went to bed early.

Today, for once, I was up before Raphaeli. I dressed in khaki and packed and handed my house over to Roger Makin for the week I shall be away. I drove to Caserta, typed some letters and then, with my typewriter and travelling stationery box, I took off with General Beaumont Nesbitt and four staff for Corsica. We flew over Anzio battlefield and saw Rome in the distance. Soon after we passed over the Island of Monte Cristo which stands, steep and exciting as a Grimm's fairy castle, in the sea. Lying in the frill of bays along the edge of Corsica were hundreds of small craft. We flew into a larger bay and saw Ajaccio huddled away on the far side within a horseshoe of mountains. The little landing ground below us glittered with aircraft.

General Rattay, the US local Commander, had sent his open car to meet us. We thanked the pilot and drove away in the sunshine along a two-track tarmac road skirting the sea. We passed the harbour which was crammed with ships and landing craft. It reminded me of a country town on market day with everything tied head to tail. Ajaccio looked very French. There were a few shops, mostly empty, some large public buildings and a smart little esplanade. In the streets I saw American, French and British troops, Goums with dusky faces, Circassians in red hats, and Corsicans – sallow, weather-beaten people. There were Yugoslavs, who work on the island, and Italians too. The locals sat on benches under neat clipped trees and watched the passers by. I went straight to Ronald Fleming's house to see if he could put me up. He is doing liaison work here. Mr Churchill and General Jumbo are going to stay with Admiral Cunningham on a ship in the harbour. I have instructions to find and prepare a house for them in case they have to stay in Ajaccio longer than we expect and do not want to work cooped up on the ship.

I dined with General Rattay and was delighted to find General Devers, who will command in the South of France, and his staff there. General Rattay has a monster moustache and kind little eyes. He is an American of Hungarian descent. One of his Aides is a white Russian and the other a Pole, so we were an international party. We sat in the garden and Napoleon, a little super-accelerated boar was brought out for us to see. He bared his teeth in a comic grin and made little charges at our ankles. He looked distinctly like General Rattay. The house was very ornate: gilt, marble and red wallpaper everywhere – as French Colonial as can be. We talked of hunting parties in Morocco and of General Patton's advance in France, and of Florence which we have captured.

13 August 1944   *Ajaccio*

I was woken by planes zooming overhead. I hurried over to the villa we are preparing. It belongs to M. Pietri, an old friend of Clemenceau's, and is modern, comfortable and gay. There is a fine head of *le tigre* in the salon. All the morning I searched for sheets, spoons and glasses, tested plugs and lights and collected rations. Now there is a heavy guard on the gate. I picked flowers in the scorching sun and arranged bowls of hybiscus, datura and heavenly blue convolvulus. When everything was ready I drove down to the aerodrome to meet 'Freedom'. I whiled away an hour watching Spitfires taking off and landing. The runway was so rough they bounced tremendously. Someone was skylarking in a scout plane. Two Walruses were parked nearby. 'Freedom' made a perfect landing and General Jumbo in shirtsleeves and Admiral Cunningham, immaculate in white, climbed out. They stopped to tell me of their trip to Bastia where they saw troops embarking today. They drove off waving. Then I went over to talk to Penny the pilot and gave him lists and letters explaining our needs and the set-up here. I watched him take off for Caserta.

Back in the jeep the American driver told me that he and most other soldiers will vote for Roosevelt. Passing the harbour the troops on the landing craft waved and whistled. Funny that I should know where they are going when they don't. This evening I climbed up to the roof and looked out to sea. Away on the horizon was a thin black line. More and more ships are coming in. Over the red roofs of the gaily coloured houses the mountains were turning deep shadowed blue. Everywhere I looked there was movement. Launches zipped the water, army trucks rattled along, Spitfires were circling to land. Old French women pottered along the streets in their black frocks. I wondered what they thought about it all. Behind me, on the edge of the town, was a statue guarded by two great eagles. It was neither ostentatious nor ornamented. Even from where I stood it was easy to see that the man at the top of the plain white steps was Napoleon.

I went down to my room and sat on my bed and thought about it all while I waited for the water to be turned on. There is a shortage here and during the day taps do not run nor plugs pull.

14 August 1944   *Ajaccio*

Today General Jumbo and Admiral Cunningham sailed early to see the ships assembling for the attack.[1] I did some typing

---

[1.] On the South of France.

and odd jobs and at three o'clock set out for the aerodrome to meet 'Freedom' and collect luggage. I got spattered with tar off the road on the way down. I recognised 'Freedom' in the air because she is still painted with brown and green desert camouflage. She slipped up the runway, turned in banks of dust and came to a standstill. The door opened and a small, plump figure stepped out. Mr Winston Churchill had arrived to see the invasion launched on the south coast of France. He was wearing a white tropical suit, no tie and a sun helmet. I had never seen him before. An American soldier standing beside me said to his mate, 'See? I told you he was coming. Won't Eleanor be mad?' The Prime Minister shook hands with the Prefect, General Rattay and the French Governor and then stumped off to his car. I walked over to the plane. Mark and Commander Thompson were laughing because, on the way over, Mr Churchill had gone up to the front of the plane and had discovered one of General Jumbo's Indo-Chinese servants in the kitchen. He came back saying that, for a moment, he thought there was a Jap on board.

Some of the Prime Minister's staff, General Beaumont Nesbitt, Mark, Ronald Fleming and I dined together at Villa Pietri. We talked of our landing which will begin tonight and of the big battle of Falaise. Mark told me that the Prime Minister's staff grumbled when they were staying in Naples because the bath water was cold. I enjoyed telling them that there is a water shortage here and they will be lucky to have one at all. People so often write to us saying that they envy us our 'comfortable Mediterranean life' but when visitors arrive from London they talk of weekends and Sundays and hot bath water and many things which we have long since forgotten.

15 August 1944   *Ajaccio*

Early this morning I went up on the roof to watch Mr Churchill's destroyer sail. Hundreds of bombers were returning from the coast of France. I counted up to sixty and gave up as new waves came over.

General Jumbo and Admiral Cunningham had a clear day.

Their work was done, their orders given. While they waited to hear how the landing had gone they visited the house where Napoleon was born and then returned to their ship to wait for signals. I spent a busy morning typing things and fixing things, and helping the orderlies to lay the table and collect enough chairs for the big lunch party at Villa Pietri. At one o'clock General Jumbo, Admiral Cunningham, General Rattay and all their staffs arrived. The first news of our landing is good. The RAF gave the enemy such a pasting that little or no aerial opposition was met. Red, white and blue parachutes and great gliders are lying in the fields behind the Riviera where our airborne troops landed safely. Every minute our positions on the beaches are growing stronger. Admiral Cunningham mixed his special tomato juice and sherry cocktail and told me of his day at sea yesterday. He explained how hundreds of ships and craft left Malta, Naples, Algiers, Ajaccio and other ports according to their respective speeds. They all met at the appointed place at the right time. The LTCs, which are slow, started first. At lunch we talked of boar hunting and Clemenceau, but all of us were really thinking of the troops on the Riviera coast. After lunch we listened to the BBC news and then General Jumbo and Admiral Cunningham returned to the ship to follow the landing on their maps. The Aides and I had the afternoon off. We drove west from the town and swam out through shallow green water to some flat rocks where a cormorant had a nest.

17 August 1944   *Ajaccio–Caserta*

We flew from Ajaccio to Venafro airfield, near Cassino, where General Jumbo had arranged a meeting with General Alexander. There was no aerodrome, just a windsock on a strip of rough ground between the mountains.

Back in the office there was a great deal to do. Mr Churchill and his staff are still with us. Despatches have to be typed, signals drafted and preparations made for a conference in Rome. General Clark padded into my room in his crêpe rubber soles and walked up and down while he told me his

268

news. I had to ask him to stop; I was still feeling airsick after our rough journey and he made me dizzy. Last night he dined with Mr Churchill who wore white linen trousers and carpet slippers with PM stitched on them. Commander Thompson went bathing with Mr Churchill at Ischia and said the Prime Minister was very active in the water, but it was hard to see which way up he was . . .

19 August 1944   *Naples*

We have had two tremendously busy days in the office but this evening I reached home early, at eight o'clock. At Villa Pina I found Lonj, the Indo-Chinaman, standing on the verandah looking very sad and far away. I asked him if something was wrong, but he said, 'No, Madame La Comtesse, it is just that I think of my home.' I asked him about his family. He was very shy at first but after a little he began slowly, half in French and half in English, to tell me his story.

> When the war started in Europe I was in my village Thien Hoa in north Indo-China. There were no newspapers or radio in my village but we knew something had happened when one afternoon couriers arrived and gave a paper to the Mayor. It was harvest time and nearly all the village were working in the fields. When they heard about the couriers everybody went back to their houses – suddenly we were anxious. Some days later proclamations were stuck on the walls saying Hitler had begun war. No one knew what Hitler was. After a bit we think perhaps Hitler is a bad thing because all our horses and bicycles are taken away.
>
> In the villages, but not in the towns, the Indo-Chinese were mobilised. First they asked for volunteers but nobody wanted to go, so it became forced. All the young men of poor families had to go but rich people gave money to the Mayor to withhold their names. A man came round with our names on a list and orders to go to the Mandarin, who is like a Prefect and has authority over the district. He is much more important than the Mayor. He told me to go to the town for a medical visit. My mother did not eat for two days. Perhaps my father was sad but he never spoke of it. After two or three days I went to Bac Ninh. The Mayor went in a *pousse-pousse*, which is a

rickshaw. We all walked. My village is on the edge of a hill beside a river.

I was not very strong and thought the medicals would say I could not go to the war but the requisitioning officer was short of people and said I should go just the same. My Mother came to see me and was very sad. She gave me a thick jersey because she said there is no sun in France and lots of Indo-Chinese there get ill. Many people came to the town for medicals – they applied tobacco to their eyes to make them red, hoping the doctor would say they had bad eyes. After a time the doctor knew and they were not successful.

We were put on a train in cattle trucks, and went for two or three hours to the port Haiphong. Five or six hundred of us were put in warehouse sheds. We slept on the floor. Lots of people tried to run away. Indo-Chinese and French police guarded the doors. I had told my Mother that they would treat me well but now I could not write to her because I discovered how bad it was.

One morning early we left in a big boat called the *Cap Padarin*. I had seasickness. We were peasants and accustomed to working in the fields for fourteen or fifteen hours a day and used to eating a great deal. Now we did not get enough food. Some of my companions asked the officers on the ship to turn round and go back to Haiphong. One day, when they made a distribution of soup in the Red Sea in a very big bowl, everybody pushed because there was never sufficient and one man near the bowl was pushed into the boiling soup. He died as a result. Nobody was sorry for him on the ship. They all said he was greedy. There was not much love on the ship because when you are hungry you are not very kind.

We arrived at Marseilles. It was bizarre, because a month before we had been amongst our own people and now when we walked in the streets there were strangers who looked at us with astonishment. Once again we were put in cattle trucks. I was unhappy because my friend must go to Bordeaux and I must go to Toulouse. We were like brothers. That was in November 1939.

At Toulouse in a great munition factory we worked in three shifts. It was a powder factory – explosives. It was strange in France to see French women working. We were quite astonished because in Indo-China French women never work but behave like little queens and we did not like them. In Toulouse the French were very kind to us and we decided

that *Liberté, Fraternité* and *Egalité* had a signification, but
unhappily only in France. I learnt to speak a little French.

We thought the French would win the war in one year. My
Mother and sister wrote that they hoped I would be back in
time to help them with the harvest. But in May we became
anxious. From our camp we could see the refugees passing
interminably down the road. Then one day the French threw
the powder we had been making into the river – three or
four months' work. It was to prevent the Germans getting it.
When Marshal Pétain asked for an armistice it was a very
great shock to discover that the Germans were more powerful
than the French. We wondered what would happen to us.

In July 1940 we were sent to Marseilles to wait for ships to
be repatriated. We stayed there seven months. Each day we
were taken to the forest to cut down trees. Then one day
we were told that fourteen hundred of us would leave the
next day. Those that were not coming, thousands of them,
gave us messages for their mothers and wives and sisters. I
became so confused I forgot them all. The Suez Canal was
shut because of the English so we must go round Africa. It
was a voyage of three months. Conditions were lamentable on
the boat but everybody was happy. In the evening we sang
this song that I had last heard sung on the day of my
departure by the young girl I am to marry in Thien Hoa. I
will make it for you in French:

> Vers le soir je me'en vais cueillir des feuilles de mûrier
> Des feuilles de mûrier j'oublie d'en cueillir:
> Je me souviens des mots d'amour.
>
> Les oiseaux chantent sur la montagne de l'est.
> Des singes d'un arbre a l'autre, se répondent.
> Qui prend soin de mon bien aimé?
>
> Regarde, j'ai dans les mains le livre à couverture d'or,
> Autant mon livre a de caractères,
> Autant mon coeur a d'amour pour toi.
>
> O mon bien aimé, tu ne sais donc pas
> Que je te suis encore plus fidèle
> Que ne l'est ton image dans le miroir.
>
> Je fais le serment d'être à toi pour toujours
> Car si la feuille de mûrier est sèche
> De quoi le ver à soie se nourrira-t-il?

Our boat called at Algiers, Casablanca and Dakar. When we
had left Dakar a week we were caught by an English warship.

English came to manoeuvre our ship and we were taken to
Durban where we were put in a concentration camp,
between the Italian prisoners' camp and the German
prisoners' camp. Many Indo-Chinese wished to fight for the
English but the Commandant was Vichy. He said that if we
fought for England he would wire to Indo-China where the
Commandant was Vichy too and there would be troubles for
our families. We had received no letters from our families
since France. The only break to our monotony was when a
German prisoner escaped. The Italians were very content to
be prisoners. After ten months we were moved to
Pietermaritzburg. The Germans and Italians came too. In
January 1943 I asked if I could work for the English on
Madagascar. I thought nothing could be worse than a prison
camp but when I reached Madagascar I wished I had
remained a prisoner. I found myself in the kingdom of
mosquitoes. Everyone had yellow fever or malaria and we had
no protection, no mosquito nets. The English gave me plenty of
clothes at Durban but my baggage had been put by mistake on
a boat which went to Syria so I arrived at Tamatave with
nothing. There had been a great cyclone and the whole town
was destroyed. The fighting had just finished in Madagascar.

I was no longer a prisoner. I was an ally. I lived in a camp
and was sent every day to cut branches off trees in a forest. Each
man had to cut forty branches. I was weak because I had fever
and so I gave a negro a few francs to cut for me and I carried
it home to the sergeant who was very content. One day that
negro took me to see his tribal Chief. In Madagascar there
are more cows than there are men and the Chief of the tribes
had thousands of cattle. When I came he killed one to
honour me. They roasted it on a fire and danced round it.
This reminded me of the film *Tarzan* which I had seen in
France. I thought it only happened on films. The negroes
respect strangers and they have curiosity – they asked me
where my home was. I pointed to the east. The Chief had
many wives. He was rich.

One day when I had been in Madagascar about ten months
there came an English Colonel of Liaison. He asked for four
Indo-Chinese who would work for an English General. After a
long conference, my three comrades Van Ha, Van Thanh,
Phi and I decided it might perhaps be better to go than rot in
this place. When our friends saw the good uniforms the
English gave they said we were right to leave. At Christmas
time 1943 we left Madagascar and went by boat to Mombasa

where we stayed for two months. Then we went by train to a place called Siroti, a little post in Central Africa. From the train we were astonished to see antelope and zebras. They looked very funny. At first we thought they belonged to some private property, but then we saw many more, and monkeys. We were in the jungle. I was very tired and had seen enough of them, but Van Ha woke me up each time he saw them. At Siroti there were only a few Europeans and when strangers arrived they were very well treated. It was the first time in my life that a waiter served me. They gave me a big dinner and the waiter stood by. Van Ha asked me, as I could speak a little English, to tell the waiter to go away because so long as he remained there he could not maintain his dignity and enjoy his dinner. We had the habitude of eating a great deal. Van Ha went to wash up the plates after dinner but he was told there was a boy to do that already. Each morning a big native knocked at the door and brought me my breakfast in bed. Afterwards we collected our little money left to give to the waiters. We would rather have eaten alone and kept our money because we were short – but we had our dignity.

On the third day we left in a military lorry and travelled through small bushes. The country was desolate. Sometimes we saw a naked negro with a spear. It was not a good route. We travelled by day and camped at night and on the third morning came to Juba. There we got into a boat and went to Khartoum. I had a relapse of malaria and was put in a military hospital. I was very ill and that I am alive still is due to the care of the doctors and nurses. Van Ha and the others went on without me. It was hot and there were sand storms. All the time I thought of my friends. After a month I went on a train to Wadi Halfa and by boat to Aswan. From there I went by train to Cairo. I expected to see my friends but I found they had gone to Algiers with the English General. I waited in camp for a month. There I became anxious that I would not find my friends again. In May 1944 I was sent from Alexandria on a boat which called at Naples before it reached Algiers. When I arrived at the house of the General I found my three friends, Van Ha, Van Thanh and Phi. Corporal Robins was with them. He did not say anything but pushed a knife and fork in my hands. I thought they must be in a great hurry in this house but afterwards I learnt it was only Corporal Robins. My chief work in Algiers was to keep the garden nice. This made me content. I came to Naples in an aeroplane. I had air sickness. When they told me at Villa Rivalta that I must get

ready to go to the Villa Pina I consulted Antonio, the Italian
prisoner . . .

'Lonj, are you happy here?' I asked.

'Sufficiently, Madame La Comtesse,' he replied with great
politeness, 'But you will understand that I cannot enjoy myself
till the war is over and I return to Thien Hoa where my family
await me.' He padded off softly into the garden.

21 August 1944   *Naples – Rome*

Our American driver, Parker, who comes from Texas, picked
me up at 7 a.m. We drove slowly through the slums of Naples
because the streets were so crowded with workers waiting for a
hopelessly inadequate supply of trams. The poverty and squa-
lor are heartbreaking. People live in garages and alleys and
ghastly houses. The only bright things to be seen are the
onions and red vegetables and little birds in cages that hang
from the walls. Children, with bare bottoms and no shoes, play
in the sickening filth of the streets, building, with their good
imaginations, castles of manure. Men walk along bent nearly
double under the bundles of faggots and vegetables they carry.
Donkey carts creak by festooned with scarecrow human beings,
their limbs and faces bony with undernourishment. Despite it
all the people in these slums seem gay and kind. Here a smiling father leads his tiny grubby child across the cobbled street
– there some women sit laughing in a doorway as they patiently
delouse each other's heads.

We turned off on to the Appian Way which the Army calls
'Highway Seven'. It is a fine straight tarmac road with trees on
either side. After an hour or so we came upon traces of war.
First there were farmhouses with their walls chipped and riddled with bullet holes. Then there were blind, vacant-faced
buildings, their red tiled roofs tilted at rakish angles, and
houses with one side blown clean off exposing the rooms like
dolls' houses with their fronts open. As we advanced it grew
worse. Chimneys stood black and solitary where once there
were homes. We drove through the half-cleared streets of Min-
274

turno and Formia between gigantic heaps of rubble. Parker told me that many people are buried in the debris. Strands of matted telegraph wires, ripped steel, and telegraph poles hanging like broken asparagus, lined our way. These little towns, built between the mountains and the sea, must have been pleasant places to live in a year ago. Now they are terrible to see. They have been bombarded from sea, land and air, and now their inhabitants sleep in holes and any shelter they can find.

We crossed the Pontine Marshes. In places the road is still only just above the level of the water. On the trees and houses dark marks, sometimes up to the first storey, show how deep the water rose when the Germans flooded it. Beyond the marshes the ground is pock-marked with shell holes and the trees are black and broken. In the Alban Hills we made a great detour because the main road is still impassable. Littorio aerodrome, just outside Rome, was a sorry sight. Stacks of strafed hulks, like prehistoric monsters, were piled on one side. The buildings were ruins.

When we drove into Rome we found ourselves in pre-war Europe. The magnificent yellow buildings are undamaged, the streets clean, the shops filled with lovely things. Pretty girls walked along the streets in silk frocks and stockings. At the Grand Hotel the Union Jack, the Stars and Stripes and the Italian flag hung from the balcony. I had a rush to turn one of the sitting rooms that had been reserved for General Jumbo into an office. When he arrived there was a crisis. Our ADC had sent the General's best uniform to be pressed and it was lost somewhere in the basement. The General, who was due to lunch at the Embassy with Sir Noel Charles, our Ambassador, Mr Churchill, Lord Moyne, General Paget and Mr Leeper, gave us what the Americans call 'Billy Hell'. All through the afternoon I typed reports, programmes and signals but when General Jumbo went to a meeting at six o'clock we staff were given a couple of hours off to see Rome. It is a lovely city.

We were so busy in Rome that I did not see much of the city. General Jumbo attended a series of meetings and had an audience with the Pope who impressed him very much. I learnt that the aristocracy in Rome have suffered little from the war. With the help of the black market they live at pre-war standards and, except for transport, the German and now the British occupations have caused them no hardship. The poor people, on the other hand, have had to live on their bread ration which is now two hundred grams a day. As they can get little else to eat they are very near starvation point. Next winter will be terrible in Italy.

Parker and I drove back to Naples on Highway Six because we wanted to see Cassino. The heat and dust were awful. I sat soaked in sweat. Always we followed the tracks of war – villages blackened and broken by bombardment, olive groves like petrified forests and avenues of trees shot down to stumps. There were busted guns and tanks and graves beside the road. At the southern end of the Liri Valley, where the road runs parallel to a range of bare mountains, we came upon notices saying, 'Do not stop', 'Do not go a yard on either side', 'Mines. Mines. Mines'. A few minutes later Parker pulled the car up with a jerk. The scene that lay before us was so startling that for a while we just sat and stared. Rising sheer above us Monastery Hill towered at seventeen hundred feet. Before us stretched what once had been Cassino.

26 August 1944   Caserta

Paris has been liberated. I am too busy to keep my diary. Besides an avalanche of work we have a spate of visitors to look after – Mr Attlee, the Deputy Prime Minister; Sir James Grigg, Secretary of State for War; General Weeks, Deputy CIGS, and Mr Churchill who has returned to Villa Rivalta from Rome.

Turkey has declared war on the Axis. The Riveria is now in our hands.

A Roumanian, who has escaped from Bucharest in his own aircraft has arrived at Caserta. We are discussing with him how we can rescue Allied air crews from Roumania.

31 August 1944   *Caserta*

Myron C. Taylor, Roosevelt's Personal Representative to the Vatican, flew down today to discuss with General Jumbo relief for the Italians. There has been a poor harvest in North Africa which will greatly add to our food difficulties. We will be short of five hundred thousand tons of wheat by the New Year.

6 September 1944   *Caserta*

Allied troops are approaching the frontiers of Germany. Hitler has called for a People's war. Brussels has been liberated. The Russians are in Ploesti.

Lady MacMichael, who is on her way home to England from Palestine, dined with me. Douglas Fairbanks came and brought Brian Aherne who, with Cartherine Cornell, is touring this Theatre. They are acting in *The Barretts of Wimpole Street* at the tiny theatre in Caserta Palace.

After dinner Lady MacMichael told us how she and Sir Harold were nearly murdered on the Jerusalem–Tel Aviv road. They were driving down to the coast to attend a farewell ceremony. They set out in the old Rolls with two police out-riders in front and a police car following close behind. A few miles out of Jerusalem, where the road spirals down the mountains, they were ambushed. The attack was well timed and took place on a wide bend. The outriders in front were engaged when they were out of sight and the police car was attacked after the Rolls had passed, also out of sight. The Rolls was caught in the middle of the bend, on one side was a sheer precipice, on the other an overhanging cliff. A strip of burning oil blazed across the road and brought them to a standstill. The driver, with great presence of mind, rammed the big car into the left side of the road where it was better protected from the tommy gun bullets that rained down on them, and less easy to push over the precipice on the other side. They had a very narrow escape – the High Commissioner was hit and so was Ken Nicholl and the driver. The band of extremists who planned and carried out this attack were traced to a Jewish village a mile away from the road. The whole village must have been involved in this attempt for none of the assassins was ever handed over. It is interesting to think that our 'Intolerant British Government' only fined this village two hundred pounds for their attempt on the lives of our Government representatives.

16 September 1944   *Caserta*

News is coming in so thick and fast that it is becoming increasingly difficult to take it in. Here, we are discussing the withdrawal of German troops from Greece. The German Garrison there still holds on but as the Balkans slide back one after another into Allied hands they are faced with the risk of being cut off. The Germans must either evacuate Greece and the islands now or fight their way out. We are waiting and preparing either to push them out at a moment opportune to ourselves or take over immediately on their departure when Greece may be faced with starvation and inflation. General Scobie will command the forces we are sending there.

In the hills behind Caserta pale pink dwarf cyclamen are growing in the woods. They have elegant red stems about three inches high. I have dug up some of their fat brown bulbs and the leaf mould they grow in and given them to Raphaeli to plant in my garden.

General Anders, General Bouciewicz and Major Lubienski dined with me. The Poles are now having a well-earned rest. They have been fighting in Italy for eight months without a break. General Anders told me he is deeply anxious for Poland. For weeks a gigantic battle has swayed in and around

Warsaw. Inside what remains of that city the Polish Underground Movement, led by General Bor-Komarowski, have fought unceasingly against terrible odds and brutality. Outside the city the Red Army are hacking their way through the suburbs. We have managed to fly in a few loads of food and ammunition to these gallant people but not nearly sufficient to really help them. It is ghastly to think that they cannot expect much better treatment from the Russians than they got from the Germans. The wives and families of my three guests are all in Warsaw. I hated to see their distress. We talked in French of many things – of our times together in Baghdad, Cairo and Algiers, of Ali Khan's Teheran which won the St Leger today. We talked of Mr Churchill, whom General Anders admires very much, and General Carton de Wiart who is well loved in Poland. After dinner General Anders told me of the battle of Cassino. He said, 'It was more than a battle. On the marshes before Cassino you felt as if the Germans would see if you moved your eyes.' Then he told me how the Poles stormed Monte Cassino. I was very proud to listen.[1]

18 September 1944   *Naples*

This morning I watched Raphaeli planting seeds. First he took off his boots and put on his spectacles, then he mixed two kinds of soil in a pot. All the time he sang his jerky little tune to himself. He took a long time collecting and looking at the seeds and when he had finished sowing them he stumped off to hide them in a kind of wig-wam he has made in the bushes. I sat in my dressing gown on a bench behind his rakes, secateurs

[1] The Warsaw rising by the Polish 'Home Army', the Polish underground against the Germans, began on 1 August. Conducted with desperate courage under the command of General Bor-Komarowski it was finally (October) suppressed by the Germans with remorseless savagery. About one fifth of the population of Warsaw were killed. Many of the bravest of the Poles died, while the Soviet Army, already in Warsaw's suburbs, remained inactive. By Stalin's orders they gave no assistance to the fighting Poles and rejected all applications from the Western Powers to use Russian-occupied airfields for aircraft recovery after dropping supplies. It suited Stalin's book, of course, that the most vigorous and patriotic Poles should be exterminated and on this occasion the Germans did it for him.

and tools. When he had finished he fetched me a spray of white jasmine and went off to do the watering.

In Rome today a Fascist called Caruso, who used to be head of the Rome Fascist Police, was tried. An ex-warder, who turned King's Evidence, was seized by the excited mob, torn from the guard room, beaten up and lynched. Finally he was flung into the Tiber where a boatman beat him on the head till it was quite certain he was dead. Then he was hung up outside his own prison.

Douglas Fairbanks dined with me. He came to say goodbye because he is returning to America. We talked about my old friend, the Chinese River Gunboat, *Aphis*. He was on her during the South of France landing when she sank a German corvette. Since I last heard of her she has had many adventures: she took part in the Pantelleria, the Sicily and the Italy landings at Reggio and Pizzo. Before the South of France landing she had a complete overhaul and is now like a new ship, fitted with a radar set. Her speed is now fourteen knots.

20 September 1944   *Caserta*

Roger Makin dined with me. After dinner I sat sewing with Coco on my shoulder and he told me the most appalling story of Lublin. He said that the Germans take Jews there by train and gas them at the rate of about two thousand a day. They burn their bodies and sell their clothes and belongings in a neighbouring shop.

22 September 1944   *Caserta*

After a tremendous battle the Eighth Army have taken Rimini. Despite the German retreats in Russia and France General Kesselring's troops have been fighting fanatically to hold the carefully prepared Gothic Line between Pisa and Rimini. We have mauled the Germans badly and we are wondering if they will fall back on to the slopes of the Alps. The Fascist Divisions with them must be beginning to think.

Fitzroy Maclean flew in from Serbia where he has been living in the mountains with the guerrillas. He told me that we have bombed the railway there so thoroughly that he does not think the Germans will be able to get out. If Tito's people catch them alive there will be an unholy massacre.

Captain Burk, who works along the passage in the Secretariat of General Staff, told me today that he is in trouble: his feet are so large that he cannot get any boots to fit them. As his last pair are nearly worn through it is being considered whether he should be returned to the States. I suggested that he might get some boots from the American coloured troops whose feet look so large, but he told me sadly that he has already tried this, to no avail. Several coloured soldiers have been returned to the States because there were no boots large enough for them. I asked him if he had tried our police who are famous for their big feet. I telephoned Mark Sykes, the Provost Marshal, who was most sympathetic and promised to send me the biggest pair of boots he could get from the Police Depot. This evening they arrived and Capt. Burk came over to my office to try them on. An enthusiastic crowd of English and Americans accompanied him. For once we were ahead of the Americans: the boots were too large. I promised to get him a size smaller and he departed in great spirits. Boots for Burk! Bundles for Britain! Anglo-American relations are soaring.

24 September 1944   *Caserta*

The Hungarian First Army Commander Nadoy has escaped from Hungary by plane and crash landed in Italy. He brought peace overtures to Caserta from the Hungarian Government and the Regent. They say they will assist us if we can ensure that British and American troops occupy Hungary as well as Russians after the war. He told us that there are seven Hungarian Divisions and eight German Divisions in Hungary. They are poor troops and ill equipped.

We are all very anxious about our Airborne Division at Nijmegen.[1]

In Caserta we are discussing with the bearded representatives of EAM and ELAS (Greek Communists and Democrats), whether they will set aside their political quarrels and help us deal with the German garrisons instead of fighting each other.

The Balkans are in a superb muddle. In Bucharest and Sofia, which are now under Russian control, Americans are having their jeeps and watches taken off them by Russian soldiers. The situation is such that they can now only go out accompanied by a Russian officer. In Bulgaria problems are arising between the Bulgars and Greeks over Thrace. The Germans are trying to drive the Bulgars off the Rupel Pass, Macedonia, probably to keep the Russians off. Meanwhile Tito has disappeared from his Headquarters on Vis under the nose of our liaison officers. Probably he has gone to Moscow or Bucharest to meet the Russians. The latter have sent a 'Cultural Mission' into Yugoslavia!

Today we flew to Rome for a conference. General Jumbo read *The Adventures of Marco Polo*. I sat up in front with Penny the pilot. We saw a lot of hospital planes returning from the Front. Dan and I lunched together. Rome looked lovely. The shops are full of flowers. We flew back through a storm across Anzio battlefield. It is awful to get only glimpses of Dan.

There is a great deal of correspondence going on about the troops' beer. There is a shortage. To get each man a bottle a

[1.] Operation 'Market Garden', the combined ground and airborne attack to get across the Rhine at Arnhem and Nijmegen, had finally failed at Arnhem on 25 September. A large number of the British 1st Airborne Division were prisoners. The bridge across the Waal at Nijmegen was, however, in British hands.

week we have to get eight hundred thousand bottles distributed round the Theatre weekly. Apart from the fact that beer cannot be produced in England at the peace-time rate, Australia cannot assist us because she needs all she can produce for her own troops in the Pacific.

This evening Crown Prince Paul of Greece paid me a visit. He talked of his trip to London and of his wife and children. He laughed a lot when I told him that Lizzie Lezard had parachuted into the South of France and landed on a casino. I sat up late talking to Whitaker. Tomorrow, he is going home on *Python*, which means his time overseas has expired. During the last five years he has shared all our troubles and jokes. We shall miss him dreadfully.

8 October 1944   *Caserta*

Mr Churchill, Mr Eden, General Ismay, General Alan Brooke, Major-General Jacob, Brigadier Peak and a large staff arrived from England this morning on their way to Moscow. I think they are going to discuss Poland and the Far East. At 6 a.m. two of the Prime Minister's secretaries arrived at my house for breakfast and baths. One of them, Miss Minto, is an old friend of mine. Long ago we worked together in the War Office typists' pool. The other, Miss Layton, is a Canadian. She came to England when the war broke out and got a job at 10 Downing Street where she has been ever since. We swapped news about our jobs. They told me they often worked through the night. Mr Churchill frequently dictates straight on to the typewriter. I was pleased to get news of Miss Roads who for years was in charge of all War Office secretaries. She retired just before the war but in spite of her age managed to get back to the War Office where she is now. That I am an accurate shorthand typist is entirely due to her obstinacy.

Down at Villa Rivalta General Alexander and General Jumbo were talking to the CIGS about the ammunition shortage in Italy which is now very serious. Mr Churchill, Mr Macmillan and Mr Leeper were seeing the Greek Prime Minister. At nine-thirty we drove through the rain to Pomigliano aerodrome.

Dakotas were taking off with supplies for Greece. They left at the rate of about one every two minutes; there seemed to be dozens of them. Miss Layton and Miss Minto showed me the Liberator they are travelling in. It has seven bunks. We walked over to Mr Churchill's York which has a comfortable bedroom and a sitting room lined with green leather. In the kitchen two stewards were preparing lobster for lunch. 'From Naples?' I asked.

'No, Madame, Billingsgate,' they replied with scorn. I watched the party take off. Tonight they will be in Egypt and tomorrow or the next day in Moscow. Most of our staff, who have been up since 4 a.m. and had bristly chins, hurried off to shave. I got a newspaper on the aerodrome and then drove to the office. Wendell Willkie is dying in New York. The fighting in France is very fierce . . .

9 October 1944   Caserta

Tex McCrary came to see me. He had just returned from Bucharest which he said is an attractive city full of Leicas, silk stockings and caviar. He told me that the Russians in Bucharest are taking a very arrogant attitude towards British and Americans. They refuse to allow Allied Officers to see Ploesti though, as Tex said, 'We were the party who bombed it.' He confirmed all the stories I had already heard of the Russians holding up our officers and men and removing their private possessions and military equipment.

10 October 1944   Caserta

I work long hours and find the rent on an interesting job is high and exacting. I leave my house at seven-forty each day and return twelve hours later. In the interval I have the fun of being 'in the know' and seeing the great come and go, but along with it there is a deal of carbon paper and drudge and a lot of bores.

In this large family, General Jumbo and his Generals, the ADCs and personal assistants, the clerks, typists, chauffeurs, cooks, waiters and despatch riders who comprise his personal staff, I am the only civilian. We deal with 50 per cent Americans, and a large number of foreigners. Last week I dined with Hungarians, Roumanians, Greeks, Poles and Americans. Besides the unending stream of visitors there is always office work to be done and Messes to be run. It is strange to be a woman and a civilian in these circumstances for I have no rank or status and can say what I like to everyone. But equally I am often left behind on trips and conferences and dinners for these two reasons. I hear the clerks' chatter, the Aides tell me of their love affairs, I type General Jumbo's most private letters and keep the confidences of chauffeurs and kings alike but I am neither fish nor fowl nor good red herring and find it confusing sometimes. Purdah is not so far away.

11 October 1944 *Caserta*

The Poles in Italy are keeping two weeks' mourning for Warsaw. The fate of Poland, and particularly Warsaw where most of their families are, has been a deep agony for them. For once neither their gaiety nor their elegant manners could hide it. It is comforting to remember that though Catherine the Great of Russia used the throne of Poland as a lavatory seat – she died on it.

13 October 1944 *Caserta*

Aachen, after ignoring our ultimatum, is now being bombarded from land and air. It must be a veritable Hades. The Germans look as if they are going to fight to the finish. Thank Heavens the war is being fought out on their doorstep for a change.

This morning we heard that Greek Partisans had captured Athens. Mr Macmillan flew there today. The Greek Government and General Scobie are already on their way by ship.

General Clark returned from a trip to the north and came to see General Jumbo. While he was waiting he described to me the road from Florence to San Benedetto, in Alpe. 'It rises to three thousand feet. The Royal Engineers' work there is magnificent. They have built up the road on the cliff sides which the Germans blew up and have put Bailey bridges back over the gorges. Guns have been placed on the corners of the road because there is nowhere else to fix them. All traffic is stopped at a distance when they fire, otherwise the windows get broken. It is terrible for the wounded – they have to be carried down from the hilltops to the main roads. Sometimes this means a two-hour run in a jeep over rocks and potholes.' He told me about General Kesselring's counter-attack in the north. The Germans are fighting magnificently.

14 October 1944   Caserta

The death of Field Marshal Rommel has been announced. Strangely, we are all sorry to hear this. He was a great soldier and a gentleman. Most of us admired him and, like Aosta, we respected him.[1]

17 October 1944   Caserta

At the moment our three main problems are: the shortage of ammunition and reinforcements for the Eighth Army; mine-sweeping at the entrance of ports in Greece, which is proving very costly; and food for the population of Italy. There have been food riots in Palermo and we are afraid the same thing will happen in Florence.

At first when we began to work with the Americans we liked them for their generous manners and enthusiasm, and for their ridiculous jokes. When we got to know them a little better we found their know-all and show-off attitude rather a trial. But now, after working with them for many months, we have almost forgotten they are Americans. We have grown accustomed to their exuberance and they are getting used to our cold exteriors. They know our faults and we theirs. We have learnt a

[1]. Assumed by Hitler to have been involved in the plot to assassinate him in July, Rommel was given the choice of taking poison or standing trial before a People's Court. He chose the former. It was given out (14 October) as a heart attack.

lot from each other. There is not one of us, in our office anyway, who does not like them. We are apt to forget that America is a continent. And they, that we are not just a small island, but a Commonwealth.

There was something in the air this morning and the something was the Prime Minister returning from Moscow. There was a great bustle in our office. After lunch I drove to Naples to see that all was well at Villa Rivalta and the cottage in the garden which has been prepared for the overflow of guests. I bought some flowers to try and cheer up that dismal house. The garden was full of soldiers on guard. In the kitchen the cooks were preparing a big dinner. Fires were burning in all the rooms. I went round with Sergeant Trayler who is a wonderful organiser. He had forgotten nothing. Then I went out into the drive to wait. All our staff had gone to the aerodrome. I talked to Mark Sykes, the Provost Marshal, and he told me of the elaborate security arrangements the police have made for this visit. I asked him about his family at home and he told me that his wife is totally blind. One gets a great shock when one discovers that cheerful people like Mark Sykes have such tragedies. In the war we meet people superficially because we are always in a hurry. Also we meet many people, sometimes hundreds a day, so it is difficult to take in who they are and what they do, let alone anything else, like their miseries and tragedies.

The first car drew up with a wide sweep and General Jumbo and Mr Churchill stepped out. General Alexander and the CIGS came next. It was dusk when the last two cars arrived with the six typists. I gave them tea in the cottage and then carried their six black cases filled with papers from the conference over to the office in Rivalta while they had a wash. In the hall I met General John Harding. He told me that he was worried about the constant drain on General Alexander's resources. The Germans are fighting hard in North Italy and our troops

287

are very weary. The weather is all against us. General Alexander can ill afford to hand over divisions to other theatres.

At six o'clock the Prime Minister, the CIGS, General Alexander and General Jumbo and some others went into conference. In the next room, surrounded by black boxes and looking completely exhausted, sat Mr Drysdale. He prepares all the papers for meetings. I fetched him a whisky. Further along the passage Brigadiers Calthorpe, Peak and Oliver were sitting in the Map Room with Miss Bright. They told me about Russia while I poured them out drinks and then I went along to the drawing room to see Commander Thompson who was talking to Mark. He told us that Marshal Stalin was very friendly and had made three unprecedented appearances – he went to the ballet, dined at the British Embassy and saw Mr Churchill off at the aerodrome. The Russians greatly appreciate the aid we are still sending them via the Persian Gulf and by the North Atlantic route. We talked about supply, the weapon of tomorrow. Russia will need a lot of help to rehabilitate . . .

I wandered off to find the secretaries. The house was teeming with people. I listened to their varied descriptions of Russia. Slowly I pieced it together. The secretaries were upstairs in Mr Churchill's sitting room; we sat on tables and boxes as there were not enough chairs. They told me they had stayed in M. Molotov's villa outside Moscow. Charming Russian women had looked after them. Miss Minto described the command performance at the ballet – the magnificent opera house, relic of the Czars, and the audience dressed in rags. When Mr Churchill and Marshal Stalin appeared in the royal box everyone stood up and shouted and waved. They cheered and cheered. It seemed as if the ballet would never start. Then all five secretaries began to talk at once, of vodka and gigantic fifteen-course meals, of the miserable shops and the Kremlin. They had been to a ball in the Crimea and danced on a concrete floor with potholes in it. 'The Russians danced beautifully and were very gay.'

Miss Layton told me that she was duty secretary to the Prime Minister on the way home. When they landed in the Crimea she enquired where the lavatory was and was conducted to a hut nearby. On leaving it she was greatly embarrassed to find a queue waiting outside – the Prime Minister, the Foreign Secretary and the Chief of General Staff. At the end of a long day she was appalled to discover that she must dine at the official party and would be the only woman present. She arranged with her friends the detectives to sit between them at the far end of the table from the great ones. It was an immense banquet – course after course was brought in, toast after toast was drunk; the Russians thought nothing of drinking twenty vodkas. She knew she might have to work afterwards. It became a nightmare. After dinner there were speeches and more toasts. When Mr Churchill rose to speak he said, 'I shall toast the ladies. Miss Layton, your very good health.' He spoke of the great contribution Miss Layton and the other secretaries had made. They had journeyed with him to conferences in Canada, Egypt and Russia. They typed for him in London in the blitz. They worked in cars and aeroplanes and often throughout the night. When he sat down everyone clapped and called, 'Speech, speech.' Poor Miss Layton was covered with confusion. 'For me,' she said, 'it was a very great moment but I was so overcome I only managed to say, "Thank you very much, Mr Churchill." '

22 October 1944 *Caserta*

I was told there was no need for me to go to the aerodrome this morning so I breakfasted on my verandah in the sun. Before long I saw outriders racing along the road hundreds of feet below me. They were followed by the convoy of cars carrying the Prime Minister and his party to Pomigliano. I was surprised to see General Jumbo's big Lincoln was empty and his flag flying on the grey Humber which Olroyd drives. Later Olroyd came to take me to the office and told me that he had been lined up at the front door of Villa Rivalta as number two car. When the Prime Minister came out he said that he wanted to talk to Field Marshal Brooke, General Alexander and General Jumbo and so the Humber, which holds four in the back, was called up. 'You could have knocked me down with a feather,' said Olroyd. 'General Wilson and General Alexander didn't half look funny on the little seats. Ee, by goom I was in such a fuss I nivver thowt the car would start. But nivver mind, I got the stoomp.' He fished out of his pocket the butt of a cigar. 'The missus will be ower the moon,' he laughed.

24 October 1944   *Caserta – Athens*

Bill Corbauld, our new ADC, and I took off in a Dakota[1] at ten this morning from Marchianese with Sergeants Trayler, Macdonald and Clark. We flew over Bari and Otranto to the Ionian Sea. I was so tired I slept all the way which was a great disappointment – I wanted to see the Isles of Greece. When I woke we were circling Kalamaki aerodrome. I was horrified to see the black marks of shell holes on the runways. I hoped our crew would not land on the wrong strip. We loaded all the food and office gear we had brought on to a truck and drove between pepper trees into Athens. Sergeant Trayler and Sergeant Macdonald knew the way to General Mazaraki's house. They were in Greece with General Jumbo in 1941.

Madame Mazaraki gave us a wonderful welcome. She said that she was pleased to have the General's Mess in her house again and apologised profusely because the Germans had taken most of her furniture away. She explained that she and her family had moved down to the basement so that the General could have as much room and privacy as he wanted. I insisted that General Jumbo would not like her to do that but she replied that all the arrangements were made and they were too happy to mind a few discomforts – 'The Germans are gone. That is all that matters to us,' she said.

Later I took some letters and messages from General Jumbo to General Scobie, who is commanding our troops in Greece. While I was waiting to see him his ADC gave me a cigarette

[1.] In Greece, where (as elsewhere) resistance against the Germans had been conducted by mutually distrustful Communist and anti-Communist forces, the Germans had withdrawn in early October and Communists (ELAS) occupied many places, imposing a reign of terror. There was universal rejoicing at liberation, but fear of serious internal trouble.

and, to my horror, he lit it with a five-million drachma note. 'Don't look so shocked,' he said. 'the inflation is getting worse every day. All the Greeks light their cigarettes with these – if they can get the cigarettes.' He gave me a whole set of drachma notes – all quite worthless. As I was leaving the General's room an old Brigadier whom I had not met before came up to me and said, 'I think it is a disgrace that you, a woman and a civilian, should be here joy-riding. You ought to be ashamed of yourself and so ought General Wilson for letting you come.'

I dined with General Scobie and his staff in a suite of rooms which the German Commander occuped ten days ago. He told me that the Germans have left a lot of agents behind to do sabotage and stir up trouble. Though the food shortage in Athens is very serious the shops are filled with luxury goods, watches, cameras, etc. It is clear that the Germans did all they could to make the people they conquered relax rather than resist. There was plenty to tempt the quislings and plenty to fear for those who dared defy them. Back in my room at the Grande Bretagne Hotel I lay awake and wondered what Athens was like a fortnight ago . . .

25 October 1944   *Athens*

Early this morning I walked out of the hotel, turned right past the memorial to the Greek Unknown Warrior, past the Temple of Jupiter to the Mazarakis' villa. Sergeant Trayler and I went all over the house. We managed to fix it so that everyone had a bed, a table and a chair. After we had shifted the furniture around, made the beds and hung towels I unpacked the stationery and files and saw that the telephones worked in the little room we are using as an office. Later I went to Kala-maki aerodrome. In Greece the atmosphere seems very clear. The bare mountains and the blue sea looked lovely in the strong sunlight. All about the field were busted German air-craft. A Guard of Honour was lined up. General Jumbo filled the doorway of 'Freedom' and waddled a little as he came down the steps. Admiral Cunningham was with him. He inspected the Guard and then shook hands with people who had come to meet him. This is a day General Jumbo has looked forward to for a very long time. We drove in a long crocodile of cars slowly into Athens. I went with some Greeks. We made a little tour of the town. People on the sidewalks clapped and waved when the General passed.

At three o'clock General Jumbo paid an official call on the Prime Minister who came to the Mazarakis' house at three-thirty to return it. I spent a busy afternoon in the office, mostly telephoning. Mr Eden and some financial experts were staying at the Embassy. General Jumbo is attending a meeting on inflation this evening. On my way to dinner, when the car turned the bend by the Temple of Jupiter, I saw the most wonderful sight: the Parthenon had been floodlit. It seemed to hang in the black velvet sky – a golden temple.

26 October 1944   Athens

This morning General Jumbo went to see Piraeus and the Twenty-Third Army Brigade. I worked in the office and arranged the house for the press party tonight. The British Embassy kept telephoning about the press release on Mr Eden's visit. At midday I went to the flower market to buy flowers for the party. There I met our ADC Bill Corbauld, who was in a dilemma. The wreath he had ordered for General Jumbo to place on the Unknown Warrior's Tomb at twelve-thirty today has gone astray somewhere between the flower market and the Mazarakis' house.

Outside the Grande Bretagne Hotel I met my old friend Colonel Zigantes of the Greek Sacred Squadron. He had just returned home after three years and insisted that I join him for a drink. We sat in a corner of the crowded bar and drank ouzo. He toasted Great Britain and I toasted Great Greece. Each time the door opened there were cries of joy and welcome as old friends met. I could not understand what they said, but I could see very well how they felt. Colonel Zigantes, his big brown face creased with smiles, kept getting up to welcome people. He always returned to my table wiping his eyeglass. 'You see,' he said, 'this is such a wonderful day for us. All

292

these are wonderful days.' When I left he took off his Sacred Squadron badge and pinned it on my jacket.

At six-thirty the war correspondents arrived and crowded into the old-fashioned room – the same room where in 1941 General Jumbo gave the order for the evacuation of the British Forces from Greece. Stiff French chairs were pushed back against the walls; the green curtains were drawn; in a glass case the swords and pistols of old General Mazaraki lay beside his blue and gold uniform. After a while someone tapped on a table and General Jumbo began to talk in a fat straightforward way. He explained how, in 1941, the Greek Government had informed him that the situation was desperate, Germans were pouring in from the north, Piraeus had been heavily bombed, the Greek Prime Minister had committed suicide. The Greeks thought it would be best for the British to leave and return later. General Jumbo said that in that dark hour the spirit of the Greek people was something he would never forget. They waved goodbye to our troops with courage and goodwill. They shouted 'Come back again' and threw flowers at our troops as they marched away.

In this war, he continued, the Greeks had suffered greatly. They had fought hard and well against the Italians and Germans who had superior numbers and weapons. For three long years and more they had resisted the German occupation despite terrible reprisals. Their villages had been razed to the ground, their heroes shot, thousands had starved. But they held on and waited till our victories in the west and the south had pinched the Germans out of Greece. This week they had welcomed us back to Athens with the same spirit as before. General Jumbo said he hoped the great sacrifices and courage of the Greeks would not go unrewarded but unless something was done quickly to help them they would once more face starvation.

We staff gave a dinner party for the Phrances and Benski families at the Grande Bretagne Hotel. We took food because there was none to be had otherwise. Our guests were pathetically excited over our rations. They said, 'Do you mind if we eat an awful lot? We have not seen meat for so long.' They all had second helpings. Afterwards they took us to their flat. Some of

293

their friends and a guitarist joined us and we all sat round the empty fireplace and sang their national songs. It was very gay. One of the party said to me, 'Excuse if I sing too loud. It gives me much pleasure. You see we have all had Germans billeted in our houses. One of the things we hated most was the sound of their boots along the streets and on our staircases.'

Several of the women at the party spoke English. I asked them about the German occupation. They said there had been a curfew at eight-thirty every night so the evenings had seemed endless: there was little food; radios were not allowed; nor could they visit one another. It was dangerous to talk freely lest your German lodger should overhear.

By day someone had to go out to try and find food but when they were in the streets or trams there was always the risk that the Germans would cordon off a space where they happened to be and say, 'We'll take you, and you, and you.' Then they would be taken out and shot as a reprisal for something the Greek Resistance had done, no matter whether they were connected with it or not. 'So whenever anyone went out you were not sure if you would ever see them again. It was a nightmare.' The Greeks explained to me that one of the reasons for the tremendous political dissentions in Greece today was that during the German occupation no schools or universities were allowed. The young men and boys had nothing to talk about. No news came in from outside the country. They became absorbed in politics and began to take very definite sides, either to the right or left. Fuel for revolution.

I shall never forget the gaiety and hospitality of these people. Though they had not been able to buy clothes for a long time and cosmetics are an exorbitant price, they were chic and neatly dressed. Today a Max Factor lipstick costs seven pounds sterling in Athens. I drove home in an open jeep with Colonel Zigantes and the guitarist. We made a great noise singing 'Lili Marlene'. The streets were strangely empty. People have not yet got used to going out after 8.30 p.m.

All day there have been conferences on supply and currency. Air Marshal Slessor, Lord Moyne, Mr Macmillan, Mr Eden, Mr Leeper, General Scobie, Admiral Cunningham and General Jumbo attended the discussions. Piraeus has been badly damaged by the Germans which will add to our difficulties of getting food into the country. General Jumbo gave a lunch party for M. Papandreou at the Mess. I had mine on a tray in the office. Afterwards I escaped for an hour and jeeped up the curling road to the Acropolis. A cold wind was whipping grey clouds across the sky. The Parthenon and the view across the red brown roofs and narrow streets of Athens is superb.

Madame Mazaraki came to tea with General Jumbo. She told us about the first winter of the German occupation when the Athenians died in such numbers that vans toured the streets picking up corpses where they had fallen. 'The hospitals were filled with dying children – sometimes there were as many as three in each bed. We could do nothing for them except give them a little warm water and watch them die. It was terrible for old people who lived alone – often they died and were not found till days later when someone chanced to visit them.' Madame Mazaraki told me about the hideous things which had happened in the country: whole villages were burned down and the villagers were lucky if they were shot instead of being burned inside their homes. With tears pouring down her cheeks she described to me how, a couple of weeks ago, all Athens watched the Swastika being taken down from the high mast on the Parthenon: 'The greatest moment in our lives was when we saw our blue and white flag being hoisted up there against the sky.'

Today was a day of celebration and ceremonies. It was the fourth anniversary of the Italian Invasion of Greece. General Jumbo and the ADCs went to the Cathedral for a Thanksgiving Service and afterwards joined in the parade at the Tomb of the

Unknown Warrior. I watched from the roof of the Grande Bretagne Hotel. Below me was a vast crowd: every roof, window and balcony was black with people and along the streets political parties marched with banners and pictures of the King of Greece, Mr Churchill and the Hammer and Sickle. Members of EAM yelled '*Kapa, kapa, epselum*', as they marched. Round the Tomb of the Unknown Warrior lines of Evzones, the Greek Royal Guard in their white frilly skirts and red slippers, and nurses in white stood in a great V. British and Greek sailors, soldiers and airmen marched past and Greek girl soldiers, in khaki with kepis and cartridge belts, went with them. There was a priest in a great purple cloak. I watched with a war correspondent who explained to me who some of the people were. He told me that George Jellicoe has done well in Greece and when he comes to Athens he gets a great reception – the Greeks shout 'Jeelico' and clap whenever they see him.

Back at the General's Mess I found Madame Mazaraki waiting for me. She led me down into the basement to a dark cellar where she introduced me to her son Jan, who was hiding there in a crate. She explained that he is a Royalist and that the Communists have sworn to kill him. He is twenty years old. For some time he has been hiding in the mountains. Now he has come to Athens to see his family; he knows it is safe when General Jumbo is here and there is a British Guard round the house. She explained to me that during the long years of occupation the youth of Greece had no wireless or newspapers, and heard nothing of the outside world; there were no schools or universities and so they became absorbed in politics. 'And now, when peace has come, the country is split with political dissension, the young men feel violently about it and are prepared to fight each other. It is a catastrophe.' She begged me to ask General Jumbo to take Jan back with us to Italy so that he might join the Greek Brigades there and fight for his King and Country instead of being hunted like an outlaw in Greece. I told her we cannot involve General Jumbo in this but I would try to help. I made her promise to tell no one of our talk. I went off to find our orderlies who always help if they can. I needed a spare battle-dress. They produced three and I chose the smallest. Back in the cellar I tried it on Jan – it was a bit big for him but adequate.

At 5.30 a.m. I hurried to the Mazaraki house and the usual bustle of departure began: papers, equipment and luggage were loaded into our cars, together with the orderlies and Jan. Endless people came unexpectedly to say goodbye. We all hugged Madame Mazaraki. With the General, Admiral Cunningham and staff we drove to Kalamaki where Sergeant Trayler told me that all cargo and orderlies were aboard our second Dakota. We climbed into 'Freedom' and both planes took off. I watched the Parthenon disappear and looked down on the Corinth Canal. Admiral Cunningham turned his swivel chair to tell me the Germans had done everything possible to render the canal impassable: they'd rammed a ship across its entrance and then blown up two bridges which caused a huge tonnage of earth to slide into the water. 'It will take a long time to clear,' he said, and explained that normally a destroyer could pass through if great care was taken to navigate lest the propellors got caught on the sides. A cruiser cannot get through.

Through wisps of cloud we flew on. General Jumbo put his Sherlock Holmes down on his tummy and fell asleep. The Aides gossiped about Athens: 'Nearly all the dancers at the Argentina Night Club had collaborated with the Germans . . . We swapped cigarettes for sponges . . .' We climbed to about 15,000 feet because the weather was bad. Admiral Cunningham turned his chair again, lit a cigarette and talked about his forty-five years at sea; his wife has been very ill; his second son went down in a submarine . . . Sergeant Trayler brought sherry and sandwiches and General Jumbo woke up and began reading his book again.

I thought of Jan – flying for the first time, entering a new world of which he knows nothing and nobody. Through the billowing clouds we bumped down on to the runway at Marchianese. I drove with the General straight to the office where we

297

learned there had been a great battle in the Pacific[1] and the Japanese fleet had been badly knocked about. A mountain of work awaited us. Mark, forever kind, had taken Jan to the Kennels Mess where we would all lunch. He would get in touch with Greek forces north of us to arrange for Jan to join them.

At lunch Jan was so shy he could hardly move but he wolfed the food which clearly astounded him. When a car arrived to take him north he led me aside, fished in his pockets and handed me five gold sovereigns to keep safe for him, a crumpled note to send to his mother, and a small antique revolver, inlaid with silver, which he explained, with difficulty, his mother wanted me to keep forever. It was the pistol General Mazaraki always carried. I tried to refuse it but he clutched my arm and said, 'It's my mother's wish – an order – you have to keep.' As he reached the car he turned and said, 'I also a great soldier will be.' His small figure in a too big battle-dress, with tears pouring down his cheeks, left me aghast at the tragedy of war. Before I began the General's work I sent a signal to Madame Mazaraki and signed it Jan Ranfurly – taking care only she could understand it.

2 November 1944   *Caserta*

A gruesome lunch at the Kennels: Jack Wintour, who had just arrived from Yugoslavia, described his experiences in Montenegro with the Partisans where he travelled mostly by horse and considered himself lucky to sleep with a roof over his head. He told us that appalling things are going on in Yugoslavia; 'In some parts of Europe, it seems,' said Jack, 'we have gone back two thousand years. I cannot tell you half the things they do – the Ustaschis, quislings and fascists – most of their tortures are unmentionable. Slitting children's throats in front of their parents and cutting them up and making the mothers eat their hearts is a mild incident where I come from. The other day in Bosnia a hospital which housed some hundred wounded was attacked at night and all the patients had their throats slit.'

[1] The Battle of Leyte Gulf, Admiral Halsey's great victory.

After that the conversation turned to trench warfare in North Italy. Chris Sinclair, who is on leave from that front, told us, 'We have to eat, sleep and do everything else in the trenches. The British are pretty clean on the whole, but the Germans – how they smell. Taking over their trenches makes you vomit.' He told us that the Germans are diabolically clever at fixing booby traps – they often fix them on dead men and sometimes even on the wounded. One of their tricks is to put a booby trap in an obvious place with another well concealed just in front of it so that when people go to render the first useless they get killed on the way . . . I could not finish my lunch so slipped away and walked to the office through the woods. When I think of the nightmare things that are being done every day in Europe, not only by our enemies but by our Allies, I feel there is no hope for humanity.

5 November 1944   *Caserta*

Today news came that Field Marshal Sir John Dill, head of the British Joint Staff Mission in Washington, has died.[1] I was dreadfully sorry to hear this. I remember him in Cairo, a fine-looking man with kind and charming manners. He and his wife have done a great job in Washington. It will be hard to replace them.

Cheese, meat, sugar, coffee, tea and matches are to be sent to Greece immediately. Stabilisation of the drachma should begin on November 10th.

Bill Maclean and Julian Amery arrived today from Albania where they have been working behind the lines for nine months.

Penny, our pilot, dined with me. He told me about the Battle of Britain. He talked fast and enthusiastically and drew pictures and plans for me on my writing block. I felt proud to listen.

---

[1] Dill had been CIGS before Brooke, and probably did as much as any man for Anglo-American understanding.

News has just reached us that Lord Moyne, who succeeded Mr Casey as Minister of State in Cairo, has been murdered. He was returning from his office at lunchtime. As he got out of his car two gunmen, who were hiding in his little garden, shot him. He fell, riddled with bullets and died almost immediately. His chauffeur, a good friend of ours, was also killed.

Lord Moyne was sixty-four. He was Secretary of State for the Colonies and Leader of the House of Lords. He came to the Middle East with Mr Casey and was in Cairo all through 1943 with us. I used to dine with him often. He was always interesting and always kind. He was one of those rare people who had taken the trouble to go and see for himself – he had travelled all over the world, studying our Empire and Colonial administration, collecting birds and flowers and rare animals. Often he went in his own yacht. In Cairo his two main interests were Abyssinia and Palestine. We are all sad, and horrified by this news. We have lost a very good man, and yet another friend.

President Roosevelt has won the Presidential Election for the fourth time.

Yesterday was my thirty-first birthday. It was a warm sunny morning and Raphaeli carried his canaries out into the garden. A puff of cloud or white smoke hung over Vesuvius. On the way to work Olroyd told me about a gang of British and American deserters and some Italians, who have been doing armed hold-ups on the main roads. Sometimes they are dressed as military police and travel in a jeep. They halt cars, like a check post, and then rob the owners. Olroyd said he won't stop for anyone.

At Marchianese the fields sparkled with frost. I saw a Fortress taking off. Around the palace everyone was bustling to work. An Italian was calling to his imperturbable white ox as he ploughed the green strip by the stables. Up in the office General Jumbo dictated some letters in his plain, unhurried way. As I was leaving his room, he said, 'You have a nasty cough. You'd better get some Faymel Syrup.' Then he talked about coughs in the Boer War for a while. He is always kind and considerate to me. After work I went to an Italian cinema to see Charlie Chaplin and Jack Oakie in *The Great Dictator*. The ex-fascist audience seemed to enjoy it very much – I could scarcely hear the jokes for their laughter.

Today I heard that Lancaster planes have sunk the enemy's largest battleship, the *Tirpitz*, in Tromsoe Fiord. Mr Churchill is in France with General de Gaulle. Himmler has made a speech for Hitler and we are all wondering what has become of the Führer. News from Holland is terrible. Fifty per cent of her land is flooded as a result of war and five million of her nine million inhabitants may have to be evacuated. Air Marshal Sir T. Leigh Mallory, who was due to arrive here from England today, has not turned up.

20 November 1944   *Caserta*

Today the headlines in the newspapers are: 'Allies batter Siegfried Line. Pipe Line miracle reaches Burma. Four Armies fight in Reich.'

Meanwhile telegrams are coming in reporting a crisis in Belgium similar to the one in Greece. Resistance groups in both these countries do not want to lay down their arms. The Allies are doing their best to distribute food and steady the local currencies but unrest and party politics make this difficult.

Three Italian Partisans lunched with us at the Kennels. They all represented different politics so, as we could not pronounce their names, we called them M. Le Communiste, M. L'Indépendant and M. Le Capitaliste. They were a delightful trio and we had an uproarious lunch, everyone talking their own politics as hard as they could. M. Le Communiste had a

tragic face. He spoke good English and told me that he had
been in prison for eight years. His mother and father are still
in hiding. One of his brothers is now in Fascist hands – the
other has already been killed. I talked to him about the slums
of Naples and asked him how they could be cleaned up. He
told me that it would take years and years to do that. M. L'Indépendant spoke no French or English but the others translated
for him and he got on very well and nearly died of laughter
when he heard his own jokes being translated into English. M.
Le Capitaliste, a fat beaming little man who seemed to have
put all the gold he possessed into his teeth, kept us all amused.
He told me that very shortly they are to go back behind the
lines. This afternoon they are seeing General Jumbo.

22 *November 1944*   *Caserta*

This morning Mark brought a bombshell into my room in the
shape of a telegram. It came from London and stated that
General Jumbo is to succeed Field Marshal Dill in Washington
as head of the British Joint Staff Mission. The news is secret so I
cannot tell Dan or discuss it with anyone. If General Jumbo
asks me to go to Washington I cannot very well refuse. This
would mean that I shall be separated once again from Dan.
Though we do not see each other very often we can telephone
whenever we like, letters only take a day or two and when we
get leave we can be together. No news could depress me more
than this. Another separation at this stage in the war is an awful
thought.

23 *November 1944*   *Caserta*

This morning General Jumbo rang for me and told me that he
would like me to go with him to Washington. He said he was
taking only three personal staff. He stumped up and down the
room as he talked. His shoes squeaked. I asked him whether I
must decide at once because I would like to discuss it with Dan.
General Jumbo said he was going to London tomorrow so I
could go to Rome and consult Dan. I congratulated him on his

new appointment. He said he would be very sorry to leave the Mediterranean.

General Alexander, who is taking over Supreme Allied Command of the Mediterranean from General Jumbo, flew down to discuss the hand-over. After spending a year fighting his way up Italy I don't suppose he relishes the idea of returning to live in Caserta. Bill Cunningham, his Military Assistant, and Mark had a brief session on the hand-over of staffs, Messes, cars, planes, etc. General Alexander is bringing most of his own staff, from Generals to orderlies, with him.

I dined with Jock Whitney and Tex McCrary for their Thanksgiving Day party in the Cascade Camp. Before dinner Jock showed me his caravan. It was filled with new books, hunting knives, superb photographs of flying, a backgammon board and such like. Jock opened a tin of foie gras and mixed some excellent Martinis, and with the wireless on we were as comfortable and cheerful as can be. I asked them what they were giving thanks for and they told me I was horribly ignorant – they were celebrating their departure from England long ago. I told them I would celebrate for the same reason. After dinner in the Cascade Mess we went over to the Camp Club which is made out of a couple of Nissen huts joined together and lined with bamboo. At one end there was a bar, at the other a big fire. Tex and Jock introduced me to all their friends: 'The Sheriff', their Provost Marshal, a great towering amiable person; 'The Judge', the US Judge Advocate, a cheerful plump man. I danced with Willie Wyler, who made the film *Mrs Miniver.* He was celebrating in a big way because his birthplace, Mulhouse, had just been liberated by the Allies. He insisted on dancing with one foot in a waste-paper basket. I have seldom enjoyed myself more. Only one of the Americans, a blond German-looking man whose name I do not know, was unfriendly. He came over and told me at some length how he detested the British and that he hoped Russia would 'get' us. When the Club closed at eleven-thirty we went over to the Sheriff's hut and played backgammon.

General Jumbo flew to London yesterday. Mr Churchill sent his York for him. There was so much work to be done in the office that I could not get away till today. Telegrams on the ammunition situation are still coming in and going out. The British Eighth and the American Fifth Armies are faced with a serious shortage. I was so tired that I fell asleep on my way out to dine with Admiral Hewitt who commands the Eighth US Fleet. He was giving a party for his old friend 'Pop' who is returning home. We sat at a long dining table on which there were three huge birthday cakes with candles. After dinner Admiral Hewitt made a little speech for 'Pop' and 'Pop', who looked dreadfully sad to be leaving the Admiral's staff, made one back. I sat next to Admiral Hewitt who told me about the carrier war in the Pacific. He also talked about his wife whom he is very proud of. They have been married for thirty-five years. Afterwards we danced. Admiral Hewitt dances à la Sir Roger de Coverley.

This morning I drove to Rome. All the way I wondered what I ought to do about Washington. Dan has been a prisoner for three and a half years and the one thing in the world we don't want is to be separated . . . General Jumbo has been kind to all of us so I do not want to let him down . . . If I were in uniform, I should have to go . . . I found Dan at his office. He was so pleased and excited that I had two days leave that at first I could not tell him why I had come. After lunch, when we went back to work, I rang up Daphne and told her the news. She said, 'I wouldn't go, but do you think you will be evacuated again for being in the same Theatre as Dan once General Jumbo has left?' I spent a miserable afternoon wandering about Rome.

It was awful telling Dan. He said that I would have to go if General Jumbo wanted me. Personal things mustn't matter in a war and perhaps it would not be for very long. We went out to dinner sunk in gloom.

The newspapers have the news: 'Wilson for Washington'. It is also announced that General Alexander has been made a Field Marshal and General Mark Clark is to take over Allied Armies in Italy.

For the last two days I have done my utmost to be gay. Dan has taken me dancing, and riding before breakfast. I have been buying Christmas presents, but it all makes me very sad.

General Jumbo returned from England. He told me he had had a most successful visit. He is going to Washington very soon. He asked me what Dan and I had decided about Washington. I gave him this note which Dan had written to him:

> Allied Commission, Rome.
> 27.11.44.

> Thank you very much for your message that you sent to me with Hermione. I am proud that you should have asked her to go with you, and have told her to accept, hoping that in this way we can repay you in some measure for your great kindness to her when I was a prisoner.
>
>   She will be leaving me and all her friends, but I know that you will do everything possible to look after her, and to bring us together again as soon as such a thing becomes a possibility.

Lately, like Raphaeli, I have been getting up with the sun. There is so much to do. At Villa Pina I am struggling with a mass of washing and mending and I have begun to pack my things. I am spring-cleaning the house for whoever comes next. I am anxious for Raphaeli and Italia. What will become of them? In the office we are clearing up our files and papers and packing a great wooden box of office equipment which will go by sea to America. Christmas is looming so there are many personal letters to write and parcels to send. Besides routine work and the hand-over I have become inundated with invitations from people who know I am going away. And all the time, at the back of my mind, are personal worries: this horrible separation from Dan . . . Daphne, who is trying to get into Allied Commission in Rome . . . Mummy, who is ill and lonely in Switzerland and who will be dismayed when she learns I am going to America. She had so hoped that when Italy was liberated we would be able to pay her a visit across the Alps. Meanwhile in these Headquarters there is the usual air of expectancy and unrest which goes with a change of command. General Jumbo's Generals, staff officers, drivers, orderlies and Mess staff are all wondering what will become of them when General Jumbo leaves and Field Marshal Alexander arrives with his own people.

For days the crisis in Greece has been growing steadily worse. M. Papandreou is trying to carry out the Disarmament Programme but the Communists will not play. General Scobie has had leaflets dropped from the air calling for a united Greece and rehabilitation. Now civil war has broken out. Yesterday the police fired on a mob and fifteen were killed. Our Parachute Brigade, which was embarking at Piraeus, will have to stay in Greece. Two more Infantry Battalions are being dispatched from Taranto at once. Today a fierce telegram arrived from Mr Churchill saying that General Jumbo has not kept him sufficiently informed about all this.

This morning General Jumbo gave me this letter to send on to Dan:

5th December, 1944.

Thank you for your letter which Hermione gave me on my return. It is very kind of you to say that she can come with me to Washington and I much appreciate your magnanimity over it. In a way it may be better for you both as there is always carping and criticism over wives and husbands serving together in a theatre of war. I will do my best to look after her in Washington and am sure she will be the greatest help to me.

I think you must arrange with Allied Commission that you

pay Liaison visits there from time to time. All good luck to you.

Penny, our pilot, brought me two bananas from Gibraltar for Coco. The old bird was very pleased – he has not seen one since we left Africa.

7 December 1944   Rome

Yesterday morning General Jumbo flew to Florence where the Rifle Brigade were giving him a farewell party. He took with him all his 'black button' staff. I drove to Rome to help prepare for his farewell press party today. I passed through Cassino where the grass is beginning to grow again. Peasants were digging amongst the ruins searching for their belongings. They looked very pathetic in their thin clothes in the rain. A puff of yellow dust hung in the air where a mine had gone off but they seemed quite unperturbed. I spent a lovely evening with Dan. For once the water was hot at the Grand Hotel. A great luxury. The newspapers are full of a speech Mr Stettinius has made in Washington regarding Italy and Greece. He says, 'Hands off, Britain.'[1]

Today the weather was so bad we did not think General Jumbo would be able to fly down to Rome. I spent a busy morning in the sitting room I have turned into an office at the Grand Hotel. Signals from London and Athens are being relayed here about the Greek trouble. ELAS are fighting our troops who are trying to restore law and order. General Gammell, our Chief of Staff, rang up from Caserta and dictated a long note on Greece for General Jumbo to use at the press conference. The line was bad. General Jumbo arrived after lunch and at once began dictating his speech. There was only just time to type it out. This is often the way. Sometimes I wait all day with nothing but filing to do and then I get a mass of

[1.] There was strong Anglo-American disagreement about Greece, the Americans refusing to accept the danger of Communist dominance and suspecting the British of playing Balkan politics. Churchill, with a personal visit at Christmas, saved Greece.

dictation and have to type it out in minimum time. Down in the big lounge, which has been cleared of civilians, General Jumbo addressed a crowd of Mediterranean war correspondents for the last time. He wore breeches and boots. He stood with his feet together. He has surprisingly elegant legs. For a while General Jumbo spoke of his five years in the Mediterranean and then there was a rustle of notebooks and interest when he started talking about Greece. Afterwards cocktails and sandwiches were handed round. I always enjoy meeting war correspondents. They see things for themselves – we don't.

Dan and I dined at the British Embassy with Sir Noel and Lady Charles. In the middle of dinner the Ambassador was called to the telephone. He came back looking very pleased and told us that Bonomi has formed a new Government. Food is still the main problem in Italy. We are so short of shipping that it does not look as if we will be able to maintain the three hundred grammes of bread per day per person.

10 December 1944   *Caserta*

Today Mark gave me a copy of this letter which he is sending to Lord Harding, Military Assistant to the Adjutant General, at the War Office:

General Jumbo tells me that your General has said you would require listed particulars of all personnel being taken by General Jumbo to America, and so herewith:

C/Sgt. Trayler F.H.	Rifle Brigade	Mess Caterer
Cpl. Gelblum I.	Palestine Buffs	Storeman
Tran Lonj	Indo-Chinese	Houseboy
VanThanh	Indo-Chinese	Houseboy

The above are proceeding by sea from NAPLES direct to the U.S.A. on 13 December.

| W/Sgt. McDonald J. | R.A.S.C. | Personal Driver to Gen. Wilson |
| A/Sgt. Porta J.C. | A.C.C. | Personal Cook to Gen. Wilson |

L/Cpl. Nicol W.	R.A.S.C.	Staff Car Driver
Rfn. Robinson L.	K.R.R.C.	Personal Waiter to Gen. Wilson
Achmed Mohammed Amar	Sudanese	Personal Servant & Valet to Gen. Wilson
Dinh Van Ha	Indo-Chinese	Valet to myself.

The above are proceeding to U.K. by air on 12 December and then by sea with Gen. Wilson to U.S.A. on 28 December.

The officers accompanying General Wilson to England are Major P. M. Wilson and Capt. Egleston, both Rifle Brigade. The former is due for leave and posting. The latter, on completion of his duty with General Jumbo in England, is returning to the 1st Bn., The Rifle Brigade. Hermione Ranfurly is coming with us also, leaving here by air on 17 December, and then by sea to U.S.A. 28 December. Necessary posting orders have been issued for all above through normal 'A', M.S., and GHQ 2nd Echelon channels. I am looking forward very much to seeing you and this time we really will get that dinner together.

All morning I typed for General Jumbo lists of the contents and value of his luggage. He asked for four copies: one for himself, one for the Insurance Company and two for Lady Wilson. There were eight long lists and General Jumbo had written them all out on notepaper in his own writing. They reminded me of packing to go to school:

> Two pairs Gumboots
> Two pairs Pants (1 thick 1 thin)
> Two pairs Marching Boots (1 old, 1 new)
> Seven silver spoons
> One Dogrobber suit
> Etc.

It is amusing watching a change of High Command from close quarters. Feelings run very strong. Careerists watch every move like vultures. Great and small are apprehensive as to what will become of them. Down the long stone passages of the Palace one hears snatches of conversation . . . 'Alex? huh. An Irish bull in the Anglo-American china shop.' . . . 'Jumbo? Fat slug. Should have been retired after the Boer War . . .' 'I'm for Alex.

A brilliant soldier.' 'I'm for Jumbo. Such a wise man.' . . . So it goes on. The Generals themselves are not altogether oblivious of this. Amongst the two personal staffs there is bound to be a clash of loyalties for I have never yet met a PA or an ADC who did not think his own General the best of all Generals.

12 December 1944   *Caserta*

I drove early to Pomigliano airfield. American police and British Marines were lined up as a Guard of Honour and all the British and American Service Commanders were waiting by the Prime Minister's York which has been sent for General Jumbo.

General Jumbo arrived at 9 a.m. He put his cane in his mouth while he struggled out of his mackintosh and then walked across the runway to inspect the Guard of Honour. Achmed, the Sudanese servant, was busy putting luggage into the plane. For the first time since I have known him his headdress was awry. Van Ha, the Indo-Chinese batman, who was going too, stood staring at the VIPs. General Jumbo came over to the plane, asked if Achmed was in, and then shook hands with everyone including his two American outriders. He turned to me: 'Have a happy week with Dan,' he said, 'but don't arrive late in London – you mustn't miss the boat.' Water splashed high as the York ran along the runway. We all waved. General Jumbo had left the Mediterranean Command.

I said goodbye to Admiral Hewitt and General Eaker on the aerodrome and drove with Admiral Cunningham to Caserta. The two outriders were fascinating to watch as they weaved and swayed through the traffic. We went like hell. I spent the morning climbing up and down the long staircases and crossing the wide courtyards of the Palace, saying goodbye to people and thanking them for their many kindnesses to me. On the fifth floor, in Air Marshal Slessor's office, John Orme and Nigel Maynard were struggling with ETAs of VIPs (expected time of arrival of very important people). Their telephones rang unceasingly. These two have worked in close liaison with us since Algiers. The Air Marshal limped out of his room to wish me good luck. Next door Major Mason, General Eaker's henchman and another great ally of ours, presented me with a photograph of his master. Across the courtyard on the third floor I visited Mr Macmillan and all his staff. Their rooms are lined with lovely Italian pictures.

Nearby in the United States Political Adviser's Office Mr Offie gave me a fine farewell present: a permit to take Coco with me to America. 'Parrot priority,' he grinned. I first met Mr Offie in Jerusalem with Mr Bullitt. Short, dark, with large prominent teeth, wherever he goes there is laughter. He is very intelligent and always well informed. I shall miss Offie. Down on the ground floor Mark Sykes, the Provost Marshal, told me he was leaving too. The orderlies, despatch riders, clerks, messengers, the policemen at the door – I was sorry to say goodbye to them all. In the Secretariat of General Staff, Ed Bastion who, when we first came to Algiers, survived our English idiosyncrasies to become a great friend, took me round his office. Few people work harder than the American girls in his Secretariat. Somehow they always manage to look attractive. 'When you go to a hairdresser in the States,' they told me, 'ask them to give you the works. They'll fix you so you won't know yourself.' Lastly I went to my old office. Already it looked changed. Bill Cunningham and Rupert Clarke, Alex's staff, were awfully nice to me. I had tea with Sergeant Pell and the orderlies who are staying on.

Back at Villa Pina I presented Raphaeli with an American mackintosh I had bought for him. He put it on very slowly and said it was too *piccolo*. Italia made encouraging noises. He had two coats on already so of course it was too small. We made him take them off and then took him to look at himself in the long mirror in my bedroom. He was suitably impressed and departed smiling. I tried to explain to Italia that I am going to America but she did not understand very well.

13 December 1944   *Caserta – Rome*

Today I got up at six and finished packing. Corporal Isaacs arrived with a lorry to fetch my luggage and Lonj, who is going by boat from Naples to America. I got a lift to Rome in a plane with my small airmail suitcase. Dan is having his Christmas leave now so that we can be together all the time. I cannot believe that I am going away . . .

21 December 1944   *Rome – Caserta*

Today I said goodbye to Dan. It was awful. Daphne came with me to Naples which helped a lot.

Dan and I had a wonderful time in Rome. We rode in the Borghesi Gardens with the old Marcello Orlando, and jumped the little fences in the indoor riding school. We bought each other Christmas presents and danced each night in the Ambassadors Hotel. We visited St Peter's and dined with Dan's ex-gaoler, Gussie Richardo. It was strange to hear them comparing notes from both sides of the bars. Then, on the 17th, just when I was packing to go to Caserta, John Orme telephoned to say that the plane which was taking me to London had not arrived so he thought it would be best if he asked General Eaker to give me a lift in his Fortress on the 22nd. I hope General Jumbo will not be cross because I am late.

22 December 1944   *Caserta*

This morning Daphne and I got up at dawn. After breakfast we went into the garden to say goodbye to Raphaeli. He was sweeping in his new mackintosh. Big tears rolled down his old cheeks. Italia had brought all her children to see us off. I have arranged with the new owner of Villa Pina to take her on so at least they will be well fed.

It was still dark when we reached Marchianese. We found Earl Hormell in the ops room. 'Not going today,' he said. 'Weather's bad over France. Come drink coffee in our canteen.' We sat on high stools. 'What do you think of the German push?' he asked. He laughed when we told him we knew nothing of it. 'Been on leave with Dan.' He laughed. 'That explains that.' He fetched a newspaper and we read of the

312

German breakthrough in the Ardennes.[1] In spite of this startling news Charlie Chaplin had managed to take up two columns on the front page of the *Stars and Stripes* newspaper. We telephoned John Orme and explained that the flight was off and we had nowhere to go. He said Air Marshal Slessor was in Malta so we could spend the day in his hut and he felt sure General Eaker would allow us to sleep in one of his guest huts at the Cascade Camp. It was an agonisingly cold day so after lunch we went to a camp movie to try and get warm.

John Orme joined us for dinner. He said the weather had improved and General Eaker would take off at day-break tomorrow. He brought with him a letter for me – covered with important-looking seals. I read it and then the others did too. This was the letter:

Office of the War Cabinet, London, S.W.1.
15th December, 1944.

Dear Hermione,

It is with a sad pen that I write you this letter to say I will not be able after all to take you to Washington with my private office.

Hester has decided that she will come out there, and it has been represented to her very strongly from the highest circles that your presence there on my staff will react unfavourably as regards her position with high-placed Americans which is regarded of extreme importance at this juncture.

To react against this opinion, which has also been put to me since I got inside this building, will only lead to trouble and might affect one's standing with certain individuals. It would be hopeless to start on the wrong foot and there is no alternative but to bow to the wind which means that you must drop out of the team.

I am afraid you are too well known; if you had a name like Smith, the question would never have come up probably. Snobbish, if you like.

[1.] On 16 December, in a last extraordinary effort, the Germans – three Armies, twenty divisions (including twelve Panzer) started a westward offensive through the Ardennes. By Boxing Day its strength was spent.

Meanwhile, I have got so much into the machinery of State that one's personal wishes cease to count.

I cannot thank you enough for all your help and loyalty to me since Baghdad days and it is sad that we will no longer be working together. I hope you will elect to stay in Rome and be with Dan after all his generosity that he would let you go to America.

Good luck to you,
Yours ever, H. Maitland Wilson.

'Reprieve,' said Daphne. 'But now you are in a nice fix: you've been officially posted out of this Theatre; your luggage is half-way across the Atlantic; your house has been handed over; you have no job, no references and I bet you've not been paid.' I began to laugh. John Orme said he wished Air Marshal Slessor was here – his advice would be a great help. 'You see,' he said, 'I'm afraid people are going to think you've baled out on General Jumbo at the last moment.'

We telephoned Dan in Rome and after some discussion the four of us agreed it would be best for me to go to London in the morning and get a reference, my pay, arrange for my luggage to be retrieved and, if possible, obtain official permission to return to the Mediterranean Theatre. Of course I would never be allowed to work in Rome with Dan as General Jumbo suggested in his letter. The big risk now is that if I go to England I may not be able to get back again.

23 December 1944   *Caserta – Paris*

I scribbled a note to Dan and set off for the airfield. Oranges and lemons, which General Eaker is taking for friends in England, were being loaded on to 'Star Duster'. The engines roared and Caserta slipped away beneath us. The palace looked marvellous from the sky.

It was dreadfully cold and General Eaker brought me a rug. 'You'll love Washington and Washington will love you,' he shouted against the roar of the engines. I felt dreadfully embarrassed: I could not shout back that I am not going to

Washington and embark on the rigmarole of why – so I just grinned. He handed me coffee and sandwiches and then climbed into one of the four bunks to read his book. He is a specially nice man.

For a couple of hours we flew through clouds. When they cleared I moved into the tail of the plane where there is a sheet glass window. I looked down on the fields and forests of France and much flooding. A fellow passenger, who works in the Caserta Map Room, joined me and told me of the great battle which is raging in Luxemburg. He drew diagrams of what he called 'The Bulge'. 'Probably this is the Germans' last fling,' he said.

We landed on an aerodrome near Paris. It has been badly bombed. As soon as we turned off the runway 'Star Duster' sank up to her axles in mud. Weather reports were bad. We were informed there was no hope of reaching England today. A jeep came alongside the plane and General Eaker and I climbed in, leaving poor Major Mason to struggle with the cargo of fruit which had to be put in a refrigerator for the night. General Eaker told me that he was going to stay with General Spaatz[1] at Air Headquarters outside Paris and would be delighted if I would go too – he felt sure General Spaatz would fit me in somewhere. We had not driven very far when we were stopped at a cross-roads by French guards. They asked to see our identity cards and took a thorough look over the car. They told us they were looking for German parachutists dressed in Allied uniforms. Soon after we were stopped again, this time by American Military Police with tommy guns. They asked to see our papers and questioned us closely. Altogether we were stopped half a dozen times.

General Spaatz gave us a great welcome. He was playing gin rummy. He is a man of about fifty, lean faced and wiry. He has an alert, rather severe expression till he smiles when he looks almost rakishly gay. He did not seem in the least surprised to see me and soon made me feel at home. His ADC Secretary, Captain Sally Bagby, a very pretty slim girl dressed in uniform,

[1] Chief of US Air Forces.

315

told me that usually General Spaatz and his staff live in the trailers on the lawn and use the villa as a Mess. They had moved into the house for Christmas because the security people are worried about the German parachutists who are landing around Paris. She said I could sleep in her trailer and took me over the frosted lawn to show it to me. It has a broad comfortable bed across the width of one end and is fitted with an electric reading lamp, a wireless and a writing table. Through a partition there is a wash basin, hanging cupboard and a lavatory. It is beautifully fitted and gay.

I was sitting by the fire in the hall reading the local newspapers when General Spaatz was called to the telephone. He came into the room holding his playing cards in one hand and a whisky and soda in the other. I watched him figuring out which he would put down so that he could take up the telephone. I guessed it was General Eisenhower or Air Chief Marshal Tedder on the other end. General Spaatz kept saying, 'Fine, Fine.' Then he listened for a while and replied: 'OK. We'll put it all in one place tomorrow and give them the works. If that doesn't stop them nothing will.' He hung up, took up his cards and turned to me: 'Weather's cleared, there'll be a massacre tomorrow,' he said and went back to his gin rummy game. I sat and watched the flames flick round the logs on the fire. What a strange war it is, I thought. You hear a man talking on the telephone – and he is talking about the weather. It all sounds so unimportant, so casual, but the result is terrible. It means that thousands of people are going to be killed tomorrow. It means, as General Spaatz said, a massacre. The weather has cleared – we are going to bomb the Bulge tomorrow . . . I tried to comfort myself that if we didn't kill them the Germans would kill us.

There were eighteen Americans at dinner in the Mess. We talked of all sorts of things – of Christmas, and General Spaatz's Fortress which crashed at Bovingdon today. It was completely wrecked. We teased Major Mason about his oranges and lemons and discussed the *New York Herald Tribune* – a Paris edition is now being printed here. I listened to the Americans talking in their short colloquial phrases. Nobody discussed the bombing tomorrow but I knew, by odd remarks that were tossed across the table, that they were all thinking of it.

24 December 1944   *Christmas Eve*   *Paris – London*

When I woke the caravan was very cold and the lawn outside white and thick with frost. At breakfast in the Mess the Americans teased me: 'Of all the antiquated, barbaric habits you British persist in – the use of toast racks is the worst: toast should be hot. The quickest way to cool it is to put it in your damnable toast racks.'

I said goodbye to everybody and thanked General Eaker and General Spaatz for their great kindness to me. General Spaatz said, 'You are welcome at my Headquarters any time – temporarily or permanently – but you'll have to learn to play gin rummy.' He laughed and departed to concentrate on The Bulge. The two Generals have decided to spend Christmas together.

Maccy, Smithy the pilot and I set off to collect the citrus and get 'Star Duster' out of the frozen mud. It took ages. We flew over Paris and when the mist cleared I saw many shell holes and much bomb damage along our route. In the morning sunshine England looked superb – we passed over Windsor Castle and Ascot Racecourse and landed at Bovingdon. I kept thinking of the slaughter going on across the Channel but none of us spoke of it.

The Americans passed straight through Passport and Customs control but I was put through all the formalities and my luggage was thoroughly searched. This made Macey and Smithy laugh. We drove into London which seemed rather empty – many people must have gone away for Christmas. They dropped me at Claridge's.

25 December 1944   *Christmas Day*   *London*

Mr Churchill and Mr Eden flew to Greece today to try to find a solution to the troubles there. Dynamite has been found under General Scobie's Headquarters in Athens. I stayed in the hotel because it is so cold and because I hoped Mark would contact me and take my problems to General Jumbo. I listened to the King's speech.

26 *December 1944*   *Boxing Day*   *London*

Today Mark came to see me. He had just arrived from Washington and found my message. He had not yet seen the General and was surprised that I am not going to America and appalled that Lady Wilson is going. He was already a bit depressed about Washington because, he said, he thinks it will be mainly a diplomatic and social job. Now he is dismayed that Lady Wilson will go: 'She is a Holy Terror,' he said. 'Poor General Jumbo – what a fate to have that job with such a wife and a *malade-imaginaire* son in tow.' I explained my predicament and he promised to get me a reference from the General and my wages, and arrange for my luggage to be returned quickly. But he was not sure that he can do anything about my posting or my return to Italy. 'What a filthy way to treat you – no notice, no pay, no reference and now you've no job, no billet and no luggage. What on earth are you going to do?' he asked.

'First I must get back to the war,' I said. We both laughed and he hurried off. Mark is always kind and very efficient. I felt cheered up.

31 *December 1944*   *New Year's Eve*   *London*

The last day of 1944 – 366 days of terrible fighting on land, sea and air – and of unforgettable heroism and tragedy. It seems unbelievable that for five and a quarter years we've all left our homes and happiness behind to concentrate on conflict. We can never get those years back – or all the friends we've lost. Pray God the New Year will bring victory and peace so we can all have private lives again.

11

Finale

1 January 1945   *London*

Mark sent me a reference from General Jumbo, who has been made a Field Marshal:

> Lady Ranfurly has been my personal secretary for a period of two and a half years. Apart from being an extremely proficient shorthand stenographer her many other capabilities have been of great value and assistance to me during this period.
>
> Her keen mind and energy together with her large circle of acquaintances and friends, have provided me in the office with much useful information. Her tact, discretion and rigid regard for security have been exemplary.
>
> It is with great regret that I now release her on my appointment as head of the British Joint Staff Mission in Washington where it is impossible for her to accompany me. I can confidently recommend her to anyone requiring a first-class secretary.
>
> H. MAITLAND WILSON Field Marshal.

Mark wrote: 'I asked Patrick why his Father had treated you so badly and he said, "Oh, it's just that my Mother says she won't go to America unless my Father sacks Hermione – but anyway I do not think my Mother will go at all." '

I've visited – briefly – all Dan and my immediate relations. It is wonderful that Cynthia is so much better. Aunt Puss and I drove to Marlborough House to collect the Princess Royal and take her to dine at the Ritz. For a long time we talked about prisoners of war. HRH is very anxious about her son who is in prison in Germany.[1]

The Nazis are holding him and other well-known prisoners, maybe as hostages. After dinner, when we were talking about Greece, a fat woman went up to HRH and asked her the way to the lavatory.

8 January 1945   *London*

Today Whitaker arrived to see me. He had come from Leeds where he is now canteen manager in a big Russian camp. He told me that the 2500 Russians there had been doing forced labour for the Germans in Axis-occupied countries, and he thought they were being kept in this camp because it was not certain whether they had collaborated or not. 'When they arrived they were in an awful mess, their feet were tied up with rags and string as their boots were much too large for them. When we issued them with three pairs of socks each they insisted on wearing them all at the same time. Then they complained that their boots were too small. They nearly went mad when we gave them chocolate. They have been given British uniforms and get the same rations as our troops – turkeys for Christmas and everything. They are allowed five shillings a week – spending money. They are a mixed lot, Mongolians and such like.'

Whitaker and I went to see Laurence Olivier in the film *Henry V.* Whitaker had hardly sat down when his seat broke. He is fatter than ever.

I dined with Freya Stark who has been on a lecture tour in America. Next week she is going to India. I was delighted to see her again. She is as vital and amusing as ever.

---

[1] Viscount Lascelles, now Earl of Harewood, imprisoned at Colditz.

A secretary rang up this morning to say Lord Beaverbrook hoped I would lunch with him today. 'Must be a mistake,' I said, 'he doesn't know me.'

The secretary replied, 'Oh, I know that. But he wants to know you.' She gave me his address. I found Lord Beaverbrook in a comfortable modern flat in Park Lane – he was younger and shorter than I expected. I asked him why he'd asked me to lunch. 'From curiosity,' he replied, 'Why did you come?'

'From curiosity,' I said.

We had an excellent lunch and all the time he volleyed questions at me: was I a real stenographer; where had I worked before the war; was I happily married; why had I no children; what did I know about him? Wherever possible I asked him the same questions back. It was very funny – in no time we had a card index of each other.

After lunch we sat in his study where he has a dictaphone, a few books, and a picture of William Penn. I told him Dan was the nearest living descendant of William Penn. After that we talked about Anglo-American relations. He said, 'You can't force friendship. Best to leave the Americans to come and make friends with us if they want to – otherwise, leave them alone and stop insincerities.' We were interrupted by the telephone and he spoke about the Wages Bill and then our funny staccato conversation began again. Just as I was leaving at three-thirty he offered me a job. Gratefully I refused it: 'I must go back to the war,' I said. I like Lord Beaverbrook and enjoyed our laughing lunch.

The Russians continue to advance through Poland and Silesia. There has been a big Allied landing in the East Indies – Luzon has been captured. In France and Belgium the Germans are retreating.

Today, by chance, I met General Carton de Wiart in St James's Street. He told me that he is leaving for Chunking in two days' time. I tried my best not to look excited when he told me that he had his own aeroplane. I asked him if he would give me a lift and drop me off somewhere in the Mediterranean. He said that, provided I had the right papers, he would be delighted. 'But don't forget', he added cheerfully, 'that I'm a gremlin. Aeroplanes always seem to crash when I'm in them.'

I had tea with Lord Gowrie whom I last saw in Australia before the war. He told me a little about the Pacific war and asked many questions about poor Pat. It was a very sad conversation.

Tomorrow is our sixth wedding anniversary.

18 January 1945   *London – Marseilles*

Early this morning I bought all the newspapers I could carry – people overseas enjoy an up-to-date newspaper more than most things. General Carton de Wiart and Lady Violet Seymour, wife of our Ambassador to China, picked me up at Claridge's at 7 a.m. On the way to Northolt I felt somewhat apprehensive lest my papers prove inadequate. Perhaps General Carton guessed this for he told me that if there was any trouble he did not want to be involved and would turn his blind eye. We found General Wavell's son, Archie John, and Julian Amery waiting for us on the aerodrome. After a long wait our luggage was weighed and we passed through the Security people. I read *The Times* as we flew over France: in Western Europe we are advancing fast; in Italy the battle is static.

Towards midday we flew over the snow-capped peaks of the Alpes-Maritimes and soon after crossed flooded marshes to the Mediterranean. We landed at Istres, a desolate place near Marseilles, where we were told that we must spend the night because the weather was bad. We dined in the Transit Mess which was filled with travellers stranded like ourselves. General Carton was charming to them all. I have seldom met anyone with such kind manners. Lady Violet told me about Chunking. It is a damp place, often shrouded in mist. The electric power is weak so it is also rather dark. Nevertheless she is happy there.

There are lovely walks in the hills and the Chinese people are delightful. She and I slept in a primitive little hut comprising two bare rooms with a chair and three camp beds in each. I funked washing in the ice cold water and slept in my fur coat.

19 January 1945   *Istres – Naples – Rome*

Early this morning we took off along a flare path. We were buffeted about by wind and clouds and soon poor Archie John Wavell was sick. The pilot's cocker spaniel, which is going to China, looked very miserable. We flew blind nearly all the way to Pomigliano where we lunched at the airfield buffet. I watched them take off and turn out to sea. They have a long journey ahead of them; tonight in Cairo, tomorrow in Aden. Archie John will get off in India and the rest of them will fly over the Hump to Chunking.

I got a lift to Caserta and went straight to my old office. Field Marshal Alexander was away in Greece so I paid a courtesy call on his Chief of Staff, General John Harding, to explain why I had come back. He told me that as far as he is concerned it was all right, but he hoped the evacuation boys would not catch up with me. He advised me not to get a job in Rome as Dan was there – that would be asking for trouble. He told me his news: we have countered the recent Kesselring offensive – the situation in Greece has improved . . .

I visited Air Marshal Slessor's office where John and Nigel arranged a lift for me in a car going to Rome and promised to telephone Dan that I was coming. Then I went up to the Cascade Camp to see Mary Alice Jaqua who is leaving in the morning for two weeks' leave in America. She was very kind. 'If you're stuck you can always share my hut,' she said. 'Or my job for that matter.'

It seemed a long way to Rome. We tore along the Appian Way down avenues of eucalyptus trees with white-painted trunks. The bombed towns and villages looked ghostly in our great headlights. Twice we were stopped by Military Police with tommy guns. They had put a barrier across the road to catch gangster deserters. It was pouring with rain and bitterly cold. I found Dan and Daphne waiting for me at the Albergo Victoria. We sat up half the night swopping news and discussing how I can get another job. It is wonderful to be back.

24 January 1945   *Naples*

Two days ago I came to stay with Admiral Cunningham at Villa Emma. It is a lovely house standing on the edge of the sea. Even when the windows are shut one can hear the waves breaking on the rocks below. Inside it has been completely modernised: each bedroom has its own tiled bathroom. Three charming Maltese servants keep it spick and span.

I have been looking for a job and a billet. Today a miracle happened. Air Marshal Slessor[1] sent for me. He told me that his ADC, Nigel Maynard, is leaving to go on active service and he would like me to fill his place. I accepted gratefully. He said that I would do part secretarial work and part ADC work: I must run Air House in Naples, look after his hut at the Cascade Camp, organise cars and stores and help John Orme in the office. He told me that General Eaker has invited me to live in the Cascade Camp where a new Nissen hut is being built for Mary Alice which I can share with her. He asked me about my wages. When I told him what I had been getting he was surprised and said, 'You were getting less than the average typist but you held the highest woman's job in this Theatre. Amazing!' We both laughed. He said I was overdue for promotion and he would make me a Senior Civil Assistant. I am to start work tomorrow. I telephoned Dan to tell him this wonderful news. On my way back through Naples I collected Coco from Villa Rivalta. He had not forgotten me.

25 January 1945   *Caserta*

Today, on my way to work, I dumped my luggage and Coco at Air House where I am to live until Mary Alice's Nissen hut is

[1] Sir John Slessor was Commander-in-Chief RAF Mediterranean and Middle East, and also deputy to General Eaker, C-in-C Mediterranean Allied Air Forces. Later Chief of the Air Staff.

ready. A bare, unattractive house, it is used, like Villa Rivalta, mostly for official entertaining and VIP visitors. I talked to the Corporal in charge of the orderlies and the RAF guard. They were all so nice to me and to Coco.

At Caserta I found John Orme and Nigel very busy with 'Cricket Signals'. This is the code name for Mr Churchill and Mr Roosevelt's meeting at Malta, preliminary of the Three Power Conference which is going to be held at Yalta. The weather is bad and conflicting telegrams are pouring in about the fleet of planes which are taking English and American staffs to Malta. John gave me a pile of RAF files to read.

In the afternoon Nigel and I toured the RAF set-up. First we went round the offices in the palace and I met the American and British staffs I shall work with. I saw the Air Room, the War Room and the Signals Office. Next we visited Marchianese – the RAF stores, the motor workshops, the Flight Office, the Ops Room and the Pay Office. I saw Air Marshal Slessor's Mitchell plane and was introduced to the crew and Corporal Topley the fitter. Lastly, at the Cascade Camp, Nigel showed me the orderly room, the men's quarters, the guest huts and the car park. I took a notebook with me and wrote down all the new names and a lot of RAF words which are Greek to me. I dined in the Cascade Mess where I met General Eaker and 'Macey dear'. They gave me a kind welcome. After dinner I drove back to Naples. Corporal Strait, the driver, talked about the Battle of Britain when he refuelled Hurricane Fighters in Essex. In his quiet Worcestershire voice he drew me a wonderful picture of those hectic days when they did everything at the double and pilots had no time to get out of their planes for refuelling. He talked of armourers and mechanics, dogfights and vapour trails – of the fun, the thrill and tragedy of it.

1 February 1945   *Caserta*

All this week we have been desperately busy. We have had a lot of work in connection with a Court of Enquiry on two British Members of Parliment who have been lost whilst flying between Taranto and Greece. Signals about the Malta meeting still pour in. Mr Churchill, Mr Roosevelt and the Combined Chiefs of Staff have arrived there safely. Mr Averill Harriman flew over from the meeting to visit General Eaker at the Cascade Camp. Today Air Marshal Slessor flew to Malta. I gave him a note to give to Mark, who is there with Field Marshal Jumbo, begging him to hurry up my luggage. I am short of clothes, and the cold here is frightful. Meanwhile Nigel has been handing over to me and packing up. Today he left. It is tough luck on John Orme that I am new when we are so busy – I am still more of a liability than a help. To add to our troubles the drains have gone wrong in the palace and the water has been cut off. Quicklime is the order of the day.

3 February 1945   *Caserta*

Air Marshal Slessor returned from Malta. He brought sad news: Barney Charlesworth[1] was killed on his way to 'Cricket' – the York he was travelling in crashed near Lampedusa Island.

The air transport arrangements to and from Malta were superb: the arrival and departure of the great fleet of aeroplanes went like clockwork. They took off at only a few minute intervals on their one hop flight to the Black Sea. Credit for this goes largely to Whitney Straight. Mr Harry Hopkins and Mr Stettinius stopped, on their way to Yalta, to lunch here with General Eaker.

Randolph Churchill paid me a visit, full of gossip from Malta. 'The Prime Minister had received a telegram from Stalin at Yalta saying "Here I am. Where are you?" The Prime Minister's valet had left Churchill's handkerchiefs behind which caused a major rumpus . . .' Randolph always refers to his father as the Prime Minister or Churchill, and I always interrupt and say, 'Oh, you mean Daddy.' Randolph is so often rude to high and low that we enjoy teasing him. For all his nuisance value and rudeness I am fond of Randolph – he reminds me of nursery days when often I was disgracefully rude to Nannie. He's never grown up.

[1] ADC to General Brooke, CIGS.

326

Spring is coming – the Italian office cleaner has put a small jam jar of snowdrops on my desk.

4 February 1945   Caserta

I dined with John Orme. He is very clever, well informed and easy to work with. He told me about Harry Hopkins who, in the early days of the war, had been one of Britain's most valuable friends: he believed we should build bombers at a time when most people wanted to concentrate on fighters. The fact that he saw this so far ahead has been an enormous help to the Allies' war effort. John told me that the RAF Bomber Command sent 1400 aircraft to bomb Germany on Thursday and yesterday 1000 American Flying Fortresses bombed Berlin with incendiaries and high explosives.

John is sad because Wing Commander Guy Gibson has been reported killed. He was the leader of the raid on the Mohne and Eder Dams in Germany – one of our finest pilots who'd won the VC, DSO, and DFC.

11 February 1945   Caserta

Yesterday General Cabbell, American Director of Air Operations, Mediterranean Theatre, arrived back from Yalta. He told me that the Russians had arranged the conference well but their transport was rotten. The Americans were billeted in the old Czar's Summer Palace. Mr Roosevelt went by ship to Malta and from there in a Skymaster which was specially fitted with an electric lift.

15 February 1945   Caserta

A spate of visitors has descended on us and we have been busy arranging accommodation and transport for them. Yesterday Air Marshal Leckie, Canadian Air Chief of Staff, arrived an hour early which upset our timetable. Sir Ronald Adam, Adjutant General, is staying with Field Marshal Alex. He has been touring India and Burma. His PA told me they had been within fiteen miles of Mandalay which is still held by the Japanese. General Marshall is staying with General McNarney in the camp above ours.

A note came from Mark, written at Yalta.

> . . . Mr Roosevelt looks absolutely worn out and even Mr Churchill looks a bit tired. Marshal Stalin is the only one who looks fit. I wish you could have seen Sir Alan Brooke, with a school history book in his hand, explaining the Battle of Balaclava to an audience of Field Marshals. We stood on a little ridge on the end of that famous battlefield where the Charge of the Light Brigade took place. All around us were the twisted remains of German anti-tank guns, a Russian-German battle was fought here in this war . . .

Today I prepared Air House for Dr Subasic, Prime Minister of Yugoslavia and General Velebit, who are on their way to Belgrade with the Yugoslav Government. They arrived with their wives just before 8 p.m., and we had to hurry to get to the Resident Minister's house in time for an official dinner. I had to be hostess and sat between Dr Subasic and General John Harding. Conversation was rather slow to start with but Mr Offie, who was sitting nearby, soon rectified that: 'Is it true that the Queen Mother runs the Yugoslav Government?' he asked, his black eyes glinting wickedly.

'Mr Offie is the most dangerous man in Italy,' I warned Dr Subasic. Suddenly the Prime Minister, who had been silent, began to chatter. He talked very fast with his head on one side and his hands waving. In excellent English and amid bursts of laughter he soon routed Mr Offie. General Harding told me that the Poles are terribly upset by the Yalta Conference decisions. General Anders is quite distraught. In this Theatre a censorship ban has been put on this, so there will be no press comment.

16 February 1945   *Caserta*

I got up very early so that I could have a bath. As there is no key in the bathroom door I thought it best to steal a march on the

Yugoslavs. After breakfast we drove with a police escort through Naples. I went with Dr Subasic. He is a sweet old man with a head like a turnip. He talked about his job. He said, 'I must be like a pioneer and try to turn the Yugoslav political jungle into a park.' He told me that his wife was a great help to him in England – she speaks excellent English. He is very proud of her. He described a long journey he made in the last war across Russia to England.

When we reached Pomigliano the Yugoslav Ministers were standing in a row near the runway. The gay little Minister of Home Affairs introduced me to his colleagues: 'This is the Minister of Finance. The four bulging briefcases he carries represent four years of inflation. This sad-looking man is the Minister of Education and Culture. He has no briefcase because all his affairs are abstract . . .' I shook hands with them and watched them take off. I had just time to drive to Marchianese with two cars to meet the French Air Delegation who have come to discuss re-forming the French Air Force. To my great surprise and delight Dan was with them. He is Liaison Officer in charge of the party. After I had been to the NAAFI to pick up stores I returned to help John in the office.

This evening, when Dan and I were on our way to see Mary Alice, we met General Eaker walking across the Cascade Camp in his red dressing gown. He had just come from the bath hut nearby. He invited us into his hut to listen to the new record Mary Alice brought him from America. It is called 'Rum and Coca Cola'. He talked about the immense carrier-borne air attack on Japan. When we left he gave me a banana for Coco.

In the Cascade Camp General Eaker is everyone's best friend. Quiet, kind and very considerate he is loved by Americans and English alike. He is like the father of a large family, always impartial but always the boss. The Americans call him 'The Old Man', but he isn't very old. He has an English batman and a black spaniel.

I took my suitcase and Coco in his cage to Caserta this morning. Mary Alice was already installed in our hut and had made her room attractive. So far I have a bed, a wardrobe and two chairs. 'Action Jackson', the charming American who runs the camp, has promised to try and find me a chest of drawers. In the middle of the room is a black oil stove. I shall need it: a tremendous gale is blowing and many of the palace windows have blown in. Back in the office the telephone never stopped: General McCreery must go to England at once where his Mother is dying; Air Marshal Slessor must have his papers for the Supreme Allied Commanders' meeting; Air Vice Marshal Mills must be met at Marchianese. Fitzroy and Randolph have arrived; and a press delegation from America is due. General Anders is in Naples waiting to go to London . . . He has asked to see me.

I dined at the hunting lodge. When I arrived Field Marshal Alex, Generals Harding, Robertson and Lemnitzer were standing round the fire. All their medal ribbons were new – it looked rather gay. I felt shy because I had not had time to tidy. Each time I meet Field Marshal Alex I am surprised at how small he is. Tonight he wore a new tunic made of British warm overcoat material. He looked tired. At dinner he told me of his childhood in Ireland – he lives close by Dan's family home at Dungannon. He talked about poaching and ferreting and then switched to Burma. With his chin in the air and his head tilted he talks in a shy, hesitating way as if he were trying to remember or forget something. He is charming.

On my other side sat John Harding. We talked of our old friend Bonner Fellers who is now working for General MacArthur in the Pacific Theatre. Opposite me was General Robertson, bluff, tall and old fashioned. He has a nice laugh. He looked at me disapprovingly. General Lemnitzer seemed as happy in this English household as I am in the Cascade Camp. When English and Americans work together it is surprising how quickly they forget their different nationalities and habits. He laughed when I told him how mystified I was when I

330

first breakfasted in the Cascade Mess and the waiter enquired whether I would like eggs 'up or over'. After dinner General Alexander stood up and toasted his American Aide, John Grimley, who is returning to the States tomorrow. He made an awkward little speech in a flat voice but it was so shy and honest that it was impressive. Back in the sitting room, which is now very bare, I thought of Sergeant Trayler: he always filled it with flowers. Field Marshal Alexander discussed moving the Headquarters to Rome. Knowing that Air Marshal Slessor and Admiral Cunningham are very opposed to this idea I was glad when he changed the subject. At ten o'clock John Harding went off to do some work and I went with John Grimley to the Kennels Mess where I found the Aides and Randolph playing Jean Sablon records on the gramophone. This little Mess has changed a lot since we used it. They have put asbestos sheets over the lovely old curly tiled roof and built in the big open chimney place. The clock now hangs in an orthodox place – we kept it under the refectory table so that we could look at it without embarrassing our guests. One of the nightmares of being on a Personal Staff is that we live to a rigid timetable.

20 February 1945   *Caserta*

Today Field Marshal Alexander and Air Marshal Slessor flew to Belgrade to meet Tito. They took a fighter escort. I went to see General Anders. He is terribly shaken by Yalta decisions.

I dined with Mr Macmillan at his villa in Naples. It was so cold that I sat in my overcoat. Mr Macmillan mimicked Lord Beaverbrook who is a friend of his. He does it very cleverly. In loose battledress trousers, an old tweed coat and tin-rimmed spectacles Mr Macmillan looks like a shaggy Edwardian. It is always fun and funny to see the Macmillans.

22 February 1945   *Caserta*

After dinner I was invited to the Sheriff's hut. Air Marshal Slessor, Thornton Wilder, the Judge and a tall fair young man

331

were sitting round the fire talking about 'combat trips'. The drawl of their voices and the clink of ice made a comfortable atmosphere. The Sheriff introduced me to the stranger and I asked him where he came from. 'He could tell you a great story, Hermione,' said the Sheriff. 'He went on the Tokyo raid.' It took a lot of persuading to get that diffident young man to tell us about it.

In 1942, when he was training in the States, he was asked if he would volunteer for a very dangerous mission. He was not told what it was. For weeks he and other picked men trained in South Carolina. He said, 'We had a tough education practising short take-offs and low altitude bombing – studying navigation, careful gas checking and meteorology.'

'Getting a fully loaded B25 off a short runway at fifty-five or sixty mph is quite a job,' said the Sheriff. For a while Air Marshal Slessor and the stranger talked about extra gas tanks, 'the twenty per cent job' they used instead of Norden sights, and wings fitted with ice boots. I got lost in a maze of technical terms. I took advantage of the interruption to borrow the Sheriff's bedroom slippers – my shoes were pinching. Then the young man continued his story.

They were given several chances to back out and each time they were warned of the danger of their mission. Colonel Dolittle visited them several times to see how they were getting on. At the end of March their training was finished and they flew over to the west coast where sixteen B25s were loaded on to an aircraft carrier – the *Hornet*. Only then did Colonel Dolittle tell them what they were going to do. The *Hornet* would take them to within 400 miles of Tokyo. They would take off the flight deck, fly in low over Japan and then make for landing strips on the Chinese mainland. Once again, Colonel Dolittle gave them a chance to back out. Nobody did. 'You know Dolittle?' the Sheriff asked Air Marshal Slessor.

'Well,' said Air Marshal Slessor, 'I have the deepest admiration for him.' Once again everyone started talking. 'Please go on,' I said.

On the aircraft carrier they studied maps of Japan and China, pictures of Tokyo and silhouettes. The crews were allotted targets at Tokyo, Yokohama, Nogoya, Kobe and Osaka. The *Hornet* had a big convoy under the command of Admiral Halsey. The Navy made them very comfortable. Early on April 18th, when they were still 1800 miles from the Japanese coast – a good ten hours ahead of the scheduled take-off – they spotted an enemy ship. Because of the risk that it might have flashed back a message to its base before it was sunk, there was no alternative but to take off immediately. The young man said, 'To get a twenty-five-thousand-pound bomber off half the flight deck of an aircraft carrier in a rough sea is a bit of a job and I don't mind telling you I was scared. Colonel Dolittle went first, his left wing over the edge of the *Hornet* and his right wheel aimed at the white line they had painted for us on the deck. The seconds seemed eternity. We made it.'

None of us spoke when the Sheriff filled up our glasses and the stranger went on with his story. 'We flew in low over Japan but we had to climb to fifteen hundred feet over the target area lest we blow ourselves up. The enemy was taken completely by surprise. In a few seconds we had dropped our bombs and were over the sea again, heading west. We were so short of fuel that we decided to make for Siberia. We landed safely, fifty miles from Vladivostok, and were interned by the Russians.'

Afterwards the Sheriff explained to me that this raid was a big bluff that worked: the Japs could not tell whether the American bombers had come from China, an aircraft carrier or an Island in the Pacific, and so were forced to tie up part of their military and air strength to defend their mainland. He told me that the *Hornet* was sunk later in 1942, in the battle of Santa Cruz.

'What a brave and magnificent story,' I said. 'Please tell me how many crews survived and how you got out of Russia?'

'Another time,' said Air Marshal Slessor. 'Tomorrow there will be much work to do and plenty of news and we all need sleep.' I thanked the Sheriff for inviting me, the pilot for telling me his story, and said goodnight to everyone and made for my hut. Before I get into bed I always wash my stockings and scribble in my Diary.

23 February 1945   *Caserta*

This whole camp is buzzing with talk of Allied air raids over Germany yesterday. Probably it was the biggest air onslaught yet – some say as many as 6000 planes may have taken part. We could be nearing the end of this ghastly war – news from nearly all fronts is encouraging: the Russians are not far from Berlin, Allied ground forces are advancing in Europe, Burma and the Far East. News is coming in so fast I can no longer take it in – far less write it down.

Casualties everywhere must be stupendous. Wreckage of buildings and their often beautiful contents is incalculable – like Dresden. And what can be the fate of animals – horses, cattle, pigs, sheep, goats, poultry, dogs and cats? Even if they are not killed or wounded can anyone still feed them under such a rain of terror?

26 February 1945   *Caserta*

It rained in the night and the wind screamed through the thin doors of our hut and rattled the wooden shutters. I was cold when I woke up and I longed for a bath. There is no stopper to the basin in my hut and only a cold tap. A busy day: much office work, shopping for stores, stationery and fresh food. I attended an evening party for American press women. I was lucky because I met and had a long talk with Toni Fresell who is an ace photographer. She started photography using only a Box Brownie and took a lot of fashion pictures out of doors. Now she is famous. Tall, slight, with short curly hair and very charming, she is keen to go to Greece. We all dined in General McNarney's Mess which is a big conservatory with a red and blue parachute hung from the ceiling to keep the sun off in summer.

Air Marshal Slessor told me this evening that he is leaving this Theatre at the end of March to work at the Air Ministry in

London. He said I can go with him as his PA if I like. I must consult Dan. He also told me he has to go on a tour round the Mediterranean soon for meetings and is taking me to cope with minutes, files and ADC work. Lucky I told no one I am afraid of flying.

7 March 1945   *Caserta*

Dressed in my battle-dress I went ahead with the luggage to Marchianese. Sergeant Topley the Fitter stowed it away in the bomb bay of the B25. Air Marshal Slessor arrived and climbed into the co-pilot's seat. I sat in the back with two RAF Liaison Officers, Ben the Wireless Operator and Sergeant Dodd the batman. Before I had time to be afraid we were airborne. At an astonishing speed we crossed dykes, avenues and strips of plough, skirted Vesuvius, left snow peaks on our left and the Sorrento Peninsula on our right and sped on. It was bitterly cold and I shivered in my sheepskin coat. As we flashed across the shallow blue of the shore to the dark blue of the Adriatic I struggled into my Mae West. At about four miles a minute it did not take long to fly past Patnos, the Corinth Canal and land at Kalamaki. A.V.M. Mills and Air Commodore Tuttle met us, and took us to RAF Headquarters in Athens where a conference was held to discuss re-equipping the Greek Air Force, which was represented by Wing Commander Platsis, M. Velos and Group Captain Alexandris. I had to take the minutes but there was an echo in the bare conference room and the Greeks sat with their backs to me and spoke in broken English, so it was a nightmare making notes. After the conference we had a quick lunch – bully beef and Greek wine. Wing Commander Platsis told me that the Mazarakis' house was totally destroyed by Communists last winter. The Greeks presented me with a bottle of ouzo and then we flew off again.

Back in the plane everyone went to sleep except our pilot, Ben the Wireless Operator and me. We flew fast eastwards through cloud. I read the newspapers: news from all fronts is good: the Allies are crossing the Rhine; in Burma we've crossed the Irawaddy and taken Meiktila[1] – so we are approaching Mandalay; Flying Fortresses are bombing Tokyo; the Russians are very close to Berlin . . . I was amazed at how soon we were over Egypt – its brilliant green cultivations and shining canals, with the Nile on one side and the Desert, burnished by the setting sun, on the other. We circled the great installations and workshops of Heliopolis and thudded down on the landing strip at 112 miles per hour. No wonder airmen like Mitchell Bombers – they travel so fast.

A police escort convoyed us through the teeming streets of Cairo. There has been trouble here lately. I was entranced to see again trams festooned with people, the gharries, the water sellers, even the beggars . . . At Air House there were telephone calls to make, papers to sort and orders for tomorrow to write down, so it was late when I drove off to stay with Geoffrey and Virginia Fielden at their lovely flat in Garden City. They, and their Sofragi, gave me a great welcome. It was wonderful to have a bath.

8 March 1945   *Cairo*

This morning I walked across Garden City to GHQ. The lame sentry at the gate said, 'Away very long time, Lady,' and let me in without asking for my pass. This time I walked through the RAF entrance. I had a struggle to transcribe the notes I took in Athens and cursed Wing Commander Platsis for his broken accent. All day Air Marshal Slessor was in conference. I worked in a little office which was really a bathroom. After work I visited Freddie Hoffman who is now manager of the Metropole Hotel. He misses our troops. 'It's all rather dull now,' he said. 'No gharry races in the streets, nobody swings from the chandeliers any more, no Ranfurlys to hide in the honeymoon suite.' We talked about Wingate and he asked after his favour-

---

[1] This was General Slim's brilliant offensive operation 'Extended Capital' which took the Fourteenth Army across the Irawaddy and would capture Mandalay on 20 March. But the Japanese were to counter-attack at Meiktila in the next weeks and were not beaten there until the end of the month. Then the advance on Rangoon began.

ite officers. I hated to tell him of those who are dead. I made him promise to come and work in England when the war ends. Then I went to see Mo. He's been very ill and looked older but with a huge grin he regaled me with accounts of his latest battles with the 'damn bad cook'.

10 March 1945   *Cairo–Jerusalem*

Yesterday Sergent Dodd and I went shopping. In Caserta it is a point of honour that anyone who goes on a trip does shopping for those left behind. My list was long. In Circurel, Sednaui and Orosdibak and the shoe shop street we bought sunglasses, suspenders, bathmats for General Eaker, underclothes for Dan, and handbags, pillows, sponges, lipsticks, fountain pens and slippers for other people. In the Musqi I bought silk for Mary Alice from my old Persian friend Agoni who plied us with coffee and news. With the help of the RAF Welfare Officer we chose a watch for Air Marshal Slessor who has broken his. There we also collected kümmel, tobacco and razor blades. Like an idiot I had not brought an empty suitcase so we became overwhelmed with paper bags and parcels. I hoped that some of them won't get broken in our bomb bay.

Early this morning we flew to Lydda. As I was getting out of the plane my zip-fastener broke – a major disaster as my battle-dress depends on it. We drove up the familiar road to Jerusalem and slowed down to look at the corner where the MacMichaels were ambushed. As soon as I walked into Air House I began to feel the uneasy atmosphere of Jerusalem and smelt the cockroachy smell all Jerusalem buildings have and I wondered how I'd managed to live for fifteen months in this strange unhappy place.

We had a busy day of conferences; Palestine Government officials came for lunch; and before dinner Air Marshal Cochrane and Whitney Straight arrived. Listening to these men talking I suddenly realised why I like serving in the Air Force: their people talk of time and distance in a new way – they know no boundaries – just like the birds.

We dined at Government House with Lord Gort. There is a

chain barrier in the arched gateway now – trouble is expected in Palestine. As we crunched over the gravel to the front door and found Mardell waiting there it all came back to me: the red leather boxes going back and forth, waiting for news of Dan and from the Desert, deciphering in the night . . . Lord Gort met us at the end of the long passage: 'Very pleased you could come, very pleased you could come,' he said in his simple and charming way, like a small boy at a party. At dinner, after remembering Fuad my mouse, he told me the situation here is much the same with both Jews and Arabs uncompromising. There is very little the British administration can do except stay here and try to maintain law and order. He told me he walks around Jerusalem unescorted because he thinks it best for the people to know he is around and not afraid. He also talked about Malta. He loves the people there. It would be impossible not to like and admire Lord Gort.

After dinner I asked if I might go to the kitchen and see my old friends. I learned that fat Said has retired, that Assad has been promoted – now he is a clerk. Mardell's daughter has a baby. Mohammed the kavass is on leave in the Sudan. Back in the great sitting room, surrounded by bowls of deep blue lupins, I talked with General Darcy who had just been to see a school for Polish orphans near Jerusalem. He said it was terribly pathetic: the children were starting life in a foreign country; they knew nothing of home life; there was nowhere for them to go in the holidays so there were no holidays. When we returned to Air House at eleven-thirty I had to mend my zip-fastener. The wind howled and buffeted over the hills and I felt glad we are leaving in the morning.

11 March 1945   *Jerusalem–Baghdad*

We bought some spring flowers from the children on the road to Lydda. At the airport Corporal Topley told me that last night, when he was working on the plane, he got thirsty and took a swig at the bottle I had left by my seat – he mistook it for water. 'I thought I'd be dead in the morning,' he grinned. No wonder. He had drunk one third of the bottle of ouzo the

338

Greeks gave me. Poor Corporal Topley. We flew to Habbanyeh through dark, glowering clouds. Lightning jerked across the sky. I took two anti-airsick pills and slept in snatches. When we landed we found a smart Iraqi guard of honour lined up. A band was playing. We were met by Air Vice Marshal George and his wife Betty, whom I knew in Ankara. She looked as lovely as ever. On the way to their house we visited the stables. I was so pleased to see Arab ponies again.

After work I walked aross the garden to the Tigris. It is in flood; its fast brown water churning up against the banks. Iraqis were squatting on the bund watching it. Already the summer sun has turned the grass brown. I looked across the flat country to the thin horizon. In the distance I could hear the magpies and the birds that go 'Pyrhh'. Iraq has a tranquillity all of its own. I love it.

12 March 1945   *Baghdad–Cyprus–Caserta*

I got up at 6 a.m. local time which is 4 a.m. Italian time and walked out across the garden to the river. Iraq looks its best in the early sun. At breakfast the bacon was too salt. I acquired a thirst which came with me all day.

'Two thousand miles to go before teatime. I have wired our ETA to Caserta,' Phil the pilot told me as I helped Corporal Topley in with the luggage. We took off in a headwind and flew over miles of mottled wilderness seeing only a few Bedouin tents, a cover caravan and some emergency landing grounds. Clouds hid Syria. We landed in a storm on Cyprus to refuel. I paddled through the pools on the asphalt to the NAAFI to collect food for the crew. They made us sandwiches by placing a poached egg between two slices of bread and butter. Great courage is needed to eat these. I ate mine in the control tower while Air Marshal Slessor talked to the station Commander. Through the sheet glass windows I saw Beaufighters. This is a training school.

We flew south for a while to avoid bad weather and then turned west over the Greek islands and skirted the toe of Italy. Probably it was too rough to cross the mountains. The Sorrento coast looked superb in the low sun. We landed at four-thirty, exactly as Robby, the Australian navigator, had calculated. Air Marshal Garrod landed just behind us in a Dakota from England. I collected all our parcels and luggage, and the two sacks of oranges and grapefruit we got in Palestine, and hurried off to my hut to change. 'Whitaker, Whitaker,' shrieked Coco as I opened the door. I had just time to telephone Dan in Rome before going over to the Cascade Club to help John Orme with Air Marshal Slessor's farewell party. He and I tried out the cocktails, lit the fire and distributed cigarettes. People began to arrive: General Eaker just back from Hungary, Admiral Hewitt, looking like a buccaneer, and all the British and American staffs. We took many of the guests to dine in our Mess and it was long after midnight before I got back to my hut which was chaotic. As I cleared the parcels off my bed my mind flitted over the last few days: important and interesting meetings; glimpsing the Middle East again and watching Air Marshal Slessor at work – always kind and ready to laugh, he is immensely able and quick at making decisions. He is the most dynamic person I have worked for. He is handing over to Air Marshal Garrod and then returning to London to be Air Member for Personnel at the Air Ministry. I am to stay on here for a month to help Air Marshal Garrod settle and then I am to go to London to be PA to Air Marshal Slessor. This fits in well with Dan's plans because he is being sent home soon under 'Python', which means he has done more than five years' overseas service. This is a miraculous coincidence for us.

15 March 1945   *Caserta*

General Eaker gave a farewell dinner last night for Air Marshal Slessor and made an excellent speech to honour him which showed how really sad he is that their work together must end.

Today a great crowd went to Marchianese to see Air Marshal Slessor off. He took John Orme and his crew – Phil, Robby and Ben – with him. There was a guard of honour and an escort of twelve fighters for the Mitchell. Poor Sergeant Topley, the fitter, was dreadfully sad to see 'his' plane leave. We stood together and waved as it took off. 'Macey dear', forever kind, insisted we drive back with him to his tent to have a slice of his beautiful brandy cake which he 'waters' with brandy once a week. He had noticed Sergeant Topley's sad face when the Mitchell took off.

For days the sun has been shining down on Italy and blossom is out everywhere – cherry, apricot and blackthorn. Magnolias and camelias are coming out too. Crocus and aconites have made carpets of colour in the grass.

22 March 1945   Caserta

We are bombing Berlin nearly every night. And the RAF have a new and awful bomb – I was told it weighs nearly ten tons.

Macey arrived in my office this morning to say General Eaker has been appointed second in command to General Arnold in Washington. Macey looked dreadfully depressed: 'Who is that man who holds up the world?' he asked.

'Atlas,' I suggested.

'That's the guy,' said Maccy, 'I feel like him – just a bit overloaded. I'll leave you my cake,' he promised as he hurried off. Poor Macey, I know what he is in for in the next two days: General Eaker's letters and personal messages are largely his responsibility. He'll have accounts to settle, the office to hand over to his successor, his master's and his own packing to do, the disposal of everything from planes to spaniel puppies, farewell parties to arrange, a torrent of questions from his General's staff about what will happen to them – and so on. It's not all roses looking after a VIP.

Later General Eaker paid Mary Alice and me a visit in our hut to tell us that General Cannon, whom the Americans call 'Uncle Joe', is taking his place. 'Things will go on just as before so don't either of you worry,' he said and hurried away. Mary Alice is very sad that her 'family' is leaving. In the war we are all ostriches of a kind and hide our heads in our immediate jobs and surroundings. When these break up we feel lost and uneasy. Our background is gone and we are alone in the war again. To be a good servant one must sink one's personality,

341

tastes and preferences and learn those of our masters so that, like good retrievers, we fetch and carry automatically without being asked. When our master leaves we have to start all over again and then, generally, we get caught in a tangle of loyalties because the new man changes everything round, thinks differently, talks differently, works differently and isn't used to trusting us. It must be the same for the Air Squadrons which are going to be split up and distributed to new units. They must hate being strangers and starting again when for so long they have worked as a team.

24 March 1945   Caserta

Confirmation of my promotion has arrived – now I am a Senior Civil Servant. Except for pay this will make no difference to me or anyone. I still do much the same work as I did for Sir Harold MacMichael and General Jumbo. Luckily there are no rules or regulations to go with this pompous little title so I can help with anything I am asked to do or what I see needs doing.

Last night, after work, there were two farewell parties for General Eaker – one in the RAF Camp and one in the Cascade Camp. He spoke well at both – said he wished he could take us all with him but he will only take Macey. 'Uncle Joe' Cannon was there. He has intensely blue eyes and his nose is very small because he has smashed it so often in flying accidents. It is said he once landed his plane on another plane. We asked him to remember to land on Marchianese with his wheels down. He is a famous flier. At dinner the Generals talked of the Allied bombers which flew yesterday from Foggia to bomb Berlin. Sadly eight did not return. 'Uncle Joe' has been commanding the American Air Force operating in Northern Italy. He told me about his Headquarters in Florence and said he was very sad to leave an operational Command.

Very early today Mary Alice and I hurried down to Marchianese to say goodbye to General Eaker. There was a huge crowd on the runway. Mr Offie arrived late, laughing as he ran. He looked very funny in his city suit with his big teeth shining in the sun. General Eaker shook hands with everyone and flew off in his Dakota, 'Yardbird'. Macey and the General's British orderlies will follow him tomorrow.

Later Air Marshal Garrod flew up to Rome to watch the South Africa v England rugger match and took me along to see Dan. We spent a lovely afternoon together.

Allied forces under General Montgomery have begun to cross the Rhine. Forty thousand airborne troops have landed in two hours.

28 March 1945   *Caserta*

So many papers come into our office that it is quite impossible to read them all. Signals pour in from General Eisenhower in France, from Air Marshal Slessor in London and from the Combined Chiefs of Staff. Intelligence summaries report that the state of Germany is terrible. The Allied Armies have advanced to within eighty miles south-west of Berlin. The Red Army have begun their battle for Vienna. In North Italy we are progressing well. In the Pacific and Burma we go steadily forward. Other telegrams give air targets, many of them oil, and large-scale enemy trooping.

There are reports from Crete where the Germans must surrender soon: that unless we take them off the Island it is likely that they will be slaughtered wholesale by the Cretans. This involves International Law. We are terribly short of shipping so do not want to use it for this, but if we don't the Germans may take reprisals on our prisoners.

Telegrams from Bulgaria, Yugoslavia and Albania report that the internal situation of these countries is becoming daily more involved. Food of course is the greatest problem. In Italy there will be trouble if the currency is not adjusted soon. From Greece and Egypt come telegrams asking for planes to help build up their own Air Forces. Meanwhile in the Mediterranean the questions of Civil Air taking over from Military Air and the rolling up of Operational Squadrons are being discussed.

I lunched with Mr Offie. Afterwards we walked back to work through the Cascade Gardens. He told me he had thirteen

343

brothers and sisters. His father was Italian. Offie has had an interesting life; he began as a grocer's errand boy and has worked his way up to a high place in the US Political Adviser's office here. As usual he was in excellent spirits. He told me that whenever he gets depressed or feels bad tempered he goes to bed and sleeps till he feels cheerful again.

At dinner I sat next to Air Vice Marshal Stevenson who has just arrived from Roumania. He admires young King Michael, who he says stands almost alone against a rule of tyranny in his country, where the Russians are slowly gaining control of everything. He described tremendous shooting parties and told me that, though the King invites the Russians to shoot with him frequently, they poach his land regularly. When the King spoke to a Russian General about this he was told that the offenders would be punished by death. The King was horrified and explained that nothing so drastic was necessary – but he would be grateful if the poaching would stop because it will spoil the shooting for everybody.

6 April 1945   Caserta

The Russians have denounced their Five Year Pact with Japan and M. Molotov has handed a note to the Japanese.

Dan came down from Rome today. We had a picnic lunch – bully sandwiches and ginger biscuits, with Mr Macmillan in his office. This evening after work we went to see the Sheriff. He had just returned from a combat trip. He told us all about it. 'You must understand the excitement of it – flying north and crossing our lines and theirs. You go up and over,' he said, spiralling his huge hands. 'There are puffs and puffs of smoke, little white ones and little black ones and tracer too. All the time the pilot shifts the plane about. The crew are intent and busy and a little afraid. I was afraid too,' he added, nodding his big head.

Dan and I sat up late discussing plans. He does not know exactly when he is going home but we know I am due to join Air Marshal Slessor at the Air Ministry at the beginning of May and have been promised a week's leave between my two jobs.

We decided I should break my journey on the way home and try to visit Mummy in Switzerland. We have worried about her because, ever since war broke out, she has been ill and alone – cut off from family and friends. Dan said I'd have to get permission to do this and also obtain a visa for Switzerland. I longed to spend my week's leave with Dan but he said he might have to go home any time now when I'm working, or even after I am to start work in London, so this was the best plan. Anyway I'd have to go to Rome to get to France, so tonight won't be 'Goodbye'.

13 April 1945   *Caserta*

Last night it rained so heavily that I thought the roof of our hut would cave in. This morning there was a lake on my floor. I walked across the sodden lawn – carrying my shoes – to the Mess hut for breakfast. When I pushed open the door it seemed very silent inside. I ordered fruit juice, eggs over and coffee and reached for my newssheet. I read it from start to finish and then folded it up and put it in my pocket.

| VOLUME III | SIGNAL CORPS | FRIDAY |
| NO. 131 | BULLETIN | 13 APR. 1945 |

| ALLIED FORCE HEADQUARTERS | OFFICE OF THE |
| | CHIEF SIGNAL OFFICER |

WASHINGTON: THE WHITE HOUSE ANNOUNCED LATE
YESTERDAY THAT PRESIDENT FRANKLIN DELANO
ROOSEVELT HAD DIED AT 3.35 P.M. CENTRAL WAR TIME
AT WARM SPRINGS, GA., OF A GENERAL
HEMORRHAGE. HARRY S TRUMAN WAS SWORN IN AND
BECAME THE 33RD PRESIDENT OF THE UNITED
STATES WHEN HE REPEATED THE OATH BEFORE CHIEF
JUSTICE HARLAN STONE AT 5.09 EWT.

Mr Roosevelt died at his summer cottage at the health resort where he had been resting for more than a week, his second stay at the foundation in four months. Stephen Early, Presidential secretary, informed reporters of the unexpected death.

He said Mrs Roosevelt, Admiral Ross McIntyre, the President's physician, and he would leave Washington by air yesterday afternoon for Warm Springs. The official White House statement said:

Vice President Truman has been notified. He was called to the White House and informed by Mrs Roosevelt. The Secretary of State has been advised. A cabinet meeting has been called. The four Roosevelt boys in the service have been sent a message by their mother which said, 'President slept away this afternoon. He did his job to the end as he would want to do. Bless you all and all our love, Mother.' Funeral services will be held Saturday afternoon in the East Room of the White House. Internment will be at Hyde Park Sunday afternoon. No detailed arrangements or exact times have been decided upon as yet.

The details surrounding the death of the country's only third-term president were dramatically given to nearly 100 reporters assembled at the White House by Admiral McIntyre. He said:

This is a tough one for me to have to give you. At 1505 Eastern War Time I had a call here from Warm Springs telling me that the President fainted while having his portrait done. The President was coming back next week. I asked Dr James Paullin to go to Warm Springs this afternoon when I heard of the fainting. I called in thirty minutes and they said it was a very serious thing. Commander Howard Bruen, who is doctor down there, said it was a cerebral hemorrhage. I notified everyone here at the White House and contacted Steve Early, who came in at once. As we were talking over plans to go down to Warm Springs, the phone rang again. It was Bruen to say that the President was just about the same, but he (Bruen) was suddenly called away. A few minutes later he came back to tell me at 3.45 . . .

At this point the Admiral broke down. Veteran Washington correspondents crowded around him had tears streaming down their faces. Finally McIntyre resumed, 'came very suddenly'.

Simultaneously, Bruen in Warm Springs gave further details

of the shocking news and said a 'massive cerebral hemorrhage' caused the death. He said he saw the President in the morning when he was in excellent spirits. He was sitting in a chair while sketches were being made of him by an architect. He suddenly complained of a very severe occipital headache, which is in the back of the head. Within a very few minutes he lost consciousness. Bruen added, 'He was seen by me at 1.30 p.m., fifteen minutes after the episode had started. He did not regain consciousness and died at 3.35 p.m.'

Roosevelt, who was born in Hyde Park, NY, on Jan 30, 1882, died in the bedroom of his little white bungalow at Top Pine Mountain where he had been visiting for twenty years to take treatment for infantile paralysis, with which he had been stricken in 1921. Last night members of his cabinet began assembling for an emergency session. First to arrive were Miss Frances Perkins, Secretary of Labor, and Harold Ickes, Secretary of the Interior. Acting President Truman announced last night that the San Francisco Conference will go on as scheduled.

15 April 1945   *Caserta – Rome*

I was packed and had said my goodbyes and was sitting in our hut with Mary Alice and Coco when we heard a familiar voice calling across the garden. It was 'Macey dear'. He and General Eaker have flown 20,000 miles in thirteen days. When they left here two weeks ago they flew to England and on to the United States. From there they flew to Hawaii, the Philippines, China, Burma, India and Egypt. Now they are on their way back to the States. Soon the General joined us and we sat listening to their global news and opening the lovely parcels they had brought us from America. It was late when I climbed into the car that was taking me to Rome. When I arrived at the hotel, Dan told me he has got my visa for Switzerland but I will not be able to get a seat on an aeroplane to Marseilles for four days. This is glorious news – we'll be together every minute except when he is working.

Dan saw me off at Ciampino at nine o'clock yesterday morning. I took a small suitcase and carried Coco in a plastic bag with a zip-fastener to give him air. We still don't know when Dan will sail for home and have had a bet on who will reach London first. Hardly had I sat down in the Dakota when Coco began to chew his way out of his bag. By midday, when we reached Marseilles, there was very little of it left and the zip was broken.

Once through Customs I made enquiries as to how to reach the Swiss frontier and was told there were no planes going to Lyons today so my best bet was to catch a train. I got a lift into Marseilles with an American who told me I would be very lucky to reach Switzerland. I let Coco out of his bag in the car – his feathers were all mussed up and he was very angry. He grumbled and preened himself all the way. The American talked about Bermuda. At the station I swopped part of my air ticket for a railway warrant and then went in search of something to put Coco in. At Miprix I bought a wooden box with a sliding lid for sixty-five francs. When Coco climbed out of his bag on to the counter he caused quite a sensation in the shop. I put him into the box and immediately he began to gnaw the lid which I had to keep ajar so that he could breathe.

It was fun to see a big French train again and to watch porters in blue linen tunics hurrying about. I leaned out of the window of my third-class carriage and watched a crowd of American and French soldiers on the platform. Opposite me the hands of the big station clock jerked out the minutes. When they reached 7.30 p.m. we started. There were an American lieutenant and two sergeants in my compartment. Coco sat on the window rail and once he fell off his perch when we went through a tunnel. Chestnut trees, prison camps and familiar French advertisements flashed past the window. All the way I saw the desolate ruins of war. The train stopped at nearly every station. At three o'clock in the morning we reached Lyons. The Americans and I hauled our luggage to the rail transport office where we enquired how to get to our destinations. People were sleeping all over the station, on the platforms, on the benches, and on their luggage. I stepped over a jigsaw of bodies. I learned that there was no direct train to Switzerland – because the railway had been bombed. The one train of the week was leaving in the morning to go via Grenoble but there was little hope of my getting on it because it was always overcrowded and people were often left behind. Leaving my luggage with the Americans, who camped at the foot of the RTO stairway with Coco in his box on their knees, I went in search of a telephone. I consulted the aerodrome, the transit hotel and grumpy duty officers. They all told me the same tale – the only certain way of getting to the Swiss Frontier was by car. Major Vick alone could fix that. Each time I asked where I could contact Major Vick they told me they did not know and hung up. At last I found him. He did not seem surprised to be woken up and told me to go to the transit hotel across the square where he would meet me at nine o'clock and check my credentials. If they were in order he might be able to help me. It was 5 a.m. when I returned to the Americans. They had all fallen asleep and I had not the heart to wake them but I wanted to thank them. I slipped away with my suitcase and Coco. Eventually I found the transit hotel and woke the concierge. I managed to get a bath.

I was drinking coffee when Major Vick walked into the little salon. Short, dark and enigmatic, he asked me a dozen questions in a curt, taciturn way: where was I going; what authority did I carry; could he see my passport; and what the devil was that ominous noise in that wooden box? Sheepishly I pulled back the lid and Coco, looking very irate, stepped out. Major Vick told me he had a car leaving for the Swiss Frontier in ten minutes' time – I could go in it if I liked. I said, 'Thank you very much but . . .'

'Well?' he asked brusquely. I explained that I did not think I would be allowed to take Coco into Switzerland and wondered whether he would look after him while I was away. Major Vick was so surprised that he began to laugh. I handed over my dilapidated bag of sunflower seeds and Coco; then I climbed into a Ford car and drove off up the Valley of the Rhône. It was 9 a.m.

The young French driver told me he is in the Maquis. He is twenty-four. Before the war he lived in Paris. When the Germans came he took a 'holiday' and travelled by a roundabout route to Lyons. It was difficult to get into the Maquis. Any enquiries you made might well be reported, spies were everywhere: you could not even rely on your friends. Besides this the people of the Maquis had to be cautious lest you were a phoney or a 'plant'. Eventually he contacted the Resistance Movement through a blacksmith and went to live in the mountains. At night they came down to the valleys to raid and sabotage German garrisons and equipment. This young man told me his tale very simply and in great detail. He was very impressive. It was better to be killed than captured, he told me in a final matter-of-fact way, as if he had accepted the fact a long time ago. He described what the Germans had done to some of his friends who were tortured to give the names of the people they worked with.

We drove under chestnut trees beside the Rhône. There were cowslips and white puffy-headed dandelions in the fields. After some hours we reached mountains; lilac and wistaria grew on the houses, lumber lay in great piles beside the road. Now and then we came on bombed or burnt out villages and German tanks. But we never saw another car on our long drive north. When we came to the high-wire fence that runs between Switzerland and France I thought of Dan and his friends – of all fugitives. How many desperate people tried to struggle through those evil-looking barbs? At Annemasse the frontier was almost deserted. I said goodbye to my new friend and lugged my bag to the French Customs. They did not bother to open it. Then I walked a few yards down the empty street to the Swiss Customs who delved deep and found nothing.

Switzerland looked like paradise. I told the taxi driver to go slowly so that I should not miss a thing. Regiments of red, white and yellow tulips lined Lake Geneva; the streets were clean; people sat on benches doing nothing. No one hurried. At the station there was a mass of porters, the buffet was filled with

350

food and on the walls were new timetables and lovely travel posters. All civilisation seemed to be centred in that station. I telephoned Mummy at Vevey. I had not warned her that I was coming lest something stopped me and she be disappointed. When she came to the telephone I listened to her voice saying, 'Hello. Hello. Hello. Who is there?' Suddenly I could not speak. My voice would not come. I was afraid she would cut off . . . It was so marvellous to hear her voice.

The electric train hissed and started. I sat by the window in a third-class carriage. As I looked across the fields of daffodils to the lake water and the snow mountains beyond, I thought; all round this little country the war is still going on – I was on an island of peace. I put my luggage through the window at Vevey and ran down the steps to the platform. Mummy was waiting for me; she looked as young and pretty as ever. Six and a half years slithered away into nothing . . .

29 April 1945   *Vevey – Lyons*

Mummy and I spent a wonderful week together. Her hotel looks out towards the Dentes du Midi. There was a magnolia tree under her window. We went shopping in Montreux: bought elastic braces and garters and silk handkerchiefs for Dan, and a travelling clock from M. Dubois, whose little shop is filled with every kind of watch, and grandfather, alarm and cuckoo clocks. We ate chocolate cake in the patisserie by the lake. The man in the antique shop gave us a paper bag full of blue gentians from the mountains. We went by funiculaire to Les Plyades to see the fields of narcissi. It was cold at the top – great slabs of snow had been cut away to make a path.

All the week we read every scrap of news in the papers: terrible descriptions of Nazi concentration camps at Buchenwald and Belsen – the news that Mussolini had been captured in Northern Italy, and Marshal Pétain had been arrested on the Swiss Frontier. We learned that the Russian and US Forces had linked up on the Elbe near Torgau. Today there is a rumour that Himmler had offered unconditional surrender to Great Britain and the United States.

I said goodbye to Mummy – her big blue eyes full of tears. It was awful. I taxied down the steep hill to the station. Shafts of sun were pouring through the mountains. The lake water was grey. I telephoned Mummy from a callbox on the platform. The train was crowded with peasants in their Sunday clothes.

I looked out of the window and thought of peace. I have almost forgotten what it was like. The taxi driver who took me to the frontier told me that he will get drunk when Hitler is dead. He has bought two bottles of whisky for this purpose long ago – they cost him seventy francs each. Once across the frontier I cadged a lift in a van to the Hotel Nationali, Annemasse, where I had a rendezvous with Major Vick's car. I found no car and no message.

All day I waited in the public bar of that little hotel. The rest of it had been taken over by the military. I watched the French proprietor and his wife eat an enormous meal. I was very hungry but they said they could only sell food to soldiers. French people, in their Sunday clothes, came in and out. Four locals sat in a corner playing cards with their hats on. There was a picture of General de Gaulle on the wall. Occasionally the proprietor turned the wireless on to hear the news: the Allies are thirty-five kilometres from Munich and Venice. We have joined up with the Russians near Linz. Mussolini's body is on view in Milan where he and his companions were shot yesterday. I had tried and failed to telephone Lyons and I wondered about Major Vick: had he forgotten me? who is he? who does he work for? Perhaps he has eaten Coco . . . At last a Polish Liaison Officer came in and spoke to me in English. He telephoned Major Vick on a military line and came back with the good news that the car was on its way.

At seven o'clock in the evening a young English officer and a girl picked me up. I climbed into the back of their little car with my luggage. We drove through the mountains in the gathering darkness. Every time we drove over a pothole my head hit the roof. 'It is snowing in the mountains,' they told me. They knew every house and village on the way but I did not like to ask them why. We passed through one village where, they told us, there had been a clash between some German troops and the Maquis. Some of the Maquis were wounded and captured. The Germans took them on stretchers, laid them out in the main street and ordered all the inhabitants to line the road. They then drove tanks over the wounded French.

We reached their villa in Lyons at 10.15 p.m. We dined on bully beef, bread and marmalade. I found Coco in their sitting room perched on the top of what remained of his wooden box. He came and sat on my shoulder and clucked with pleasure. Just before midnight Major Vick walked in. In his curt, businesslike way he told me he had arranged a lift for me to Paris in the morning. I must start at 5 a.m. My curiosity overcame me: 'Are you French or English, and what is your job?' I asked.

'For once,' he laughed, 'I am not going to help you.' He dropped me back at the transit hotel.

30 April 1945   *Lyons – Paris – London*

A Frenchman called Tournier collected Coco and me at 5 a.m. We drove out of Lyons in the sombre grey of pre-dawn, crossed the Rhône and the Saône, and with the dawn came to lovely rolling country. Coco sat on the back of my seat and whistled. Tournier had a bad eye but all the shops were closed so we could do nothing about it. He told me about his war as he hurried across France. He talked about General de Gaulle and his young English master, Le Commandant Archibald. We passed within twenty miles of Vichy and we made a detour to look at some bombed villages. We came through the Forest of Fontainebleau to Paris, where Tournier dropped me at the Ritz. I left Coco with the concierge while I went to Air Transport Command to see if I could get a seat on a plane.

I called at Arthur Forbes's office and found he was away, but General Wood, who works with him, was there. Together we took Coco to Arthur's house where I left him in charge of Arthur's housekeeper. It was dreadful leaving him behind. Afterwards General Wood took me back to his flat. He had just returned from a trip to Germany where he had visited two concentration camps. Sitting in his luxury flat, with the sun shining outside on the Champs Elysées and the gramophone playing dance tunes, I looked at the appalling photographs he had taken with his Leica camera and listened to his description of piles of corpses, 'like busted sawdust dolls', and torture implements.

I took off at dusk in a Dakota filled with young Americans, who told me they were aircrews who had force landed over North-East Germany and had been taken by the Russians who returned them via Persia. They were very interesting but it was hard to hear against the roar of the engines. At midnight we landed at Bovingdon on a flare path. It was freezing. A big bus took us through country lanes to London. We arrived at 2 a.m.

12

On Target

Late last night it was announced that Hitler is dead. Reinforced by this wonderful news early today I continued my seach for somewhere for Dan and me to live. This is proving difficult: London is overcrowded. Agents have nothing to offer at a price we could afford; hotels are booked solid for months. So far I've walked miles round central London to no avail. I've also spent a lot of time queueing; to get an identity card, a ration card and a card to get into the Air Ministry.

I contacted Arthur Forbes, who was as kind and amusing as ever. He was undaunted when I told him I'd left Coco in his Paris flat and said he could send him back to me easily via his air transport network. 'As soon as I return to Paris I'll arrange it. I always presumed you had named him after me so it's the least I can do,' he said. Arthur was called Coco as a child – but I can't remember why.

This evening I learned that Berlin surrendered to the Russians at 3 p.m. today – and the German armies in Italy signed their unconditional surrender in our old office in Caserta.

I've started work for Air Marshal Slessor at Adastral House, Kingsway. I have a desk on the fourth floor in a room with two Permanent Civil Servants, Mr Havell and Mr Davis, who are trying to teach me the intricacies of the Air Ministry. We are working on promotions, retirements, postings, manning, honours and awards, rehabilitation of the Air Force and demobilisation. Our room is very cold because the windows are covered with light canvas material as the glass was blown out when a bomb landed nearby. The walls are black with grime from bomb blast. The roar of traffic in the street below makes it difficult to hear on the telephone. I start work at 9 a.m. and leave at 7 p.m. Air Marshal Slessor gets here at eight and seldom goes home before eight at night. I go back and forth by bus. We work on Saturdays but not on Sundays.

London and its inhabitants seem very sombre, which is not surprising after all they've been through. But it's sad. Wherever you go there are bombed buildings and people with rather dismal faces, drab clothes and, often, dreary conversations.

I dined with David Stirling who is just back from Colditz prison in Germany. He looks thinner but fit. He talked about going to the Far East war. After dinner we were joined by Peter Stirling and Fitzroy. They were all in high spirits and made me laugh. They brought the news that the Fourteenth Army has captured Rangoon and that Hitler and Goebbels are thought to have committed suicide but no bodies have been found. 'Not surprising,' said Peter. 'There is no food in Berlin so probably Himmler ate them.' Peter is being posted to Budapest. Mo will go with him but presently is on leave in the Sudan, visiting his 'damn bad wife'.

8 *May 1945* London

Today the people of London and their children and thousands of visitors took to the streets and parks to celebrate victory in Europe. Flags flew from all the buildings. Shop windows were stuffed with red, white and blue clothes, flowers and materials.

Planes flew overhead, and streamers, ticker tape and paper poured out of windows. There was no traffic because people filled the streets and pavements. I walked to the office and found only Air Marshal Slessor there. 'It's a National Holiday – you shouldn't have come,' he said. 'Supposing I stay and help till lunchtime,' I said and added, 'besides it's a brilliant time to throw some of your more boring papers out of our windows.' Before I left I peeled the canvas off one window and emptied the contents of five waste paper baskets on to Kingsway. I longed to be more generous but did not dare.

I eased my way into the Strand and progressed at snail's pace towards Trafalgar Square. It was a good-natured multitude and except for the sounds of feet and voices there was a silence over London – a silence loaded with emotion. A few people were crying and a few were laughing but the majority trudged forward silently. No one pushed. It took ages to reach Trafalgar Square which was already overcrowded – the steps, lions and lamp-posts were coated with people. I looked down on White-hall which appeared to be paved with heads. Someone said, 'They are waiting for Mr Churchill.'

I drifted with the current along the Mall. As we drew nearer to Buckingham Palace I could hear people shouting, 'We want our King.' Around three o'clock Mr Churchill's voice came over amplifiers announcing that Germany has surrendered and hostilities will end at midnight. The dense crowds cheered and cheered and cheered again, stamped their feet, clapped, waved and threw hats in the air. Around five o'clock the Royal Family and Mr Churchill came out on the balcony and it seemed as if every voice in the world was cheering. I felt desperately sorry Dan was not with me.

Through a giant carnival of dancing, singing and laughing people I slowly made my way home with a thousand thoughts rushing through my head – of the lands, the skies and the seas I'd seen; of the marvellous people I'd met; of the wounded, the dead, the animals, the flowers, of the jokes and the tears; the hopes and the fears; of those terrible, frightening, yet tri-umphant years . . .

Marvellous. Coco has arrived. I collected him from a young pilot in Chelsea who had flown him over in a smart metal box with 'Explosive' painted on the lid. He was touchingly pleased to see me and I am overjoyed to get him back. Luckily I'd bought a cage for him only yesterday, and some bananas.

I am impatient for Dan to arrive and can't think what delays him. And I am impatient to find somewhere for us to live. As agencies produce nothing we can afford, I continue to explore areas of central London on foot each evening after work. I look for 'To Let' boards. So far no luck – only altercations with tarts who tend to think I'm after their beats.

Since most secrets need no longer be kept a flood of interesting news, on radio, in newspapers and from friends, is pouring in about Germans surrendering in Norway, Czechoslovakia, Austria, the Channel Islands, Denmark, Holland and Greece. Meanwhile our thoughts and prayers are beamed on the Far East where terrible fighting continues. Our Forces are in the thick of this. It seems that, slowly but surely, the Allies are winning that war too. Flying Fortresses, sometimes five hundred at a time, are bombing Tokyo and other targets.

Yesterday the King and all the Royal Family and other European Royals – and Diplomats and Service Chiefs, and Mr Churchill with Ministers, plus some workers and housewives – went to St Paul's Cathedral to thank God for our Victory.

Miracles do happen. Last night, after dining with Mrs Stirling in South Audley Street, I took a short cut and found myself in a mews called Red Place which runs into Green Street, Mayfair. There I saw a board advertising 'Unfurnished Maisonette to Let'. Though it was late I knocked on the door and amazingly it opened. I was shown the first and second floors which had their own front door: upstairs two bedrooms and a bathroom; downstairs a small dining room, nice sitting room and a sensible kitchen. And the price was very reasonable. There and then I signed the lease. The landlord said I could move in today. I was so pleased and excited that I accidentally kissed him goodbye. I am over the moon. Dan and I have a home again. This morning I telephoned the Pantechnicon and fixed for our furniture to come this evening.

26 May 1945   *London*

On Thursday I put on my prettiest clothes and arrived at King's Cross Station an hour early for Dan's train. 'When the train glides in,' I thought, 'it will be the end of all our misery – the beginning of living happily ever after . . .'

I saw him a long way down the platform. I stood and watched him, just like I did a long time ago, on sand, at Rehovoth. Heaven . . . is being together.

28 May 1945   *London*

Dan is delighted with Red Place and to see his furniture again. And he was amused to see the pile of our wedding presents – some of them still in their boxes or tissue paper. He had a ghastly journey by boat from Naples – twenty officers to a cabin. It took three weeks to reach England.

We telephoned Whitaker at the Russian Camp near Leeds; he is hoping to join us very soon. 'You see,' he said, 'as promised I didn't desert in this war.' And he added, 'As soon as I reach London I'm going to hire-purchase an Upright Piano.' Yesterday – my day off – we moved all the furniture around, hung curtains and unpacked everything. Our home is now very comfortable – even pretty.

Rations have been cut because, it is said, there is a danger of famine in Europe next winter. Himmler was captured in Lüneburg – a suitable place to find him. He, rather cleverly, managed to commit suicide when being searched.

We invited Air Marshal and Lady Slessor to dine with us at
Claridge's. David Stirling came too. We talked about the Far
East war – where David wants to go – and about our new
'Caretaker' Government. Air Marshal Slessor told us about his
tour of the Ruhr from which he has just returned. He said, 'No
one in England can know how terrible the bombing of Germany was. I flew over Essen, which is about the size of Reading,
at five hundred feet and the sight below was fantastically
terrible. Now it is flat. The works there were gigantic but now
are just rubble. How the Germans managed to keep fighting us
after that one cannot imagine. The Gestapo alone could have
organised it. Next winter in Europe is going to be frightful.'

After dinner we were joined by Mr Saltzburger of the *New
York Times* who had just returned from Russia where, he said,
he saw nothing much except that Tito had a colossal welcome
there. Mr Saltzburger has an ugly voice but he was interesting
about what is happening in Poland, Hungary and Yugoslavia.
We had a laugh over Lord Haw Haw being captured.

At the office there is much talk of Wing Commander McKin-
ley flying a Lancaster 'Aries' from Yukon across the North
Magnetic Pole to Iceland. He had a crew of ten. It took twenty
hours and twenty minutes to cross the top of the world.

Before the war Dan worked in the City but now he is too old
to start where he left off, so he is puzzling what he should do,
but first he must get demobbed, obtain food and other permits
and collect his car from Melton. It won't be easy for him – or
for anyone else – to find a job.

12 July 1945   *London*

This morning we all leaned out of the office windows to see
General Eisenhower drive by on his way to the Guildhall where
he will receive the Freedom of the City of London.

Wonderful news: the Australians are in Borneo. This is very
important because of oil.

Two of our greatest war secrets have been made public –

Pluto and Fido: the first the underwater pipe lines invented to keep our Forces supplied with oil; the second, invented to disperse fog, which was vital to the RAF and Allied planes.

Dan continues to canvass for the Conservatives in the coming election. He has spent a lot of time in the East End, particularly in Wapping. He says the people are charming to him in spite of it being a Labour area. Though every citizen adores Churchill, Dan thinks the public will vote for Labour this time.

This evening we went to see the film on Belsen. It was incredibly horrible – beyond our wildest imaginations of atrocity and evil. I had to come out before the end I was so upset. How can anyone ever forgive the Germans?

After dinner the Regent of Iraq brought Nuri Pasha[1] to see us. We showed them a clever escape kit – a tiny cigarette lighter containing maps and a compass. They were also intrigued with my collection of guns, especially the Mauser pistol. Nuri Pasha liked Coco very much and walked around the room with him on his shoulder. He was delighted to learn he came from the grain shop in Baghdad.

15 July 1945   *London*

Hurrah! Today Dan was demobbed.

The last of my Great Aunts has died. We used to say: 'Nothing but Death'll part us from Ethel.' Now it has happened we are sad. Though she had a beard, a moustache, a voice like a corncrake and wore astonishing clothes we all loved her because she was interested in everything, never shocked or surprised, and her thin, high-pitched laugh was the eighth wonder of the world. I laugh even to remember it. She had many unusual friends, among them Virginia Woolf.

Letters from Washington all tell the same story: Mark, exasperated, has left Field Marshal Jumbo and hopes to go to the Far East war; Lonj wrote to me in French – asking our help. He

---

[1.] Nuri Pasha, Iraqi Prime Minister, was murdered in the Iraq Revolution of July 1958.

and Thanh are being given tickets to Liverpool and ten pounds each as they are no longer wanted, but they don't know how to get back to Indo-China; Driver Dunbar wrote, 'A reign of terror here! Now the very nice Chef has finally revolted because the menus are often altered five or six times in a morning. Last week he announced, "I'll cook nothing in this house today," and the family had to go to an hotel to eat.'

After dinner we set off on foot for Piccadilly. For the first time since September 1st, 1939, the lights of London have been switched on. Huge crowds with their children arrived in the West End. So many of the children had never seen London lit up before. We had a lovely time.

Mr Churchill and President Truman have arrived in Berlin for the conference at Potsdam. Stalin is due to arrive soon.

Dan says we must have Lonj and Thanh to stay in our spare room till we can discover how the Military can get them back to Indo-China.

24 July 1945   London

Yesterday the trial of Marshal Pétain began. Newspapers are full of this. Not surprisingly the French court became a shambles and had to be cleared. The old Marshal seems to have been the only one to remain dignified. What a little life they can take from this eighty-nine-year-old man if he is proved to be a traitor.

26 July 1945   London

Labour has won the election and Mr Attlee will be Prime Minister. I feel a bit sorry for him – it won't be easy to succeed a hero like Churchill; ghastly to be faced with the repair of our country – to help the thousands returning from the war, all needing a job; and frightful to have to raise money from a weary, bereaved and poor population.

In San Francisco a Charter has been signed by representatives of fifty nations to try and guard peace and fair play in the world. It will be called United Nations.

Lovely news: Dan has got a job – a good one – in the City. He is to start work in September. And I have got two weeks' leave. We want to go to Scotland in the car if we can get enough petrol.

At teatime Whitaker arrived, wreathed in smiles. He is going to work for us as before. We gave him a huge welcome and then he bustled off to Oxford Street saying he had urgent business there. We did not need to ask what that was. An upright piano is looming.

A Mitchell plane has crashed into the Empire State Building. Three lifts dropped about 1000 feet. The plane stuck half in, half out of the skyscraper. How can they get it out?

After a busy morning in the office I hurried along the Strand to meet Dan and George Jellicoe for lunch at the Savoy Grill. I found them bent over the *Midday Standard* at a nice corner table. They hardly looked up when I arrived but moved the paper so I could read it too.

Across the front page, in huge letters, was one word – 'OBLITERATION'. In aghast silence we read that the Allies had dropped an Atom bomb on Hiroshima last Monday at 1.30 a.m. Four square miles, or sixty per cent of the city, were wiped out by the incredible pressure and heat. All living things were destroyed. Since then, from Guam, General Spaatz, US Air Force, has announced that reconnaissance photos, taken as soon as the seven-and-a-half-mile high mountain of dust and smoke had cleared, show the heart of the city swept as though by a bulldozer with awful thoroughness. It is rumoured that the bomb weighed only five hundred pounds

Throughout lunch we talked of this news which eclipsed anything we had ever heard in our lives. It seemed to us that all modern inventions, even Navies, Armies and Air Forces are now out of date, dwarfed by this appalling weapon.

Walter Monckton wandered over and sat down at our table: 'This is the biggest thing which has happened since Christ came,' he said. 'The heat, the driving power of this thing, is vast. If one tenth of one per cent can completely destroy four and one tenth square miles then a full dose could destroy four thousand square miles. It means we could change the weather, melt the poles – and every aspect of trade and civilisation as we know them could be altered. This discovery is so huge that there is little one can think of that it might not change.'

On another page of the *Standard* the heading was: 'Japanese General escaped on an elephant in Burma.'

10 August 1945   *London*

Dan went by train to Melton to collect his car. I lunched with John Wyndham at Boulestins – prawns and pigeons. Suddenly the head waiter came to our table and said, 'Japan has surrendered.' Apparently Tokyo radio announced that Japan, via Switzerland and Sweden, has applied to surrender provided their Emperor may remain on his throne. Washington, Moscow and London have not yet announced Peace.

Only seventy-odd hours ago we heard that the first Atom bomb was dropped on Hiroshima. It is thought that casualties were between 100,000 and 150,000 people. Only thirty-six hours ago the Russians declared war on Japan. A second Atom bomb has been dropped on Nagasaki, the great Japanese Naval Base, smoke still hides the extent of the damage. So far we only know that flames could be seen for 250 miles.

Walking back to the office, with paper cascading from office windows and swirling in gusts along the streets, and people on the roofs and balconies singing and shouting, I felt terribly sad. It is so wonderful that World War II is over, and no wonder people celebrate, but what we have all done – to defend ourselves and to win the war – is too frightful for words.

August 1945   *Upper Loch Torridon, Scotland*

Dan, Andrew the Ghillie and I set off early this morning. We took the mountain track through the wood. Cobwebs glittered on the grass and brambles, rabbits thumped their warnings and hustled away into the bushes.

Soon we began wading up steep heathered hills, catching our toes in roots and tufts, leaving deep marks in the peat hags. Andrew went easily ahead – his rifle slung on his shoulder, his lunch bulging his pocket. Several times I slumped to the ground and looked back at the blue loch water below. I wondered if I was tired after the long drive from London yesterday – or am just lazy. How does one know the difference? I counted three out loud to make myself get up, and each time Andrew looked back and grinned.

Presently we reached bare rock and began to climb. It took ages to reach the top. There we lay in the sun and spied for stags through a telescope while we ate our lunch, each with a halo of midges. Deer were grazing in a corrie far beyond and below us and through the long hot afternoon we made a great detour and stalked them, finally crawling to get in range. Dan fired, and missed. I was glad – the stag was so beautiful.

Index

366

374